THE
GREAT
PERSUASION

THE
GREAT
PERSUASION

Reinventing Free Markets
since the Depression

ANGUS BURGIN

HARVARD UNIVERSITY PRESS
Cambridge, Massachusetts
London, England · 2012

Copyright © 2012 by the President and Fellows of Harvard College
All rights reserved
Printed in the United States of America

Library of Congress Cataloging-in-Publication Data

Burgin, Angus.
The great persuasion : reinventing free markets since the Depression / Angus Burgin.
    p.   cm.
Includes bibliographical references and index.
ISBN 978-0-674-05813-2 (alk. paper)
1. Free enterprise. 2. Capitalism. 3. Economic policy. I. Title.
HB95.B867   2012
330.12'2—dc23   2012015061

For Kate

CONTENTS

THE
GREAT
PERSUASION

INTRODUCTION
The End of Laissez-Faire

In the late fall of 1924, John Maynard Keynes strode into the Examination Schools in Oxford and announced that the political economy of the civilized world was approaching, as his lecture title boldly proclaimed, the end of laissez-faire. Although he was only forty-one years old, Keynes had already accumulated a range of experiences that uniquely traversed the cloistered world of Oxbridge economists and practical affairs. After a childhood passed in a household at the center of Cambridge academic life, he had been elected to a prize fellowship at King's College at the age of twenty-five and had been appointed editor of the *Economic Journal* less than three years later; his career as a civil servant had taken him from a junior clerkship at the India Office to a position as the chief representative for the Treasury at the peace conference in Versailles. Now he was turning his attention to the development of a coherent theory of political economy to supplant the fading doctrines of the preceding century.[1] "We do not dance even yet to a new tune," he told the attendees. "But change is in the air."[2]

The very idea of laissez-faire, Keynes believed, was a perversion of the views expressed by its purported advocates. "The phrase *laissez-faire* is not to be found in the works of Adam Smith, of Ricardo, or of Malthus," he reminded his audience. "Even the idea is not present in a dogmatic form in any of these authors." Rather, it represented "what the popularisers and the vulgarisers said."[3] Those who sought to relay economic ideas to the untutored masses deliberately reduced them to abstract tenets that appealed to those with a limited capacity to understand.[4] Having absorbed those shrunken lessons, the public had come to "regard the simplified hypothesis as health, and the further complications as disease."[5] The result was a growing gulf between popular assumption and academic opinion. Despite the lingering popularity of the idea of laissez-faire and the widely shared assumption that it was the prevailing view of most economists, for more than fifty years the world's leading practitioners of the profession had applied it only as, in the words of John Elliott Cairnes, a "handy rule of practice" with "no scientific basis whatever."[6] Keynes provided a sweeping list of the "complications" to the application of laissez-faire that most economists accepted and attempted to incorporate into their analysis, including "when overhead costs or joint costs are present," "when internal economies tend to the aggregation of production," "when the time required for adjustments is long," "when ignorance prevails over knowledge," and "when monopolies and combinations interfere with equality in bargaining."[7] Such a list implicitly encompassed vast segments of the free-enterprise economy. In other words, laissez-faire was dead, and only the public had yet to know.

Keynes identified several reasons for the continued prevalence of laissez-faire despite what he perceived to be its intellectual bankruptcy. Foremost, its primary alternatives in the ideological arena—protectionism and Marxism—had "obvious scientific deficiencies" that made them easy for the advocates of laissez-faire to dismantle in a convincing fashion. He spared no sympathy for Marxism in particular, marveling at "how a doctrine so illogical and so dull can have exercised so powerful and enduring an influence over the minds of men, and, through them, the events of history."[8] Economists struggled to overcome a public prejudice in favor of laissez-faire through arguments that were either sophisticated or facile. Those who sought to advocate for a market system tempered by intricate restraints found themselves, because of the complexity of their views, at a decided rhetorical disadvantage. And if opinion devolved, as it often did, into a competition among abstract generalities, the concept of an unadulterated laissez-faire was easier to accept than its equally simple-minded alternatives. Finally, a presumption in favor of unhindered markets maintained a close "conformity with the needs and wishes of the business world of the day."[9] Advocates of laissez-faire had wealthy and influential benefactors who could always ensure it a prominent hearing in the venues of political power.

Keynes was confident that despite all its inherent advantages, the dominance of laissez-faire in the public sphere was gradually drawing to a close. His certainty in this regard was attributable, in part, to his famous faith in the capacity of economic ideas to filter down, over time, to the practice of everyday life. Sooner or later, he believed, the near unanimity of economists' critiques of laissez-faire would manifest itself in the assumptions shared by the public at large. Perhaps more important, the institutional structure of business was working to mitigate the preeminence of the profit motive. The disassociation between ownership and management in modern organizations inspired, in Keynes's view, a diminishing emphasis on dividends. Managers weighed improvements in the bottom line against the potential disapprobation of their customers or a broader public and increasingly prioritized the latter. Businesses "are, as time goes on, socialising themselves," Keynes concluded. "The battle of Socialism against unlimited private profit is being won in detail hour by hour."[10] The weight of economic opinion and institutional practice were converging to overturn economic assumptions that had lasted long past their due. To argue against laissez-faire was to assault a "lethargic monster" that, in Keynes's terms, had "ruled over us rather by hereditary right than by personal merit."[11] He did not doubt that it would be slain.

Keynes did not live to develop a comprehensive statement of his political views. Although "The End of Laissez-Faire" made gestures toward the elaboration of an emerging social philosophy, it was, as his preeminent biographer has noted, far too abbreviated and incomplete to be treated as a Keynesian manifesto.[12] A figure of his significance could little be expected to explain and justify his worldview during a university lecture that was comfortably endured in a single sitting. Nevertheless, it provides as good an introduction as any other to his advocacy of a market system saved from its worst excesses. Keynes articulated an understanding of capitalism as a mode of social organization that demonstrated both irreplaceable merits and undeniable flaws. "For my part," he told his audience, "I think that Capitalism, wisely managed, can probably be made more efficient for attaining economic ends than any alternative system yet in sight, but that in itself it is in many ways extremely objectionable."[13] He envisioned a public sector that would engage in limited but forceful interventions to ameliorate the problems that were engendered when individuals were left to act alone. "The important thing for Government is not to do things which individuals are doing already, and to do them a little better or a little worse," he explained, "but to do those things which at present are not done at all."[14] Such interventions would help mitigate the failures of the market without doing violence to its essential underpinnings. His proposed modifications, he asserted, were in no way "seriously incompatible with what seems to me to be the essential characteristic of Capitalism, namely the dependence upon an intense appeal to the money-making and money-loving instincts of individuals as the main motive force of the economic machine."[15] The end of laissez-faire did not signify to Keynes the end of marketplace life. It was, he believed, a mode of preservation through restraint.

Keynes's lecture stands as both a prescient forecast and a founding document of an era when a conviction that markets required extensive oversight was broadly shared. Even at the height of the 1920s, the reviews that Keynes's lecture received within the economics profession expressed dissatisfaction with the generosity with which he treated laissez-faire.[16] After the onset of the Great Depression at the decade's end, the remaining popular support for free markets rapidly dissipated. Governments enacted a range of policies—from the adoption of new tariffs to the abandonment of the gold standard and the implementation of extensive social programs—that, in Eric Hobsbawm's sweeping terms, "destroyed economic liberalism for half a century."[17] The prestige of the economics profession, which had conspicuously failed to predict the onset of the crisis, plummeted from the highs of the preceding decade to an unprecedented low.[18] Even the economists who are now remembered as the Depression years' most committed allies of free markets eventually became convinced that the era of their feasibility had passed. The letters of the University of Chicago economist Frank Knight are a testament to the depths to which laissez-faire had fallen. "We cannot go back to laissez faire in economics even in this country," he wrote to a colleague in the summer of 1933. "Now it seems to me inevitable that we must go over to a controlled system," he wrote later that year, adding that his only question was "whether any sort of liberty, especially freedom of consumption and intellectual freedom, can be maintained to a significant extent."[19] The 1930s were an era when even many of the economics profession's most strident advocates of marketplace freedoms accepted that they would need to be curtailed to a substantial degree.

The predictions in "The End of Laissez-Faire," for all their manifest foresight, went unfulfilled in one crucial respect. Keynes was right that the public acceptance of laissez-faire was on the cusp of a precipitous decline, but he was wrong to assume that the change would be permanent. Advocacy of free markets entered a period of reconsideration and retrenchment during the Great Depression, but it by no means arrived at an "end." Instead, the story of the half century after the onset of economic crisis is in part one of its triumphant return. By the 1980s debates in the Anglo-American public sphere were permeated with the assumption that the workings of the free market should be protected from governmental attempts to intervene. Recipients of the economics profession's highest honors were calling for a comprehensive rollback of the public sector, a thriving community of generously funded policy institutes had formed in support of free-market ideas, and a host of journals, magazines, and newspapers had embraced identities as public proselytizers for laissez-faire. The president of the United States and the prime minister of the United Kingdom perceived themselves as stalwart allies of the free market and cited its preeminent philosophers in justification of their political ideals.[20] Keynesianism, rather than laissez-faire, had come to seem a relic of a rapidly receding economic world.

The events that precipitated this evolution in popular assumptions about political economy are only beginning to be understood. Their narrative relies, ironically, on precisely the relationship between ideas and political change that Keynes cited as a rationale for his confidence that laissez-faire was on the wane. The shift in popular approaches to the market occurred on many levels, and many actors and institutions played constitutive roles, but it could not have occurred without the committed efforts of a transnational community of ideas. Much as Keynes worked, with manifest success, to develop and disseminate an understanding of advantageous ways in which the public sector could intervene, a network of philosophers, economists, journalists, and private foundations across the Atlantic world coalesced with the common goal of reversing the growth of government and rebuilding public support for free-market ideas. As distant colleagues they had weathered depression and war; in future years they would experience perceptions of public irrelevance, impediments to academic advancement, countless political defeats, and, eventually, an extraordinarily rapid institutional and ideological ascent. In the process they sought to construct a new philosophy of the free market and remained resolutely convinced of the capacity of their abstract discussions—over time and with the aid of external events—to transform the practice of popular politics. This is the story of the community they built, the ideas they advocated, and the enduring legacy of their attempt to reconstitute the theory and practice of capitalism.

Despite the central role market advocates have played in American politics during the past three decades, the narrative of their return to prominence has proved difficult to unravel. For many years observers struggled to explain how and why the celebration of markets and the condemnation of planning regained a hold on the popular imagination after an extended period of dormancy.[21] They expressed confusion at the populist embrace of economic policies that seem to redound to the disadvantage of the poor.[22] And they saw little coherence in a political coalition that urged the preservation of social traditions while supporting a free-market system that often served, with ruthless efficiency, to undermine them.[23] The most influential explanations of these phenomena long emphasized social factors that lurked beneath the abstract language of political and economic ideals, including anxieties over declining status in a fast-changing cultural and technological environment and a desire to create a color-blind language capable of preserving racial privileges that seemed in danger of falling away.[24] But in the absence of a convincing account of the development of conservative ideas, it will remain difficult to understand the contours of a movement that has exerted broad influence over the structure of public debate.

Few would contest that the conservative movement was inflected by social and racial anxieties, supported by many who were unlikely to benefit from its economic proposals, and characterized by the simultaneous advocacy of contradictory views. These interpretive models, however, shroud important aspects of the movement behind an analytic veil. A social philosophy is rarely comprehended by reducing its arguments to social or material interests, or by distilling its tenets into rigidly formalized schemes. The *homo economicus* is useful only as a formal abstraction, and few of us would withstand an interpretive procedure that ceased with the judgment that there were points of apparent conflict among aspects of our stated worldview. Our experience of the social environment is relentlessly complex, and our political perspectives are formed through a dynamic and ever-changing interaction among abstract idealism, purposive strategy, emotive inclination, and intuitive response. They are provisional responses to an always-incomprehensible world. Understanding why individuals believe what they do and evaluating the comparative validity of their beliefs require a mode of analysis that acknowledges the entangled nature of the problems it attempts to address.

In recent years serious critical studies have emerged on several of the conservative intellectual movement's most challenging and influential figures, including Leo Strauss, Friedrich Hayek, Whittaker Chambers, and Ayn Rand.[25] Research into the development of conservatism at the grassroots level has yielded an earnest and sustained attempt to understand its subjects' worldviews.[26] New interpretations have clarified the social and cultural origins of the potent combination of free-market advocacy and evangelical Christianity.[27] And a proliferating literature has commenced the formidable task of chronicling the institutional structures that helped foster and propagate conservatism in the public sphere. This emerging research has begun to unravel the complex points of intersection that developed during the twentieth century among businesspeople, financial institutions, political associations, and free-market advocates.[28] It has illuminated the relationship between the Cold War, the Rand Corporation, and the rise of rational-choice theory in contemporary policy discourse.[29] It has identified the institutional levers that conservatives maneuvered to transform the practice of the legal profession.[30] And it has helped clarify the essential role played by the popular proselytizers in the expansive orbit of the *National Review*.[31] Cumulatively, these contributions represent a paradigm shift in the way the history of conservatism is written. Ideas and intellectuals are now broadly acknowledged to have played a constitutive role in the conservative turn, and advocacy organizations have been assimilated as essential components of its instigation of political change.[32]

This book provides both a contribution to this developing literature and an implicit revision. It takes the detailed analysis of conservative ideas out of the realm of intellectual biography, where it has largely remained, and situates the major figures in dialogue with one another. By focusing on networks and processes of intellectual exchange, it devotes substantial attention to institutional context without inferring that the environment exerts hegemonic force over the generation and propagation of ideas. And it abandons the close observance of national boundaries that has continued to define the parameters of research into the origins of the conservative movement. The result is a narrative that examines how its central figures developed, explained, and justified their beliefs; how they alternately influenced and opposed one another's opinions; how they navigated the perilous relationship between politics and philosophy; and how, over time, their assumptions and arguments discreetly but decisively transformed. It approaches ideas neither as abstractions that unfold in a realm wholly distinct from politics nor as mere tools that are invoked to engender a desired change. The leading figures of the conservative intellectual world engaged, like most of us, in quiet and at times unreflective acts of navigation across the porous boundary between the two.

As Keynes concluded "The End of Laissez-Faire," he reminded his audience that discussions of abstract economic theory often serve as proxies for debates over the kind of world in which we want to live. The problems of economics cannot easily be severed from the problems of philosophy. The "fiercest contests and the most deeply felt divisions of opinion," he predicted, "are likely to be waged in the coming years not round technical questions, where the arguments on either side are mainly economic, but round those which, for want of better words, may be called psychological or, perhaps, moral."[33] Debates over economic policy occur on two levels: they encompass considerations of both how to achieve specified ends with maximum efficiency and what the ends themselves should be. Advocates of a particular approach to political economy rarely achieve much traction in the political arena without devoting close attention and rhetorical emphasis to the latter. Endeavors to transform economic policy almost invariably demand the capacity to reframe the meaning that members of a community derive from, and ascribe to, their world.

In the midst of the Great Depression, market advocates were acutely aware that the social philosophy of the free market inspired little support within either academic institutions or popular politics. They sought to overcome their isolation by establishing networks of sympathizers who could work in conjunction to reexamine the philosophical foundations of their ideas and reconstruct the public presentation of their arguments. Over time they formalized these connections, developing recurrent venues for the interchange of ideas, institutional organs for the dissemination of policy positions, and funding bodies for the provision of financial support. Many of these new organizational forms emerged out of the membership of the Mont Pèlerin Society, a group founded by Friedrich Hayek in 1947 to provide an international gathering place for leading philosophers, economists, journalists, politicians, and philanthropists who supported the market mechanism.[34] Although this society has received only limited attention from scholars, it has long been cited as a progenitor of the social philosophy that has become known as "neoliberalism" and as a point of origin for the elaborate network of policy institutes that inspired and advised the resurgent Anglo-American conservative leadership of the late twentieth century.[35] Its members played a decisive role in the construction of the contemporary market-centered world.

An exploration of the rhetoric of the society's members in its early years reveals a movement far less doctrinaire than the conventional narrative would indicate. What emerges is a growing awareness of a set of complex tensions confronted by market advocates in the postwar era. Early members of the society desired to establish philosophical foundations for marketplace freedoms but expressed deep skepticism toward the intolerance and irrationality of unsubstantiated political absolutes. They sought to reach out to the religious believers and the economically disadvantaged individuals whom they believed nineteenth-century market advocates had mistakenly eschewed but demonstrated hostility toward theological dogmatism and the redistributive state. They glorified the achievements of capitalism but at times expressed dismay at its cultural and moral effects. They valorized liberty but maintained the vital need for collective moral traditions. They defended capitalism as a theory of individual choice but expressed deep suspicion of the implications of political democracy. Their similarities accentuated, rather than elided, the points of difference that drove them apart.

As a result of the retrenchment that accompanied the onset of the Depression and persisted through World War II, all the assumptions that this community ostensibly shared were subject to reconsideration. The financial crisis and subsequent political instability left them broadly convinced of the need for a social philosophy that transcended the abstract dictates of laissez-faire: they agreed that if capitalism was going to be saved from the pressures that were continuously eroding its foundations, its core assumptions would need to be rebuilt. But they disagreed sharply and continuously when the conversation turned to identifying those aspects of the capitalist order that were sacred and those that could be revised, or those morals that might be coded as absolute and the mechanisms of enforcement that would make them so. The postwar conservative intellectual world, with all its points of implicit unanimity and internecine discord, developed out of this atmosphere of uncertainty. That these problems were posed by cosmopolitan intellectuals from around the Atlantic world, engaging together in earnest inquiry into the philosophical foundations of their social order, complicates the common assumption that the conservative project was parochial in its origins and strategic in its intent. It was the product of a collapsed rather than a rigidified worldview.

The state of uncertainty that characterized market advocacy in the 1930s and 1940s was evident in, and to some extent precipitated by, an inability to build consensus about conceptual apparatuses that many saw as ambiguous or obsolete. "Terms like 'liberalism' or 'democracy,' 'capitalism' or 'socialism,' today no longer stand for coherent systems of ideas," Hayek observed shortly after the conclusion of World War II. He saw them instead as "aggregations of quite heterogeneous principles and facts" that had become linked to certain words by means of a "historical accident."[36] Today we continually resort to anachronism when we rely on labels of this kind. As will become apparent, in the interwar and early postwar years "neoliberalism" held a valence, on the rare occasions when the term was employed, that diverged significantly from that associated with it today.[37] The word "libertarian" was unfamiliar to most members of the society and was only infrequently used. The society's members were almost unanimous in their rejection of "conservatism," which they associated with the preservation of a status quo that they sought to overcome. "Traditionalism" and "neoconservatism" were to emerge as political signifiers only in an unforeseeable future. Occasional attempts to rehabilitate the concept of "Whiggism" were impaired by its archaic undertones. And the word "liberal"—otherwise a favorite— had been irrevocably altered by its increasing association with a progressive worldview. It is sometimes possible to use these terms without distorting their contemporary valences: most of the early members of the Mont Pèlerin Society believed that they were reconsidering the foundations of liberalism in order to prevent its further decline, and free-market economists became active participants in a world of conservative publications, policy makers, and advocacy groups in the postwar United States.[38] But these gestures at classification should not obscure the sense of unease, uncertainty, and discord that structured these communities and their vocabularies of dissent. We cannot rely on static renditions of the philosophies of the present if we wish to understand the dynamics of an earlier time.

The more strident market advocacy of recent years emerged only after an extended period of contestation and debate. Over time the economic and political crises of the 1930s receded, academic disciplines grew increasingly specialized, and free-market economists found new champions in print media and popular politics. Attempts to reinvent the philosophy of liberalism and move beyond the static dictates of laissez-faire lost the sense of urgency that had impelled them in earlier years. A younger generation of economists came of age, oriented toward the mathematical language of postwar economics and responsive to the political debates of the Cold War public sphere.[39] By the early 1960s Milton Friedman had emerged as the central figure of this new cohort, reframing a number of problems central to the economics profession and expounding the virtues of the market to a popular audience in unconditional terms. The dissemination of his ideas was made possible by the presence of audiences more receptive to free markets, and institutions better equipped to advocate for them, than had been available at the outset of his career. He took advantage of these opportunities to abandon the equivocations of his predecessors and imbue the rhetoric of market advocacy with a renewed sense of certainty. Capitalism, he argued, was an engine of prosperity that rewarded merit and produced superior outcomes in all but the rarest cases, and the many ills of modern life were products of misguided constraints on its workings rather than demonstrations of its flaws. Friedman's confident language signaled that the moral quandaries and programmatic ambiguities of an earlier generation had been left behind, and a great persuasion had begun.

The narrative of the Mont Pèlerin Society is one of interrelated failure and success. Its members established for themselves an extraordinarily ambitious philosophical program that they proved unable to achieve. What began in a grand gesture of unity soon broke apart into factions with differences that its internal dialogues served to exacerbate rather than resolve. At the same time, the society's attempt to rehabilitate free markets in the public sphere yielded, in part through the concerted actions of its members, spectacular results. Together, they helped precipitate a global policy transformation with implications that will continue to reverberate for decades to come. To chart the transmission of ideas across generations and into politics is necessarily to find patterns of distortion, and the intersection of these dual narratives of decline and ascent inspired a sense of conflict among those who were present at the society's creation. As they grew older, many of its founders came to view the emboldened market advocacy of its later members as a violation of its original ideals. They looked with mingled admiration and disapprobation at the world that Milton Friedman had wrought. The story of the Mont Pèlerin Society is sometimes cited as an exemplar of that rare phenomenon: a group of intellectuals who managed to have a palpable impact on the politics of their time. It is told less often as a parable of the perils, in the exercise of ideological influence, of success.

1

MARKET ADVOCACY IN A TIME OF CRISIS

In the spring of 1933, nearly a decade after Keynes had proclaimed the end of laissez-faire, Friedrich Hayek ascended to the podium for his inaugural lecture at the London School of Economics (LSE). His subject, like Keynes's, was the shift away from classical economics, but in all other respects the circumstances of his presentation markedly differed. In the intervening years the world had descended into a state of severe depression, casting the established paradigms of the economics profession's leading figures into doubt even as they assumed increasing prominence in the public sphere. In contrast to Keynes's genteel Oxford environs, Hayek's audience consisted of members of an institution that was not yet four decades old, still populated largely by occasional students, and bordering a slum.[1] Hayek himself was seventeen years Keynes's junior and little known outside small circles of social scientists in England and his native Austria. His speech was distinguished by a thick Viennese accent that many in his audience struggled to follow.[2] And although Hayek agreed with Keynes that the social philosophy of the free market was in eclipse, the purpose of his remarks was to lament rather than to celebrate its decline.

Among Hayek's audience were a number of economists who sympathized with his views, including Edwin Cannan, an aging conservative who had shaped the department at the LSE largely in his image, and Lionel Robbins, Cannan's young protégé, who had invited Hayek on the visit that led to an offer of a professorship. Surveying the crowd, Hayek was quick to acknowledge that support for the workings of the free market was not uncommon within the economics profession. The problem, he said, was that their ideas had demonstrated no capacity to influence a broader public. He saw little difference between planning and socialism, and few public officials appeared willing to question the merits of planning. "In this sense," he sadly concluded, "there are, of course, very few people left to-day who are not socialists." Popular opposition led the dissenting economist to feel "hopelessly out of tune with his time, giving unpractical advice to which the public is not disposed to listen and having no influence upon contemporary events."[3] He believed that his colleagues possessed scientific knowledge with obvious relevance to the world situation but lacked opportunities to bridge the divide between theory and practice.

Hayek was in the early stages of a career in which he would often feel that his views ran against the tenor of the times, but at no other period was the contrast as stark as in the early 1930s. As governments adopted increasingly radical approaches to an extraordinary economic crisis, academic opponents of government intervention felt ever more marginalized. Around the Atlantic world they clustered in academic environments that prided themselves on fostering opinions that challenged the mainstream, including Hayek's own London School of Economics, the University of Chicago, and the Institute for International Studies in Geneva. The leading economists in each of these institutions expressed despair at the trajectory of public opinion. Even before Hayek's arrival in London, Lionel Robbins had decided that economic reasoning would never be grasped by a broader public. "The hope that Economics will ever become something which the layman can comprehend without training," he asserted in 1930, "is doomed for ever to frustration."[4] In Chicago, Frank Knight had entered into a depression that lasted for much of the decade, precipitated in part by a sense that failures of public deliberation had rendered democracy an unsustainable form of government. By 1934 he believed that there likely remained "a decade or two at the most before we see the end of anything like freedom of inquiry in the United States and all the rest of the liberal European world where it has not already been sunk."[5] Prior to his arrival in Geneva, the displaced German sociologist and economist Wilhelm Röpke had concluded that the time had come to "recognise that the case of Liberalism and Capitalism is lost strategically even where it is still undefeated tactically."[6] Economists who supported the free-enterprise system perceived themselves to be the final defenders of a social philosophy that was in the midst of passing away.

Although these lamentations at times drifted into an apocalyptic excess, their grim tone was not unjustified. This was a period of extraordinary isolation for academic opponents of government intervention. Popular magazines and newspapers were quick to dismiss their views as the prattle of outmoded cranks. Conservative political parties, confronting the specters of communism and fascism in the international environment even as they struggled to cope with economic crises at home, no longer provided reliable havens for economic orthodoxy. Established industries, eager to maintain protective tariffs and negotiate monopoly advantages with regulatory bodies, remained untrustworthy allies at best.[7] And despite Hayek's words to the contrary, even within the economics profession market advocates were increasingly disregarded. Among American social scientists the left-leaning historicism of institutionalist economics remained a powerful force, and in England Keynes had become the preeminent economist in both the academic world and the public imagination.[8] Soon after the publication of *The General Theory of Employment, Interest, and Money* in 1936, Keynesianism had permeated economics departments on both sides of the Atlantic. Economists in London and Chicago found ever fewer allies within both the profession and the public.

In the Anglo-American world since the onset of the Industrial Revolution, the marginalization of market advocates during the early and middle years of the 1930s remains a singular event. This can be attributed in part to the loss of trust in markets that tends to accompany the onset of severe financial crisis. But while events seem to shape the horizons of a discursive world, their hold on the ideological life of a community is not complete. However dismayed economists may feel at the level of public debate, their ideas, arguments, and assumptions all help frame its content and structure. This influence is most palpable in periods of uncertainty, when settled assumptions can suddenly become objects of debate within a broadened public sphere. Hayek's frustrations can be attributed in part to the tenor of the times and in part to the rhetorical force of the message that he and his colleagues conveyed.

Although the market advocates at the LSE and the University of Chicago shared a skepticism about the accelerating government interventions of the time, their opinions were rarely united and often opposed. In London, Lionel Robbins and Friedrich Hayek initially espoused an extraordinarily constrained vision of the government's ability to redress the economic crisis. Blaming the downturn primarily on a business cycle that had become overstimulated by government interference, they argued that further interventions would only repeat the same disastrous pattern. Although their views developed pockets of influence, by the mid-1930s their council of quietism was increasingly ignored by a public and a profession that were eager to find positive solutions to a seemingly intractable crisis. In Chicago, Frank Knight, Jacob Viner, and Henry Simons developed a more moderate response to the events of the time. All three were quick to denounce the excesses of laissez-faire, and they varyingly embraced the prospect of public works projects, progressive taxation, social insurance, and vigorous antitrust policies. This brought them much closer to the profession's mainstream than their colleagues in London, but made it difficult for others to associate them with any ascertainable doctrine or plan. Considered in conjunction, the economists in London and Chicago reveal a world of market advocacy that was very much in disarray. Some corners held firm to reactionary extremes that few were willing to follow; others much more readily made concessions but proved incapable of articulating a coherent oppositional worldview.

The leading figures on both shores remained reluctant to endanger their scientific authority by wading into venues of popular debate, and instead sought to leverage their influence primarily among their colleagues in the profession. They also shared no institution in which they could discuss their ideas, develop new rhetorical strategies, establish networks of communication, or assist younger colleagues who were sympathetic to their views. Instead, they pursued their ideas in discrete universities in separate countries, connected only by the lectures or personal friendships that occasionally inspired them to make the slow journey across the Atlantic. In some cases they devoted as much energy to attacking one another as they did to contesting those with whom they more vociferously disagreed. Their ideas remained fragmented, and they failed to adopt anything resembling a common voice. Businesses demonstrated little interest in funding the world of ideas, and few in the academic world made any efforts to identify themselves as members of a purposive group.[9] Without finding rhetorical traction among themselves or significant sources of institutional support, they had little capacity to influence a public that was already being courted by ideological communities that were better organized and shared a more cohesive point of view.

Hayek was a thoughtful observer of institutional dynamics, and he came to view the challenges he and his colleagues faced as an opportunity to learn lessons that would prove valuable in future years. In his inaugural lecture in 1933, he was already tempering his pessimistic views on contemporary politics with optimistic pronouncements about long-term processes of ideological change. Public opinion, he informed his audience, "can clearly be traced to the economists of a generation or so ago. So the fact is, not that the teaching of the economist has no influence at all; on the contrary, it may be very powerful." His colleagues simply needed to remember that "it takes a long time to make its influence felt."[10] The problems that they identified during a challenging decade would help them shape the structure of market advocacy in the years that followed. Frustrated by their persistent fragmentation and isolation, they began to work together in the late 1930s to construct organizations in which they could develop and propagate their ideas. In the process, they turned their attention to the problems that continued to divide them: the foundations of their social-scientific methodology, the relationship between their economic analyses and their social philosophy, the degree and structure of those forms of government intervention that they might find acceptable, and the rhetorical strategies that would best enable them to persuade others to adopt their worldviews. Their activities helped frame the public life of ideas in the final decades of the twentieth century, as growing segments of the population came to believe that markets provided a constitutive freedom and that attempts to intervene in their dictates and adjudications were almost invariably misguided. The extraordinary successes of market advocates in the decades since the Great Depression were made possible, in part, by the failures they experienced in its early years.

During the early 1930s the London School of Economics became widely known as a center for economists who believed that the government could not contribute to the resolution of the ongoing crisis. Even as leading conservative economists across the Atlantic world advocated for public works and other emergency measures, Lionel Robbins and his colleagues dwelled on the dangers of intervention and the absence of quick solutions. For a brief period they captured the attention of the profession with their youth, their charisma, and the relative audacity of their views. The Economics Department at the LSE became a dynamic center within an increasingly prominent field, and students and faculty sensed that their discussions held a significance that extended well beyond the walls of their seminar rooms. By the end of the decade the sense of excitement that had permeated their discussions had dissipated. Some faculty, like Hayek, appeared increasingly irrelevant within a profession that had become preoccupied with other concerns; others, like Robbins, had already begun the process of bringing their views into closer alignment with the economic mainstream. Although the rapid ascent of Hayek and Robbins signified that the foundations of market advocacy were beginning to shift, their equally abrupt decline suggested that market advocates would need to reconstruct their message if they hoped to sustain public support for their ideas.

The LSE's emergence as an institutional home for a reactionary economics struck many observers as a peculiar development. The university had been founded by members of the Fabian Society less than forty years before, under the theory that a thorough education in economics and political science would serve to further the spread of socialism. Its structure manifested a set of commitments that made the Fabians unusual among their socialist peers. As George Bernard Shaw wrote in a retrospective on the group, they were unabashedly elitist, perceiving themselves as "a minority of cultural snobs and genuinely scientific Socialist tacticians" who had "no time to spend on the conversion and elementary Socialist education of illiterates and political novices."[11] They were committed to a policy of intellectual openness, believing that their ideas would achieve "Permeation" if they were shared with unwelcoming audiences rather than just the converted.[12] And they eschewed the language of revolution, preferring to pursue social change through, in the words of Sidney Webb, "the inevitability of gradualness."[13] Thus the LSE focused on advanced training in the social sciences rather than elementary education for workers and the masses; it welcomed a faculty and student body that represented a broad range of views rather than demanding adherence to a particular ideological perspective; and it sought to cultivate a capacity for critical reasoning rather than radical action.

By the early 1930s the Fabians could look back on their commitments to elitism, openness, and gradualism with some appreciation for their successes. In his introduction to a 1931 reissue of *Fabian Essays,* Shaw noted the "air of amazing advance in our political circumstances." A Fabian Socialist served as prime minister, two of the society's original essayists were in the House of Lords, and Parliament itself "swarm[ed] with Fabians."[14] Further, the LSE was flourishing. In the two decades after 1919, its full-time teaching staff more than quadrupled, and the percentage of students considered "occasional" had halved.[15] Its rapidly expanding infrastructure earned the school the epithet "the empire on which the concrete never set."[16] And its students, who represented a broader range of nationalities and more varied economic backgrounds than their counterparts at Oxford and Cambridge, were widely known for their socialist leanings.

Much of the school's dynamism was attributable to its commitment to open intellectual inquiry and the sometimes heterodox appointments that institutional mandate inspired. The cost of such a mandate, of course, was a lack of control over the political opinions of the faculty. At times this resulted in peculiar ideological discontinuities: the school's first director, for example, later went on to serve as a Conservative member of Parliament.[17] The disparity the Fabians found most vexing, however, was the reactionary reputation of the school's growing body of economists. Beatrice Webb, one of the school's founders, sprinkled her diary entries throughout the 1930s with disdainful references to the theories that had become associated with its economics faculty. Although in personal interactions she found Robbins "good looking" and "pleasant," in intellectual matters she found him and his colleagues to be "dogmatic and theoretical," "ultra individualist apologists for profit making Capitalism," "fanatical individualist economists," followers of the "*laisser faire* of Nassau Senior and Herbert Spencer," and, quite simply, "our antithesis at the School."[18] The Fabians' commitment to ideological openness led the institution they founded to harbor advocates of precisely the economic theories that it had been established to overcome.

As is often the case, the intellectual trajectory of the department can be traced back to a single appointment: the arrival of Edwin Cannan as the school's first chair of political economy in 1907. Cannan shared some important similarities with the founders of the institution, including a belief that societies should change "slower than oak-trees" rather than through the "sudden efforts of inspired geniuses."[19] But unlike the Fabians, his commitment to gradualism emerged from a deeply conservative sensibility. Cannan attributed his support for the market mechanism to skepticism about the available alternatives rather than any ardent enthusiasm for its workings. "Modern civilization, nearly all civilization, is based on the principle of making things pleasant for those who please the market and unpleasant for those who fail to do so," he observed in *An Economist's Protest,* "and whatever defects this principle may have, it is better than none."[20] When Cannan had the opportunity to choose between established practice and an emerging alternative, he almost always opted for the former. Thus he became one of the most prominent academic advocates of the return to the gold standard at its prewar level in the 1920s, a position that would harm his reputation in later years.[21] He expressed dismay at economists' increasingly technical methodologies during the final stages of his career, arguing that his colleagues worshipped abstract figures "like the stone and wooden idols of the more degraded religions."[22] And he absolutely despised Keynes's newfangled theories, calling him the "second most mischievous pseudo-economist, Marx being the first and the rest nowhere."[23]

Cannan did not have the conventional attributes of an institution builder. Throughout his tenure at the LSE he maintained only a part-time affiliation, commuting to his teaching engagements from a residence in Oxford. His mastery of the discipline did not extend to readings far beyond the shores of England, and even his most devoted disciples were quick to acknowledge his distinctly parochial sensibility.[24] His teaching focused on the critical analysis of his predecessors' doctrines rather than the elaboration and propagation of his own.[25] He was also, as Lionel Robbins recalled, "a poor lecturer, apt to mumble into his beard or, when he spoke up, not necessarily in full control of the tonality of his voice." Putting it gently, Robbins concluded that Cannan "made no concessions to the convenience of his hearers."[26] This assessment was not his alone. T. E. Gregory recalled Cannan's "very difficult delivery" and his "habit of looking over our heads into a distant corner of the room, so that much of what he said was altogether missed by us, in both senses of the word."[27] These qualities served to narrow his range of disciples considerably and to lead his public influence to pale in comparison with that of Keynes, his younger and more dynamic counterpart in Cambridge. Nevertheless, Cannan was the most prominent remaining defender of economic orthodoxy in England, and to a small cadre of students his contrarian sensibility lent him a certain charisma. Lionel Robbins recalled, "At L.S.E. and within its sphere of contacts, his ascendancy was paramount. We revered him. We hung on his words. We conned over his every piece of writing. He represented for us archetypal mature wisdom in his subject."[28] Over time, as his students ascended to teaching posts of their own, the LSE's Economics Department became known for offering conservative alternatives to the more progressive proposals emanating from Cambridge.[29] Long after the profession had left Cannan behind, scholars would identify the market advocacy associated with the economists at the LSE as an outgrowth of his singular personality.[30]

But if Cannan's appointment helps explain how the LSE fell into its unlikely role as an institutional home for conservative economics, it does not account for the extremity of its leading professors' views in the early 1930s. Although Lionel Robbins had been converted from guild socialism to market advocacy in part by Cannan's teachings, his views departed from those of his mentor in a number of significant ways. Most important, he read German easily and extensively and familiarized himself with a broad international literature that remained largely obscure to his predecessor. While Cannan had struggled to register his dissatisfactions with Marshallian economics in terms derived from other British economists, Robbins discovered an alternative intellectual tradition in Austria that directly addressed many of his concerns. As his colleagues at the LSE observed, Robbins was not a particularly innovative thinker; his great skill lay in his capacity to aggregate and synthesize the scholarly achievements of others.[31] In a discipline that remained distinctly insular, however, he achieved significant originality by elaborating on the insights of foreign sources that his colleagues found largely obscure.[32] While Cannan's distinctly British sensibility had cultivated an environment at the LSE that was friendly to conservatism, the ideas that defined its leading professors' views in the early years of the Great Depression were imported from abroad.

The Austrian tradition that Robbins uncovered had been established by Carl Menger, one of the three developers of marginal-utility theory, in the middle years of the nineteenth century. It was characterized, in part, by a commitment to theoretical abstraction. Menger had clarified his methodological views during a bitter dispute, which became known as the *Methodenstreit,* with the German economist Gustav von Schmoller. Schmoller argued that economists should devote the majority of their attention to the accumulation of vast sets of data, from which they would eventually use induction to arrive at their analysis. Menger did not deny the benefits of historical information or inductive reasoning, but he believed that economic theory emerged primarily through deductions from first principles. And while Schmoller used his accumulated data to advocate for reform, Menger's respect for the organic logic of the market led him to express suspicions of plans to bring about rapid or dramatic social change.[33] Although Menger was no ideologue, his elaboration of the abstract workings of the price mechanism implied a suspicion of excessive interference in its activities, and many of his successors became known for their market-oriented sensibilities.

The most strident market advocate among them was Ludwig von Mises, an economist for the Vienna Chamber of Commerce who questioned the capacity of socialism to establish a rational pricing system for goods. Although Mises acknowledged that work-arounds might be developed to identify appropriate prices for consumer goods, he argued in an influential 1920 article that state ownership would render the construction, or even the simulation, of a competitive market for production goods impossible. In the absence of such a market, there was no way to determine how to allocate resources efficiently. "There is only groping in the dark," he wrote. "Socialism is the abolition of rational economy."[34] Mises followed this article with *Die Gemeinwirtschaft,* a book that provided a much more extensive economic and cultural critique of the socialist worldview and ignited a debate between socialist and free-market economists that persisted for decades.[35] Robbins read the book within a year of its publication and shortly thereafter corresponded with Mises to inquire about the possibility of translating part of it into English.[36]

Robbins's readings in Austrian economists from Menger to Mises helped him develop the views that defined his scholarship in the early 1930s. Unlike Cannan, he was passionately committed to abstraction, arguing in his most famous work that economic analysis proceeded primarily through the deductive rather than the inductive method.[37] Austrian capital theory, as expounded by Eugen von Böhm-Bawerk, helped convince him that government meddling in interest rates had far-reaching ancillary effects on the business cycle that could do grievous harm to the economy. And Mises's critique of socialism and corresponding defense of the efficiency of the market helped lead him to the conclusion that attempts to interfere with the price mechanism were almost always misguided. Robbins's appointment to the LSE faculty in 1929 therefore represented not merely a perpetuation but a significant extension of the opposition to Keynes and Cambridge that had characterized the department under Cannan's leadership.

The extent of Robbins's disagreements with Keynes emerged on a very public stage soon after he joined the faculty of the LSE. The Labour government under Ramsay MacDonald convened the Economic Advisory Council in 1930 with the goal of developing policy proposals to counteract the persistent unemployment that had plagued the British economy throughout the 1920s. The council quickly realized that it was confronting a global economic slump of extraordinary proportions, and Keynes, as a leading member, persuaded MacDonald to allow him to establish a separate Committee of Economists to examine the causes of and potential solutions to the developing crisis. He had just completed *A Treatise on Money*, which attributed England's persistent unemployment problems in part to an excess of savings over investment, and proposed a program of public works as one remedy.[38] Citing the distortions that wage rigidity was creating within a framework of free trade, Keynes was also beginning to warm to the idea of a tariff.[39] He privately assured MacDonald that the committee would produce a unanimous memorandum, and he expected it to conform largely to his views.[40] Robbins was surprised and honored to receive an invitation to join the new group. Presumably Keynes wanted it to demonstrate some ideological diversity and expected that Robbins's relative youth would make him somewhat deferential to his more senior colleagues. It did not take long for Robbins to disabuse Keynes of that notion. Citing an international literature that was largely unfamiliar to the other members of the committee, Robbins argued that many of the group's central assumptions were ill founded. He encouraged them to solicit the opinions of younger scholars from other countries, suggesting as one possibility the Austrian economist Friedrich Hayek, who had recently written an article criticizing public works proposals in the United States.[41] The Austrian capital theory expounded by Hayek, Robbins believed, would demonstrate that the slump was caused by an excessive investment in fixed capital provoked by artificially low rates of interest rather than the depressive effects of an artificially high rate of interest that Keynes had blamed in the *Treatise*.[42] Robbins argued that the government, rather than accepting wage rigidity as a given and trying to encourage investment, should promote flexibility and avoid artificial stimulations that ran the risk of provoking another unsustainable boom. He was appalled by Keynes's suggestion of a moderate tariff and deeply skeptical of the benefits of any program of public works. Keynes was dismayed by Robbins's intransigence and expressed little interest in soliciting opinions from foreign scholars. Although other members of the committee were sympathetic to some of Robbins's criticisms, he stood alone in his refusal to sign a compromise memorandum, demanding instead to submit a minority report.[43] Keynes's failure to achieve unanimity represented a significant setback in his attempts to leverage the prestige of the profession in support of his public policy views, and his outrage at Robbins's insubordination set the stage for a decade of intense disagreements between Cambridge and the LSE.

Shortly before engaging in these public disputes with Keynes, Robbins had arranged for Hayek to present a series of lectures at the LSE in January 1931.[44] The fortuitous timing led some to conclude that Robbins was drawing on Austria for intellectual reinforcements. "While the controversy about public works was developing," the Cambridge economist Joan Robinson recalled, "Professor Robbins sent to Vienna for a member of the Austrian school to provide a counter-attraction to Keynes."[45] As a star pupil of the distinguished economist Friedrich von Wieser and one of the most active members of a regular *Privatseminar* on economic theory and social-scientific methodology that Ludwig von Mises held for young Viennese intellectuals beginning in 1924, Hayek had developed an impressive range of connections throughout the Austrian academic world. He also was unusually discursive in Anglo-American political economy, in part because of connections formed during an extended research visit to New York City in 1923–1924 and at international conferences in subsequent years. Nevertheless, at the time he was still a young and little-published economist caught within an Austrian academic system that was notorious for making the journey to a professorship lengthy and penurious. Outside his native country Hayek's scholarship remained largely obscure.

The faculty and students at the LSE saw this visitor as a "discovery" of Robbins's, and his lectures proved a source of "great excitement." During four gatherings Hayek presented to packed crowds the incipient work that would be published shortly thereafter as *Prices and Production*. Many in the audience struggled to understand Hayek's argument, finding his accent heavy, his presentation largely "non-followable," and his ideas confusingly "tangled."[46] His first lecture, however, demonstrated a knowledge of the history of British monetary theory that would have been extraordinary in a native scholar, let alone one who had been educated within a different national tradition. Further, he drew extensively on ideas from Austrian capital theory that were novel to many members of the audience; although they were difficult for scholars unfamiliar with its antecedents to understand, they appeared to hold the potential to address urgent problems in the study of business cycles. Like Keynes, Hayek relied on the Swedish economist Knut Wicksell's distinction between the natural rate of interest and the market rate of interest, and analyzed the influence of the lending activities of banks on the relationship between them. Hayek's grounding in capital theory, however, led him to dwell on the effects of a divergence between the two rates on the period of production. He believed that when the market rate dipped below the natural rate, longer-term methods of production would appear to become more profitable, and companies would shift their investments away from capital goods that yielded consumer products in the short term. Over time consumers would respond to this shift by bidding up the relative prices of goods that were currently available; in this new environment the market rate of interest would rise, businesses would abandon their investments in more roundabout methods of production, and a crisis would commence.[47] Crucially, this line of reasoning suggested to Hayek that any "artificial stimulants" would further disrupt the relationship between the market rate of interest and the natural rate of interest, sowing the seeds of "new disturbances and new crises." The only solution to a depression, he suggested in *Prices and Production,* was "to leave it to time to effect a permanent cure by the slow process of adapting the structure of production to the means available for capital purposes."[48] Hayek concluded with an argument that the current unsettled state of monetary theory made any movement away from the gold standard unwise, and that attempts to intervene in a prolonged depression with targeted public expenditures would distort the pattern of investment and thereby prolong stagnation.[49] The best way for governments to respond to the economic crisis, in his bleak assessment, was to do nothing at all.

Robbins immediately recognized Hayek as a powerful ally in his arguments against public expenditures, credit expansion, and tariffs. He made his enthusiasm very clear when the LSE's director, William Beveridge, suggested that Hayek might be an appropriate choice for the long-vacant Tooke Chair of Economic Science that Jacob Viner had just declined.[50] Hayek, who had engaged in idle daydreams about the possibility of a professorship in London, was flatly astonished at his good fortune in receiving the offer.[51] As the longtime hub of the financial world and an increasingly dynamic center for economic thought, it seemed an ideal situation. "I mean, if you are at thirty-two a professor at the London School of Economics," he later told an interviewer, "you don't have any further ambitions."[52] He also felt an immediate affinity for the cultural life of his adopted country. It provided a social framework, he observed, where people seemed to "understand what your needs are at the moment without mentioning them." This genteel sensibility and the complex messages it was capable of conveying through formal conventions alone made Austria seem foreign by comparison. "It was like stepping into a warm bath," he remarked, "where the atmosphere is the same temperature as your body."[53]

Hayek's arrival helped establish the LSE as a center for economists who dissented from the views associated with Keynes and Cambridge. Within six months of his visiting lectures, he published the first of two lengthy critiques of Keynes's *Treatise on Money* in the LSE's journal, *Economica*. He excoriated Keynes for the total absence of capital theory from his analysis. Keynes conceded the criticism but then turned to an attack on Hayek, ridiculing his assumption that there was an "automatic mechanism in the economic system" to equalize the rates of savings and investment.[54] Hayek, in turn, replied by observing that Keynes failed to provide a coherent explanation of the causes that led the rates of savings and investment to diverge. Keynes acknowledged that his analysis required further revisions, but he indicated in private correspondence with Hayek that there was "a better way to spend one's time than in controversy."[55] His colleague Piero Sraffa then continued the assault, arguing in a devastating journal article that Hayek's theory relied on a strangely simplified conception of money and that his assumption that there was a single natural rate of interest was absurd.[56] Over time the tone of these disputes became increasingly vitriolic. Keynes described *Prices and Production* as "one of the most frightful muddles I have ever read," and Sraffa added that Hayek built up "a terrific steamhammer in order to crack a nut—and then he does not crack it."[57] By the end of 1932 Hayek was widely recognized as the leading theoretical opponent of Keynes's ideas, but neither had emerged with his arguments unscathed.

While Hayek's writings strengthened the department's opposition to Keynes's ideas, his international connections augmented its reputation for cosmopolitanism. The list of visitors to the LSE in the 1930s included leading figures from a broad range of national backgrounds, such as Erik Lindahl, Bertil Ohlin, and Ragnar Frisch from Scandinavia, Constantino Bresciani-Turroni from Italy, Frank Knight and Jacob Viner from the University of Chicago, William Rappard from Switzerland, and Hayek's Austrian acquaintances Gottfried Haberler, Fritz Machlup, and Joseph Schumpeter.[58] These visitors discovered a department that maintained much of the closeness and conviviality that had defined the LSE in its more haphazard early years: Hayek, Robbins, and their colleague Arnold Plant lived near one another in Hampstead Garden Suburb and freely shared books and conversation outside university hours, members of the department gathered for tea in the common room on a daily basis, and most of the leading figures convened regularly for a grand seminar in which new work was presented and critiqued.[59] The obvious importance of economics in the contemporary political environment combined with the youthfulness of the department's leading figures to create a sense of exhilaration among its students and lecturers. As Nicholas Kaldor later recalled, the early 1930s at the LSE were "a time of endless discussions which went on at all hours of the day and night," pervaded by an "atmosphere of creative tension" that subsequent generations would struggle to comprehend.[60]

Despite the importance of Hayek's arrival, it remained clear to all that Robbins was the department's dominant personality. He taught the foundational course that introduced incoming students to the subject, convened the seminar in which members of the department shared their new work, and oversaw the department's primary administrative tasks. His personal charisma, dedication to his students, broad mastery of the contemporary literature, and bureaucratic capabilities were widely recognized. With the publication of *The Great Depression* in 1934, Robbins synthesized many of his and Hayek's policy recommendations in a form that could be approached by a general reader. While Hayek's writings at that time remained highly abstruse and challenging for even graduate students in economics to understand, Robbins's prose was fluid, clear, and occasionally dramatic. Denying the common narrative that attributed the recent collapse largely to failures of the market mechanism, Robbins instead cited interventionary policies as the primary culprit. "The cartelisation of industry, the growth of the strength of trade unions, the multiplication of State controls, have created an economic structure which, whatever its ethical or aesthetic superiority, is certainly much less capable of rapid adaptation to change than was the older more competitive system," he wrote. "This puts it very mildly."[61] He worried, on the one hand, about the "impediments to enterprise" created by these interventions and, on the other hand, about the possibility of an unsustainable inflationary boom created by the attempts to address the Depression with a massive program of public works.[62] His policy recommendations included restoring the international gold standard, dramatically reducing restrictions on international trade, preventing trade unions from blocking those who were willing to accept a lower wage, and relaying a clear message that failing businesses would not be saved from bankruptcy.[63] On a grand historical scale he framed his analysis as a celebration of the free-market system that he attributed to England before the Great War and a lamentation of the departures from it that had accumulated since that time.[64]

Both Hayek and Robbins very clearly identified what they were arguing against. In Robbins's terms, it was not the conditions of capitalism that had precipitated the present crisis, but rather their negation.[65] He wanted to roll back a range of reforms that disrupted credit cycles and diminished businesses' abilities to adapt to changing conditions. Hayek, too, saw his message at this point in his career as primarily critical. In his inaugural lecture he stated that it was "probably no exaggeration to say that economics developed mainly as the outcome of the investigation and refutation of successive Utopian proposals." He situated himself within a long line of practitioners who were experts in demonstrating that attempts to redress the "undesirable effects of the existing system" were "based upon a complete disregard of those forces which actually enabled it to work."[66] Neither held any pretensions that the capitalist system was ideal, or even that its workings would allow for a swift resolution to the present crisis. When Robbins came under sharp criticism for his failure to provide a route out of the Depression, he responded by arguing that the development of such a road map was not within his purview. "If I see a man who has lost his way in a powder factory, about to strike a match, it is surely not incumbent on me to hold my peace because I do not know the way out myself," he explained in a 1932 letter to the *Economist*. "And, in fact, I do not know any 'way out' by means of grandiose policies. It is the grandiose policies which have brought us to our present position."[67] At this point in their careers, Hayek and Robbins both concentrated their energies on critical inquiries into the economic implications of political philosophies and policy proposals pursued by others rather than the development of their own. They focused on discrediting rather than constructing a social ideal, and as a result the tenor of their rhetoric was overwhelmingly negative.

The bleakness of Hayek's and Robbins's assessment of their prospects was further exacerbated by the arrival of Keynes's *General Theory of Employment, Interest, and Money* in 1936. Until that point economics at Cambridge had been impeded by lingering defects in *A Treatise on Money* that Keynes himself had acknowledged. By abandoning the assumption that total output was given and turning his attention toward the level of aggregate demand, however, he dramatically shifted the framework of discussion and created a much more robust explanation for the problem of stable equilibrium below full employment.[68] To its initial readers, *The General Theory* seemed to have been constructed to address precisely the situation that the economies of England and the United States were confronting, and to offer a clear road map to the solution of the crisis. Further, its arguments in favor of loose credit, increased public expenditure, and restrictions on trade appeared to validate populist approaches to economic policy. This enraged economists who held opposing views; in correspondence with his colleague Jacob Viner, the Chicago economist Frank Knight wrote that Keynes was "taking the side of the man-in-the-street," lending succor to "anti-intellectual" views, and "passing the keys of the citadel out of the window to the Philistines hammering at the gates."[69] Keynes had the additional advantage of endorsing these popular sentiments in a highly abstruse form. Although it was soon simplified by his colleagues and successors, his language in the book seemed to many economists willfully obscure. Viner observed in his review of *The General Theory,* "No old term for an old concept is used when a new one can be coined, and if old terms are used new meanings are generally assigned to them."[70] (Privately he admitted that he found its terminology "terrifying.")[71] This combination of timeliness, esotericism, and support for prevailing opinion proved extraordinarily potent because the book appeared to present a vitally important message on which much academic work remained to be done. As Albert Hirschman has observed, Keynes "managed to present common sense in paradox's clothing and in fact made his theory doubly attractive: it satisfied at the same time the intellectuals' craving for populism and their taste for difficulty and paradox."[72]

Although *The General Theory* had little immediate impact on public policy, it swept through the profession with, in the terms of the MIT economist Paul Samuelson, "the unexpected virulence of a disease first attacking and decimating an isolated tribe of South Sea islanders."[73] Even Keynes's critics acknowledged the broad influence of his work on young scholars in the field. Reviewing the book from his position at Harvard, Joseph Schumpeter recounted "the expectations of the best of our students, the impatience they displayed at the delay in getting hold of their copies, the eagerness with which they devoured them, and the interest manifested by all sectors of Anglo-American communities that are up to this kind of reading."[74] Despite the distinct lack of enthusiasm among the department's leading professors, graduate students and young faculty at the LSE shared in the excitement. Tibor Scitovsky recalled that "most of the students" there "avidly read it, day and night," and were "bowled over" by its analysis.[75] They shared a venue to exchange ideas with students in Cambridge through a joint seminar that Hayek's student Abba Lerner had established in 1933, which increasingly became a site of evangelical conversion. Lerner himself became a Keynesian after spending six months in Cambridge in 1934–1935.[76]

The General Theory was intended as an assault on the entire edifice of orthodox economic theory, but Keynes was not above sending, as Alvin Hansen observed in a prominent review, "many a dart at the neo-Viennese and London school."[77] He drew particular attention to the contrast between its optimistic and constructive approach and the much bleaker and more defeatist perspective in the work associated with the LSE. "The right remedy for the trade cycle is not to be found in abolishing booms and thus keeping us permanently in a semi-slump," Keynes observed, "but in abolishing slumps and thus keeping us permanently in a quasi-boom."[78] Keynes's mocking treatment of Hayek's ideas quickly became common even within seminars at the LSE. After converting to Keynesianism while on a fellowship in the United States during the 1934–1935 academic year, Hayek's younger colleague Nicholas Kaldor began making sarcastic interjections in seminars that became increasingly notorious within the school.[79] In the midst of this atmosphere, Hayek made the devastating decision not to submit a review of *The General Theory*. He later cited many grounds for his inaction, including a disinclination to renew engagement with a scholar who seemed to hold ever-shifting views, a desire to wait until the publication of a revised version of his own capital theory, and a reluctance to discredit Keynes when many of the other leading economists seemed much worse.[80] Regardless of the reasons, his decision seemed to many an admission of defeat.

Hayek faced the prohibitive challenge of advocating for quiescence in the face of an economic catastrophe that Keynes claimed he could solve. His colleague John Hicks later observed, "It is in its application to deflationary slumps that the Hayek theory is at its worst; and it is a terrible fact that it was in just such conditions—in 1931–2—that it was first propounded."[81] Hicks recalled that in the absence of a forceful reply to Keynes, Hayek's theories gradually "slipped through our fingers" as economists turned their focus toward what they perceived to be more urgent problems.[82] Students at the LSE were hesitant to accept a theory that seemed to offer no clear route out of the crisis. In Scitovsky's terms, they felt that they were being taught a mode of economics that was "very remote from economic reality."[83] Milton Friedman, who was a graduate student at Columbia and the University of Chicago at the time, recounted that he and his generation were not convinced by the proposition that "you just have to let the bottom drop out of the world." He concluded that by encouraging a "do-nothing policy both in Britain and the United States," Hayek and Robbins "did harm."[84] Hayek's dwindling collection of graduate students abandoned work they had commenced under him to redirect their studies toward problems raised by Keynes. By the end of the decade only two or three Hayekians were left at the LSE.[85] After the campus relocated to Cambridge during World War II, one of his few remaining students recalled that "most of the younger economists of the time thought that Hayek on employment and output was out of date, was out of fashion. They didn't take it very seriously."[86] The magnum opus he published in 1941, *The Pure Theory of Capital*, went largely ignored. Hayek himself, noting the profession's turn toward macroeconomics and econometrics after the publication of *The General Theory*, acknowledged that he became perceived as "old-fashioned, with no sympathy for modern ideas."[87]

As he confronted this hostile professional and political environment, Lionel Robbins began to reassess his line of analysis. Working alongside Keynes during the war, he moderated and in some cases reversed the uncompromising stances he had adopted earlier in his career. "Up to a point," Hayek later recalled, "Robbins was won over by Keynes to semi-Keynesian views."[88] Robbins made his conversion official in a series of talks delivered in Cambridge in the spring of 1947. In three lectures he expressed some support for progressive taxation of the wealthy and redistribution of income to the poor, an expansive interpretation of public goods, and a vigorous regulatory authority.[89] Most astonishingly, he acknowledged the "profound limitations" of the private-enterprise system "as an instrument for maintaining reasonable constancy of *aggregate* demand."[90] It was the job of public policy, he asserted, to redress these limitations. In later years Robbins would argue that he always accepted a vigorous role for the government, and that his writings from the early 1930s simply failed to make that sufficiently clear.[91] In his 1947 lectures, however, he acknowledged that his understanding of the government's role in managing demand was the product of a "change of point of view." He quite explicitly renounced his earlier arguments against government responsibility for aggregate demand, attributing them to his prior adherence to an intellectual tradition with "a tendency to ignore certain deep-seated possibilities of disharmony, in a way which, I now think, led sometimes to superficiality and sometimes to positive error."[92] He even went so far as to appropriate, with some caveats, the term "planning" to describe his perspective.[93] In a retrospective on his career, he called his arguments with Keynes against government stimulation of the economy "the greatest mistake of my professional career" and said that *The Great Depression* was a book he "would willingly see forgotten." Although he was not willing to renounce the entirety of his analysis of the causes of the Depression, he conceded that "to treat what developed subsequently in the way which I then thought valid was as unsuitable as denying blankets and stimulants to a drunk who has fallen into an icy pond, on the ground that his original trouble was overheating."[94]

By the late 1930s the approach to economics that Hayek and Robbins had incubated at the LSE was no longer prevalent even within their own department. Robbins was beginning to abandon his previous positions, while Hayek increasingly directed his attention to problems unrelated to his prior work on monetary theory. Hayek had foreshadowed the difficulties that precipitated this decline in his inaugural remarks at the LSE, which acknowledged that market advocates tended to dwell too much on criticisms of proposals for reform and to focus too little on elaborations of their own positive vision. At the time he saw this as an unfortunate necessity, driven by the broad range of state activities that were being justified with woefully ill-considered invocations of economic theory. Similar exigencies had led the classical economists to allow "the impression to gain ground that *laissez-faire* was their ultimate and only conclusion," an interpretation that he found both incorrect and harmful to their popular influence. He thought that it would eventually be important to turn his attention to "the positive part of the economist's task, the delimitation of the field within which collective action is not only unobjectionable but actually a useful means of obtaining the desired ends."[95] Facing increasing professional and political irrelevance in the wake of the Keynesian revolution, Hayek decided that the time had come for him to begin to elaborate on his own positive vision. Market advocates, he determined, would need to do a better job of expounding the virtues of markets along with the vices of intervention, and of clarifying those points where moderation of the market mechanism would be necessary and beneficial. This line of inquiry would precipitate a dramatic shift in his professional identity, and would lay the early groundwork for a social transformation that he continued to envision even in the midst of his increasing marginalization. Although Hayek's writings on the immediate prospects for the economy were unfailingly grim, he retained an extraordinary confidence in the capacity of his ideas to alter the long-term course of events. Here, at least, he found it salutary for any sources of discouragement to be ignored.

During the 1930s the leading economists at the LSE saw their counterparts at the University of Chicago as their closest intellectual and ideological allies outside Vienna. They invited two of Chicago's most prominent figures, Jacob Viner and Frank Knight, to give lectures in London, and they cultivated a network of relationships between the departments that spanned the Atlantic.[96] The strongest of these connections was between Lionel Robbins and Jacob Viner, who recounted their first meeting in 1927 in terms more often used for romance than for discussions of theory. "I went for a walk with Robbins," Viner wrote to his wife the following day, "still debating theory, until 1:30 in a beautiful starlit night among the spires and towers of Oxford."[97] Robbins recalled needing to awaken the porter "like a defaulting undergraduate" on their return. In a later retrospective on Viner's career, Robbins described him as "the outstanding *all-rounder* of his time in our profession."[98] Friedrich Hayek had first met Frank Knight before moving to London, and wrote in 1936 that despite their occasional differences he could find "no other author with whom I feel myself so much in agreement."[99] Robbins, too, expressed particular admiration for Knight's work, assigning his treatise *Risk, Uncertainty and Profit* as an introductory textbook in economic theory and assisting with the publication of his collection of essays, *The Ethics of Competition*.[100] In 1937 Robbins told Viner that he was convinced that the economics faculty in Chicago was "easily the most important group in the world."[101]

It is easy to understand why economists at the LSE would have seen the faculty of the University of Chicago as engaged in a similar endeavor on the other side of the Atlantic. Chicago economists had developed a reputation as leading opponents of the economic policies associated with the New Deal. Several of them were highly critical of institutionalism, a methodology that relied on precisely the modes of inductive reasoning that Robbins had denounced.[102] After Keynes published his *General Theory,* some of the sharpest criticism of his ideas emanated from their department.[103] Chicago also developed a reputation for inculcating a conservative approach to political economy among its graduate students, who included Milton Friedman, George Stigler, and Aaron Director. Friedman later recalled that the "core" of his and his wife Rose's conservatism was attributable to the "common influence" of their time in the department. Its intellectual atmosphere, he indicated, led students to admire the "strength of the price system" and to feel "rather negative towards socialism, socialist economics."[104] Chicago seemed to be the last redoubt of economic sentiments that the rest of the profession was fast leaving behind.[105]

A closer consideration of the Chicago economists' writings, however, reveals that their assessments of their ideas did not always accord with those of their students and peers. The three leading market advocates at Chicago in the interwar years, Frank Knight, Jacob Viner, and Henry Simons, were all eager to distance their approach to political economy from the more extreme views associated with their colleagues in Austria and London. They saw themselves as moderate by comparison. Frank Knight made his opinion clear in a review of Robbins's *Economic Planning and International Order* in 1938, which descended into outright mockery. "We confront a picture of laisser faire bordering on the conception of a world-wide anarchist utopia," he remarked, "a vision of universal freedom and brotherhood, if only governments would cease from troubling and politicians go out and die, except for police functions." In contrast to Robbins, he believed that the preservation of "human liberties" was "likely to call for considerably more in a political way than mere negative contraction and retrenchment of activity."[106] In a letter to Walter Lippmann in 1937, Henry Simons put his dissatisfactions in still stronger terms. Ludwig von Mises's and Lionel Robbins's "notions regarding the proper spheres of governmental action, and the limitations of economic planning, are often fanatically extreme," he wrote, "and their contribution to the liberal cause, on balance, is probably a disservice."[107] Viner's friendship with Robbins softened his tone, but he, too, expressed concerns in private correspondence about the need for a "stabilizing influence" at the LSE to counteract its economists' "doctrinaire tendencies with respect to methods of analysis or selection of premises."[108] Their opinions did not diminish with the passage of time. In the early 1940s Viner referred to Mises's recent work as "really eccentric or crank economics," and Knight found it "slightly impatient and dogmatic" and often simply "contrary to facts."[109] Upon encountering Hayek's

Road to Serfdom several years later, Viner wrote to a friend that the book "overargues his case" and was riddled with "dogmas," and Knight told the publisher that it insufficiently recognized "the necessity, as well as political inevitability, of a wide range of governmental activity in relation to economic life in the future," instead dealing "only with the simpler fallacies."[110] They could hardly have made their opinions clearer. Although they shared with their colleagues in London an inclination to defend markets against excessive or ill-conceived interventions, they believed that the government had an essential role to play in the modern economy. Further, they worried that the extremity of the views associated with the LSE was rhetorically ill advised, distilling market advocacy into an unforgiving absolutism that was more likely to persuade readers of their opponents' views than their own.

The most influential of the market advocates at Chicago during the interwar years was Frank Knight. Knight has long been remembered as the "sage and oracle" of Chicago economics and one of the most prominent academic critics of the economic policies associated with the Roosevelt years.[111] His unusual background led him to stand out, both intellectually and interpersonally, from disciplinary norms. After growing up as the oldest of eleven children in an evangelical family in rural Illinois, he went on to pursue graduate training in German philosophy at Cornell before switching disciplines to economics because of an "ingrained skepticism" that one of his advisers said would "destroy the true philosophic spirit wherever he touches it."[112] As a teacher he was a phenomenon who, students recall, "dominated the intellectual atmosphere."[113] Smoking a corncob pipe and presenting unremitting critiques of economists past and present in a distinctive midwestern drawl, he became well known for revealing "scattered fragments of a complete philosophical system" in graduate courses that the student newspaper suggested be renamed "Frank Knight I" and "Frank Knight II."[114] Despite their notoriously diffuse presentation, these lectures were credited with transforming incoming socialists into nascent libertarians in an act of political alchemy often cited as the origin of the Chicago School.[115] George Stigler recalled Knight as his most influential professor at Chicago, and Milton Friedman remembered him as a "revered teacher" and one of the department's "stars"; both were considered by their peers to be members of a Knight affinity group that behaved, at times, like "Swiss guards."[116] Knight's unsparing criticisms of the naïveté of social reformers made him a notorious opponent of progressive economists and left an indelible mark on his students' approaches to political economy.

Attempts to harden Knight's oppositional remarks into a unitary social philosophy, however, run the risk of imparting a selective order to the deliberate messiness of Knight's worldview. His writings have never neatly aligned with his imputed role as a dedicated advocate of free enterprise. Instead, he perceived himself to be primarily a critic, more comfortable exposing the obfuscations of other theorists' systems than constructing his own.[117] He lived, as he acknowledged in *Risk, Uncertainty and Profit,* in "a world full of contradiction and paradox," and his primary instinct as a scholar was to expose these qualities where he perceived them to be elided.[118] His one philosophical absolute was a refusal to indulge in the uncritical adoption of absolutes.[119] "There is always a principle, plausible and even sound within limits, to justify any possible course of action and, of course, the opposite one," he explained in his 1950 presidential address before the American Economic Association. Like cookery, he continued, economic theory "calls for enough and not too much, far enough and not too far, in any direction."[120] Throughout his career he refused to extol the virtues of markets without drawing attention to their limitations, or to observe those limitations without enumerating the costs inherent in any attempt to overcome them.

Knight worried, in particular, about the moral life of market-centered societies. It was neither common nor desirable, he observed, for individuals to decide how to act on the basis of rational calculations of their own financial interests. Even those at the highest levels of business enterprise pursued profit more out of a love of competition than a desire for monetary gain. He wrote in *Risk, Uncertainty and Profit* that they "consume in order to produce rather than produce in order to consume, in so far as they do either. The real motive is the desire to excel, to win at a game, the biggest and most fascinating game yet invented, not excepting even statecraft and war."[121] Indeed, actions pursued purely for interests that economists would define as "rational" were widely considered abhorrent. The "rational, economic, criticism of values gives results repugnant to all common sense," he observed in his 1922 essay "Ethics and the Economic Interpretation," and the "economic man is the selfish, ruthless object of moral condemnation."[122] Market societies encourage such undesirable behaviors while discouraging the production of values not reflected by the price mechanism. "In a social order where all values are reduced to the money measure in the degree that this is true of modern industrial nations," he wrote the following year, "a considerable fraction of the most noble and sensitive characters will lead unhappy and even futile lives."[123] Knight believed that a capitalist society could sustain itself only to the extent that it consisted of individuals whose behavior departed from the norms it incentivized.

Knight's concerns about the morals of capitalism led him to express deep skepticism about any social vision that failed to suppress its potential excesses. He explained his reservations in reviewing an article by Hayek in 1949. Neither "freedom nor truth can be treated as an absolute," he wrote. "They conflict with beauty and morality and other values, and with one another, necessitating 'marginal' comparison and compromise, and correct proportioning."[124] He concluded that a social system that prioritized the market above all else would become imbalanced and prone to collapse. This should not be taken to mean, however, that he believed that any other system could solve the persistent tensions between a society's moral and material welfare. In a 1933 letter to Walter Smith, an economist at Williams College, he explained his peculiar synthesis of radicalism and conservatism. "Trying to look as deep as possible into fundamentals, I feel that both the radicals and conservatives are right," he wrote. "On the one hand, the old system had got to where its workings could not be tolerated, and there is absolutely no use in thinking of going back to it. On the other hand, it just doesn't seem real to me that any convention of the best minds could do much in the way of designing a new system to order."[125] Knight saw his world as consisting of desperately bad alternatives, which allowed him to advocate the market system despite a distaste for its effects and a growing conviction that it was piloting itself toward collapse. "I'm very curious as to what alternative to the profit-system you can think of that wouldn't be worse," he wrote to a colleague two decades later. "I've been trying to think of one for a half-century or so, without success."[126] He demonstrated the radical's capacity to lament the inadequacies of the present world and to yearn for a better one, but he lacked the ability to believe that the necessary options existed or that the desired changes might come to be. In the context of the 1930s, Knight's misgivings about alternative forms of social organization led him to be perceived as a market advocate. In stark contrast to some of his colleagues in London, however, his support for the market mechanism was both reluctant and restrained.

Although Chicago's reputation and intellectual atmosphere were defined largely by Knight's singular personality, Jacob Viner played the central role in its graduate education. Viner first developed his professional reputation through influential and densely erudite treatises on international trade and the history of economic thought. He then rose to public prominence in a role in the Treasury Department that forced him to spend much of the 1930s shuffling between Chicago and Washington. Within the department he was best known for his severe classroom demeanor. Like many universities in that period, Chicago accepted vast numbers of graduate students and sifted them over time through a policy of encouraged and enforced attrition. Viner's Economics 301, which became known as the premier graduate course on economic theory in the country, was designed to play the central role in this process, and he appeared to perform it with relish.[127] The student newspaper reported that he adopted a "hard-boiled" approach to teaching that reminded students of the Spanish Inquisition.[128] Paul Samuelson recalled that the course was "celebrated for Viner's ferocious manhandling of students, in which he not only reduced women to tears but on his good days drove returned paratroopers into hysteria and paralysis."[129] Students recalled him as "scornful of inferior people" and "an expert in intellectual evisceration and skinning," whose "self-appointed task in life seemed to be that of destroying confidence in students." But a compliment from Viner, one student recalled, was to be "treasured for one may be sure it was a genuine one from a most competent critic."[130] The department's reputation for theoretical rigor derived largely from his influence.[131]

At times Viner was represented in the popular press as a hard-line conservative economist. One newspaper columnist in 1936 wrote that he was "so far over to the Right in his views, in one sense, that he is as lonesome as Ibsen's master builder. He is of the let-nature-take-its-course school, against artificial price stimulants or controls."[132] Viner himself acknowledged in an interview later in his life that he might have been regarded by some within the Roosevelt government as an internal "saboteur."[133] When he directly addressed matters of public policy, however, he strongly emphasized his departures from anything resembling laissez-faire. His rhetoric was particularly strident in regard to limitations on the powers amassed by large corporations. "Nothing in the history of American business," he reminded his audience in a 1931 speech, "justifies undue confidence on the part of the American public that it can trust big business to take care of the community without supervision, regulation or eternal vigilance."[134] Although he took pains to acknowledge that size had some benefits, he identified "*the* important economic issue of our day" as the fact that "the mere *size* of business units tends almost inevitably to result in attempts to escape the impact of competition which have important—and in my opinion highly undesirable—consequences for the operation of the economic system."[135] He also strongly believed that democracy should take precedence over the dictates of economic theory. If the public wanted direct controls, he expressed the opinion that economists should set about developing efficient implementations rather than expressing frustration at perceived theoretical deficiencies. Satisfying such demands promoted confidence and stability in the economic system, which, Viner believed, held priority over governmental adherence in all cases to abstract economic theory.[136] His sympathy with certain aspects of the progressive critique of corporate power, in addition to his commitment to practical economic policy making and the maintenance of social and economic stability, led him to adopt a flexible and contextual approach to the problems he confronted.

Viner shared an instinctual support for free markets with Robbins, but he was much more willing to abandon his conservative inclinations to accommodate situational complexities and the political tenor of the time. "While I am more of a defeatist than you," he confided to his close friend in 1940, "and am more disposed to be content when the lesser of evils is chosen instead of the true good, I am wholly and admiringly with you in your aims."[137] Robbins recognized and respected Viner's reluctance to align himself with any abstract doctrine. "Jack was not a believer in any orthodox creed," Robbins wrote in a retrospective on Viner's career. "But he believed passionately in the liberal values: equality before the law, the maximum freedom for the individual compatible with similar privileges for his fellows, sympathy and help for the unfortunate."[138] Viner's ideological flexibility gained him a reputation for equanimity and respect for multiple points of view. One publication asserted in 1935 that "the Treasury's short, red-headed chief brain truster takes pride in the fact that he holds no iron-bound theories, belongs to no special school of economic thought, has never lacked the ability to tack quickly and expertly in any wind."[139] He cultivated the public persona of a scholar who eschewed the temptations of dogma in order to remain, in journalists' terms, a "middle-of-the-roader."[140] Although his language lacked Frank Knight's intensity of expression or deliberately paradoxical form, he shared with his colleague an inclination to defend market advocates from both their detractors and their own excesses.

Henry Simons had been a student of Knight's at the University of Iowa and was both younger and far less distinguished within the discipline than his senior colleagues. His publication record was slim and primarily oriented toward popular consumption. Students remember him as having been "not liked in the economics department," and George Stigler later recalled controversy over whether a scholar who "had written two book reviews in the previous twelve years could get tenure."[141] He was also plagued by health problems, which culminated in his death due to an excessive ingestion of sleeping pills in 1946, in what was termed an accident but believed by many to have been a suicide.[142] His fragile health left him an indifferent classroom teacher, defined largely by an outward appearance of indolence and a lack of interest in his less capable students' ideas.[143] Nevertheless, his strong engagement in matters of contemporary political debate, his unconventional points of view, and his greater proximity to the graduate students in both age and position garnered for him substantial influence. As a bachelor through much of his time at Chicago, he would gather with students in Hanley's tavern on a weekly basis, where he came to play a central role in the doctoral experiences of many students who never took a course with him during their time at the university.[144]

Like Knight and Viner, Simons was quick to remind his profession and the broader public that the virtues of markets were not easily replaced.[145] He was the first significant American economist to refer to himself as a "libertarian," and in his writings on the New Deal he expressed a strong conviction that even small acts of government intervention could inaugurate a gradual slide from a free economy to authoritarianism.[146] He firmly believed, as he indicated in 1938, "that the main direction of New Deal policies is toward authoritarian collectivism."[147] The strength of Simons's market advocacy led George Stigler to claim that his pamphlet "A Positive Program for Laissez-Faire" established him as "the forerunner of what the public and much of the economics profession now take to be the central position of the Chicago School—a devotion to private (competitive) markets to organize the production and consumption of goods, with only limited economic functions for the state."[148]

But also like his colleagues, Simons believed that powerful brakes were necessary to avert the perils associated with unhindered competition.

Through targeted acts of regulation and redistribution, he believed, the government could curb the cartelization and corresponding destabilization of the modern economic environment without excessively interfering with competitive business endeavors. His "positive program" suggested, for instance, that the government implement a "steeply progressive" income tax, which he believed would combat the concentration of economic power without obstructing the free play of marketplace competition. "Confining my remarks to matters of taxation, I may sound to you like a full-fledged New Dealer, or something worse," he acknowledged in a speech before an audience of Republicans in 1938. "My criticism of the Roosevelt administration, in this special field, is that it has been unduly backward and diffident about reform."[149] And like Viner, he assailed the increasing centrality of giant corporations within the modern economic system, proposing a series of dramatic steps to discourage consolidation and return the basic structure of American business to a smaller scale. Simons's "positive program" presumed that the "great enemy of democracy is monopoly, in all its forms," and proposed counteracting this through a "complete 'new deal' with respect to the private corporation," which involved eliminating horizontal and restricting vertical integrations, as well as nationalizing "both the railroads and the utilities, and all other industries in which it is impossible to maintain effectively competitive conditions."[150] He further proposed "direct limitations upon size, for the purpose of preventing unnecessary concentrations of power," asserting in justification that "we *have* created Frankensteins. The best single remedy lies in drastic narrowing of corporate powers, with the purpose of facilitating use of the corporate form for the organization of enterprise and production, while preventing its use for sheer aggregation of businesses and concentration of power."[151] Cumulatively, these ideas amounted to a complete reinvention of the corporate form that Simons hoped would counteract a trend toward consolidation and reshape the American economy around competitive small producers. "The corporation is, I think, simply running away with our enterprise system," he wrote to the Norwegian journalist Trygve Hoff in 1939.[152] He believed that the preservation of capitalism required a full-scale assault on its largest enterprises.

Simons was both more politically engaged and a more strident public defender of capitalist forms of social organization than either Viner or Knight. As market advocacy began to gain traction after World War II, some of its leading figures therefore turned to his work in the hope of finding support for their ideas. They were appalled at what they discovered. Leonard Read, the director of the libertarian institute, the Foundation for Economic Education, wrote to one of Simons's colleagues in 1947 that his book was too "loaded with the advocacy of collectivistic ideas" to be of use to him.[153] William F. Buckley Jr. had a similar reaction, writing that Simons's program "would give to the state unprecedented power" and provided "a sure program for the destruction of the free economy."[154] Decades later Ronald Coase reiterated these opinions, finding "A Positive Program for Laissez-Faire" to be a "highly interventionist pamphlet" that sought to use antitrust to "restructure American industry" and "reform things by nationalization."[155] Meanwhile, Ralph Nader cited Simons's unsparing attacks on the corporate form as an unlikely source of inspiration for his own assaults on concentrations of economic power.[156] Such responses provide a reminder that the stridency of the later Chicago School was a product of change rather than constancy. Although the early Chicago economists viewed themselves as defenders of capitalism in a social environment that had rapidly turned hostile, they were convinced that it was a system that required moderation, regulation, and restraint. They were drawn to it more by skepticism of the available alternatives than by any confidence in the desirability of the market ideal.

One further difference distinguished the faculty at Chicago from their colleagues in London: they did not conceive of themselves as a purposive group. Although some of their students would go on to ascribe a retrospective coherence to their time at Chicago, Knight, Viner, and Simons demonstrated only limited affinity for one another and little sense that they considered themselves members of an ideological community. Years later Knight recalled the greatly differing interests of the Chicago economists in those years, declaring flatly that there was no "Midway monolith." Viner emphasized that he was never a conscious participant in any "school," and that if one existed, his membership would have been tenuous.[157] "In the 1930s economics appeared to be a little different at the University of Chicago than elsewhere, but the same statement could be made about most major universities," George Stigler explained. The "Chicago School," he asserted, did not yet exist; after all, Knight was "severely critical of the ethical basis of a competitive economy," much of Simons's program "was almost as harmonious with socialism as with private-enterprise capitalism," and Jacob Viner "rebelled against doctrinaire or simplified or 'extreme' positions."[158] Chicago economists in the interwar years were fashioned into a group through the loose reflections of certain students, colleagues, and successors, but one can accept the term only by denying the contrary impressions of its ostensible members.

In their personal interactions they expressed little mutual warmth, virtually no belief that they held allied perspectives, and some skepticism about one another's worldviews. The relationship between Knight and Viner is emblematic. When Knight was at the University of Iowa in the 1920s, they engaged in a notably warm correspondence, expressing a shared appreciation for theory that distinguished their methodologies from the historicist inclinations of their peers.[159] By 1927, however, Viner began to criticize Knight's increasing preoccupation with the assumptions that lay at the foundations of social-scientific analysis. It was "crazy," Viner told him, to believe "that metaphysical adventures offer the only scope for your talents."[160] Privately he wrote to his former mentor at Harvard that Knight was "wasting himself in his metaphysical speculations."[161] Knight responded by saying that such criticisms made him "wince," arguing that he was inquiring into precisely the "things on which economists primarily and especially need to be straightened out."[162] This pattern of intermittently friendly and fraught conflict over fundamentals persisted after Knight's arrival at the University of Chicago. In one of the few surviving letters between them from the 1930s, Knight expressed his exasperation at differences in their interpretation of economic theory that had emerged during their discussions of the curriculum. He declared that robbing banks was "a less dishonest way of making a living" than publishing on economic theory amid such disagreement on fundamentals, and expressed his unwillingness to peddle "as science what is either unintelligible or fallacious to my peers in the profession."[163] Their quarrels carried over to graduate teaching, in which students were sometimes asked to shuffle between classrooms as proxies in ongoing arguments and were often driven to despair over whose tastes to indulge in oral exams.[164] They were not close personal friends and communicated rarely in the years after Viner's postwar transfer to Princeton.

The relationship between Viner and Simons was distinctly colder. As early as 1925 Viner was expressing reservations about Simons's capabilities, writing to Knight that although he had "no misgivings as to his intellectual capacity," he was skeptical of Simons's "capacity for sustained effort not yielding constant mental exhilaration."[165] After Simons and Knight made the transition from Iowa to Chicago, Viner's impressions of his younger colleague solidified. In 1935 he wrote to J. M. Clark that on "the role of competition, Henry Simons could be counted on to give a forceful, well written, dogmatic, and highly simplified exposition of whatever view he happened to hold at the moment."[166] In evaluating Simons's dissertation in 1937 Viner adopted a less judicious tone, insisting that it be "put on the Library shelves" only under the condition "that several hundred of the abusive adjectives applied to those who do not agree with him be removed."[167] On at least one occasion he voted not to grant Simons tenure, setting himself in direct opposition to Knight.[168] To Viner, the role of the academic was to provide dispassionate and, to the extent possible, objective analysis divorced from political ideology or rhetorical devices. He believed that Simons's work contravened these professional ideals, and he never altered this impression or perceived him as a peer or ally.

Of the three, Knight and Simons had the closest relationship. Knight demonstrated a pattern of allying himself with younger students and colleagues, such as Harry Gideonse and Aaron Director, and attempting to shepherd them through a sometimes hostile department. He had served as a mentor to Simons in Iowa and continued to provide support and encouragement in Chicago even while his younger colleague suffered through a debilitating illness and a sustained inability to complete his dissertation or publish academic research. The other members of the department did not share Knight's enthusiasms. In 1935 Knight wrote to Viner to indicate that the department's treatment of Director had "finished any sentiment of attachment or loyalty I felt for the group," and to notify him that "if anything of the sort happens to Simons, I will decidedly prefer to be somewhere else rather than here." But even as Knight served as a valuable mentor and advocate for Simons, his imposing personality and wholly divergent intellectual interests meant that he was not quite a peer. At times Simons chafed at his mentor's tendency toward abstraction and apocalyptic pronouncements, privately observing that he was exasperated at Knight's melancholy fixation on "the futility of struggle against deep historic forces of disintegration."[169] After Aaron Director left the department, Simons wrote that despite Knight's presence he felt, "*qua* economist, quite alone."[170]

The complex network of relationships among Knight, Viner, and Simons reveals that the Chicago economists in this period did not perceive themselves to be part of a coherent group that agreed on any particular agenda. Their allegiances with one another were attributable more to common intellectual opponents than to an established theoretical or ideological program. They shared a distrust for the rapid growth of the interventionary state and the progressive orientation toward radical social experimentation, but little else. They remained distanced from one another, both personally and intellectually, and did not actively view themselves as a "school" or even as loosely affiliated allies in a political battle. Further, their political ideas and approaches to political economy were deeply ambivalent, and all diverged sharply from anything resembling a strict adherence to the dictates of the market. They were not hesitant to condemn colleagues whose adherence to ideological principles was perceived to be excessively dogmatic, and each was willing to concede roles and purposes for governmental intervention that strayed far from the ideas characteristic of their colleagues in London. They operated in an environment in which their professional colleagues and the broader population believed overwhelmingly that markets needed to be restrained. They were willing to accept this critique to a substantial degree, and correspondingly incorporated substantial competitive restraints into their visions of an ideal political economy. As a result of this lack of coherence and this ready willingness to make broad concessions to the critics of laissez-faire, they did not share a movement culture during the Roosevelt years. Market advocacy in the United States during the 1930s was dispersed, concessionary, politically abstemious, and deeply conflicted in its conception of the social ideal.

To assert that the early Chicago economists did not perceive themselves to be part of a coherent school, did not espouse a consistent ideological program, and did not even identify one another as peers engaged in a common endeavor is not to argue that they failed to have a decisive impact on their students and the economics profession during its most transformative years. Students' recollections of their educations at Chicago often take the form of a conversion narrative, even if the missionaries were reluctant and perhaps even unwitting in their roles. Time and again students remember entering Chicago as passionate socialists and departing as ardent advocates of the capitalist order. James Buchanan's experience is exemplary. After arriving at Chicago with a strong socialist orientation, he enrolled in Frank Knight's course on price theory. Knight was "not an ideologue, and he made no attempt to convert anybody," Buchanan recalls, but nevertheless, "within six weeks after enrollment in Frank Knight's course in price theory, I had been converted into a zealous advocate of the market order."[171] It was, as Milton Friedman recalled, not a process of transmitting specific policies or approaches to economic theory, but rather one of passing on a "general outlook or general philosophy."[172] The faculty at Chicago at the time held some views that ran contrary to accepted convention in the broader profession, and their students embraced and extended that heterodoxy with renewed energy and a revolutionary zeal. Hence it was not unreasonable for Paul Samuelson to refer to Frank Knight on his passing as "one of America's most influential intellectuals," even if "few people would recognize his name."[173]

Milton Friedman, who himself went to Chicago with no notable political convictions and the modest goal of becoming an actuary, aptly described the atmosphere that made the conflicted teachings of the department's professors assume a kind of coherence in the minds of their students. "You have to recognize what the environment was at the time" beyond the confines of the department, he urged scholars in later years. The "general intellectual atmosphere was strongly prosocialist. It was strongly in favor of government going all the way to take over the whole economy." In that context the faculty's restrained defenses of the competitive economy and cogent explications of the value of price theory appeared to students as radical validations of the freedom of markets. Friedman's shock on rereading Henry Simons four decades later serves as a moving demonstration of the transformation of the broader profession, and the nation as a whole, in the intervening years. "I've gone back and reread the *Positive Program* and been astounded at what I read. To think that I thought at the time that it was strongly pro free market in its orientation!"[174] Clearly the Chicago "School" did not exist in the minds of its putative leaders during the years between the Great Depression and the end of World War II. It had begun to take form, however, in the minds of their students, and the effects of that formation turned out to be far more potent than anything they alone could have achieved.

The early 1930s were a time of extraordinary ideological fluidity across the Atlantic world. By 1933 fascism was ascendant in both Italy and Germany, and the Communist government of the Soviet Union appeared to have weathered the decade's early tribulations with greater stability than its capitalist counterparts. Powerful movements had emerged on the far left and right in American politics, and both advocates and adversaries wondered whether this new extremism might represent the vanguard of a coming transformation. This was an environment in which

Keynes's novel proposals and Roosevelt's unprecedented experiments could appear to some as conservative gestures, adopted as the minimal measures possible to save capitalist democracies from an otherwise impending collapse.[175] Milton Friedman was right to emphasize that the tenor of the times largely accounted for the conservative reputations that some ascribed to his mentors at Chicago. In a period when radicalism seemed to have become the norm, even a limited defense of the market mechanism was seen by some as symbolic of a deeply reactionary worldview.

Discussions of political economy have long traversed an uneasy boundary between the abstract theories of academic economists and the public rhetoric of political ideologues. In the early 1930s the tensions inherent in this terrain were exacerbated by the instability of international politics. Contemporary political debates compelled defenders of the market mechanism to reflect on the social philosophy that undergirded their support for free markets and to consider how best to frame their ideas in order to influence public opinion. It is all the more extraordinary, then, that the leading market advocates of the time resolutely refused to relate their ideas to a holistic worldview and regularly eschewed opportunities to engage in political activities. Despite their many differences, economists in Chicago and London shared a deep skepticism about attempts to relate economic ideas to political philosophy and chastised their opponents for blurring the boundaries between the two. In the midst of unprecedented political change, they did not seek to relate their economic analysis to a coherent ideology; in a public sphere dominated by competing perspectives, they largely abstained from opportunities to promote their own.

At the LSE the reluctance to connect economics to a broader political philosophy was undergirded by a prohibition against the use of economic reasoning to support any ethical propositions. Although Lionel Robbins had a number of predecessors in both English and Austrian political economy, he provided the classic statement of this view in his major work, *An Essay on the Nature and Significance of Economic Science,* which he first published in 1932. Positioning himself against the common notion that economics was the study of material welfare, Robbins argued instead that it was "the science which studies human behaviour as a relationship between ends and scarce means which have alternative uses."[176] Economics had no particular contribution to make to discussions over which ends society should pursue, and such inquiries should be left to the study of ethics or aesthetics.[177] Economists, he determined, were "entirely neutral between ends."[178] Their role was to determine how to pursue predetermined goals with the greatest possible efficiency. Drawing on works by Menger and Mises, Robbins provided a forceful critique of the historicist belief that the study of economic behavior had a dynamic and inextricable relationship with the social, cultural, and institutional environment that conditioned the objects of study. He went so far as to argue that any engagement with questions of ends stepped beyond the boundaries of economics as a science and improperly lever- aged the prestige of the discipline to address questions on which it had no contribution to make.

Robbins did not intend for his dictum to mean, as some at the time insinuated, that economists should refrain from any form of public engagement or philosophical argumentation.[179] His major publications in the 1930s, including *The Great Depression* and *Economic Planning and the International Order,* were written to appeal to a general audience, and during the decade he may have been the most politically engaged of all the market advocates in Chicago and London. Rather, he was making the more limited claim that economists could not draw on their scientific work to arrive at any normative conclusions. If economists determined that free trade would lead more efficiently to the well-being of the poor than protectionism, it would be appropriate for them to indicate as much, but they should not connect that analysis to any broader assertions about the ends that society should share. "Economics cannot tell you whether you ought to do a certain thing," he asserted in his inaugural lecture at the LSE. Robbins's advice, to the extent that it was followed, served as a rhetorical straitjacket. Political debate, particularly in times of duress, relies heavily on the invocation of norms. Economists who adopt a self-denying ordinance in regard to discussions of philosophical ends limit their public speech on economic matters to the discursive realm of technocratic expertise. As progressive reformers had discovered a generation earlier, the hold of scientific efficiency on the popular imagination is not strong. Robbins himself seemed comfortable with this fate. "I am inclined to think that if we as economists devote ourselves too much to attempts at popularisation," he indicated in the same lecture, "we shall be doing our science a disservice, and limiting its chances of beneficial influence."[180] He believed that economists should embrace, rather than combat, a restrictively defined role for their contributions to the public sphere.

Frank Knight disagreed with Robbins's claim that economics was a science concerned exclusively with the study of means rather than ends. In a footnote to an article in 1934, he referred to this aspect of *Essay on the Nature and Significance of Economic Science* as "unfortunate."[181] He did, however, agree with the conclusion that economists' attempts to adopt persuasive rhetoric in the political realm were a transgression of their academic responsibilities. Knight's concerns were not with the definition of economics but rather with the nature of rhetoric. Knight saw a capacity for free and mutual interchange as central to any democratic polity and believed that any resort to persuasion would contaminate the discursive environment.[182] He explained his position in a preface to the 1933 reissue of *Risk, Uncertainty and Profit*. "Discussion must be contrasted with persuasion, with any attempt to influence directly the acts, or beliefs, or sentiments, of others," he wrote. The latter "is the basic error, or heresy, of modern civilization, and represents a kind of original sin."[183] Shortly thereafter he clarified that "the very concept of discussion excludes all use of force, including persuasion, in any form."[184] This stark claim left Knight with the challenge of determining how one could adopt a language from which persuasion had been expunged. His quarrel was with the nature of language itself: he was not willing to accept the intentional elisions that are entailed in the process of expressing thought and experience in discernible signs. He regretted the linguistic mandate of reducing a complex world to much simpler sentences.

In his prose Knight responded to this problem by adopting a relentlessly paradoxical style that drew attention to its own elisions in order to gesture toward truths that resisted linguistic reduction. Needless to say, this approach remained uncommon within the economics profession. Knight found himself, as he wrote in private correspondence in 1933, "bitterly disappointed and disgusted" with his colleagues within the discipline, seeing them as thinly disguised polemicists who leveraged their academic status to influence public debate on issues that remained controversial within the profession.[185] The "headlong plunge of my colleagues in the social science professions here and elsewhere into political activity," he asserted in a letter the following year, "seems to me the suicide of science."[186] It at once debased public debate and eroded the public's already-limited trust in the authority of experts. In a spirit of deliberate contrast, Knight worked hard to embody the restrained public persona that he found lacking in his peers. He pointedly avoided all speeches and public events that had a bearing on contemporary policy debates, and he directed his writings toward a scholarly audience.[187]

Jacob Viner was not troubled by the concerns about the nature of rhetoric that had led Knight to avoid public engagement. He was intensely protective of his mantle of academic objectivity, however, and anxious to honor the expectation of disinterestedness that he ascribed to the institutions that employed him. These goals led him, like Knight, to maintain a wary stance toward organizations that were formed to pursue a political goal. His continued refusal to accept the offer of membership in the American Jewish Committee in the midst of World War II, despite his Jewish heritage and the increasingly pressing nature of its cause, demonstrates the seriousness of his reservations. There was no element of the committee's program, he acknowledged, to which he "could not heartily subscribe." Nevertheless, his usefulness "would be seriously diminished" if he accepted any commitments beyond his "wholly objective work as an economist." This might seem like "excessive squeamishness," he acknowledged, but he could align himself with no "narrower loyalties than my American one."[188] Viner's invocation of the importance of national service helps provide some explanation for his willingness, despite his reverence for analytic detachment, to accept government work in the Roosevelt administration. He remained frustrated and dissatisfied by the work, characteristically remarking to Lionel Robbins on a brief return to academia in 1935 that he found it "peculiarly pleasurable" to reenter "discussion of things which don't matter except to scholars."[189] He felt some commitment to fulfill civic obligations when called upon and was reluctantly willing to set aside his academic identity when asked to contribute to the country's governance. He was consistently unwilling to do so, however, in the active support of any narrower cause.

Despite their personal and professional differences, Knight and Viner both sought to distance themselves from partisan debate and therefore held aloof from organizations they perceived to have an ideological agenda. They adopted this disinterested stance in deliberate opposition to the approach of their interventionist colleagues, whom they consistently criticized for their frequent engagements in politics and their willingness to validate matters of opinion with the mantle of science. Many of their students would choose to protest the growth in the scope of governance by entering the political fray themselves. Knight and Viner,

however, remained devoted to an alternative model, one in which economists labor to acknowledge contrary interpretations of the available
data and refuse to employ their prestige to advocate a particular approach to political economy on the public stage.

In the early 1930s Hayek, too, was reluctant to connect economic
analysis to any social or political ideology. He aligned himself with Robbins's methodological views, agreeing with his colleague's argument that
economists should avoid claims to normative expertise. His inaugural
lecture explicitly praised Robbins for having "so effectively impressed
upon us, that science by itself can never prove what ought to be done."
He also agreed with Robbins's contention that the philosophical limitations of economics should not prevent its practitioners from participating in political debates. Because the economist's tools were needed to
determine "the best policy" for achieving ends that were widely shared,
Hayek concluded that it would be appropriate for economists to criticize proposals for social improvement if they "were not conducive to the
desired end" or "policies of a radically different nature would bring
about the desired result."[190] This represented a significant restriction on
his political role, and Hayek attempted to observe it in his writings during the first half of the decade. His disputes with Keynes in economic
journals attracted broad attention within the profession, and he did not
shy away from contributing to the ongoing socialist calculation debates.
In both cases, however, he focused on analytic questions and avoided
explicit invocations of broader philosophical claims. His writing was
still thematically abstruse, stylistically Germanic, and preoccupied with
problems in capital theory that even many economists found difficult to
comprehend.[191]

Hayek began to question his approach to problems at the intersection
of politics, philosophy, and economics during the second half of the decade, as he struggled to overcome increasing public and professional
skepticism of his ideas. In a methodological shift that he saw as crucial
to his subsequent development, he arrived at the conclusion that certain
forms of economic analysis need to be subjected to empirical verification. An encounter with Karl Popper's *Logik der Forschung* convinced
him that empirical methods were particularly important when economists moved from considering the actions of a single individual to those
of several members of a group.[192] The concept of equilibrium, he argued
in his 1936 lecture "Economics and Knowledge," relied on assumptions about group behaviors that were rarely verified or even acknowl-

edged.[193] Hayek saw this presentation as the beginning of his own "original development," and its emphasis on the need for empirical foundations as a clear break from his mentor Ludwig von Mises's insistence on the a priori foundations of economic analysis. (He was surprised that the notoriously thin-skinned Mises never seemed to perceive it as such.)[194] The phenomenon that economists most needed to illuminate in order to understand group behavior, Hayek believed, was the acquisition and division of knowledge: "How can the combination of fragments of knowledge existing in different minds bring about results which, if they were to be brought about deliberately, would require a knowledge on the part of the directing mind which no single person can possess?"[195] He saw this as the central insight of Smith's "invisible hand," the motivating question of the social sciences, and a problem that economists were uniquely equipped to address. In shifting his attention to this line of inquiry, Hayek was initiating a project that led him far astray from the narrow modes of economic analysis that he had employed in his early works on capital theory. This was a subject that required him to address questions related to social-scientific methodology, political philosophy, and the law, and to relate his conclusions in these fields to his economic views. Although he maintained the skepticism about direct political engagement that he had expressed early in his career, he no longer could claim to be disinterested regarding normative concerns. He was not disturbed by this transformation in his role. By the end of the decade he was convinced that his ideas would become persuasive to others only if they were connected to a worldview that they found compelling. In pursuit of this goal, he dedicated the remainder of his career primarily to the development, elaboration, and propagation of a social philosophy that would ground his economic arguments within a broader theory of knowledge. He sought to distance himself from direct engagement in the pressing political problems of the day but openly oriented his work toward a long-term goal of generating ideological change.

In Chicago, Henry Simons also arrived at the conclusion that market advocates needed to do more to connect their economic ideas to a broader political philosophy. In this endeavor he came to see Hayek as a mentor and model. "There is no one now writing," he wrote to Charles Anderson of Macmillan, "who, in my opinion, can equal Hayek in that crucial area common to economics and politics."[196] He shared Hayek's goal of pursuing this line of inquiry without directly connecting himself to partisan debates. "I cherish my academic independence and zealously avoid identification or affiliation with any political faction," he explained in a 1940 letter to Irving Fisher.[197] Of all the leading market advocates in the economics profession during the 1930s, however, he was the least rigid in his interpretation of academic disinterestedness. He readily accepted invitations to give public lectures on matters of relevance to politics. His essays had a consistent political orientation and a strong rhetorical dimension, and his only major book, the posthumously published *Economic Policy for a Free Society*, consisted of a loosely related collection of political tracts. Although he was anxious to avoid association with any ideological dogma, he openly positioned himself as a policy thinker concerned primarily with ideas that were relevant to contemporary political problems.

In pursuing his political goals, Simons strategically framed the presentation of his ideas in order to maximize their rhetorical effect. By proposing a graduated income tax, for instance, Simons believed that he gained reformist credibility without needing to sacrifice matters of foundational principle. "We old fashioned liberals have, at best, a hard time avoiding popular classification as reactionaries," he wrote to Frank Knox at the *Chicago Daily News* in 1939. "Taxation, notably as to exempt securities and capital gains, is one of the few areas where we can talk in what is recognized to be 'progressive' language—without compromising at all on our free-market position."[198] He demonstrated a similar degree of tactical self-consciousness in his discussions of corporate power. "The present size of our great corporations, whatever the real economic effects, does place the economist liberal at an awful disadvantage in any discussion or debate," he wrote to Trygve Hoff in 1939.[199] In attacking the size of modern corporations, Simons hoped to undermine a persuasive component of progressive economic critiques. Further, he was willing to think of himself as part of a self-conscious coalition that shared certain defined political goals. "We liberals must stick together," he wrote in one letter, "and not dissipate our small influence by arguing too vigorously the particular points on which we may disagree."[200]

In the final years of his life, Simons began working on the idea of establishing an institute of political economy at the University of Chicago that would foster inquiries into the economic and political foundations of the free market. In an initial memorandum proposing the idea, he was the first to try to link the ideas of his colleagues and their students together as a group that practiced something definable as "Chicago economics," invoking a tradition of market advocacy that he hoped to preserve and extend.[201] "There should, I submit, be at least one university in the United States where this political-intellectual tradition is substantially and competently represented," he argued, "and represented not merely by individual professors but also by a small group really functioning as a social-intellectual group."[202] Simons's project demonstrated the extent to which market advocates within the economics profession had shifted their position on public engagement during the 1930s. Although they continued to distance themselves from contemporary political debates, they recognized the need to form institutions capable of fostering and propagating their ideas. They grew less wary of connecting their economic ideas to a broader social philosophy and came to see that project as crucial in generating popular and professional support. And they proved increasingly willing to consider how best to frame their positions rhetorically to convince those who were otherwise inclined to be skeptical.

In the years surrounding World War II, the dispersion that had characterized market advocacy after the onset of the Great Depression gave way to an incipient period of network formation and institution building. Small groups of entrepreneurial intellectuals responded to the failures of the early 1930s by initiating the development of organizational structures, philosophical programs, and rhetorical frameworks in support of their views. Hayek, Simons, and their colleagues came to realize that an absence of institutional assistance constrained their capacity to support and learn from one another, hobbled their ability to build a movement culture, and left their voices scattered and disconsonant. They were acutely aware of the rhetorical defeats of the preceding years: the most vociferous defenders of the market mechanism had done little to explain how it could provide an acceptable solution to the pressing problems posed by the economic crisis, and its more moderate advocates had couched their arguments in too many qualifications to offer a coherent alternative. An unwillingness to connect their ideas to a broader worldview had consigned them to technocratic impotence in a political environment characterized by passionate ideological contestation. In attempting to develop a new approach, they began to lay the groundwork for an era in which market advocates achieved rapidly growing influence in both popular politics and the academic world.

Although the new generation of market advocates would succeed spectacularly in cultivating popular and professional support for their ideas, their approach never gained the acceptance or endorsement of their predecessors. The architects of the economics departments at the University of Chicago and the London School of Economics expressed increasing discomfort with the philosophical and rhetorical shifts initiated by their colleagues and students. Edwin Cannan passed away in 1935, but he had already become wary of Hayek and suspicious of his influence on the school. The recent arrival "has corrupted them all, and ought to be deported," he wrote in private correspondence with characteristic acidity. The ideas Hayek had imported from Austria, Cannan worried, were turning his colleagues into a "gang of defeatists."[203] Viner repeatedly refused to affiliate himself with Hayek's efforts to form institutions in defense of the free market.[204] Late in his life Frank Knight expressed growing dissatisfaction with what he perceived to be the rhetorical excesses of the new generation of market advocates. They were, he wrote to a former student, "hurting the cause by going to extremes."[205] Cannan, Viner, and Knight remained dispositional conservatives, inclined to distrust both novel attempts at social engineering and excessive credulousness in regard to the workings of the market. They were suspicious of political engagement and the effects it could have on the quality and complexity of academic analysis. Their support for the price mechanism was born more of dismay at the alternatives than of admiration for its moral, cultural, or informational effects. Although their measured approach proved ineffective in preventing the rapid expansion of the state, that was not the standard by which they hoped to be judged. In the midst of the Great Depression, they saw the points where politics and economics intersected less as a source of opportunity than as a cause for regret.

2

ENTREPRENEURIAL IDEAS

The publication of Walter Lippmann's *Inquiry into the Principles of the Good Society* in 1937 sent seismic waves through the Depression era's nascent network of academic supporters of free markets. Through his column "Today and Tomorrow," syndicated in more than 100 newspapers and read by more than ten million Americans, Lippmann had become, in one reviewer's terms, the nation's "genial companion of the breakfast table," a role that garnered his opinions an extraordinary breadth of influence.[1] For economists and political theorists who remained acutely aware of the unpopularity of their views and their inability to gain a foothold in the popular imagination, Lippmann's apparent embrace of free-market principles and repudiation of economic planning were transformative events. As the proofs circulated in advance of publication, these academics began to write Lippmann letters from locations around the Atlantic world to express grateful approbation of his newfound role. The book, William Rappard wrote from the Institute of International Studies in Geneva, was "a most remarkable work, and one the publication of which will, I am sure, be a real landmark in the history of our times."[2] Henry Simons wrote from the University of Chicago that it was a "magnificent contribution to the liberal cause," and that he was "urging it upon all my literate friends."[3] Decades later, on the cusp of the publication of *The Constitution of Liberty*, Friedrich Hayek declared the magnum opus of his political philosophy to be "the final outcome" of a "trend of thought which may be said to have started twenty-two years ago when I read *The Good Society*."[4] The book's combination of political stridency and popular success precipitated a change in the self-perception of the academics whose influence on *The Good Society* Lippmann readily acknowledged.[5] Intellectuals who had largely confined their critiques to academic circles began to see themselves as engaged in a broader political struggle and as participants, however dispersed, in an emerging movement.

In the decade after the publication of the book, this developing movement culture manifested itself in a variety of institutional forms. The first international gathering to discuss "neoliberal" ideas was held in Paris in August 1938, in celebration of the publication of a French translation of Lippmann's book. In subsequent years the Centre International d'Études pour la Rénovation du Libéralisme was founded in Paris; the Free Market Study was established in association with the Economics Department at the University of Chicago; Wilhelm Röpke worked from Geneva, ultimately without success, to raise money to support an international journal of liberal ideas; and Friedrich Hayek prepared the groundwork for the first meeting of what became the Mont Pèlerin Society in Switzerland in 1947. Many of these attempts were to varying degrees uncertain, lurching, and transient, and until the establishment of the Mont Pèlerin Society none of the institutions managed to fulfill their original mandates or to become established on a permanent basis. But the experimental activities of this period demonstrate the nature of the commitment that these individuals believed they shared; the motivations that impelled them to overcome their hesitations and embrace new identities as popular champions of particular political views; and the peculiar entrepreneurial process through which academic intellectuals attempted to find institutional forms capable of translating unpopular ideas into eventual, if distant, political praxis.

This awkward transition from dispersion to coherence played a foundational role in the postwar rebirth of liberalism.[6] Although it progressed fitfully, with a variety of false starts and unrealized endeavors, certain commonalities emerged. First, the intellectuals in this period, with a few vocal but marginalized exceptions, were broadly committed to a significant overhaul of what they perceived to be traditional liberalism. If one of their primary opponents was "collectivism," they reserved nearly commensurate vitriol for their denunciations of laissez-faire. Second, their endeavors to create lasting institutions were defined by an effort to assemble broad coalitions. A feeling of isolation and marginalization led them to emphasize commonalities rather than differences, and a shared critique of opposing ideologies allowed them to elide the differences that distinguished their own. Third, they perceived their roles as public intellectuals to be one of precipitating long-term ideological change, and they rebelled forcefully against institutional structures that risked sacrificing the mantle of academic objectivity in favor of more immediate political aims. Finally, they relied heavily on international organizations to develop the movement culture that enabled them to work in concert in pursuit of a common goal. This is a narrative about a network of small groups, which were isolated in specific universities and commensurately marginalized from national debate, developing the capacity to act as a broad and diverse community by conceiving of their project in supranational terms. Contemporary scholarship often treats community and global society in antipodal terms, but in the case of ideologies in abeyance the very possibility of community can depend on structures developed on a global scale.

Although the participants in the "Colloque Lippmann" are often referred to as neoliberals, the precise meaning of the term has long remained unclear.[7] Jamie Peck has observed, "Neoliberalism was a mix of prejudice, practice and principle from the get-go. It did not rest on a set of immutable laws, but a matrix of overlapping convictions, orientations and aversions, draped in the unifying rhetoric of market liberalism."[8] It is extremely difficult to treat in a sophisticated manner a concept that cannot be firmly identified or defined. For many years attempts to do so remained the province primarily of social scientists, who overwhelmingly focused on the period of increasing neoliberal influence over economic policy that began in the early 1970s.[9] One notable exception was Michel Foucault, whose lectures at the Collège de France in 1979 devoted close attention to the early strands of neoliberalism and its varied meanings in different national contexts.[10] The publication of Foucault's lectures in 2004 inspired renewed attention to the decades when the term "neoliberalism" came into common parlance, and a realization that its emergence was characterized by conflict as much as by consensus.[11] A closer examination of the processes through which it began to transition from marginalization to influence will help us interpret the set of prejudices, practices, and principles that fall under the ambiguous rubric today. Attempts to understand the origins of neoliberalism require both a critical analysis of ideas and a detailed examination of the organizational structures that abstract theorists leveraged in their attempts to generate political change.

The eventual successes of the neoliberal movement have made it challenging for contemporary readers to recognize the sense of uncertainty that impelled its early years. Between the two world wars it remained very much in abeyance, as a limited cohort of advocates struggled both to define their ideas and to prepare them for an eventual resurgence.[12]

They fell into quarrels with one another even as they sought to defend a worldview that seemed in the midst of a precipitous decline. However halting and imperfectly considered, their actions cultivated a sense of solidarity and developed networks of communication that persisted beyond the collapse of the institutions they built. The sense of crisis that brought them together would continue to inspire their shared project long after its specific conditions had fallen away.

In the years that preceded the publication of *The Good Society,* Walter Lippmann did not seem a likely advocate for free-market ideas. He had become known early in his career, through both his books and his long-time association with the *New Republic,* as an advocate of scientific management and interventionary economic policies. Having helped arrange the serialization of *The Economic Consequences of the Peace* in the *New Republic* more than a decade earlier, Lippmann maintained a close friendship with John Maynard Keynes that he later recalled as "one of the happiest of my life."[13] And after a period of initial skepticism, he had openly embraced Franklin Roosevelt's economic program, telling him in the period between the election and the inauguration that he "may have no alternative but to assume dictatorial powers" and vigorously advocating the policies of the early New Deal.[14] Lippmann's only link to economic conservatism was through a recent institutional affiliation: in the fall of 1931 his career as executive editor of the *New York World* concluded with the newspaper's demise, and he accepted a new position as a columnist at the staunchly Republican *New York Herald Tribune.* The editor of the *Herald Tribune,* Ogden Reid, had wooed Lippmann with offers of a substantial salary and—despite the newspaper's reputation and constituency—full control over the content of his columns.[15] The new employer provoked some concern among Lippmann's progressive colleagues: "Don't let the Bankers get you," William Allen White warned him as he transitioned to his new position.[16] But even as the early 1930s witnessed dramatic changes in Lippmann's institutional affiliation and readership, his tone and themes seemed to maintain the fierce independence and eclectic progressivism that had defined his writing in the preceding years.

Once Lippmann delivered the Godkin Lectures at Harvard in May 1934, however, it became apparent that his perspective on both the New Deal and economic planning was beginning to change. Like his earlier work, these lectures manifested an unremitting skepticism about the practicability of laissez-faire, which he analogized to "a man condemned who is reprieved repeatedly because he works miracles." Lippmann argued that capitalism was sustained by the rising standard of living it enabled, but that improvements in living conditions had increased the price of social order from the full dinner pail to the two-car garage in a matter of decades. Such an order, he concluded, "is inherently unstable."[17] But his perspective was inflected by a new goal: he hoped to identify, in light of this instability, a foundation on which to preserve the viability of a capitalist economy. His attention now centered on the task of generating a "defense of liberty" that was grounded, unlike its nineteenth-century predecessors, in "positive convictions and affirmative principles."[18] This would require identifying a "form of control" that was "compatible with the variability, the complexity, and the dynamic character of the capitalist order."[19] For this vision Lippmann adopted the uneasy label "free collectivism," which he described as the doctrine of a state that maintained responsibility for "the operation of the economic order *as a whole*" while preserving "within very wide limits the liberty of private transactions."[20] Although he had not yet developed an apposite language or a set of specific policy proposals to reinforce his vision, he was clearly advocating a project to save the capitalist order by delimiting and restraining its most troubling abuses.

By the time Lippmann published *The Good Society*, which was partially serialized in the *Atlantic Monthly* before its final publication in the fall of 1937, he had traveled further along the path that the Godkin Lectures had set.[21] The transformation was partially inspired, he acknowledged in the opening pages of the book, by his readings in Austrian economics, and in particular by a volume edited by Hayek and published in 1935, *Collectivist Economic Planning*.[22] "In a crude way I had discerned the inherent difficulty of the planned economy," Lippmann wrote to Hayek as the final proofs of the book were being submitted to the publisher, "but without the help I have received from you and from Professor von Mises, I could never have developed the argument."[23] On the American side Lippmann had been "greatly helped" by his readings of Henry Simons's essays and pamphlets, and the two of them had initiated an active correspondence.[24] His policy vision had not dramatically transformed from the vague suggestions he had propagated in the Godkin Lectures, but these readings had convinced him that the terms in which he expressed his advocacy needed to be refined. Gone were all references to "free collectivism": in *The Good Society* all activities that could fall under the rubric of "planning" were expressly reviled. This transition inspired sharp critiques from Lippmann's journalistic and academic colleagues, who ascribed the shifts in his perspective to the subtle pressures exerted by his new institutional environment. The most savage of these assessments came in a private letter from the historian Charles Beard to Maury Maverick, a Democratic congressman from Texas who had been asked to review *The Good Society* for Little, Brown. Since joining the *Herald Tribune*, Beard wrote, Lippmann had "been going Right as fast as his supple legs will take him." But he rejected "the idea that Lippmann has sold out to the rich. Some men do not sell out. They go over gradually through association. They are buttered by flattery. They sink softly into soft carpets and cushions. Having no steel in their systems, having never slept on the hard ground, they hanker after those things that tend to effeminacy, and plutocracy provides just those things." Lippmann's writing, Beard asserted, exhibited the "odor of a sickly humanism as thick as the smell of magnolia blossoms which apologists of the good old days in the South spread over the sweat of slave gangs."[25] His extraordinary vituperation reveals Hayek's grim prescience in confiding privately to Lippmann that *The Good Society* would inspire vocal enmity among the progressives he had once considered colleagues and friends.[26]

Lippmann's emphasis now fell heavily on the virtues of the market and the dangers of excessive attempts to restrict its purview. Presaging the rhetoric of market advocates in the subsequent decade, Lippmann established a stark and dispiriting binary: those who wrote on contemporary economics were either committed to freedom or to totalitarian collectivism, and he perceived the vast majority of his contemporaries to be advocates of the latter. The "premises of authoritarian collectivism have become the working beliefs, the self-evident assumptions, the unquestioned axioms . . . of nearly every effort which lays claim to being enlightened, humane, and progressive," he asserted with astonishing sweep.[27] Those who considered themselves liberals, progressives, or radicals were "almost all collectivists in their conception of the economy, authoritarians in their conception of the state, totalitarians in their conception of society."[28] This polar understanding of economic policy, and its corresponding insinuation that gradual changes in the economy led inevitably toward a dictatorial state, became the defining trope of free-market polemics in the decade that followed. It was the absolutism with which Lippmann expressed this binary that most troubled his colleagues and peers. The book, John Dewey wrote in *Common Sense,* gives "encouragement and practical support to reactionaries," in part by identifying "every form of socialism and collectivism with state or governmental socialism."[29] Lewis Mumford complained of Lippmann's "strange collectivist heresy hunt," in which he posited the only social options as a free economy and a militarized collectivism.[30] And Charles Merriam expressed his consternation about "an attempt to state a theory and formulate a practice of neo-liberalism" that demonstrated "illiberalism and intolerance toward those who differ from the new credo."[31] Lippmann's refusal to accept the legitimacy of gradations of planning lent a potent sense of urgency to his rhetoric, which in turn troubled those who did not share his manifest belief in the contemporary dangers of nuance.

But even as Lippmann's conservative turn in *The Good Society* provoked criticisms from the left, his unreserved scorn for nineteenth-century laissez-faire inspired sharp commentaries from a small cadre of otherwise grateful colleagues on the right. Lippmann railed against "Adam Smith fundamentalism," which he identified as a product of the distortionary excesses of the first half of the nineteenth century and "a philosophy of neglect and refusal to proceed with social adaptation."[32] As Henry Steele Commager observed a decade later, the book elaborates a perspective that is "closer to Huxley than to Spencer, to Ward than to Sumner," and "its most deadly attack was leveled not against government but against that perversion of classical economics which masqueraded as liberalism."[33] "Who *were* the callous Liberals of the late nineteenth century?" W. H. Hutt asked in the *South African Journal of Economics,* speculating that Lippmann was here showing a failure to overcome dubious "ideas which he absorbed as a young man and cultivated as editor of *The New Republic.*" Herbert Spencer, Hutt further complained, had become "an Aunt Sally," and those who read the much-disparaged members of the Manchester School would find them to be paragons of disinterested idealism.[34] If Lippmann's forceful advocacy of free markets and overt disparagement of all forms of economic planning antagonized contemporary progressives, his harsh criticisms of laissez-faire revealed his lingering resistance to the prospect of an unhindered market mechanism.

The multivalence of Lippmann's criticisms, and the relative ambiguity of the programmatic suggestions that he offered at the book's conclusion, inspired confusion about the substantive content of his social vision. If all forms of planning were tantamount to totalitarianism, and nineteenth-century laissez-faire was a bankrupt ideology, how could one identify an appropriate scope of intervention for the state? The distinction between collectivists and intelligent interventionists was vague at best: in critiquing the former, Lippmann appeared skeptical of virtually all forms of economic intervention; and in extolling the latter, he appeared to advocate dramatic redistributions of income and vigorous government action that paralleled many of the policies enacted in the course of the early New Deal. In an incredulous overview in the *Yale Review*, Ralph Barton Perry observed that "Mr. Lippmann could not very well have attacked the New Deal directly because, item by item, he accepts the greater part of it."[35]

The tensions between Lippmann's critique of collectivism and his positive proposals for reform are evident in the responses he received from the Department of Economics at the University of Chicago. Both Frank Knight and Henry Simons extolled the book as a major event and a brilliant contribution to contemporary debates about the appropriate scope of governmental interference in the economy, but expressed concerns that it was—paradoxically—excessively optimistic in its interpretation of the prospects for reform and insufficiently critical in its acceptance of certain laissez-faire principles. "I was a bit annoyed," Henry Simons wrote in a private letter, "both by your tribute to Keynes and by those few pages in the text which reflect his influence." Keynes was "irresponsible and untrustworthy" to members of the liberal movement, he warned, and the *General Theory* had potential as an "economic bible of a fascist movement."[36] Knight worried, in a review published in the *Journal of Political Economy*, that "many of the author's proposals of lines of reform involve difficulties which are both staggering and obvious to the student of economics, so that his suggestions seem optimistic to the point of naïvety."[37] But if Lippmann had "given Keynes more than his due," Simons continued, he might "have also been too generous toward his arch enemies in the academic world, Professors Mises and Robbins."[38] Knight echoed Simons's complaint about Lippmann's positions "taken over from the theorists of extreme laisser faire, of whom Professor von Mises is an extreme example," including an unsubstantiated assertion of the "impossibility" of effective collectivist economic planning and an inattention to the perils of monopoly.[39] These opposing criticisms reveal much about the hetorogeneous and ambiguous nature of Chicago economics in this period, as its theorists struggled, like Lippmann, to articulate forceful critiques of laissez-faire alongside uncompromising denunciations of the New Deal. They further reveal the importance that Lippmann, Knight, and Simons all attributed to the project of distancing themselves from an absolutist adherence to free markets. By couching their criticisms within strong statements of approbation, Knight and Simons expressed sympathy with Lippmann's ambition, if not his specific program, to avoid the excesses of both totalitarianism and laissez-faire.

It should be noted, however, that neither Knight nor Simons listed Hayek among those who advocated "extreme" policies in support of laissez-faire. At the time *The Good Society* was written, Hayek was beginning to turn away from his earlier focus on capital theory and toward the development of a broader social philosophy. To an extraordinary degree, *The Good Society* established the framework for the arguments adopted by market advocates in the subsequent decade, and in particular for the political project that Hayek began to conceive in the wake of its publication. "No human mind has ever understood the whole scheme of a society," Lippmann stated in *The Good Society*, in a critique of social-scientific rationalism that would become central to Hayek's thought in the ensuing decades. "At best a mind can understand its own version of the scheme, something much thinner, which bears to reality some such relation as a silhouette to a man."[40] He attributed this basic insight to eighteenth-century intellectuals, most notably Adam Smith, whose thought he sought to protect from the parodies that had emerged in the intervening years. Presaging Hayek's essays of the early 1940s, he disparaged Spencer and Mill, and contrasted the failures of nineteenth-century laissez-faire with what he perceived to be the richer and more nuanced conception of liberty that emerged in the Scottish Enlightenment. And, foreshadowing Hayek's central argument in *The Constitution of Liberty*, Lippmann argued that the power structure of the modern state should center not on a managerial bureaucracy, but rather on a carefully delimited and constantly evolving network of established laws.[41] Certainly Lippmann's work had been influenced by Hayek's body of research, and in particular the critique of the economic viability of a socialized economy that Hayek had developed in concert with Mises. But the contrary line of influence, running from Lippmann's arguments in *The Good Society* to Hayek's developing political philosophy in the subsequent decades, is still more pronounced. As Hayek began in the late 1930s to conceive of his project in broad political terms, *The Good Society* established the groundwork for the social vision he would come to expound.

Hayek's response to the proofs of *The Good Society* expressed, in contrast to the positive but somewhat more reserved reviews from Knight and Simons, an unqualified endorsement of Lippmann's arguments. Hayek wrote to Lippmann that he expected from his readings of the serialized portions of the book that he would "be in complete agreement with the critical parts," but it was "a pleasant surprise that I found myself in almost equally complete agreement, even to points of detail, with the constitution section." He went so far as to express particular enthusiasm for Lippmann's positive proposals, noting that he had "always regarded it as the fatal error of classical Liberalism that it interpreted the rule that the state should only provide a semi-permanent framework most conducive to the efficient working of private institutions as meaning that the existing legal framework must be regarded as unalterable."[42] In one of the rarest of scholarly experiences, Hayek had found a book that perfectly conformed with his evolving views. His enthusiasm was shared, with only limited qualifications, across the transatlantic network of classical liberals with whom Hayek maintained active communication during his time at the London School of Economics.[43] To have a journalist of Lippmann's stature parroting and, still more remarkably, helping form their views was an extraordinary event. As Charles Beard noted in his epistolary skewering that autumn, it "is a rare find for them to catch a Lippmann and they are tickled to death, like a child with new boots."[44]

The Good Society emerged at a time when this small collection of individuals was beginning to observe, within what had until then remained a haphazard collection of disparate voices, a growing atmosphere of consensus. In the months preceding the publication of Lippmann's book, the German economist Wilhelm Röpke wrote separate letters to Lionel Robbins, Karl Brandt, and Friedrich Hayek all lauding the apparent "convergence" of their respective views.[45] Röpke was eager to find allies: he had risen rapidly to a chair at the University of Marburg at the age of thirty, but his forthright criticism of the Nazis had cost him his job soon after the implementation of their Law to Restore the Professional Civil Service. After a short stay in Turkey, he had recently joined the faculty of William Rappard's nascent Institute for International Studies in Geneva. Although Röpke had been more open than his colleagues at the LSE to public investment as a means of combating the Great Depression, he substantially agreed with their diagnoses of the causes of the crisis and shared their anxiety about the global drift toward authoritarianism.[46] He was now eager to begin a more active exchange of ideas. Lippmann himself had noticed a similar congruence, writing in *The Good Society* that a "reëxamination is now under way by a new generation of liberal thinkers, who have been shaken out of their complacency by the debacle of liberalism and out of the easy acceptance of the collectivist alternative by the horrors of the collectivist reaction."[47] In this atmosphere the publication of a book that could capture some portion of the popular imagination was a potentially transformative event. Upon the publication of *The Good Society*, Röpke wrote directly to Lippmann to herald its appearance as a moment of transition. "I state with unmitigated enthusiasm that you have given masterful expression to ideas which are in the minds of that all too small circle of thinking Liberals and that you have added new and weighty ideas."[48] Lippmann, in publishing *The Good Society*, heralded the possible emergence of a new moment for those who had committed themselves to a revitalized liberalism: a time when what seemed to have been a desperate errand into the wilderness began to yield precursory results.

The perception that a unique opportunity was at hand inspired the pivotal question of how best to take advantage of it. Hayek, Röpke, and their peers faced the fundamental challenge of attempting to transform a felt consonance of opinion among a small network of individuals—in some cases separated, as Röpke noted in his letter to Stanford economist Karl Brandt, by "a continent and an ocean"—into a coherent movement.[49] This was further complicated by persistent ambiguities about what the goals of such a community would be. As the reviews of Lippmann's *The Good Society* had revealed, dual criticisms of laissez-faire and creeping collectivism had yet to yield a clear representation of what fiscal and social policies one could advocate. And as a community consisting primarily of academics, they remained committed to ideological change but deeply uncertain about how to transform their isolated theoretical ideas into effective political praxis.

During 1937 Hayek, Röpke, and Lippmann engaged in a correspondence that began to develop an image of the form an initial process of collaboration might take. Hayek wrote to Lippmann in April of his desire to discuss the problems they were writing about in person, and of the concomitant need to achieve "closer cooperation" among their intellectual allies in order to make their arguments "more articulate before it is too late."[50] Lippmann's reply acknowledged that the idea "interests me very much indeed," but that he was groping to determine "how one would go about it." He concluded that "the best beginning would be to identify the genuine liberals and begin to correspond with them and get them in touch with each other."[51] Hayek's response in June began the enterprise of compiling lists of those who could be counted on as collaborators in their ideological endeavor. Having spent his youth in Vienna and his subsequent career at the London School of Economics, Hayek had worked with the two principal mentors of those whom he viewed as exemplars. "The names I have included," he acknowledged, "are practically all economists, mostly people who have been at one time or another under the influence either of the late Professor Edwin Cannan or of Professor L. Mises." He also acknowledged what he described as "the interesting little group in Freiburg in Germany, led by [Walter] Eucken and one or two of his colleagues at the law faculty there"; a small congregation of sympathetic Italians centering on Luigi Einaudi; and the collection of "some of the most brilliant liberals in Europe" that had gathered at William Rappard's Institute for International Studies in Geneva. In America, Hayek lamented that only "Mr. H. C. Simons of Chicago seems to be quite untainted by collectivist ideas," while "the men with the best practical judgment among the American economists," including Jacob Viner, Alvin Hansen, and C. O. Hardy, may not "have quite realized where collectivism leads to." The list's notable lacunae aside, however, Hayek remained confident that it "would represent a bigger and better team of really liberal economists than could possibly have been found during the first quarter of this century."[52] What remained missing was an institutional structure capable of leveraging the latent capacities they shared.

Hayek's primary idea, as he articulated it to Lippmann, was to create an "international organization of liberal economists" that would center on "collaboration in some sort of international journal entirely devoted to the problems arising out of the rational construction of a 'Good Society.'"[53] Röpke, on the other hand, wanted "a thorough discussion of the main issues involved (the Agenda of Liberalism, its failures in the past, the larger sociological problems etc.)."[54] He elaborated on his idea in a letter to Lippmann in the early fall: "I believe the next step should be to organise, in one form or another, a discussion among the few people in the world whose thoughts in these matters have reached the necessary degree of maturity." He liked Hayek's idea of "a special periodical or series of pamphlets," but he worried "that an enterprise of this sort would lack the indispensable unity and direction without the personal touch and the thorough-going discussion which only a small conference could provide."

He acknowledged privately to Lippmann that he had long held a vision of what that would involve, which appears today as a strikingly prescient description of the conditions underlying the first meeting of the Mont Pèlerin Society a decade later. "Some years ago, I launched the idea of assembling the dozen of Enlightened Liberals in a solitary hotel high up in the Alps and to cross-fertilise their ideas for a week. Unfortunately, nothing has come out of it for lack of necessary funds, but I hope that something of this sort will become possible in a not too distant future."[55]

The conditions that precipitated the meeting of the Mont Pèlerin Society in April 1947 were therefore in place nearly a decade before the meeting occurred. Lippmann's *Good Society* had outlined the basic parameters of the social philosophy that Hayek would spend the years before and after the war elaborating in substantial detail. It was, in this sense, the foundational text of neoliberalism: the first work to shape the conjoint critique of economic planning and laissez-faire into a holistic and popularly compelling philosophical program. A transatlantic cohort of intellectuals who shared the basic perspectives outlined in Lippmann's book had begun to coalesce, and the core of Hayek's developing list of potential collaborators would look remarkably similar in the years after the conclusion of the war. The beginnings of a movement culture had become evident in the calls for mutual cooperation that became increasingly urgent as the summer of 1937 turned to fall. The following winter, of course, brought the Anschluss, an increasingly rapid international turn toward diplomatic breakdown, and, eventually, war. The very conditions that inspired the sense of urgency that Hayek, Röpke, and Lippmann shared would soon dramatically accentuate the difficulties of international communication and make the existence of the stable institutions they imagined impossible. In the meantime, however, there remained a small window of opportunity, and plans began to take shape for a preliminary gathering to discuss the problems and possibilities that their solitary publications had raised.

As Hayek corresponded with Lippmann and Röpke to determine the appropriate mode of organization during the summer of 1938, he put Lippmann in touch with Louis Rougier, a philosophy professor at the University of Besançon in France.[56] Rougier had received his doctorate from the Sorbonne in 1920, having already published extensively on the philosophy of physics. In 1925 he published *La scolastique et le thomisme*, a massive critique of the logical contradictions of Thomism that had required over a decade to complete.[57] During the 1920s he became the only French member of the Vienna Circle, and in 1935 he served as president of the first Congrès International de Philosophie Scientifique at the Sorbonne.[58] As the political crisis of the early 1930s accelerated, however, Rougier's attentions began to drift away from neopositivist critiques of theology and toward what he perceived to be contemporary "mystiques," or doctrines that "one would not know how to demonstrate by reason or to ground in experience, but that one accepts blindly for irrational motives."[59] He viewed this endeavor as very much connected to his previous philosophical project: an attempt to identify logical fallacies that had permeated the popular imagination, and in doing so to rescue and demarcate the proper spheres of scientific inquiry.[60]

He focused first on political "mystiques," writing a pamphlet in 1935 in which he examined the foundational myths of—among other political systems—monarchy, democracy, and totalitarianism, and briefly argued that the only remedy for the fraught relations among the competing systems was "to return to the practices of *political, economic and cultural liberalism in the framework of a constructive internationalism.*"[61] Rougier's work to this point remained primarily critical: he had done little to demonstrate what these "liberal" practices would look like, or how they would redress the tendency of political systems to rely on foundational dogmas. But on the strength of his existing body of work, in 1937 he was given the opportunity to edit the Librairie de Médicis, a new collection of books intended to promote liberalism and to combat potentially subversive political theories. The founder of the Librairie, Marie-Thérèse Génin, was an employee in the Bureau de Documentation in Paris, where her employer, the right-wing industrialist and propagandist Marcel Bourgeois, had urged her to establish a new series of books targeting public intellectuals. The "first task of propaganda," Génin wrote after the war, "is the publishing of books . . . by famous authors."[62] In a private letter to Lippmann in the summer of 1937, Rougier described the goal of the series as "to contend with marxism [*sic*], guided and planned economics and to point out the way to salvation through political and economical liberalism."[63] He was therefore explicitly charged with the task of bringing to press books that expounded a particular ideological agenda, with the ultimate goal of effecting political change through the conversion of intellectual elites.[64] He served, in this sense, as an early progenitor for the more populist conservative publishing houses—like the Henry Regnery Company, founded in 1947—that began to appear in America in the years after the war.

Rougier began to put forward a more explicit agenda in his article "Retour au libéralisme" in the *Revue de Paris* at the beginning of 1938 and a book, *Les mystiques économiques,* that followed months later. These two texts lament the apparent devolution of political debate to a choice between fascism and communism, both of which he perceived to renounce the advantages of a liberal system: namely, the division of labor, the circulation of capital, the cosmopolitanism of culture, the dignity of the individual conceived as an end, the security provided by a stable judicial system, the free choice of consumers, and the freedom of thought.[65] Criticizing, like Lippmann, the steady accumulation of gradual compromises, he argued that the contemporary liberal democracy "finds itself transformed into a totalitarian State."[66] He shared Lippmann's belief that new economic solutions would require overcoming a static adoption of laissez-faire, which he labeled "la mystique libérale."[67] And like Lippmann, he emphasized the importance of establishing a stable network of laws to protect the rights and capacities of the individual citizen against the progressive encroachment of the state.

Rougier bolstered this argument, however, with a determined critique of popular sovereignty that resonated much more closely with Lippmann's progressive valorizations of elite expertise in the early 1920s than with the populist tones of *The Good Society.*[68] The masses, Rougier argued in an unremitting list, are "ignorant and self-important," "impatient and brutal," "primitive and futurist," "iconoclastic," "conformist," "herding," and "materialist." "Their reign," he concluded, "is synonymous with commonness, vulgarity, and boredom."[69] He asserted in *Les mystiques économiques* that his current work sought to dispel economic doctrines that were "founded not in reason or experience" but rather "merely make explicit, while portraying them as scientific pseudo-demonstrations, certain sentimental attitudes, certain class prejudices, certain mental habits; in brief, certain partisan passions."[70] He hoped to find ways to overcome the failings of the mass mind. Governments, he concluded, would suffer for the intellectual incapacities of their constituents unless they created mechanisms to distance decision-making processes from the heterogeneous claims on the levers of power. Liberal societies could not sustain their dual emphases on the principle of the rights of the citizen and the principle of popular sovereignty, and he urged his readers to help the former prevail.[71]

Shortly after receiving Rougier's inquiry, Lippmann agreed to let the Librairie de Médicis publish the French version of *The Good Society*, which would join a growing list of translations that included works written or edited by, among others, Ludwig von Mises, Fritz Machlup, Lionel Robbins, and Friedrich Hayek.[72] The book was slated for publication, under the title *La cité libre*, in the summer of 1938. Rougier and Lippmann maintained a correspondence during the year, and Lippmann expressed his admiration for the contents of *Les mystiques économiques* upon its publication.[73] When Lippmann arranged a trip to Europe during the coming summer for separate reasons, Rougier perceived it as an opportunity to gather a few interested individuals to clarify "how one could organize intensive propaganda" and "launch an international crusade in favor of constructive liberalism" as it had been "defined by Lippmann, Röpke, Mises, and the London School."[74] He arranged a meeting over afternoon tea in Geneva at the end of June, including himself, Lippmann, Wilhelm Röpke, and possibly William Rappard.[75] At that meeting Rougier proposed, among other possibilities, a larger and more formal gathering at Marcel Bourgeois's home in Paris the following week.

At this point Lippmann manifested a sudden unease about the circles into which he was being rapidly assimilated. He was rarely self-reflective about the shifts in his political perspective, but his transition from progressive supporter of the New Deal to association with free-market advocates on the transatlantic politic fringes did not occur without some discomfort. Rougier exacerbated this disquiet with his constant and unabashed references to "propaganda" and his plans to host an event at the home of a politically active industrialist. Rougier's vision of intellectuals devoted to a "constructive liberalism" had a much stronger immediate political valence than that of Lippmann's other European correspondents— Hayek, Röpke, and Rappard—and their initial encounter brought Lippmann's anxieties to a breaking point. He had not realized that a planned dinner "had any purpose beyond affording an opportunity to talk over the ideas in which we are all interested." As a "matter of principle," he refused to "participate in propaganda or in political movements of any kind whatsoever," a rule that he found all the more important to observe when he was visiting a foreign nation.[76] He was far less charitable in a private letter he sent to Rappard. It was inconceivable for him to "take part in any movement, even as a silent spectator," oriented toward "domestic struggles" and financed by "special interests." He was "suspicious of Rougier" and didn't "intend to be associated with anything of that kind."[77] As a result, he thought it best not to attend the dinner. Lippmann's anxieties demonstrate a concern that was broadly shared within the emerging movement, if not by Rougier: the difficulty of establishing appropriate boundaries between discussion of a common intellectual program and active engagement in propagandistic activities. The movement's central figures shared a desire to precipitate long-term political change, and fully recognized that the purpose of a gathering would be to create conditions that would hasten the possibility of a re-birth of liberalism. But a lingering sense of decorum deterred them from overt discussions of the relationship between their ideas and immediate political action. A veil, however thin, needed to remain between their social philosophies and the world they hoped to transform.

In the ensuing weeks Rougier successfully persuaded Lippmann not to avoid future mutual endeavors, and in mid-July he sent a circular notice to potential participants in a conference centering on a discussion of Lippmann's *The Good Society* that he had scheduled for late August. The proposed "Conférence Walter Lippmann" (later formally christened the "Colloque Walter Lippmann") would be designed "to discuss the principal theses of this work relative to the decline of liberalism and to the conditions of a return to a renovated liberal order distinct from Manchester laissez faire." Propaganda was not listed as an explicit goal of the meeting, and the author of the book would be an active participant.[78] Rougier thereby succeeded in assembling a collection of twenty-six individuals, including, among others, Raymond Aron, Friedrich Hayek, Walter Lippmann, Ludwig von Mises, Michael Polanyi, Wilhelm Röpke, Jacques Rueff, and Alexander Rüstow, at a building a short walk from the Louvre during the long final weekend in August. The world was fast entering a state of crisis: Hitler had completed his annexation of Austria in the spring, and his meetings with Neville Chamberlain would begin less than three weeks later. Before Lippmann returned to America, and with a sense that the window of opportunity for effective action was rapidly closing, Rougier hoped to have established a formal program for future work on the creation of a new and constructive liberalism.

The theme of the conference, Rougier announced on its opening day, would be the attempt to build on the insights of *The Good Society* to construct a new liberalism that was "essentially progressive." The world, he believed, was caught in a destructive cycle in which democrats believed their last defense to be socialism, and capitalists believed their only recourse to be fascism. This disastrous situation could be redressed only through a liberalism that was able to sublimate the "Manchester doctrine" of *"laisser-faire, laisser-passer."* Such a version of liberalism would require a vision that fundamentally differed from those that had been applied in the recent past. To illuminate the problem, Rougier drew attention to an analogy that Lippmann had previously drawn: "To be liberal, it is not, like the 'manchestérien,' to let the cars drive in every direction, following their inclinations, which would result in difficulties and incessant accidents; it is not, like the 'planner,' to determine for each car its hour of departure and its itinerary; it is to impose the *rules of the road.*"[79] The goal for the conference was to develop a consensus around this foundational supposition, and then to begin engaging in discussions about what the specific nature of such rules would be. Lippmann supported Rougier's mandate, advocating "the necessity of renewing liberalism by turning it into a new doctrine, capable of providing questions and answers likely to satisfy everyone."[80] The liberalism Lippmann and Rougier sought to create, as one participant stated, "is not yesterday's, it will be tomorrow's: a liberalism mellowed, revised, renovated."[81] This gathering, in conjunction with the original publication of Lippmann's book, represented the inception of what is now commonly referred to as neoliberalism, in the form of a nascent community joined together to discuss the parameters of a radically reconstructed liberal doctrine. The participants in this meeting shared a commitment to attempt to save liberalism by changing it, even as the ideology seemed to be ineluctably entering the later stages of a disastrous and self-inflicted decline. It was an attempt to step outside a cycle that Frank Knight had sometimes described as an immutable law of history: the collapse, due to carefully hidden internal contradictions, of all political doctrines from within.

The first problem of the new liberalism would be to identify a term that its ideological sympathizers could apply to themselves. They could no longer consider themselves "liberals" because the use of that title would identify them with the very philosophy they were attempting to overcome. In his introduction to the published version of the "Colloque," Rougier acknowledged the emerging adoption of the terms "neoliberalism" and "neocapitalism" to describe the project they had undertaken.[82] But in the actual discussions the only references to the adoption of the prefix were negative, because participants demonstrated unease with both the problematic connotations of the term "liberalism" and the ambiguous or elided meaning of "neo."[83] The conversation circled relentlessly back on the question of what term might serve as a formal designation, and "liberalism," "neoliberalism," "individualism," "laissez-faire," and "liberalism of the left" were all variously raised and rejected.[84] The continual focus on matters of wording at the "Colloque Lippmann," which might seem at first consideration trivial, attested to the importance of developing a single rubric to encompass the various members of an ideological group. The relationship between movements and terminology is reciprocal: just as movements create terms to describe the projects they have undertaken, terms provide a conceptual umbrella around which their disparate members can unite. Later generations would develop additional allegiances around the terms "classical liberalism," "libertarianism," and "conservatism" and engage in ongoing battles about how best to define the set of beliefs they shared. The failure of the participants in the "Colloque Lippmann" at this moment to name themselves generated a problem that would plague the movement in later years, as in the absence of a shared reference its members increasingly identified themselves with divergent labels and focused intensively on the differences their respective choices entailed.

The second task of the new liberalism was to identify which aspects of "nineteenth-century" liberalism it would seek to revise. For a conference ostensibly dedicated to the subject, the ideas put forward at the "Colloque Lippmann" were remarkably vague. The participants in the conference were committed to the rehabilitation of the market mechanism and to the advocacy of a social structure that preserved—with some necessary caveats and limitations—a general framework for free discussion and exchange. But they largely agreed that the previous philosophical vehicle for this system of beliefs, which they alternately described as "liberalism" or "laissez-faire," had proved itself unsustainable as an abstract framework for the ordering of social interaction. They were therefore committed to the idea of a "revised," "progressive," "constructive," "new" liberalism without having yet identified precisely what the revisions entailed. Much as Lippmann, in *The Good Society,* struggled to outline a "positive" program that did not seem to advocate the policies that his critique of socialism condemned, the participants in the "Colloque Lippmann" had difficulties identifying constructive "revisions" that did not violate the philosophy they were attempting to save.

Most of the participants contributed little toward a solution of this problem, and the explicit discussion of positive proposals was covered only briefly in the final hours of the conference discussion. By the conclusion of the meeting, however, the German sociologist Alexander Rüstow observed that two distinct perspectives had begun to emerge.[85] One group, Rüstow said, "searches for the responsibility for the decline of liberalism in liberalism itself."[86] Rüstow himself had been engaged in such an internal critique of liberalism for much of the decade. Having been trained as a philosopher before the outbreak of World War I, he later served in the Reich Economics Ministry and the Association of German Engineering Manufacturers. After attaining a chair in Freiburg im Breisgau, he became prominent for his advocacy of a strong state that would protect the market economy while suppressing cartels and counteracting the extremes of the business cycle. Having attracted the ire of the Nazis, he followed Röpke to a position in Turkey in 1933, where he would remain until 1949.[87] In his descriptions of his position at the conference, he moved beyond economic analysis to launch a forceful moral critique of the capitalist order. Liberals—including the participants in this discussion—had forgotten, he argued, that "the most important socioeconomic task is to give the economy a form that provides to the largest possible number of men not the highest income possible, but a living situation as satisfying as possible."[88] The present economic crisis was merely a secondary symptom of "a more profound sickness in the social body."[89] Humans required both liberty and unity to flourish, but in moments of flux the latter priority was of greater import than the former. In order to rescue liberalism, it would be necessary to find a way to reconcile liberal insights with the fundamental human need for integration into a broader social organism, with stronger lines of connection than those provided by abstract reason alone. Lippmann expressed implicit agreement with Rüstow, indicating that the maximization of utility was a social good but not necessarily the only standard by which progress should be measured, although Rüstow reminded him that acknowledging this raised the unresolved question of what alternative standard one should apply.[90] This vision of a "constructive liberalism" relied on an acceptance of the idea that the problems with laissez-faire could not be addressed merely through a network of limited restrictions on the grosser excesses of the market. Rather, they demanded the abandonment of the abstract paradigm of the *homo economicus,* and the integration of the market economy into a redefined and morally renewed social order.

Another group, Rüstow argued, found "nothing essential to critique or to change in traditional liberalism" and attributed contemporary difficulties to failures to implement sufficiently liberal ideals.[91] Among the active participants in the discussion, the two central figures in this group were Jacques Rueff and Ludwig von Mises. Liberalism, Rueff argued, led to a higher standard of living, provided the economic system with a flexibility that prevented instability, and tended to maximize the welfare of the lower classes.[92] It was essential, Mises added, to hold on to the unmodified word "liberalism" as the core of their belief.[93] If Rüstow believed that liberalism required a dramatic revision of its very philosophical foundations, the members of this group appeared suspicious of the notion that it required any substantial revision at all. This uncritical adherence to liberalism was not broadly accepted within the "Colloque Lippmann," however, and its advocates remained a vocal and dissatisfied minority.[94] Hayek himself had been critical, in a letter the previous summer, of "elderly men who still cling to the old tradition, but mostly for bad reasons, and my experience with them is mostly 'God beware us of our friends!'"[95] In the years after the "Colloque Lippmann" this group found itself increasingly marginalized from the movement's ongoing debates. Mises's refusals to compromise his "pure" version of liberalism left him engaged in ever fewer dialogues, and made it impossible for him to find an academic position commensurate with his professional prestige after he fled Switzerland for the United States at the end of the decade. Mises, Fritz Machlup wrote privately to Hayek in November 1940, was a "problem child."[96] "You know how difficult it is to make him listen to an opponent's argument and discuss it in a friendly spirit," he added in another letter months later. "Now you can imagine that discussions in these times require more patience and less dogmatism—and that people do not stand for Mises' lack of the former and excess of the latter. This is why I have little hope for him."[97] Most of the participants in the "Colloque" shared a belief that the principles of traditional liberalism had proved unsustainable, and perhaps more important, that they did not present a viable option to those in positions of academic or political power.

Discussions at the "Colloque Lippmann" remained vague and broad because of both the relative brevity of the individual contributions and a general sense of uncertainty about whether the conversation should focus on a reexamination of foundational principles or a discussion of practical policies. The primary task of the meeting, however, was to establish an agenda for the future of the movement itself, and about that the participants remained in broad agreement. Lippmann stated the problem clearly, drawing on his programmatic suggestions in *The Good Society* to argue that it was crucial to determine which economic interventions should be considered necessary. Even Mises agreed that this was the central topic to consider, although it was clear that his conclusions would differ from those of many of his colleagues. "It is, in effect, without a doubt," he replied to Lippmann, "that the principal problem to study will be that of the possibilities and the limits of interventionism."[98] By demarcating the boundaries where they would restrict the extent of laissez-faire, they would seek to identify precisely what the "neo" in "neoliberalism" meant.

As the meeting wound to a close, Rougier proposed pursuing this agenda through a new institution named, at the suggestion of Marcel Bourgeois, the Centre International d'Études pour la Rénovation du Libéralisme. Rougier would manage the organization, and chapters would be established in the United States, England, and Switzerland under the respective leadership of Walter Lippmann, Friedrich Hayek, and Wilhelm Röpke.[99] Lippmann explicitly approved of the idea, and he wrote to Rougier shortly after the meeting, and again a year later, to describe the preliminary steps he had taken to establish such a group.[100] The goal of the center, Rougier revealed in a subsequent document, was to identify a role for the state that manifested *not the indifference of a spectator, but the neutrality of an arbitrator*" who would protect "the rules of the game." Its vision would be "progressive" rather than "conservative," in the sense that it would promote a social vision based on "perpetual adaptation."[101] Rougier's "Manifesto" for the center, which was lifted verbatim from a presentation Walter Lippmann delivered at the "Colloque," carved out a substantial role for state intervention, specifically identifying five areas where tax revenues should be distributed: national defense, social insurance, social services, education, and scientific research.[102] The goal was to engage in research and discussions that would further clarify and demarcate an appropriate role for the state. Such shared lines of inquiry, Rougier thought, would be strengthened by contributions from liberals committed to varying degrees of intervention, but would need to exclude nonliberals in order to "avoid falling into incoherence."[103] It would require an initial investment of 160,000 francs, three-fourths of which would be devoted to the hosting of conferences and colloquiums and the subsequent publication of the proceedings. It was vital, Rougier added, that it be self-financed, relying on "subscriptions, grants, or donations" that were "impartial, unconditional, not imposing any moral or intellectual constraint."[104]

Rougier eventually inaugurated the Paris chapter of the center in March of the following year.[105] By the summer of 1939 a conference had been

planned for late fall that would reassemble many of the original participants in the "Colloque Lippmann" to discuss how to progress.[106] But at
the beginning of September Hitler commenced his invasion of Poland,
and, as Hayek later wrote, an immediate "suspension of all efforts of this
nature" occurred.[107] Any potential for the longer-term sustainability of
the institutions that Rougier had established disappeared with his peculiar involvement in secret diplomatic negotiations with Churchill on behalf of Pétain in October 1940. In a dramatic effort to maintain a secret
Franco-British alliance, Rougier leveraged his connections with faculty
members at the London School of Economics to convince Pétain to send
him to London as an envoy. After Rougier's meetings with Churchill,
a "gentlemen's agreement" was drafted that required Pétain to avoid
making certain military concessions to the Germans and to commit to a
resumption of war once the British were able to provide needed assistance.[108] Rougier departed for New York in December of that year with a
grant from the Rockefeller Foundation to teach at the New School. His
associations with the Vichy government had branded him a collabora-
tionist among his peers, however, and his colleagues in the "Colloque
Lippmann" grew increasingly hesitant to maintain relations. Rougier,
Hayek wrote to Röpke in August 1941, is "somewhat suspected by his
co-nationals here of pro-Vichy tendencies!"[109] Röpke replied that the suspicions were "well founded indeed," and that Rougier had proven to be "a
rather malleable type."[110] Rougier's reputation was further diminished
after the war when—in a dispute followed intensively by the international
press—the British government denied Rougier's accounts of the negotiations and Rougier impugned Churchill's character in response. Although
his accounts of the negotiations would be largely vindicated decades later,
he was not allowed to teach again in France until 1955, and he was
barred from entrance into the Mont Pèlerin Society until the late 1950s.[111]

As a result of his sudden plunge into public disgrace and academic obscurity, Rougier's pivotal role in the prewar development of a movement
to rehabilitate and reconstruct liberalism has been largely forgotten.[112] At
the time, however, Rougier was broadly understood to have been the central figure in an emerging French "neoliberal" community.[113] He "did
much," Hayek recalled, "to start the movement for the revival of the basic
principles of a free society," and "it was around the group Professor Rougier had brought together that a larger international association of friends
of personal liberty was formed."[114] To the extent that an international
movement existed before the outbreak of war, it was a product of

Lippmann's synthetic "agenda" and Rougier's organizational energies. Rougier had become a paradigmatic, if early, version of the entrepreneurial policy intellectual, curtailing his established academic interests in order to focus his energies on developing institutional structures that might foster the long-term political change he envisioned. His network of contacts developed during years of travel and correspondence with sympathetic intellectuals, his lack of scruples about propagandistic activities, and his ability to gain funding from sympathetic industrialists all enabled him, in his work as an editor and a conference organizer, to establish activities that would serve as models for his successors after the war. But his willingness to prioritize ends over means, and to descend from the academic world into overtly political milieux, would ultimately lead to his exclusion from the movement that he had helped create.

Rougier's rapid disappearance from the center of the movement at the start of the war was complemented by Lippmann's drift toward other concerns. Not long after Lippmann returned home from the conference, he wrote Rougier to suggest that the international crisis meant that "the immediate problem in Europe is no longer how to save liberty but how to save the national independence of the peoples who would like to preserve their liberty." This fight, he indicated, would necessarily alter "our practical attitude on immediate questions of policy."[115] With the arrival of war came a rapid and dramatic shift in priorities away from the subjects of their earlier debates. Moreover, the cosmopolitan structure that had lent a sense of particular purpose and fellowship to the initial meeting of the "Colloque Lippmann" left its members' relations particularly susceptible to the geographic disruptions of the war. When conflict broke out, the meeting's participants were either uprooted from their home institutions or isolated from their correspondents in other areas of the world. The war, therefore, became for many of them a holding period as they attempted to maintain established contacts while planning for urgent actions if and when the conflict drew to a close.

For an initial period after the outbreak of hostilities, their concerns focused on finding safe havens for colleagues who were fleeing dangerous situations for the United States. As self-identified "liberals" and vocal antifascists, the participants in the "Colloque Lippmann" felt particularly vulnerable in the midst of the German offensive. Ludwig von Mises was one of the first to be affected: the German army sealed his apartment shortly after its arrival in Vienna in 1938 and permanently removed all his possessions shortly thereafter.[116] He fled the Institute for International Studies in Geneva, where he had taken refuge since 1934, in a desperate dash for the United States in July 1940. He managed to cross the closed Spanish border only via the direct intervention of Louis Rougier, who leveraged his influential position in the nascent Vichy regime to secure a special visa.[117] In the United States Mises struggled to find a stable academic position, finally arriving at a perpetual "visiting" appointment at New York University in February 1945.[118] Röpke decided, with some reluctance and after weighing several offers, to remain in Geneva, respecting the concerns of the institute's director, William Rappard, that "Röpke's leaving might be interpreted both here and abroad as an unfortunate symptom of defeatism."[119] Hayek, meanwhile, evacuated with the remnants of the London School of Economics to Cambridge, where he lived "largely among old men and a motley crowd of foreigners and semi-foreigners," including "no lack of orientals of all kinds" and "Europeans of practically all nationalities, but very few of real intelligence."[120] All three existed in radically transformed intellectual atmospheres, with Mises confronting the unstable life of an itinerant intellectual in New York City, Röpke waiting out the war from an uneasy perch in a surrounded Switzerland, and Hayek passing his time in an academic environment that his most distinguished colleagues had abandoned for service in London.

Their intellectual priorities had shifted, commensurately, from propagation to preservation, and the simple act of maintaining contact with the outside world became a daily struggle. Hayek, in particular, lamented his difficulties in preserving extranational relationships and sources of information. "Correspondence with America takes a very long time and is unreliable, foreign books are of course about impossible to get and one begins to be really poor," he told Röpke in April 1941. "One would not mind anything of this if one could see a definite end."[121] He relied on friends in neutral territory, like William Rappard, to keep him updated on his remaining family in Vienna.[122] And he devoted great energy to developing schemes to acquire books from Germany, from which he felt "completely cut off" to a degree one could "scarcely imagine."[123] Despite his sense that his position during the war was enviable, Hayek felt consistently oppressed by the discontinuity between the relative isolation of wartime Cambridge and his prior reliance, as a longtime émigré, on correspondence with colleagues across both the Atlantic Ocean and the German border.

The sense of panic and dismay that isolation inspired was only enhanced by the persistent conviction that the ideological program they had discussed at the "Colloque Lippmann" remained unpopular and obscure. The "trend everywhere," Röpke observed in 1939, "is decidedly in the direction of Collectivism and Totalitarianism," such that even England was "highly pathological" and the United States perhaps even worse.[124] Émigrés in the United States, like Machlup and Mises, reported that the "Veblen-Hansen ideology dominates public opinion in this country" and subsumed the entire generation of economists under the age of forty.[125] Mises was appalled by the methodological remnants of institutionalism, referring to the "haeretics [sic] who doubt whether compiling series and indexes is really a substitute for analytical research" as a "vanishing race."[126] This nearly unmitigated despair would become the animating spirit behind Hayek's *Road to Serfdom,* with its sustained tone of anguish at the "entire abandonment of the individualist tradition which has created Western civilization."[127] If the "Colloque Lippmann" was precipitated by a common belief that advocates of liberalism were lonely and that their ideas were besieged, the barriers to communication during the war and its daily record of apocalypse only heightened the experience of isolation and incapacity.

The book that Wilhelm Röpke published in the midst of the war, *The Social Crisis of Our Time,* was permeated with this sense of crisis.[128] "There is unanimous agreement," he wrote, that the current age was distinguished by its "unequalled moral and intellectual decadence," "spiritual chaos," and "boundless relativism."[129] Röpke, however, preserved some of the optimism that had accompanied the first gathering of revisionary liberals four years before. A "vanguard—perhaps small as yet and by no means very certain of itself" was formulating a "new spiritual development . . . quietly and far from the noise of the great stage of the world where the last act of the old drama is still being played out."[130] His book was intended as both a diagnosis of the ills afflicting contemporary civilization and a programmatic statement of possible solutions to be implemented in the coming years. Its brisk pace of sales—over 6,000 copies were purchased within German Switzerland alone in the first few weeks after publication, necessitating an immediate second edition—spoke to the wartime appetite for didactic assessments of the contemporary social crisis.[131]

Röpke's fundamental trope was the same as Lippmann's and Rougier's: the elimination of the "sterile alternative" between collectivism and "that brand of liberalism which developed and influenced most countries during the nineteenth century and which is so much in need of a thorough revision." Drawing on his predecessors, Röpke called for a "constructive" or "revisionist" liberalism, which he also referred to as "economic humanism" and, most controversially, the "Third Way."[132] Hayek worried that the last term, in its English-language form, invoked "those half-way houses between competition and planning which take the worst of both worlds as to discredit them with all thinking people"; and Röpke dropped it a half decade later because of a misleading titular similarity to the French Third Force coalition.[133] As the term "Third Way" implied, Röpke was committed to finding a fully differentiated alternative to both capitalism and collectivism: drawing on the social critique his colleague Alexander Rüstow had presented at the "Colloque Lippmann," he advocated a more thoroughgoing revision of the liberal project than was implied in the prior writings of Lippmann or Rougier. In his recollections of the conversations at the "Colloque Lippmann," he complained of the emphasis on "purely economic" questions, which he attributed to the "fairly crude sense of affairs" maintained by "our American friends."[134] As early as 1936 Röpke was explicitly aligning himself with Rüstow and arguing that he was "coming more and more round to the idea that the disintegration of the moral foundation of our system is the most important and most sinister aspect of the process of the present disintegration."[135] Redressing the moral collapse of the capitalist order, he believed, would require both a new theoretical framework and a willingness to adopt quite dramatic proposals in order to engender the necessary social change. In his conjoint defense of a liberal framework of competition and vigorous critique of its excesses, Röpke acknowledged, echoing Frank Knight's self-description from the preceding decade, that his program could be considered both "radical" and "conservative."[136] His "radical" proposals included forceful state interventions in the market to restore an independent agricultural peasantry, to bolster and rebuild the class of artisanal tradesmen, and to restructure manufacturing practices in order to give industrial work "the meaning, self-determination and rhythm which characterize the working life of the artisan."[137] He offered an impassioned defense of competition, but tempered that defense with an acknowledgment that he "would like to see competition shaped and controlled in such a manner that it loses all traces of its cut-throat and nerve-racking character."[138]

The Social Crisis of Our Time synthesized a number of reformist ideas that had been circulating among the transatlantic network of neoliberal intellectuals for some time: Lippmann's and Rougier's repudiations of historical laissez-faire and calls for an organized and constructive liberalism, Henry Simons's assault on large corporations, Frank Knight's ethical critiques of an abstract and unhindered competition, and Alexander Rüstow's call for a liberalism that emphasized the moral rather than merely the economic satisfaction of the citizen. It was notable, however, for the sweeping overhaul of modern industrial capitalism that its list of constructive criticisms implied. Cumulatively, Röpke's suggestions carved out an extraordinarily broad space for the economic transformation of the existing financial order. The breadth of this proposed transformation makes Hayek's response to the book all the more notable: shortly after its publication he wrote Röpke to express "almost complete agreement not only as regards the main argument but also with respect of the detail."[139] Röpke's vision, Hayek's consensus, and their joint role in the postwar establishment of the new neoliberal institutional order all testify to the depth of dissatisfaction with the traditional liberal order that "neoliberalism" at this moment entailed. The "constructive" aspects of the movement did not merely involve minor technical limitations on the free market or symbolic rhetorical gestures designed to repackage a social philosophy that had lost favor in the public arena. Rather, they were rooted in foundational dissatisfactions with the moral abstractions of *homo economicus* and a desire to adopt a social philosophy capable of reconciling a theory of competition with the extramaterial needs of humankind. The "neoliberalism" that became paradigmatic in the Anglo-American policy arena in the 1970s and 1980s looked very different from the "neoliberalism" of the late 1930s and 1940s. The history of the latter must resist the temptation of presumed continuities, and the history of the former must do more to account for the causes of the theoretical divergence between the two.

With the arrival of 1945, as the conclusion of the war seemed to be approaching, Wilhelm Röpke began making plans to reestablish the international network that had begun to form before the war. His new plan was to develop "an international monthly defending the case of humanism and liberalism (as we understand it)."[140] By the summer of the following year he had assembled, with Hayek's advice and assistance, a preliminary international committee of editors and contributors.[141] One of these editors was Benedetto Croce, whose journal *La Critica* served as an acknowledged exemplar for Röpke as he attempted to envision the structure of such a periodical. Röpke's task was complicated, however, by the fact that "Croce was a rich man, and I am not."[142] By autumn Röpke had secured a financial commitment for a preliminary period from a team of industrialists led by the well-connected itinerant Swiss businessman Albert Hunold, and was planning to publish the initial volume of a proposed quarterly under the title *Occident* early the following year.[143]

Röpke's vision for *Occident* was grounded in the belief that Europe, as the war approached its close, continued to be threatened by a "spiritual and moral danger" fostered by an environment in which "traditions, principles until now above all dispute, values and last-ditch convictions have quite ceased to function as a brake or guide for humanity." The periodical was, crucially, to serve as a vehicle for moral regeneration rather than a simple reexamination of economic and social policy. Indeed, he believed that the task he envisioned required the cooperation of all who perceived themselves to be supporters of "Humanism and Western traditions of Liberty," including "followers of every faith, members of the political Liberal, Conservative and Democrat parties, and even, where possible, moderate Socialists." He recoiled against the prospect of "hairsplitting debates" and indicated that the periodical should operate under the unwritten motto "*in necessariis unitas.*" The periodical would rely on two fundamental premises in advocating for its ideals. First, as its title implied, it would operate under the assumption "that the Western World is an intellectual unit" with "ultimate values and legacies," in which "each country represents only one instrument in the orchestra." Second, and in part as a result of its Western internationalism, it would be explicitly elitist, with articles written for an intellectual audience with a reading knowledge of English, French, and German. "It will appeal to the *upper intellectual class* and thus obviates [*sic*] vulgarisation and all concessions to the tastes of the multitude," Röpke announced. "It is not intended, therefore, to exercise direct influence on the masses, but on the other hand it will acquire prestige, which would make it a generally recognised authority, that being legitimate, cannot be ignored."[144]

Röpke's project was marked by several distinctive strategies, each of which reflects a meaningful dimension of the movement to reconstruct liberalism in the immediate postwar years. First, it relied on the notion, which he had already established in his published writings and private remarks, that nineteenth-century liberalism required a truly radical revision. The material foundations of the rational constructions posited by liberal economists needed to be discarded and wholly replaced by an entirely new social and ethical construction. Second, Röpke believed in the importance of establishing a grand coalition, encompassing individuals who shared certain broad principles but advocated programs whose specifics differed substantially. The social abandonment of traditional liberalism had both rendered an uncritical rehabilitation of liberal ideals inconceivable and proscribed the possibility of an excessively restrictive conception of the movement's membership. Mises remained a lone, if vocal, objector on this point, arguing for the exclusion of Röpke himself from any joint endeavor on the grounds that he was an "outright interventionist."[145] Third, Röpke drew on a pronounced faith in the ability of abstract intellectual discourse to inspire processes of political change. He remained entirely unapologetic about the elitist nature of his enterprise, limiting it to a trilingual audience and expecting that the mere statement of their views would command attention and commensurate action. Indeed, the very loftiness of the discussion, in the form of its "prestige," would be a crucial lever in the realization of the ideological aims the project implicitly entailed.

The distance Röpke hoped to maintain between his project and popular politics, however, ultimately left him unable to realize the vision he had worked to achieve. In the late fall of 1945 he engaged in a disagreement with Albert Hunold over the press that would be best suited to print the periodical. In the course of their argument a dispute about financing emerged: Röpke wanted absolute and unconditional control over the journal, and Hunold wanted to preserve some of the privileges of ownership in order, he said, to safeguard the investments others had entrusted to him. Röpke was unwilling to consider anything that would compromise the periodical's "complete independence which is essential since, seeing the passionate animosities such a periodical is bound to stir up, there must not even [sic] the shadow of suspicion on its financial sources."[146] Röpke's letters to his colleagues in this period demonstrate a heightened emotion and a level of vitriol that characterized his behavior in times of personal difficulty, and he temporarily refused all continued relations with Hunold on the grounds that his "frustrations" with the perceived betrayal had caused "crippling intestinal disturbances."[147] Hunold, failing to understand how Röpke could expect full ownership of an enterprise funded entirely by others, simply concluded that "it is a matter of a sickly man and that one must treat him accordingly."[148] Röpke's efforts to find 90,000 Swiss francs in separate funding to cover the first three years of the journal's existence met with no success, and his inquiries ended in the summer of 1946. If Rougier had failed in the role of institutional organizer because he was too willing to work in concert with his financial supporters, too quick to engage in direct political activities, and too insensitive to others' interpretations of his actions, Röpke failed in his attempt because of a refusal to accommodate financial backing, an apprehension at the prospect of political antagonism, and a heightened sensitivity that left him unwilling to distinguish between personal and professional differences. Several years later Röpke had the opportunity to serve as a founding member of the advisory board for a new journal that went on to have broad influence: *Ordo*, a publication focusing on social and economic regulation that was edited by his colleagues Walter Eucken and Franz Böhm. Its leading figures became known as "ordoliberals" for their attempts to steer a course between planning and laissez-faire and for the influence their prescriptions exercised on the development of the social market economy in Germany.[149] *Ordo*, however, was a more localized and parochial project, and did not have the methodological breadth or the cosmopolitan reach that Röpke had hoped to achieve in his efforts. As he confided to Hayek shortly after the German surrender, his ideological ambitions had exceeded his entrepreneurial abilities. "The fight against the Amalekites," he acknowledged, "calls for strong nerves and a thick epidermis—things I haven't got."[150]

One of the first people Röpke contacted when he began developing his plans for a new journal was Walter Lippmann. After learning of Röpke's proposal, Lippmann elected not to become involved.[151] Hayek also developed "rather the impression that [Lippmann] deliberately avoided meeting me when I was in the States last Spring," adding that "he has certainly kept very aloof from our other friends in America with whom he used to agree."[152] Together, he and Röpke concluded that Lippmann was "unpredictable," subject to "ever more doubts," and moving in the "wrong direction."[153] Despite Lippmann's central role in the movement's foundational period, he would never again engage directly and purposively with the members of their intellectual community. He extricated himself from the neoliberal movement at the very moment when it began to establish the durable structures that would lay the groundwork for its popular success. This deliberate disengagement has led most histories of neoliberalism to ignore Lippmann, like Rougier. His brief but pivotal role in its foundational years serves as a reminder that the renewal of liberalism was a more heterogeneous and uncertain project than it initially appears, from a contemporary vantage point, to have been.

The transition from the dispersion of the early 1930s to the self-conscious movement of the postwar years was achieved through a series of halting attempts to control its geographic and intellectual heterogeneity and channel it toward concerted activity. The major figures in this story—Lippmann, Rougier, Röpke, and Hayek—sought with persistence and creativity to develop the structures that they believed would be most effective at sustaining an ideology that had fallen into abeyance. The success of their endeavors relied on an entrepreneurial capacity to conceive of new modes of organization and to bear the practical difficulties and reputational risk of their implementation. The willingness of these individuals to devote their energies to the task is a testament to the importance they attributed to the mere existence of a forum for debate. Considering the goals they were attempting to achieve, they devoted remarkably little discussion or consideration to the complex relationship between ideas and politics. Their practices, however, attest to a belief that ideological change was not best precipitated by solitary individuals; the success or failure of their project would depend, they implicitly acknowledged, on a deliberate act of collaboration.

The late 1940s proved to be a unique moment of optimism within a movement that had previously tended to adopt an apocalyptic tone. The trials and restrictions of the preceding decade had fostered a sense that renewed contacts carried infinite possibilities, and the prospect of establishing durable institutions inspired a sense of momentum that had remained elusive in the past. The central figures appeared to believe that finally, after years of broken contacts and projects conceived but left undone, it would be possible to commence the philosophical task they had established for themselves shortly before the onset of war. With all distractions and disruptions concluded, the real work of reconstructing liberalism could begin.

3

PLANNING AGAINST PLANNING

In the early spring of 1945 Friedrich Hayek boarded a convoy ship to make the slow wartime journey across the Atlantic.[1] It would be his first visit to the United States in two decades, and he had reason to feel gratified by the conditions under which he would return. His new book, *The Road to Serfdom*, had achieved some notoriety after its publication in England, and demand for it was outpacing the limited rations of paper allotted to its printer.[2] After struggling to find a publisher for an American version, he had signed a contract with the University of Chicago Press, and its fall release had garnered a wave of unexpectedly high-profile reviews and successive print runs of escalating size. His editors had arranged for him to give lectures at several major American universities, providing an opportunity for him to reconnect with old colleagues and to raise his profile in economics departments that had otherwise marginalized his academic work. Hayek had not anticipated that the book would inspire this degree of interest. As an Austrian émigré, he still did not feel wholly comfortable writing in the English language, and had found it necessary to read drafts of the first few chapters aloud repeatedly in his chambers in Cambridge in order to approximate the rhythms of a native speaker.[3] He had intended the book primarily for socialist intellectuals in Great Britain and had given little thought to its potential for a popular audience or its applicability to the United States.[4] He was surprised to hear that its publication there had attracted much notice.

Upon his arrival in the United States, Hayek was stunned to discover that his celebrity had increased dramatically during his time at sea. The catalyst was an abridgment by the *Reader's Digest*. In barely two decades the *Digest* had become the most widely circulated magazine in America, and its readership numbered well over eight million. Its editors, who had recently begun including condensations of books in the final pages of the magazine, accorded *The Road to Serfdom* unusual prominence as the lead article in the April issue. This unexpected publicity had forced Hayek's publisher to create, unbeknownst to him, an entirely new schedule for his visit. A commercial lecture agency had lined up an array of public lectures across eleven states, beginning with a radio address to an overflow crowd of more than 3,000 the day after his arrival in New York.[5] Hayek maintained the cultivated reserve and unabashed elitism of a Viennese aristocrat, and did not take well to this new position. An interviewer at the time dwelled on his "purely academic" demeanor, and an observer at his first press conference recounted that he had "small, sensitive hands which he seemed at a loss to know what to do with when he was not lighting his low-slung briar pipe."[6] Decades later Hayek recalled his shock at the dictating machines and microphones that greeted him at his first public event.[7] Hayek's uneasy relationship with his popular persona had begun.

From the beginning, he found the textual life of *The Road to Serfdom* difficult to control. As he repeatedly observed, his message did not always align with its depiction in the hands of its advocates. In particular, he grew frustrated at a tendency among his more reactionary readers to disregard all his caveats and qualifications in order to represent the text as a call for a return to laissez-faire. It is not difficult to understand the source of this interpretation: much of *The Road to Serfdom*'s rhetorical force derived from its critique of central planning, and at various points Hayek did appear to advocate for the radical attenuation of the state. Drawing on his background as an Austrian émigré, he argued that fascism was a "necessary outcome" of socialist trends that were now emerging in even the liberal bastions of the Anglo-American world, and he depicted any social philosophy that disrupted "freedom in economic affairs" as a step toward the arrival of a totalitarian state. Further, he appeared to reject the possibility of a middle way, arguing that both "competition and central direction become poor and inefficient tools if they are incomplete."[8] Such absolutist language led a substantial subset of his readers to derive the message that the government should abstain from intervention altogether.

Most of these readers had encountered the text through a version that was substantially different from Hayek's own. The condensation published in the *Reader's Digest* was less an abridgment than a re-creation. Although the final product was widely attributed to Max Eastman, the magazine's founding editor, DeWitt Wallace, spent hours reworking it himself.[9] Both were drawn to the text in part for ideological reasons: Eastman was a recent convert from socialism and one of Stalinist Russia's most prominent critics, while Wallace was a staunch anticommunist who had recently guided his magazine, as the sympathetic editor of the *Saturday Review of Literature* observed, on "a conspicuous list to the extreme Right."[10] In their reworking of *The Road to Serfdom* Hayek's style was simplified and dramatized, his observations were reordered and reconnected, and new sentences were written to impart an appearance of seamlessness to disconnected snippets. As a result, many of Hayek's qualifications were lost. As one critic observed, the text itself had become an enactment of readers' tendencies to take sentences out of context in order to support their own point of view.[11] Hayek told his audiences that the *Digest*'s editors had performed a difficult task remarkably well, but he also warned them that its "faulty editing" posed a "particular danger."[12] He was acutely aware that only a slim proportion of the readers of *The Road to Serfdom* experienced the book through his own prose. No author can control readers' interpretations of his or her published texts, but Hayek had lost control over the words themselves.

Conservative politicians, journalists, and business leaders were quick to appropriate the *Reader's Digest* version as a useful aid in their efforts to roll back the New Deal state. Citing the fact that it was undoubtedly "one of the most important and significant articles in recent years," the *Digest* in a sidebar to the article had advertised reprints made available by the Book-of-the-Month Club, offering steep discounts for bulk orders.[13] Over a million orders for the reprint version were placed, many by corporations and their advocacy groups, dwarfing the 40,000 copies of the original version that had been sold. Employees of companies including General Motors and New Jersey Power and Light received copies courtesy of their managers. *Look* published a cartoon version, which was reprinted shortly thereafter in the General Electric Company's magazine. The National Association of Manufacturers, eager to expand its public relations activities as the war approached a close, mailed free copies to all of its 14,000 members. Editorials in the conservative Hearst newspapers urged "every free-acting, free-thinking, free-writing American" to read "every line," and its syndicate King Features distributed the condensed version shortly after Hayek's arrival in the country. In order to exploit this publicity, Hayek's lecture agency built his tour around presentations before chambers of commerce and bankers' associations.[14] Meanwhile, moderate business organizations like the Committee for

Economic Development chose to keep their distance because Hayek had developed a reputation as—in the words of one observer—"a made-to-order hand grenade for conservatives to hurl at planners."

Hayek had become, that commentator continued, "caught up in a war not of his own making."[15] His text became known as a partisan document arguing for the emaciation of the state, and he was variously labeled a "spokesman for the economic beliefs which flourished up to 1929," a "voice out of the old Manchester school of Cobden and Bright," and "Spencer, in modern dress."[16] One critic dedicated an entire book to the observation that *The Road to Serfdom* was a "Manifesto of the reactionaries," going so far as to argue "that Hayek's apparatus of learning is deficient, his reading incomplete; that his understanding of the economic process is bigoted, his account of history false; that his political science is almost nonexistent, his terminology misleading, his comprehension of British and American political procedure and mentality gravely defective; and that his attitude to average men and women is truculently authoritarian."[17] Hayek had become a symbolic figure, appropriated to serve as a public relations tool and source of intellectual legitimation for critics of the New Deal state and as an emblem of reactionary excess to its more numerous defenders. As the frequent invocations of Hayek in the contemporary media attest, these roles have continued to define his public image ever since.

In the decades that followed, Hayek expressed dismay at the prevalence of this interpretation. He repudiated it in his book *Law, Legislation and Liberty,* inveighed against it in his introduction to the 1976 edition of *The Road to Serfdom,* and privately wrote Paul Samuelson in 1980 to excoriate him for propounding it in his widely read textbook *Foundations of Economic Analysis.* This "myth," he told Samuelson, had "prevented people from taking my argument seriously."[18] As Hayek repeatedly reminded his interpreters, his book both renounced any claims to inevitability and assailed the "wooden insistence" with which previous generations of liberals had clung to laissez-faire.[19] Like Walter Lippmann's *Inquiry into the Principles of the Good Society* before the war, *The Road to Serfdom* was premised on a belief that one could engage in a vigorous critique of planning without rejecting government intervention altogether.

At a number of points in the book Hayek explicitly condoned a vigorous role for the state. He informed his readers that responsible governments could limit the fluctuations of the business cycle through monetary and perhaps even fiscal policy. They could provide those items, like transportation infrastructure, that the price system failed to allocate efficiently. They could maintain quite strict regulations against certain business practices by limiting working hours, requiring sanitary arrangements, proscribing the use of poisonous substances, prohibiting deforestation, preventing harmful farming methods, restricting the noise and smoke produced by factories, and imposing stringent price controls on monopolies to curtail extraordinary profits. And they could develop forms of social insurance that provided redress to victims of earthquakes and floods, that compensated victims of sickness or accidents, and that ensured a basic minimum of food, shelter, and clothing for all.[20] Hayek supported a role for the government in counteracting the business cycle, constructing new infrastructure, regulating a broad range of business activities, and administering extensive social insurance guarantees. It is not difficult to understand why he grew frustrated with those who confused this vision with what he described as "dogmatic laissez-faire."[21]

Upon its initial publication, most of the book's reviewers acknowledged that Hayek's argument countenanced a substantial role for the government. A. C. Pigou observed in the *Economic Journal* that Hayek thought that the state should do a "great deal," John Davenport pointed out in *Fortune* that his argument was compatible with a "fiscal policy aimed to eliminate the worst features of boom and slump," the *American Mercury* noted his advocacy of a "guarantee of minimum standards of living," and the *Political Science Quarterly* drew attention to his statements in favor of a "comprehensive social security organization."[22] If "a list were made of all the forms of purposive direction which are blessed in the course of the book," the *Economist* observed, "it would be seen that Professor Hayek does not want to go back, but quite a long way forward."[23] Even Keynes recognized the book's openness to public investment, writing Hayek in private correspondence that he found himself "in agreement with virtually the whole of it; and not only in agreement with it, but in a deeply moved agreement."[24] Hayek himself used radio addresses and popular interviews to draw attention to the positive aspects of his program, urging that "security against severe privations" was an essential part of any government that sought to sustain itself. Like Frank Knight, he worried that a society that failed to fulfill these basic needs would inspire uncontrollable levels of popular discontent. "I would rather have a little planning now to prevent much worse planning, and possibly authoritarian controls, later," he told one interviewer. The excesses of the free market, he observed, were not sustainable if they were left unaddressed. "We must never forget that most men will bear the risks that freedom entails only if those risks are not prohibitively great."[25]

The problem Hayek's more careful readers faced was how to reconcile all the positive programs he apparently condoned with his stark warnings about the dangers of planning and the unacceptability of a middle way. Hayek did little to resolve such questions in *The Road to Serfdom* beyond stating enigmatically that he advocated "planning for competition" rather than "planning against competition."[26] Keynes privately warned Hayek that his denunciations of laissez-faire did not align with his insinuations that any planning would lead down a "slippery path" to the socialist state.[27] Others publicly savaged him for this vagueness on what seemed to them the central question of the book: one critic found him "strangely" silent on the specific measures to which he objected, another could not find "the manner of distinguishing between good planning and bad planning," and a third observed that one would "hunt in vain" for any "concrete" vision.[28] One reviewer concluded that this muddle was a "great weakness of the book."[29] It also left Hayek's argument highly susceptible to interpretive sleights of hand, as readers emphasized his strong language in portions of the book without acknowledging the caveats couched in others. *The Road to Serfdom* demonstrated a propensity, *Harper's* noted, for being "accepted in fragments and misused for childishly partisan purposes."[30]

As his lecture tour approached its close, Hayek complained to an interviewer about a "tendency to pick and choose from what I regard as unitary philosophy." In his travels across the country, he had encountered "far too many people talking about what I am represented to have said rather than about the argument that I have actually used," so that a book "written in no party spirit" had come to be viewed almost exclusively as a partisan document. For an author who had dedicated his book without irony to "socialists of all parties," this was an unfortunate fate. In reflecting on it, Hayek quoted Lord Acton's observation that alliances formed with other "friends of freedom" often gave one's opponents "just grounds for opposition."[31] He worried that his most vociferous advocates had represented his work in a manner that, ironically, made it impossible for him to convince those inclined toward an alternative point of view. He also became concerned about the effects that his growing reputation as a reactionary agitator would have on his career as an academic economist. For decades after its publication, he maintained that his most popular book had ruined his professional career. Just as the economics profession confronted the problems of the postwar era, Hayek recalled that "Keynes died and became a saint," while "I discredited myself by publishing *The Road to Serfdom*."[32]

Nevertheless, Hayek did derive some benefits from his newfound celebrity. He departed the United States at the close of his lecture tour with a strong impression that his convictions about the dangers faced by the contemporary world and the urgent need for a revival of liberalism were widely shared. As he wrote to his colleague and friend William Rappard, "there are still many more people who feel on the whole as we do than I had ever dared to hope."[33] Hayek's newfound fame also provided him with a unique platform from which to expound his worldview. A half year after the conclusion of his lecture tour, Mises informed him that he had become one of the most famous English writers in the United States.[34] Hayek had some reservations about his new stature but also recognized that it could be leveraged to establish intellectual credibility and public support for his ideas.

Building on the successes of *The Road to Serfdom* would require an approach that overcame its limitations, of which Hayek's experiences on the lecture tour had made him acutely aware. In the future he would need to be stricter about demarcating the boundaries between intellectual debate and the public sphere. Popular audiences were quick to turn any discussion of ideas into partisan rhetoric; in the process, they did grievous harm to the complexities of his arguments and, by extension, his academic reputation. Additionally, any attempt to reframe market advocacy would need to be more thoroughly grounded in a coherent social philosophy. In the wake of a catastrophic economic crisis, many still associated skepticism about government planning with unreflective support for the market mechanism. Debates over economic policy had a tendency to devolve into an opposition between absolutes, and attempts at moderation would not be taken seriously unless they were perceived as constitutive elements of a holistic worldview. Finally, Hayek was adamant that any project to develop the philosophical foundations of a revived liberalism could not be undertaken by him alone. The public response to *The Road to Serfdom* had reminded him of the importance of transatlantic dialogue and the extent to which it had atrophied during the war. Hayek recognized that his ideas would develop a broad and durable base of support only if they were supported by intellectuals from a range of disciplines and national backgrounds. Most urgently, he sought to reconvene his growing network of allies and supporters on a more permanent basis.[35] They had last gathered in the waning days before the onset of the war, at the height of concerns about the viability of democratic capitalism in an increasingly totalitarian world. Now, amid the opportunities and indeterminacies of postwar reconstruction, Hayek turned his attention to explicating the foundations of the social philosophy they believed themselves to share.

After returning to his wartime residence in Cambridge for the summer, Hayek began to develop a plan of action. In a memorandum sent to friends, associates, and prospective funders, he explained the confluence of events that justified the establishment of a new discussion venue at this moment. "The war has divided the world into a number of intellectual islands," he wrote, "separated from each other as never before in modern history."[36] This situation was hard for all scholars, but was perhaps most devastating for those who held deeply unpopular views. As Ludwig von Mises wrote to Hayek before his lecture tour, free-market economists still felt marginalized in a world where the most influential economic figures—Veblen and Hansen in America, and Laski and Keynes in England—were best known for their criticisms of the market mechanism.[37] This constricted discourse had created what Hayek would describe as a "growing current of fatalism," in which "more and more people feel that we are ineluctably moving towards a kind of social order which nobody wants and which we have yet no power to avert."[38] By creating a single transatlantic forum, Hayek hoped to foster a sense of association among individuals who perceived themselves, within their national boundaries, to be very much alone.

In developing his vision, Hayek drew directly on the plan to develop an international liberal journal that Wilhelm Röpke had conceived and then abandoned as the war drew to a close. Like Röpke's proposed publication, this new society would aim to escape a narrow economism and would focus its attention more broadly on "the observance of universally valid moral standards in politics" and "the common background of ideas and values which a civilization needs to survive."[39] Its membership would be broad based, consisting of individuals who agreed on certain basic principles but disagreed about many present-day political issues, because Hayek found particular value in those who could speak in a language persuasive to the Left.[40] And, as he explained in "The Prospects of Freedom," a prefatory speech at Stanford the following year, it would maintain some distance from political advocacy. "The organisation which seems to be needed is something half-way between a scholarly association and a political society," he said. "It would differ from a purely scientific group in that its members would be held together by a basic agreement on the aims for which they are seeking the means. And it would differ from any political organisation in that it would not be concerned with short run policies, or even with the peculiar problems of particular countries, but with the general principles of a liberal order."[41] He described it as "a kind of International Academy of Political Philosophy," or more specifically as "a closed society, whose members would be bound together by common convictions and try both to develop this common philosophy and to spread its understanding."[42]

Not all of Hayek's correspondents approved of his institutional vision. After receiving Hayek's memorandum, Karl Popper wrote him to express deep concern at his call for the organization to be ideologically closed and defined by its members' common convictions. In his recent book *The Open Society and Its Enemies* Popper had described himself as a critical rationalist, arguing that intellectual growth emerged out of the interaction between differing systems of belief. He warned Hayek that the adoption of ideological prerequisites for membership would give the new society an appearance of dogmatism, leave it unable to recruit individuals in positions of political power, and prevent it from serving as a legitimate forum for open discussion that could mediate ideological disputes through philosophical debate.[43] Popper believed that a society following Hayek's proposed structure was in danger of solidifying points of disagreement rather than establishing a venue for productive consensus. Hayek responded that certain presuppositions were necessary as grounds for a productive conversation; otherwise the group would have no foundation from which to begin. As he would later explain in *The Constitution of Liberty*, his social theory relied on the premise that values were "not a product but a presupposition of reason," and that any effort to improve our institutions must therefore "take for granted much that we do not understand."[44] Hayek believed that there were limits to rationalism, and that some foundational values could not be left up for debate. The society would include only those members for whom these values could simply be assumed.

While Popper worried that the society's criteria for membership would be too rigid, others expressed concern that they would not be rigid enough. The most vociferous of these critics was Hayek's friend and mentor

Ludwig von Mises, who had become a lonely advocate within their intellectual community for an uncompromising laissez-faire. The "weak point" of such a society, Mises argued, was that it relied "upon the cooperation of many men who are known for their endorsement of interventionism." In doing so, he argued, the group would lend credence to the idea that advocates of freedom should place limits on the market mechanism.[45] Mises wanted his colleagues' veneration of the market to be absolute and was frustrated by their accommodationist instincts. Over the subsequent decade he would alienate many of his friends and colleagues with vitriolic attacks on their departures from ideological purity. His letters to Salvador de Madariaga, which accused his colleague of adopting "the terminology of all socialists, nationalists, supporters of dictatorship" and informed him that he did "not even know what liberalism means," were emblematic of his increasingly intransigent views.[46] Many of his peers shared William Rappard's attribution of such statements to the fact that Mises "is more than 70 years old and finds himself very isolated, personally and intellectually, in New York."[47] During the 1940s and 1950s Mises's absolutism was largely ignored by a network of colleagues who shared Hayek's assumption that their political ideals could be revived only if they were invented anew.

Even those who shared Hayek's visions for the new organization, however, expressed some concerns about the challenges it would face. The French journalist Bertrand de Jouvenel wrote Wilhelm Röpke to say that Hayek's proposal was "an excellent development" because the time had arrived for an attempt to bring together scholars who agreed on the dangers of centralization. He urged, however, that the meeting should not become a "restatement of the 'Way to Serfdom,'" suggesting instead that criticisms be left out in order for participants to focus on "the alternative."[48] His concern was that advocates of capitalism would follow the path taken by socialists a generation earlier. In their contributions to the calculation debates, Hayek and Mises had assailed socialists for focusing their energies on critiques of capitalism and failing to devote sufficient attention to the elaboration of their own worldview. Such an approach represented "good tactics," Jouvenel admitted, because criticisms of one's opponents are often more persuasive than honest discussions of the implications of one's own proposals. But an excessive focus on tactics would be myopic. If members of the nascent movement were to create a new liberalism that was very different from its historical predecessors, they would do so only through a process of vigorous contestation and debate. Their energies needed to center on the development of novel ideas rather than the advocacy of established principles, even if such a mode of discussion would necessarily render them politically impotent for an indefinite period of time. He believed that their initial goal was to identify, not to propagate, a common worldview.[49]

The responses to Hayek's memorandum revealed several challenges that his proposed organization would confront. Even at this early stage he faced strong pressures to clarify which aspects of its political philosophy would be open to debate and which would be simply presumed. Many of his friends and colleagues shared his respect for the liberal tradition and his sense that it needed to undergo a renovation and renewal, but it was not yet clear that they defined that tradition in the same way or agreed on what elements would remain sacrosanct. Additionally, Hayek would need to develop a strategy for navigating the perilous boundary between ideas and politics. Some of his correspondents perceived the proposed organization's goals to be primarily intellectual and envisioned it as an environment for open academic debate, while others believed them to be political and emphasized the presentation of a unified front. They looked to Hayek for an indication as to whether this group would be inquisitive or tactical in its approach to political and philosophical problems. As in *The Road to Serfdom*, Hayek remained vague when he was pressed to provide specific responses to questions of this kind. He was hoping to build a small community of dissenters into a substantive coalition, and may have recognized that any benefits of specificity would be outweighed by the limitations it imposed.

After determining that his friends and colleagues held sufficient interest in the prospect of establishing a new society, Hayek confronted a potentially prohibitive challenge: finding sources of funding capable of covering the expenses that such an endeavor entailed. Years before the invention of the jet engine, assembling a transatlantic community of intellectuals with limited means in a single location for over a week required a substantial financial commitment, and Hayek did not have the luxury of endowed institutions with sympathetic ideological agendas and established records of support. He needed to demonstrate the capacity to persuade funders, despite the unusual nature of his proposed project and all the related uncertainties, to trust in the feasibility and importance of its realization.

Examining how Hayek approached the problem of funding provides some insights into the status of financial support for conservative political ideas in the late 1940s. Today we live in a world with a vast array of right-wing ideological funding organizations, but in the immediate postwar period advocacy organizations with an explicit political agenda were unusual, and those with a free-market orientation were rarer still. The existing policy institutes, such as the Brookings Institution, were largely Progressive-era enterprises designed to provide "objective" advice on making government more rational and efficient. Although these organizations were by no means unfriendly to business—Brookings, in particular, was known for its critical response to the New Deal—Hayek believed that they were much more forthcoming to moderate and left-leaning intellectuals than to market advocates like himself. "While I see daily how for the international contacts of the leftish groups, and particularly the Communists, almost unlimited means seem to be available and in consequence the closest co-ordination of their systematic efforts possible," he complained to a potential funder, Jasper Crane of DuPont, in 1949, "I have so far failed to obtain any funds to speak of for similar endeavours on the liberal side."[50] The unstable patchwork of institutions and individuals that Hayek approached reveals both the challenges faced by market advocates in the immediate postwar era and the new institutional paradigms they invented in their attempts to generate long-term ideological change.

After his initial funding inquiries Hayek saw little hope for the kind of organization he was proposing. "While the general scheme had a very good reception from all the scholars I have approached," he wrote in October 1946, "there is so far no prospect of the considerable funds forthcoming which would be required to make such an undertaking worth starting."[51] Shortly thereafter, however, he identified the two sources of support that would sustain his proposed society during the first decade of its existence. The first was Albert Hunold, the Swiss businessman who had aided Wilhelm Röpke in his unsuccessful attempt to develop the liberal journal *Occident*. Once that project fell through, Hunold agreed to redirect 20,000 francs raised from other business leaders toward accommodations for visiting scholars associated with the proposed conference.[52] The second was a Kansas City charitable foundation, the Volker Fund, which agreed to cover travel costs for the American attendees.[53] Both individual corporate philanthropists and ideological foundations would become major sources of financial support for market advocates in the decades that followed. Hayek recognized them as essential resources and worked to convince them of the role abstract ideas would play in bringing about the tangible political changes they sought. He also recognized that accepting funds from individuals and organizations with an ideological orientation posed particular dangers to an organization that sought to maintain some academic distance from contemporary political debates. His challenge was to obtain their largesse while preserving the integrity of his institutional vision.

Hunold proved to be an invaluable source of both administrative and fund-raising support. He was able to draw on contacts cultivated throughout a disparate career as a schoolmaster, a university assistant, a radio commentator, a secretary of the stock exchange, a bank director, and a publicity executive in the watch industry to find a set of Swiss institutions that were willing to sponsor regional meetings. Despite his lack of substantial personal wealth, he worked doggedly to convince colleagues and connections to provide periodic support to visiting academics.[54] Further, his high degree of interest in Hayek's project led him to take on basic organizational tasks that his academic colleague was not competent to fulfill. Hayek had only limited willingness to engage in the more tedious aspects of administration, and his reservoirs of energy were not limitless; his family recalled his inability to wear a self-winding watch because of its failure to function as he sat motionless for hours in his study.[55] Hunold, in contrast, demonstrated a capacity to attach deep personal importance to the most minor administrative matters. This unique sense of investment in Hayek's enterprise both motivated him to provide essential support and provoked some concern. During Hunold's earlier collaboration on the journal *Occident*, Wilhelm Röpke had grown increasingly disillusioned with his funder's attempts to take control over aspects of the operation and his tendency to turn professional disputes into matters of personal conflict. At the time Hayek told Röpke in no uncertain terms that "the person who holds the purse strings will exercise a certain influence," and that he should not allow related concerns to lead him to abandon an essential source of support.[56] Röpke proved unwilling to accept this advice, writing Hayek later that he was "speechless" over Hunold's most recent transgressions and concluding that he was an "entirely impossible man."[57] In accepting financial and organizational support from Hunold, Hayek exhibited a greater willingness to incorporate the personal idiosyncrasies and demands of funders. In later years he experienced a falling out with Hunold that mirrored aspects of

Röpke's earlier difficulties, but at that point Hayek's society was sufficiently stable to continue without Hunold's assistance. In the meantime Hayek made a calculated decision to accept the fact that philanthropists would expect to receive some privileges in return for their support.

While Hayek relied on Hunold to arrange the site for the first meeting of his proposed society, he drew on the Volker Fund to pay the substantial travel costs of the meeting's American participants. Support for an enterprise of this kind represented a substantial departure from the fund's original mandate. It had been established in 1932 through a donation by the Kansas City furniture manufacturer William Volker, who endowed it with half his estate at the outset and much of the remainder at his death in 1947. Initially its activities were primarily oriented toward public works projects in the Kansas City area. As Volker aged, however, the organization fell increasingly under the influence of his nephew, Harold Luhnow, and its priorities began to shift. As a later statement indicated, the directors did "not feel obliged to follow in precisely the pattern William Volker established. In fact, he told them not to, but to adapt the Fund to the changing needs of changing times."[58] Luhnow, at the urging of a former Kansas City associate named Loren Miller, had become an advocate of Austrian economics, with a particular interest in Hayek and Mises. Hewing to what he referred to as the core "principles" of Volker's giving, he began to shift the recipients of the fund's largesse away from regional public works and toward philosophical advocates of economic freedom. Influenced by Hayek's contention that classical liberal ideals could not be realized without a strong intellectual base, he set out to foster the construction of that base through the strategic allocation of disbursements from his uncle's fund.[59]

Luhnow attended a talk that Hayek gave at the Economic Club of Detroit during his lecture tour for *The Road to Serfdom,* and several days later he showed up at Hayek's lodgings in Chicago to inquire whether he would be willing to write a revised version of the book tailored to audiences in the United States.[60] Hayek was leery of that possibility, but before returning to England he wrote Luhnow to ask about his willingness to help finance the first meeting of his proposed society.[61] At first Luhnow rebuffed Hayek's request. Although the specific origins of his hesitations remain unclear, the fund was reluctant to support institutions that its administrators had not conceived, and its domestic mission left it with little interest in investing directly in projects overseas. After a year of continuing inquiries, however, Luhnow wrote Hayek to inform him that the fund had decided to lend its support. Sufficient resources were now available for Hayek to plan his proposed society's initial gathering.[62]

Although support for this meeting was not inexpensive, it represented a very small subset of the fund's bottom line. During the late 1940s and 1950s the fund was dispensing over $1 million per year, and its administrators used these resources to provide support to market advocates in a variety of ways. They underwrote the salaries of Mises at New York University and Hayek at the University of Chicago, providing institutional bases in America for the most prominent international opponents of governmental intervention. They supported a series of institutions that were designed to foster communication among academics and students who opposed economic planning, including the Free Market Study at the University of Chicago, a rotating series of summer conferences and academies, and Hayek's proposed society. Through a committee of four affiliated readers—Murray Rothbard, Frank Meyer, Rose Wilder Lane, and George de Huszar—they also sought out individuals who published arguments that corresponded with their stated ideals. After performing careful analyses of prior publications, they would send unsolicited financial support as a source of encouragement for further writing and research.[63] Building on Hayek's insights about the relationship between ideas and political change, the fund's administrators designed it to provide an institutional glue that would allow disparate sympathizers to coalesce in support of an unconventional worldview.

Many of Hayek's colleagues expressed concerns about the sources of funding for his proposed endeavor, and he was quick to reassure them that "no strings of any kind have been attached."[64] In return for the financial support, however, Luhnow did expect to have some say over who would be invited to make the transatlantic journey. When he saw the list of prospective invitees, he was quick to express his displeasure over names that he thought were insufficiently forceful in their defense of the market mechanism. "Frankly," he wrote to Hayek in January 1947, "some of the reactions that I have had on one or two of your suggestions are such that I know the Directors of the Volker Charities Fund would not be interested in paying their travelling expenses anywhere."[65] Hayek quietly excised the most offensive names from a subsequent version of the list.[66] The Volker Fund had successfully leveraged its financial support to narrow the ideological horizons of the society Hayek was hoping to found. Hayek, meanwhile, proved skilled at the dual task of reassuring colleagues of the unimpeachability of the funding sources while making limited adjustments to preserve the necessary support. He had demonstrated himself to be an institution builder with a crucial combination of qualities: an entrepreneurial ability to conceive and execute complex and potentially controversial plans, an academic background and reputation that reassured his colleagues about the nature of the enterprise, and a capacity to accommodate the needs of funding organizations without appearing wholly subject to their demands.

Hayek was very explicit in his correspondence with funders about the long time horizon over which its influence should be evaluated. "I . . . freely admit," Hayek wrote, "that I neither expect immediate results nor believe that any efforts which aim at immediate results are likely to change the general trend of opinion."[67] Instead, he drew on his background at the London School of Economics to adopt a deliberately Fabian approach to the advancement of social change. The relationship between the society and its members would, Hayek hoped, be much like the relationship between a well-constructed legal order and its constituents: it would merely provide a framework that enabled the individuals involved to pursue their projects aided by the greatest possible degree of mutually beneficial interaction. "'Organisation' in the intellectual sphere must consist mainly in providing channels and facilities of communication," he wrote, "of bringing together the people whose common outlook and interests make fruitful collaboration possible, not in 'organising' the work to be done which must grow freely out of the contacts and exchange of opinions."[68] The genius of such a structure would consist in the very limitations it set on itself. Hayek believed that the most effective way to inspire social change would be to avoid any explicit attempt to pursue it.

On a Tuesday morning in the early spring of 1947, Hayek convened a group of thirty-nine colleagues in a hotel near Vevey, Switzerland, at the base of Mont Pèlerin. The room was filled with journalists, businessmen, and academics from across the Atlantic world, many of whom knew one another by reputation if not personal contact. A few had traversed great distances in order to attend, including some Americans who had never before traveled abroad.[69] In an era when transatlantic flights remained too expensive for many to afford, they had crossed the Atlantic in ocean liners and had discovered upon their arrival a Europe still ravaged by the war.[70] The winter of 1947 had brought famine, freezing weather, impassable roads, shortages of coal, and growing concerns about spiritual malaise and economic stagnation. In the midst of this devastation, Switzerland's wartime neutrality had turned it into an oasis of relative prosperity.[71] The resort where they would spend the next ten days provided a respite from a surrounding continent that was on the verge of painful and still-indeterminate reconstruction.

With the group finally assembled, Hayek delivered a speech addressing the nature of their task. This gathering, he informed them, represented a unique opportunity. Long isolated in home environments where they were "forced constantly to defend the basic elements of their beliefs," the participants now found themselves among others who shared an "agreement on fundamentals." Through sustained debate with like-minded colleagues, they would be able to develop the comprehensive revision of liberalism that books like *An Inquiry into the Principles of the Good Society* and *The Road to Serfdom* had promised but did not provide. Hayek expected this to be a difficult task because it would require "both purging traditional liberal theory of certain accidental accretions which have become attached to it in the course of time, and facing up to certain real problems which an over-simplified liberalism has shirked." In overcoming the failures of laissez-faire, Hayek urged, it would be essential to develop a social philosophy that provided a rich account of the moral dimensions of human existence. Any advocate of capitalism who understood its benefits in purely material terms or prioritized economic concerns over matters of spiritual fulfillment was bound to fail in the court of popular opinion. They would need to cast aside an arid rationalism in favor of humility and, in doing so, heal the "breach between true liberal and religious convictions" that continued to prevent "a revival of liberal forces."[72] The relative isolation of conservative intellectuals in the wake of the Great Depression had created an extraordinarily fluid ideological environment, in which market advocates were eager to recognize the limits to laissez-faire and social traditionalists were quick to acknowledge the benefits of the market mechanism. Hayek was not trying to adjudicate between static ideologies, but rather to develop one anew.

During the following ten days the participants engaged in both discussions of preordained topics and casual meals and excursions into the countryside. As with many events of this kind, the informal gatherings may have proved more important than the sessions themselves. Interactions among the attendees reflected the group's interplay between diversity and homogeneity: they shared certain commonalities of viewpoint, substantial institutional overlaps, and some personal connections to Hayek, but they came from a broad transatlantic milieu that included

France, Germany, Italy, Switzerland, the United States, Denmark, Norway, and Sweden. Participation was restricted, with the lone exception of the British historian Veronica Wedgwood, entirely to white men, but their backgrounds spanned a wide range of careers, including popular journalism, academic economics, social philosophy, corporate management, and ideological advocacy. The attendees' varied nationalities and professions enabled many new connections to be formed, and their substantial commonalities and relatively small number made it easy for networking of this kind to occur. During the conference funders established relationships with future recipients of their largesse, journalists initiated dialogues with potential sources of new ideas, and academics found areas of commonality among disparate lines of inquiry. The influence of these interactions on participants' work would continue long after they had departed Mont Pèlerin.

Perhaps their most important task was to develop a formal account of what the goal of this new organization would be. In doing so, they would have the opportunity to frame the parameters of the "new" liberalism Hayek had summoned them to construct, and to identify the points of commonality that held their sometimes divergent perspectives together. Their first draft of such a statement was written by a committee of five members, who sought to employ language that one of them described as "broad enough to be meaningful, and not detailed enough to split us up."[73] They produced a list of foundational convictions that assailed the socialist menace, lauded the virtues of the competitive market, and drew connections between economic freedoms and the "intellectual freedom" that totalitarians sought to erode. Echoing Hayek's introductory speech before the society, they also paired an emphasis on the importance of a free marketplace for both goods and ideas with appeals to the necessity of a "widely accepted moral code" governing "collective no less than private action."[74] Even in this vague initial form, their statement inspired controversy among the participants, who erupted in debate about whether it excessively or insufficiently emphasized the importance of private property, whether its reliance on the concept of a "moral code" should be expanded or removed, and whether it embraced the forward-looking language of progressivism strongly enough. Some members questioned whether their difficulties were a sign that the society's members did not share many commonalities after all. If the group could not agree "on a fairly general scheme of ideas," George Stigler remarked, "then it seems that there would be very little purpose or reason, in forming a society."[75] In its demands for both intellectual freedom and unquestioned absolutes, an atomic marketplace and a moral collectivity, the statement's expansive commission accentuated the complexities of the society's mandate.

In an attempt to resolve these tensions, Hayek enlisted Lionel Robbins to dictate a new draft of the statement after breakfast the following morning. Robbins's version, which was quickly accepted by the group, defined the society's mission primarily through the trends its members opposed, including the recent worldwide turn toward a "decline of belief in private property and the competitive market" and a denial of both "absolute moral standards" and "the desirability of the rule of law." United in their sense of opposition, the members now faced a pressing need to unravel the "essential moral and economic origins" of the "present crisis." At the outset there were several basic assumptions on which they could agree: a rejection of totalitarianism, a defense of the market mechanism, a connection between economic and intellectual freedom, and an acknowledgment of the importance of moral absolutes. But Robbins's statement cast aside the language of "convictions" in favor of an emphasis on problems that still needed to be solved. Their meetings would be charged with the task of generating "a reassertion of valid ideals" that could stand as firm bulwarks for the capitalist order against the socialist encroachments of recent years.[76] About what those ideals might be, strong disagreements had already emerged. The members of the Mont Pèlerin Society were unified in the social philosophy they opposed and the questions they sought to address, but the structure of their alternative vision remained unclear.

As a result of this lack of clarity, they spent much of their time dwelling on the ideological opponents that had brought them together. In part because of reservations about antagonizing a wartime ally, Hayek had framed his critique of totalitarianism in *The Road to Serfdom* around Nazi Germany. By the time the society gathered for its first meeting, however, his colleagues did not hesitate to identify the Soviet Union as their primary source of concern. "You only get further with the Russians," Lionel Robbins dramatically asserted, "if you treat them as though they are *not* human beings."[77] Echoing Harry Truman, who only weeks before had announced that nations faced "a fateful hour" in which they would need "to choose between alternate ways of life," the society's members took turns expressing their anxieties about Communist threats both without and within.[78] Taking the onset of World War II as a lesson in the dangers of conciliation, many of them urged that the response be aggressive and immediate. "Are we going to make the same mistakes of appeasement?" the scientist and social philosopher Michael Polanyi asked. "Or are we going to depart from this attitude, and become firm and resist all claims of communism by force?"[79] Over the summer and fall of 1947 their concerns grew still more pressing. "Doubtless you feel as I do that we are now hovering on the brink," Bertrand de Jouvenel wrote to Hayek early the following year. "The Russian menace from the outside, the Communist menace from the inside, and to defend Europe against this double offensive, the Socialists whose every idea tends to disorganize and weaken the Occident. . . . The awakening comes, all but too late."[80] They worried that a growing proportion of their contemporaries had been convinced by Communist criticisms of the capitalist system. Abstract debates about social philosophy took on new urgency in an environment in which market advocates perceived themselves to be on the verge of losing a global war of ideas.

They believed that they were entering this period of ideological combat with a potentially insurmountable disadvantage: the scorn of the intellectual establishment. In the popular wartime tract *Capitalism, Socialism and Democracy,* Joseph Schumpeter had famously complained about a tendency for capitalist economies to generate intellectuals who were hostile to the social system that produced them. In previous eras, Schumpeter wrote, intellectuals served at the pleasure of a ruling class that was quick to punish them for heretical ideas. Capitalism provided them with the printing press, the radio, an increasingly leisured and literate public, and a system of cultural and legal restraints that protected expressions of dissent. As a result, he concluded, "unlike any other type of society, capitalism inevitably and by virtue of the very logic of its civilization creates, educates and subsidizes a vested interest in social unrest."[81] Schumpeter himself, always sui generis within the economics profession, did not attend the meeting at Mont Pèlerin, but the society's members shared both his belief in the importance of intellectuals and his discouragement at their predilections. "The grand disruptive force," Bertrand de Jouvenel wrote to Hayek after the meeting, "is not the upsurge of the industrial workers, it is, in my view, and I think in yours, the creation of a vast class of professional intellectuals, receptive to ideas, dealing them out, and who have set into motion beliefs, ideals, dreams, which are wrecking our societies."[82] Ludwig von Mises juxtaposed his virulent attacks on the "simplified Marxism" and "romantic illusions" of contemporary intellectuals with calls for the development of a contrary intellectual tradition.[83] Ideas, he informed his colleagues, must be "fought by ideas."[84] The Mont Pèlerin Society was founded to counteract what its members perceived to be a contrary ideological trend, both in the international political environment and among the intellectual class.

They were acutely aware that if they were going to persuade others to adopt their worldview, they would need to differentiate their perspective from an uncompromising adherence to laissez-faire. Some of the society's early members worried that its discussions did not go far enough in this regard. The French economist Maurice Allais chose not to sign its statement of aims on the ground that its "dogmatic stance" on private property left it "much closer to the laissez-fairism of the nineteenth century than to a genuine revival of liberalism."[85] Most of his colleagues in the society, however, saw themselves as defenders of theoretical complexity against Communists and planners who advocated misleadingly simple solutions for the social ills of the time. This argument was most prominently expressed by the French social theorist Raymond Aron, who used his one recorded presentation before the society to criticize intellectuals' tendency to mindlessly denounce capitalism without interrogating whether it caused the problems they perceived. This superficial mode of analysis, he argued, helped provoke the misguided assumption that revolutions could solve the central problems of human history. "Revolutions are sometimes inevitable, but they are almost always a misfortune," he told the members. "They destroy irreplaceable goods."[86] Aron later published similar comments in *The Opium of the Intellectuals,* referring to intellectuals as "revolutionaries by profession" who passed judgment "by comparing present realities with theoretical ideals rather than with other realities."[87] The early members of the society represented their market advocacy as emerging from a skepticism about, rather than a rigid adherence to, theoretical ideals.

They were also quick to distance their ideas from reactionary sentiment and to associate them with the forward-looking language of progressivism. In *The Road to Serfdom* Hayek's vigorous condemnations of laissez-faire had served to remind his readers that his argument was not a simple restatement of ideas that had long been out of fashion. He now wanted to move toward a more specific, visionary representation of his worldview. "What we lack is a liberal Utopia," he wrote in the late 1940s, "a program which seems neither a mere defence of things as they are nor a diluted kind of socialism, but a truly liberal radicalism."[88] Frank

Knight, who had himself straddled the boundaries between a liberal sensibility and an explicitly "radical" worldview, urged the society's founding members to align their market advocacy with support for religious toleration and the mantle of humanitarianism. Perhaps the most vociferous advocate of the adoption of the language of progressivism, however, was Milton Friedman. He assailed the tendency of liberals to represent their ideas as a "defence of the status quo" and urged his colleagues to rely instead on rhetoric that was "dynamic and progressive." It was essential, he said, to relay the fact that their organization was "concerned in the progress of man's welfare."[89] In the wake of the Great Depression, no democratic polity would be compelled by the cold language of nineteenth-century market advocates. The remorseless social Darwinism associated with theorists like Herbert Spencer and William Graham Sumner had little place in a popular conversation in which so many perceived themselves as helpless victims, or potential victims, of an unhindered market.[90] It would be necessary to soften the price mechanism's sometimes rough edges and to shift its rhetorical logic of market advocacy away from an adversarial ethic and toward an emphasis on the benefits it could bestow on all.

The central mandate the society's members set for themselves was to provide, in the words of their statement of aims, a "reassertion of valid ideals." Any attempts to present a compelling alternative to the Communist worldview, to foster a contrary intellectual tradition, or to appropriate the language of progressivism would require a renewed inquiry into the philosophical foundations of capitalism. If not an unrepentant individualism, what social ideal would best justify and represent the social theory they sought to defend? How could they represent their market advocacy as part of a holistic worldview that their compatriots might conceivably share? Answering these questions would require them to reinvent, or at the very least to reground, the morals of capitalism. It was their task to provide a convincing account of the ethical foundations of a market-centered world. The early members of the Mont Pèlerin Society struggled, however, to arrive at anything resembling consensus in their responses to the problems raised by the project they had assigned to themselves. Although they found some unity in their respect for the price mechanism, they gradually discovered that this shared orientation derived from deeply incongruous worldviews.

In the late 1940s Hayek was in the midst of his own attempt to describe the philosophical foundations of the market society, a project that would consume much of his remaining career. A decade earlier he had begun publishing work that provided an epistemological justification of his economic views. He increasingly represented himself as a theorist of ignorance, arguing that each individual had only a tiny fraction of the available information about the world within which he or she operated. Given these severe constraints on the individual's capacity for comprehension, the challenge of the modern social order was to maximize the cumulative knowledge of its many constituents. Hayek was deeply suspicious of any response to these problems that relied on what he described as rationalism, "the product of an exaggerated belief in the powers of individual reason and of a consequent contempt for anything which has not been consciously designed by it or is not fully intelligible to it."[91] Instead, he advocated for a humbler sensibility that emphasized the irrationality and fallibility of humankind, an approach that he specifically associated with "English individualism."[92] Adherents of this antirationalist philosophy would respect the market as a mode of ordering social interactions that was capable of assimilating the unique knowledge of its constituents without subjecting them to any unitary plan.[93] Although they would not hesitate to limit the exercise of coercive power, they would be suspicious of attempts to rationalize an economy or society, because such enterprises tended to overemphasize the knowledge of a few individuals and thereby to constrain the contributions of the many.

Hayek was not alone in his critique of rationalism. One close ally was Michael Polanyi, a Hungarian chemist who had been appointed to a chair in physical chemistry at Manchester University in 1933. Shortly after arriving in England, Polanyi began writing articles that criticized Russian restrictions on theoretical science. These attracted the attention of the emerging transatlantic network of critics of socialism, and he accepted invitations to attend the "Colloque Lippmann" in 1938 and the first meeting of the Mont Pèlerin Society nearly a decade later. In developing his theory of knowledge, Polanyi came to extol what he referred to as "spontaneous order": the extraordinarily "delicate and complex" patterns of alignment that aggregations can assume when they reach a point of equilibrium between internal and external forces.[94] Spontaneous order was not always preferable to the imposition of an assigned plan, but Polanyi argued that it was often capable, especially in tasks involving large numbers, of producing a much more comprehensive and efficient outcome than the alternatives. His discussions of spontaneous order ranged from small particles to communities of scientists, but he indicated that the "most massive" example was that of an economic marketplace.[95] Hayek adopted the term and joined Polanyi in expressing the dangers involved in imposing order on both intellectual and economic communities.

During the 1950s Polanyi turned his attention to another failure of rationalism, developing a social philosophy that accounted for modes of knowing that could not be relayed to others through language alone.[96] Many forms of knowledge, Polanyi argued, cannot be distilled into any simple prescription. Consider, for example, the existence of skills that can be transmitted only by example from master from apprentice. He observed that many such crafts were altogether lost after remaining dormant for a single generation, citing the repeated failures of even the most sophisticated techniques of modern production "to reproduce a single violin of the kind the half-literate Stradivarius turned out as a matter of routine more than 200 years ago."[97] Knowledge of the kind that Stradivarius manifested in his work was unspecifiable. Polanyi called this "tacit knowing" and indicated that it could not be subjected to the systematic forms of criticism that were applied to articulate forms.[98] He believed that much of human life could be described in these terms, a fact that accounted "for the possession by humanity of an immense mental domain, not only of knowledge but of manners, of laws and of the many different arts which man knows how to use, comply with, enjoy or live by, without specifiably knowing their contents."[99] Polanyi's emphasis on tacit knowing led him to advocate for the decentralization of both civic and intellectual culture, but also to urge respect for established institutions and convictions that enabled such processes to unfold, even if they could not be justified using reason alone.

Polanyi's conception of knowledge influenced the views of another leading midcentury antirationalist, Michael Oakeshott.[100] Oakeshott arrived at the London School of Economics (LSE) barely a year after Hayek departed for the University of Chicago, and assumed the chair in political science that had been vacated by the death of Harold Laski. Laski had been a prolific scholar and a formidable lecturer, advocating a distinctive brand of socialism that exerted broad influence in Labour Party circles. These qualities had made him the central figure in the academic pantheon at the LSE, and the adoption of his post by Oakeshott was widely perceived as a moment of institutional transition. In contrast to Laski, Oakeshott was a reserved and careful scholar who eschewed grand pronouncements and manifested a distinctly conservative sensibility. He had produced only two books before the appointment, one of which was a guide to picking winning horses at the Derby.[101] One commentator observed, "Had the managers of the School searched the whole wide world for a man polar to Laski in temperament, in teaching, in instinct and sympathy . . . they could not have found one better fitting the specifications."[102] Oakeshott himself acknowledged in his March 1951 inaugural lecture that it was "perhaps a little ungrateful" that such a confident teacher was followed in the position by an unrepentant skeptic. He then proceeded to question the entire enterprise of political science, arguing that in politics "men sail a boundless and bottomless sea," for which "seamanship consists in using the resources of a traditional manner of behaviour in order to make a friend of every hostile occasion."[103] According to Oakeshott, one should study politics to become competent in traditional manners of behavior, not to learn abstract rules that could be universally applied. Political philosophy, he argued, "is not what may be called a 'progressive' science, accumulating solid results and reaching conclusions upon which further investigation may be based with confidence."[104] To launch such an assault on the practice of political scientists while assuming a chair in the field at the LSE was, one observer recalled, equivalent to shouting "No Popery under the very windows of St Peter's."[105]

Both Oakeshott and Polanyi were led, via their focus on knowledge that escaped the confines of the rational, to manifest a simultaneous respect for social traditions and the economic marketplace. Polanyi's critique of rationalism inspired him to valorize both the tacit knowledge embodied in networks of social tradition and the spontaneous orders that emerged out of large-scale market interactions. Oakeshott's skepticism about abstract problem solving drove him to commend "traditional" forms of knowledge and to assail government interventions that were "consciously planned and deliberately executed."[106] The modern sensibility, they feared, was excessively sanguine about its capacity to construct entirely new social orders based on rational schemes. In contrast, they saw a hidden and often unarticulated wisdom in traditional beliefs and practices and an organic logic in the apparently chaotic exchanges that were characteristic of market societies. Neither advocated a wholly unreflective adherence to traditional beliefs, nor did they believe that all restrictions and regulations should be removed from the marketplace. Rather, they were seeking to persuade their contemporaries to adopt a less rapid and less rationalist approach to political and economic change amid the uncertainties of the postwar world.

Hayek saw his social theory as very much aligned with Polanyi's and Oakeshott's. Like them, he contrasted the extent of human ignorance with the hubris of theorists who trafficked in abstractions, and he leveraged this line of analysis to emphasize the importance of respecting both social traditions and the implicit logic of the marketplace. Hayek saw this perspective as the product of a long tradition of liberal thought and often cited Lord Acton and Alexis de Tocqueville as exemplars. (His attempts to name his new organization the Acton-Tocqueville Society were rebuffed due to concerns about the choice of two Catholic noblemen.)[107] But neither Acton nor Tocqueville was a systematic thinker; Hayek looked to them for manifestations of a shared sensibility rather than for detailed justifications of his worldview. In explaining the foundations of his social philosophy, he instead adopted David Hume as his "constant companion and sage guide."[108] Hayek saw Hume as a theorist who justified both social traditions and commerce on competitive grounds. Traditions were products of extended processes of competition and had persisted because in some sense—which their beneficiaries did not always rationally comprehend—they worked. Hume's *Political Discourses* drew on this lesson to argue that wise leaders "bear a reverence to what carries the marks of age" and adjust innovations "as much as possible, to the ancient fabric."[109] At the same time, commerce enabled processes of competition to continue and helped bring about beneficial social change. The "greatness of the sovereign and the happiness of the state are, in a great measure," Hume wrote, "united with regard to trade and manufactures."[110] Hayek drew on Hume's insights to argue that both social traditions and marketplace interactions enabled individuals to benefit from a breadth of information they could not possibly hope to acquire on their own. In *The Constitution of Liberty* he explained that "civilization enables us constantly to profit from knowledge which we individually do not possess," in part by providing us with established "rules which experience has shown to serve best on the whole," and in part by allowing the "spontaneous forces of growth" to emerge out of the "freedom and unpredictability of human action."[111] He believed that support for social traditions and the free market could be jointly derived from a theory that emphasized the knowledge constraints encountered by discrete individuals.

The social theory that Hayek was working to develop, however, did not gain wide acceptance within the Mont Pèlerin Society. Many members expressed concerns about the conflicted relationship between markets and social traditions. Left unhindered, they argued, markets subverted the ethical foundations of the societies within which they existed. Frank Knight had elaborated on this argument in his classic 1923 essay "The Ethics of Competition," which pointed out the sharp divergence between the standards of value embodied in ethical norms and the prices of goods. Such divergences gradually degraded the ethical conventions of market societies and only became starker as restrictions on competition were removed. Untrammeled individualism, he wrote, "would probably tend to lower standards progressively rather than to raise them," and giving the public what it wanted generally meant "corrupting popular taste."[112] Hayek argued in response that the price mechanism was an ethically neutral arbiter, and that markets were a desirable mode of social organization precisely because they declined to dispense rewards on the basis of any uniform conception of merit.[113] Knight saw this argument as one of many Hayekian half-truths.[114] Despite Knight's sometimes vociferous criticisms of institutional economics, he inherited the institutionalists' belief in markets' ability to shape the wants and values of their participants. "An examination of the ethics of the economic system must consider the question of the kind of wants which it tends to generate or nourish," he wrote in "The Ethics of Competition."[115] Any claim for the ethical neutrality of markets simply ignored their tendency to reshape the ethical standards of the societies they operated within. The clear disparity between accepted social norms and the ethics embodied in economic behavior did not bode well, he believed, for the sustainability of market-based societies.

While Knight's work emphasized the conflicts between capitalism and standards of ethical value, other early members of the Mont Pèlerin Society drew attention to the degradation that markets engendered in the broader cultural framework of the societies within which they operated. The French journalist Bertrand de Jouvenel repeatedly expressed his concerns that this problem was not receiving sufficient attention in the society's discussions. His treatise *On Power*, published in the final year of World War II, dwelled at length on the "inharmonious behaviours" that had emerged in a society marked by rapid economic dislocations. Comparing a master saddler in the Temple quarter of Paris to his son who lived in the suburbs and worked for a massive industrial concern, Jouvenel observed that "there has been a prodigious transformation of folkways, beliefs, and sentiments, a transformation which cannot but leave its mark on the whole tone of society and in the end even affect the interplay of supply and demand."[116] He frankly stated to Hayek in 1950 that "when Capitalism triumphs there is, as I see it, a decline of culture."[117] Hayek acknowledged Jouvenel's concerns while attempting to draw his attention to capitalism's cultural advantages. "Of course I agree that capitalism is not necessarily favourable to culture, but it makes certain cultural growth possible which would probably not be possible under socialism," he wrote, directing Jouvenel's attention to its ability to foster "the growth of tradition as an impersonal, not centrally directed force."[118] Hayek saw decentralization as, on balance, beneficial to the preservation and further development of cultural forms, while Jouvenel worried that more concerted efforts were necessary to mitigate the cultural instabilities generated by the marketplace.

Even some of the society's most strident advocates of the free market acknowledged in their meetings that "high" cultural forms were unlikely to fare well in a mass-market society. No members of the group questioned Ludwig von Mises's credentials as a defender of free enterprise: he had no patience for those who defended central direction of the economy on the grounds of economic efficiency and was said to have once stormed out of one of their meetings, chaired by Milton Friedman, shouting, "You're all a bunch of socialists!"[119] Mises was quite willing, however, to acknowledge that the public sustained a distressingly limited market for the arts. "There is, in the structure of a capitalist society, little room left for the activities of the solitary philosopher, the detached poet and the lofty artist," he observed. "The majority of the buying public has no use for their products. It is these facts with which we have to deal in studying the cultural effects of capitalism."[120] Mises believed that debates over the economic efficiency of the capitalist system had been successfully concluded, but he acknowledged that critiques on the grounds of its cultural effects were very much alive.

Other members perceived a disharmony between capitalism and religion and worried that the market was shepherding in an increasingly atheistic world. Wilhelm Röpke, in particular, developed into the society's most consistent and vehement critic of a godless capitalism. When the society assembled in 1950, he presented a dystopic vision of atheistic modernity that manifested deep concerns about the implications of a free-market economy stripped of religious supports. "The dislodging of religion means the complete 'politicalisation' of existence," he wrote, leading to "the relativization of everything," "the realm of the Arbitrary," a social environment "where every kind of morality is conceivable."[121] The problem of the relationship between capitalism and religion became a central concern in his major work of the 1950s, *A Humane Economy.* Invoking Adam Smith's *Theory of Moral Sentiments,* he launched a vigorous attack on "such 'isms' as utilitarianism, progressivism, secularism, rationalism, optimism" and decried the twentieth-century "cult of man, his profane or even ungodly science and art, his technical achievements, and his State."[122] Humankind was, in his terms, *Homo religiosus,* and it would be necessary to reconcile the market with the deep spiritual longings this identity entailed.

Röpke's concerns about the cultural implications of capitalism did not end with its influence on religion. He also drew attention to the collapse of local economies, and in particular to the decline of traditional modes of agriculture, as signs of the dehumanizing influence of unregulated competition on interpersonal relationships. At the 1947 meeting he extolled "the social life of the family farm" and observed that it required economic "units smaller than would otherwise be rational for normal business standards."[123] Röpke's respect for ways of life that stood outside the pure logic of competition and his evident contempt for the "proletarian nomads" engendered by capitalist industrialization revealed deep reservations about the social effects of capitalist systems of labor. Other early members of the society expressed similar anxieties. William Orton, an economist at Smith College, wrote Hayek in 1947 to share his concern that the restoration of rural life in Europe might represent "a choice between the economic and the cultural criteria of the good life."[124] And Karl Brandt, in his presentation "Economic Strategy of Agricultural Development" during the 1954 meeting, acknowledged that the "most satisfactory combination of freedom, individual responsibility, and efficiency of operation in agriculture is achieved on family farms."[125] The members who voiced these sentiments hoped to use the society's meetings to identify regulations and reforms that would preserve spheres for market exchange without subjecting the full range of human experience to their destabilizing force. Like Hayek, they sought a consonance between markets and social traditions; unlike him, they believed that this could be achieved only through concerted efforts to protect the cultural forms that markets otherwise eroded.

Few members of the society proved as optimistic as Hayek about the preservation of moral and cultural traditions in a market-centered world.

Even those philosophers whose theories of knowledge closely aligned with Hayek's found his views too sanguine in this regard. Michael Oakeshott saw hints of rationalism in Hayek's reluctance to accept substantial limitations on the free market. "A plan to resist all planning may be better than its opposite," he wrote of *The Road to Serfdom*, "but it belongs to the same style of politics."[126] He told Hayek that he would be willing to accept membership in the Mont Pèlerin Society, but he never attended a meeting.[127] Michael Polanyi participated in several of the society's early meetings but eventually decided that there was an irreconcilable gulf between his and Hayek's worldviews. He wrote Hayek in 1955 to say that the group had "supplied invaluable impulses at a time when they were greatly needed," but that its successes had come in spite of the persistence of some "far reaching errors." His own inclinations, he gently informed his friend, were toward "a somewhat different view of Liberty" than that expounded by extreme market advocates like Jacques Rueff and Ludwig von Mises, and sometimes by Hayek himself.[128] In the environment of the mid-1940s, when support for social planning was widespread and even leading advocates of the free market were willing to countenance substantial limitations on its extent, a natural alliance formed between defenders of the market mechanism and those who sought to protect established moral and cultural norms. They were brought together by a common opposition to the implementation of rationalist plans that, they believed, would precipitate rapid and far-reaching processes of social change. The Mont Pèlerin Society's attempt to codify their shared vision, in conjunction with the increasing stridency of market advocates in the early 1950s, served to remind them of the final incommensurability of their worldviews. Hayek's attempt to identify the foundations of a new liberalism foundered amid disagreement over whether its social ideal would be fostered because of, or in spite of, the implicit ethos of the marketplace.

If the society's members were troubled by the difficulty of reconciling capitalism and social traditions, they were equally preoccupied with a second challenge that Hayek's philosophical project entailed: the need to clarify the complex relationship between capitalism and democracy. Many of them believed that the central attributes of participative governance, including democracy and freedom of speech, had developed concurrently with and largely because of the emergence of the market economy. One of the central virtues they attributed to the market was its capacity to loosen restrictions in other areas of life, and they asserted that "political freedoms" and "economic freedoms" were closely and necessarily entwined. At the same time, they acknowledged that in recent years democratically elected legislatures had supported ever more restrictive interventions in their constituents' economic activities. In the wake of the social legislation of the 1930s, protecting the free market appeared to require restrictions on popular sovereignty, and in many cases they were willing to accept such restrictions as a necessary or even constitutive component of their social ideal. Their rhetoric alternately represented capitalism and democracy as a dyad and a choice.

Frank Knight's writings in the 1930s and 1940s repeatedly referenced the close relationship between competitive markets and competitive politics. The "development of democratic political forms," he wrote in his 1935 essay "Economic Theory and Nationalism," was "an accompaniment of the growth of the automatic market organization in the economic realm."[129] Knight's understanding of this relationship was echoed by members with varying political views at the society's first gathering in 1947. Ludwig von Mises, perhaps the society's most uncompromising market advocate, argued that "economic freedom and political freedom are inextricably linked with each other. There cannot be any question of liberty and religious and intellectual tolerance where there is no economic freedom."[130] Wilhelm Röpke, who was much more sanguine about restrictions on market exchange, also identified a "very close relation" between "economic liberalism and general liberalism."[131] An assumed relationship between free markets and democratic politics pervaded the society's discussions throughout its first decade of its existence and provided a foundational premise for many of the members' contributions to its debates. The journalist William Henry Chamberlin articulated a common view among his colleagues when he declared at the 1957 meeting that there was "an inseparable historical connection between free thought and free trade, between tyranny and insecurity of private property."[132]

The close connection that members perceived between markets and democratic politics over the long sweep of modern history, however, became more complicated when they turned their attention to contemporary political concerns. Knight was quick to point out that the relationship between capitalism and democracy, though close, was inherently unstable. Democratic politics were both attributable to the market mechanism and a continuing danger to its preservation. "The notion that the general mass of mankind," he warned, "taken on the scale of a modern national state, can quickly and reliably think out and apply important constitutional changes, is tragic nonsense."[133] Unrestrained markets tended to create unsustainable inequalities in the distribution of power, but unrestrained democracy fostered the same problem to a still greater degree. Any government that sought to sustain itself would, according to Knight, need to place sharp restrictions on the number and kind of questions that were subject to popular vote. Knight's warnings about the dangers of majority rule were reiterated by his student James Buchanan, who helped establish the study of public choice after receiving his doctorate from the University of Chicago in 1949. Buchanan articulated his concerns at the 1954 meeting of the Mont Pèlerin Society, arguing that the "maintenance of free society may well depend on the removal of certain decisions from majority-vote determination," in part so that wealthier citizens would not be asked to shoulder an unreasonable tax burden for their fellow citizens.[134] But while Knight's mode of analysis was scattered, vague, and often conflicted, Buchanan's was rigidly formalized. Applying the techniques of methodological individualism to the problems of constitutional formation, Buchanan and his colleague Gordon Tullock concluded in *The Calculus of Consent* that a rational individual who sought to minimize the costs of social interdependence would not necessarily have any reason to prefer a decision-making structure based on majority rule. "At best," they wrote, "majority rule should be viewed as one among many practical expedients made necessary by the costs of securing widespread agreement on political issues when individual and group interests diverge."[135] Buchanan was frankly skeptical of the capacity of majorities to develop policies that would redress their own moral, cultural, or economic failings. "A shift of activity from the market sector cannot in itself change the nature of man," he and Tullock concluded. "The man who spends his time at the television set or in his automobile in private life," they added drily, "is not the man who is likely to vote for more taxes to finance libraries, concerts, and schools."[136]

The skepticism that Knight and his students expressed toward popular sovereignty was shared by many of the same members of the Mont Pèlerin Society who emphasized the close ties between markets and political freedoms. Wilhelm Röpke starkly warned that democracy could "lead to the worst forms of despotism and intolerance" in his wartime book *The Social Crisis of Our Time*. The market economy, he concluded, "cannot be maintained without certain protective measures and legal principles which offer security and protection to the individual," and these measures should be shielded from the popular vote.[137] And Hayek, in a lecture delivered shortly after the war drew to a close, excoriated the democratic "misconception" that "we must accept as true and binding for future development the views of the majority." For him, a central task of the society would be to identify the distinction between problems that should and should not be subjected to the majority view. Economic exchange was one subject on which democratic deliberation could not be trusted because, in matters of trade, "the majority view will always be the reactionary, stationary view."[138] Hayek made the distinction between the liberal and the "dogmatic democrat" central to his later work *The Constitution of Liberty,* arguing that liberals regard "it as important that the powers of any temporary majority be limited by long-term principles."[139] He celebrated markets as incubators of freedom while seeking to ensure that they remained protected from a democratic capacity to intervene.

The extent to which members of the society were willing to suppress popular sovereignty was laid bare in their debates over colonial policy. A number of members expressed concerns that colonies would quickly enact protectionist and redistributive policies if granted control over their own affairs, and they argued that this provided grounds for continued foreign domination of their governments. The British economist Arthur Shenfield became one of the most ardent proponents of this view. "It does no service either to liberalism or to democracy to assume that democracy is necessarily liberal or liberalism necessarily democratic," he informed his colleagues at the society's gathering in 1954.[140] Three years later he acknowledged that although in "a world completely safe for liberalism it might be right for the West to give up its bases and depart from its positions of power," in "the world as it is, to do so is to betray the hopes of liberalism." He bluntly concluded that "anti-colonialism, not colonialism," was "the problem."[141] Edmond Giscard d'Estaing, a French civil servant (and father of the future French president Valéry Giscard d'Estaing), worried that in the colonies people aspired to political sovereignty "even if they don't have any ability to assume it."[142] And Karl Brandt, an agricultural economist at the Food Research Institute at Stanford, found that "the West has no reason to be ashamed of its history of colonial expansion." He argued that for an "enlightened liberalism, the problem is not how to rid the colonial areas of the white people" but rather "how to create, as soon as possible, conditions in the colonial areas under which the white people not only can stay but where more of them can enter the areas as welcome partners and friends."[143] These calls for a renewed colonialism were not confined solely to the academic sphere; the nascent conservative magazine *National Review* enthusiastically adopted them, trumpeting the economic successes of colonial governments and lamenting the impact of their periodic defeats and departures.

In the immediate postwar years the members of the Mont Pèlerin Society faced a popular environment that was deeply hostile to their economic views. In the face of this opposition, they were quick to draw connections between economic freedoms and political liberalism, but also to distinguish political liberalism from the advocacy of government by majority rule. The members' attempts to work through the problematic relationship between capitalism and democracy resulted in some of their richest and most complicated works, but also revealed a willingness to abandon popular sovereignty altogether when the views of the public did not align with their own. As John MacCallum Scott, the secretary general of the Liberal International, invoked Edmund Burke to observe at their gathering in 1956, "Liberty, too, must be limited in order to be possessed."[144] In practice, this sometimes meant disenfranchising local populations in order to defend the market economy from their control. Although these antidemocratic inclinations were not universally shared within the Mont Pèlerin Society, they helped foster a perception that its members regarded all politics as subsidiary to the logic of the marketplace. It seemed fair to infer that freedom, for many members of this newly constituted group, was to be evaluated primarily in economic terms.

The Mont Pèlerin Society was established by a set of individuals who shared a conviction that capitalism had entered a potentially decisive moment of crisis. For all their differences, they agreed that the market system deserved to be defended from the forces that threatened its continued existence. Their debates over how best to achieve this goal continued to be shaped by the predicament that had brought them together, and they marginalized those who argued that the market system should remain free of regulations as impractical extremists. Among nearly all of the society's founding members, the term "libertarian" was either rejected or ignored. Even those who were most skeptical of government intervention recognized that the prospects of public support for a social philosophy that resembled laissez-faire remained, at best, dim. Although Hayek's attempt to cobble together a "new" liberalism can in retrospect seem peculiar or quixotic, at the time his colleagues and allies considered it a task of obvious urgency. The social philosophies that had justified capitalism and imbued it with a sense of legitimacy for much of the nineteenth century had little purchase on a public with enduring memories of the Great Depression. If the market economy was to be preserved, it would need to be presented as part of a potentially compelling worldview. Hayek established the Mont Pèlerin Society because he believed that this act of ideology formation could occur only over time, among groups of sympathetic intellectuals who shared a political goal but were shielded from the rhetorical pressures of contemporary policy debates.

Once Hayek managed to create such a venue, the debates failed to unfold as he had hoped. He discovered that he had assembled colleagues who were largely united in what they opposed but shared little agreement in their attempts to construct an alternative vision. Some of the participants regarded capitalism and tradition as twin elements of an antirationalist critique of planning, while others perceived them as at best an antagonistic pair. A number of them warned that the logic of the market would need to be restrained in order to avoid wreaking havoc on ethics, religion, agriculture, or the arts, but others believed that a desire to avoid such restrictions was precisely the goal that had brought them together. All of them struggled to explain how the free market could be implemented and protected in the midst of a hostile public without the adoption of some form of authoritarian control (a prospect that, in certain cases, several of them seemed to embrace). The unity of their opposition and the popular marginalization of their views fostered, in conjunction, an extraordinarily fluid intellectual environment. The subjects that occupied their attention during this period of uncertainty would define much of the landscape of American conservatism in the decades that followed.

During the early years of the Mont Pèlerin Society, the very existence of a conservative intellectual world was a source of skepticism. Scholars in the 1950s, observing the atmosphere of consensus that pervaded American politics, were quick to deride the intellectual credibility of their conservative contemporaries. Lionel Trilling referred in *The Liberal Imagination* to the "plain fact that nowadays there are no conservative or reactionary ideas in general circulation." To the extent that there was an orientation toward conservatism, it was attributable to "impulses," or "irritable mental gestures which seek to resemble ideas."[145] Richard Hofstadter appropriated Theodor Adorno's term "pseudo-conservative" to describe the most vocal dissenters from the postwar liberal consensus, citing "clinical evidence" of their "profound if largely unconscious hatred of our society and its ways."[146] Although historians have long since abandoned the reduction of conservative politics to psychologistic impulses, a tendency to cease inquiry into conservative ideas with an observation of their incoherence has remained. Libertarianism, traditionalism, and anticommunism have been understood as uneasy partners in a strategic alliance, formed to achieve overtly political ends; those who adhere to aspects of each of these perspectives are presumed to have engaged in insufficient reflection on the consistency of their worldviews.[147]

The early history of the Mont Pèlerin Society presents a different image of conservative ideas in the years after the war. Its members were engaged in intensive and urgent inquiries into the structure and coherence of their social philosophies. In their endeavors to piece together a worldview that accounted for the economic crises of recent years, few of them thought in static absolutes. Their attempts to identify theoretical connections between capitalism and social traditions, though in many cases incomplete or unconvincing, cannot be dismissed as acts of strategy alone. And their discussions and actions revealed a remarkable faith in the political importance of abstract ideas. Ironically, in this period it was the conservatives who patiently constructed institutions that bridged the divide between academic theories and processes of political change. Organizations like the Mont Pèlerin Society and the Volker Fund laid the groundwork for an era in which market advocates reframed and recaptured control over a broad range of public debates. Their members and beneficiaries went on to transform the economics profession, shift the parameters of journalistic analysis, guide a new generation of politicians, and establish an array of think tanks that reshaped the process of policy formation. The successes of the conservative movement in the final decades of the twentieth century can be attributed, in part, to the conviction with which its leading figures developed and propagated the ideas that contemporary intellectuals presumed them not to have.

4

NEW CONSERVATISMS

The Mont Pèlerin Society was established amid an atmosphere of crisis, in an attempt to address a set of problems that had long troubled its founding members and seemed especially pressing to them as a period of global conflict drew to an uncertain close. As the society approached the conclusion of its first decade, Hayek began to wonder whether changing circumstances had brought its value as an organization to an end. The American social environment—marked by an increasingly stable international political order, extraordinary economic growth, and a return to comparative moderation in governmental affairs—had lost the sense of urgency that had inspired him to summon the founding members to its original meeting. "Here in America," he confessed to the secretary of the society, Albert Hunold, "with the enduring prosperity and the relative reason of the Eisenhower government, the sense of the necessity of the organization is ever more fleeting."[1] The challenges posed by these developments were exacerbated, Hayek believed, by increasingly evident problems within the society itself. It had been created largely to facilitate "contact between the European and American members," but "the majority of American members have never been able to attend and are loosing [*sic*] interest," and "it tends to become increasingly a Continental European affair, which I cannot run from here and which is still kept alive only by my efforts."[2] And its conversations were now largely dominated by economists who expressed little interest in the foundational questions that had inspired Hayek to assemble the initial gathering. If members with sociological or philosophical orientations like Raymond Aron, Bertrand de Jouvenel, and Michael Polanyi "ceased to attend," he wrote to the latter in 1955, "I should probably rapidly lose interest in the proceedings and get tired of the thing."[3] Aron, Jouvenel, and Polanyi did

123

cease to attend, and Hayek grew ever more weary of his role. By early 1956 he was suggesting to colleagues that the society should celebrate its tenth anniversary and then announce its permanent cessation.[4]

Hayek's determination that the society should dissolve was the product of a peculiar combination of triumphalism and despair. It was motivated in part by his belief that an encouraging political environment and an increasing mutual awareness among free-market economists diminished the need for regular meetings. In this sense, the society's raison d'être was the victim of its unexpected and premature success. Any satisfaction derived from these victories was tempered, however, by his frustration at the continued failure of the society's internal debates to fulfill his original aspirations. A true intermingling of European and American perspectives involved a level of expense and commitment that posed a perennial and insuperable challenge; and attempts to construct a genuinely interdisciplinary community had been impeded by the gravitational force of economics, the disciplinary home to an ever-increasing proportion of its members. Hayek's disenchantment with the tenor of the society's debates was magnified in the late 1950s by his increasingly depressive epistolary tone. He found himself in a peculiar position in the Eisenhower years: the popular valence of *The Road to Serfdom* and the eclipse of Austrian business-cycle theory had marginalized him within the community of professional economists, and the relative obscurity and poor sales of his subsequent books had eroded his reputation as a public intellectual with broad popular reach. The ambiguity of his situation combined with his advancing age to leave him exhausted and, to some extent, saddened by a sense of lost opportunities in both the academic and the public spheres. He was no longer in a position to assume the entrepreneurial functions that he had performed with relish and extraordinary energy only a decade before. Instead, he concluded that if the society were to continue—a prospect he contemplated with ambivalence, at best—it would need new individuals to adopt his onetime role.

In the years after the society's tenth anniversary, the problems that had troubled Hayek began to escalate. Albert Hunold, its longtime secretary, instigated a series of disputes—later known as the "Hunold affair"—that eventually brought about an irreparable schism within its membership.[5] Despite its apparent origins in minor personal disagreements, the Hunold affair exposed divisions that had been hardening since the society's original meeting. Changes in the external political environment and the society's internal structure had gradually undermined the atmosphere of compromise and conviviality that had defined its early years, and tensions between Anglo-Americans and continental Europeans, economists and representatives of other disciplines, and libertarians and social traditionalists were increasingly central to its debates. After Hunold and a bloc of sympathizers resigned their memberships, the society adopted a narrower identity, intellectually and institutionally dominated by Anglo-Americans, unapologetically oriented toward technical economics, and inhospitable to those who did not subscribe to the near-universal preferability of free markets to the alternatives. And the central public intellectual in the society's orbit would no longer be Friedrich Hayek, who with his move to Freiburg in 1962 receded into a less active and more ceremonial role, but rather Milton Friedman, who after the publication and popular success of *Capitalism and Freedom* that year emerged as the leading advocate of free-market economics on the public scene. The transformation of the Mont Pèlerin Society signified the collapse of Hayek's ambition to create an active dialogue between economists and philosophers, the ebbing of the influence of continental Europe in the social-scientific world, and the end of the shared attempt to construct a "new" or "revised" liberalism. At the same time, it marked the ascension of economics to the top of the disciplinary pyramid, the increasing prestige of the American university and its prolific social scientists, and the revival of laissez-faire as an influential social philosophy among academic theorists and in the public sphere. The shifting power dynamic in the Mont Pèlerin Society was both a product of petty interpersonal disputes and a portent of broad changes in the conservative intellectual world.

When Hayek addressed the founding meeting of the Mont Pèlerin Society in 1947, he identified one of its central goals as helping its members escape a state of "isolation" in their home countries in which they were "forced constantly to defend the basic elements of their beliefs."[6] A half decade after its initial gathering, he acknowledged that the public had become much more receptive to advocates of free markets. "Gone are the days when the few outmoded liberals walked their paths lonely, ridiculed and without response from the young," he wrote in 1952. Classical liberalism maintained "little influence on the world of action," he admitted, "but its ideas are alive again, and once more a vital segment of the living mind." In five years the burden carried by dissident intellectuals had transitioned from keeping the flame of liberalism alive to the "staggering responsibility" of satisfying a new generation's demands for the answers it had to offer "for the great problems of our times." These rapid advances were sources of "new confidence" to Hayek as he looked toward the future of the ideas the Mont Pèlerin Society had been established to advocate.[7]

Although he was pleased by these changes in the social environment, Hayek remained uncertain whether the Mont Pèlerin Society—founded amid an atmosphere of crisis that had since been superseded—should persist. The society's remaining benefits were not, he believed, substantial enough to justify the extraordinary personal energy he needed to commit to organize each meeting. With no endowment funds, it produced a fixed annual income only through nominal membership fees that did not begin to address the cost that its gatherings entailed.[8] All external financial support was provided on a case-by-case basis, and the society did not possess any long-term financial commitments that would allow it to plan on a time frame that exceeded a single event. In part, this was a product of a deliberate strategy: in order to limit the impact of any single funding organization, the society's leadership labored to ensure that meetings were financed by a range of supporters located near the rotating sites of the annual meetings. "We always refused to take money solely from one source," Albert Hunold, the society's primary fund-raiser in its first decade, later recalled. "We insisted on a wide geographical dispersion of the different funds received," and the society never took "any money from political parties or their affiliates." The 1954 Venice meeting, for example, was financed by the Banca d'Italia, industrial organizations based in Rome and Milan, and a Venetian foundation; the 1957 St. Moritz meeting was financed by twenty-three firms throughout Switzerland; and the 1960 Kassel meeting was financed by six enterprises from five German cities.[9] The organization of each meeting required its own capital campaign and the cultivation of new regional sources of support.

In the society's early years the travel costs incurred by the American attendees were reimbursed through periodic grants from the Volker Fund. Hayek viewed this support as essential to the society's goal of fostering dialogue within a transatlantic community of intellectuals, but the fund insisted on approaching each request separately and expressed open reservations about the sustainability of its role. The fund's director, Harold Luhnow, informed Hayek in advance of the society's tenth anniversary meeting that it would support the travel expenses for six

American members and thereafter terminate its financial interest in the program. Although the society had "in the past performed an important function," Luhnow felt that its future relevance was "at best, debatable." The Volker Fund was now hosting a "growing conference program" of its own, and Luhnow was frank about his expectation that these events would fulfill the role once played by the Mont Pèlerin Society.[10] The Volker Fund never again provided assistance to the society, and by the mid-1960s it had altogether dissolved.[11]

Hayek eventually succeeded in his endeavor to find a stable source of travel funds. Beginning in 1959, the Earhart and Relm foundations, which were jointly operated out of Ann Arbor, Michigan, provided reimbursements for the travel expenses incurred by many of the society's American members. Luhnow had conceived of the Volker Fund as a supporter of libertarian causes, but the Earhart and Relm foundations sought to provide assistance to a broader range of conservative intellectuals.[12] Despite occasional ideological differences, these organizations cultivated a remarkably similar and highly distinctive mode of philanthropy. Through direct contributions to carefully chosen intellectuals and institutions, they sought to facilitate the expression of unorthodox ideas in the national conversation, and thereby to provoke long-term ideological change. In contrast to other contemporary sources of funding, they did not expect any immediate tangible return for their investments. Instead, they attempted to support viewpoints that fell outside the political and academic mainstream, and they approached "the unique and unorthodox" as "an advantage, rather than a handicap."[13] In adopting this strategy, they demonstrated an extraordinary faith in the capacity of abstract ideas to generate substantive political change. These commitments remained central to the conservative movement in subsequent decades and developed a palpable influence with the emergence of a new collection of lavishly funded think tanks in the 1970s and 1980s.[14] The sources of financial support were more modest in the 1950s, but the Earhart and Relm foundations provided overlapping grants to several institutions—including the Mont Pèlerin Society and the graduate program at the University of Chicago—that played a crucial role in defining and defending the foundational principles of postwar conservatism.

Hayek's difficulties in securing funding had been exacerbated by the society's insuperable growth. At the founding meeting in 1947, it comprised only 39 members; by 1951 that number had grown to 167, and by 1961 it had reached 258.[15] As John Jewkes observed, this rapid expansion compounded the challenge of obtaining financial support for the annual meetings.[16] Although the excessive size of the membership was widely acknowledged, it was an extraordinarily difficult problem to solve. Fritz Machlup argued in 1961 that rigid restrictions on entry would have the problematic effect of preventing the society from widely disseminating "the benefits of exposure to our views." Perhaps more importantly, the prospect of turning down an individual who had been proposed by an active member was also awkward: Machlup's colleagues "were embarrassed by having to offend some good people every year who were anxious to join but had to be rejected because of the fear of overcrowding."[17] That awkwardness was due, in part, to the impossibility of finding a standard for the evaluation of new members that did not seem on some level arbitrary. Milton Friedman expressed dismay at the absence of a "proper basis for discriminating among applicants, for admitting one person and refusing another." He filtered the problem through the lens of a characteristically economistic logic: "The general problem of course is the one that always arises with non-price rationing, and in this case I see no clear objective criteria that can replace price."[18] The members needed to decide, Jewkes observed at a council meeting in 1959, "what sort of society the Mont Pèlerin Society shall become": whether it would develop into a populist enterprise or remain restricted, as seemed increasingly unlikely, to a "limited elite."[19]

At the conclusion of the 1962 meeting, an article in *National Review* mulled over the dangers faced by the society as it added new members to its rolls. "The intimate atmosphere of a select group of intellectual peers, good friends and philosophic companions may give way to the business-like atmosphere of a professional convention," it observed. "Although the Society represents a rather broad spectrum of opinion within the libertarian fold, the present philosophic unity of the group could be affected and its intellectual strength watered down. These are the risks inherent in expansion, yet the world is moving on and this seems to be the course the Society will take."[20] Meeting participants expressed growing concerns about whether, as one wrote to Milton Friedman, "beyond a point, dilution may not only lower the standards of the annual proceedings but may deter economists who should be associated with it."[21] Once members were admitted, there seemed to be no means of controlling their contributions apart from what Friedman termed "the self-pressure which will arise from a climate of vigorous criticism," which did not always enforce a perfect consonance between the quantity and the quality of remarks.[22] As numbers became "extremely large," Friedman reluctantly concluded that it "was not feasible to have the kind of personal, informal discussion that did so much to make the first meeting a memorable one."[23] The society's very success had robbed it of the intimate and exclusive character that had lent value to its earlier gatherings. Its meetings had become, as Hayek later acknowledged, much too big.[24]

Despite Hayek's reservations about the society's changing character during the 1950s, he advocated its continued growth in order to forestall a still more troubling problem. Since the organization's founding he had endeavored to prevent it from becoming a society of economists. The high proportion of economists among its founding members, however, initiated a self-reinforcement mechanism that Hayek was unable to control. The professional networks cultivated by existing members were far more likely to include economists than members of other disciplines, and as these networks yielded a new generation of members, the society's noneconomists felt increasingly tangential to its debates. The problem, Hayek discovered, was insoluble. He found that adding too many new members limited the society's ability to monitor the quality of its members and to generate productive discussions and relationships among them, but failing to add new members led the society to become superannuated and narrowly economistic. In an attempt to solve one problem Hayek found it necessary to exacerbate another, and he ultimately felt dissatisfied on all accounts. The society, he concluded, was no longer what he had intended. The period of its conformity with his original vision had passed.[25]

Hayek's misgivings about the society were alleviated in its early years by his limited involvement in its day-to-day affairs, which were handled with devoted attention by Albert Hunold. Hunold's inability to make detailed arrangements from across the Atlantic, however, forced other members to participate more actively in the financial preparations for the Princeton meeting in 1958. They provided Hayek with an assessment of the society's expenditures that led him to grow increasingly concerned about Hunold's management. Hunold's behavior at Princeton, where he did not have the authority over administrative matters to which he had become accustomed, manifested a heightened sensitivity to his institutional prerogatives. Throughout the meeting he quibbled over minor organizational details, adopting a belligerent tone that estranged his colleagues.[26] Hayek found himself contemplating the feasibility of hiring an administrator to assume the tasks that had long been overseen by Hunold, and Hunold felt that his position in the society was threatened because of the perceived hostility of many of his fellow members. The first decade of the society's debates had been characterized, with occasional exceptions, by a formality and reticence that mirrored Hayek's aristocratic reserve, but its primary officers were no longer operating with the close harmony that had characterized their relationship in earlier years. The tensions that were now emerging within the society's leadership allowed its latent conflicts to surface, with traumatic and enduring results.

Hunold became the primary instigator of a major schism within the society for several reasons. Although many members perceived the society as a personal affiliation with only limited and occasional significance, Hunold considered it an integral part of his identity. He approached his assigned duties with extraordinary diligence, personally bankrolling many of the costs associated with the society's day-to-day management and identifying and soliciting regional businesses for the financial support that made its early meetings possible.[27] As many members readily acknowledged, the society would have been an administrative impossibility without his efforts during its first decade of existence. Even his detractors admitted that it "could not continue to live without him as secretary, as nobody else could be found who would be willing to do the same amount of work for the society . . . and would be so efficient in collecting funds for the society." By the late 1950s Hunold and the society had become interdependent. The society needed Hunold to arrange funding for its gatherings and to carry out the mundane administrative tasks that other members were unwilling to perform. Hunold, in turn, needed the society to lend meaning to his otherwise unremarkable and peripatetic business career, and to provide him with an institutional imprimatur that enabled him to solicit funding and support for his unrelated activities.[28] As Trygve Hoff wrote in 1961, "the close contact with MPS means very much for Hunolds [sic] prestige and therefore also economically."[29]

Hunold also possessed a notoriously abrupt and irascible personality, and his rhetoric lacked the soft edges that characterized the communicative styles of his academic colleagues. His close friend Wilhelm Röpke acknowledged that their "serious brawl" after the war over the establishment of the journal Occident demonstrated that "occasionally, his temperament may carry him away."[30] After only one meeting Hunold was already complaining that the society was insufficiently "aggressive" and proclaiming that it was "useless to discuss anything" with one member, Maurice Allais, who reminded him of "socialists and communists."[31] Irritability is a characteristic that only rarely diminishes with the passage of time, and Hunold grew more vocal with his complaints as the society matured. In 1959 he publicly referred to the society's recent debates as a "playground for soft-pedalling [sic] neutralism and impotent scientism which would divert our Society from its real aims and drive it into moral bankruptcy," and he privately complained that the "neutralists" among its members needed to be taken "by the horns."[32] His disenchantment with the society's direction was aggravated by an impression that his ideas and suggestions were not receiving the attention they deserved. He channeled the resulting frustration into periodic eruptions about issues of relatively trivial significance, alienating the society's other members and leading them to grow increasingly concerned about his capacity to fulfill his secretarial duties.

As his relationship with Hayek began to deteriorate, Hunold inaugurated the *Mont Pèlerin Society Quarterly,* a public journal of the society's activities. The *Quarterly* was the product of Hunold's longtime ambition to create a vehicle for the dissemination of the society's ideas in the broader political environment. Hayek's concerns about the new publication extended beyond his reservations about its creator. From the society's initial conception, Hayek had rigorously adhered to a view that it should avoid any public engagement in order to protect its identity as a philosophical enterprise. He believed that any turn toward propaganda or the proactive dissemination of its members' views would challenge its identity as a venue for serious inquiry and foundational debates. The emergence of a society publication was therefore a very serious matter, and Hayek attempted to delay the publication of the *Quarterly*'s first issue because of explicit concerns about its scope. He wrote that his "personal view is still that the Society as such should not express opinions," adding that he was deeply hesitant to "attempt anything more ambitious" than a newsletter designed "to inform members about publications by other members of the Society, about changes in membership and to communicate to all members papers presented at the meeting."[33] Hunold expressed disappointment and termed Hayek's policy "a nuisance." "If we go on like this," he proclaimed, "we shall soon be hanged by the communists." The best route to take, he decided, was "just to start such a publication in a more or less dictatorial way and create a 'fait accompli,' then wait and see what happens."[34] Within a very short time the relationship between Hayek and Hunold had deteriorated to the extent that Hunold was altogether ignoring directives from his institutional superior.

A vicious circle emerged: Hunold's contentious behavior led him to be stripped of administrative powers, and his diminished authority in turn provoked further resentment and rage. The problem was conspicuous at the society's 1959 meeting in Oxford. Antony Fisher of the Institute of Economic Affairs (IEA) hosted the event, and Hunold was appalled to learn that the IEA was in charge of all the arrangements that he had typically managed in previous years.[35] He attached great significance to a letter from the IEA insinuating that there was no need for him to bring his customary two assistants to the meeting, and he concluded that IEA affiliates were plotting to replace him as the society's secretary.[36] After the meeting he wrote an irate letter to the directors of the society in which he complained that the IEA had stolen his prerogatives "like a thief at night," leveraged the Mont Pèlerin Society to produce "propaganda" for itself, and engaged in a "conspiracy" to replace him with the IEA affiliate and nonmember Ralph Harris. He then inaugurated an unremitting campaign to prevent the society from offering Harris membership.[37]

Hayek, who had initially responded to Hunold's hostile behavior with mild exasperation, was now utterly dismayed. "I must confess," he wrote to Röpke in the winter of 1960, "that I am beginning to doubt if he is still entirely sane."[38] He was more eager than ever to step down as the society's president but had become convinced that he would first need to find a replacement for Hunold in order to leave the society on stable ground. Although he hoped to appoint a new secretary with little fuss, he decided that a public intervention was necessary after discovering that Hunold had falsely invoked his name in an attempt to incite the directors to vote against Harris's membership. Hunold had provided the society with "extraordinarily valuable services," Hayek wrote to the membership, but his "general conduct during the last year . . . convinced me that a change in the European Secretaryship has become even more important than a change in the Presidency."[39] In an astonishing demonstration of the dispute's escalation, he refused to sustain his affiliation with the society until Hunold was no longer its secretary.[40]

The society's members were faced with a difficult problem. The formal bylaws of the Mont Pèlerin Society had been designed during a more tranquil time; upon their ratification in 1947, one prescient member had worried that they were "somewhat casual" and "drafted merely for fair weather conditions."[41] In the society's early years they had been consigned to an ornamental role, as its occasional points of disagreement were managed through a process of genial consensus founded on an assumed conformance with Hayek's views. When the society was confronted with an apparently intractable dispute among the society's officers, the bylaws' limited scope and ambiguous meaning did little to identify a coherent mode of resolution. The society had entered a period of indeterminacy and constitutional crisis. The members responded by breaking into two groups—those who supported Hunold and those who did not—with each group endeavoring to obtain proxy votes to wield at the forthcoming annual meeting. Hunold wrote personally to many members in order to request the authority to vote on their behalf, occasionally expressing the nature of the dispute in demonstrably misleading terms.

Much of the society remained distant from the increasingly public conflict, but a subset of its most influential members developed very clear allegiances. The differences between Hunold's supporters and his adversaries provide a window into the organization's shifting demographics and underlying divisions. The members fissured largely along national lines. His opponents were led by a cohort of academics—including Milton Friedman, George Stigler, and Fritz Machlup—affiliated with American institutions and, in particular, the University of Chicago. Friedman believed that Hunold represented "the most reactionary and status quo ante influences in the society," and he became the central figure in "a determined movement by a group of us to get rid of Hunold as European secretary."[42] Friedman's profile within the economics profession had grown dramatically during the preceding decade, and his actions against Hunold represented his assumption of a leadership role within the society. "The key issue is that Hunold has become increasingly impossible and insubordinate," he wrote to one member, "taking over the reins in his own hands, not waiting for or following instructions or rulings from the Council of Hayek, insulting members and libelling them, etc. etc."[43] Although he had not been very active in the first decade of the society's existence, Friedman approached the dispute over Hunold with extraordinary intensity. "If we lose," he wrote to a colleague, "we shall most of us resign."[44]

Hunold's allies consisted primarily of continental Europeans, including three vice presidents of the society (Louis Baudin, Franz Böhm, and

Wilhelm Röpke). They condemned the Chicago economists' attempts to gather proxy votes from their colleagues, citing the fact that "only about one half of our American members have ever been present at a meeting of the Society" as an indication that they were "not familiar with the problems of the Society."[45] This willingness to exploit the Atlantic divide to their advantage was tempered by Röpke's rhetorical assertions that the emerging "split between America and Europe within our own Society" was "surely the very last thing we should permit." But their intransigence equaled that of their American colleagues. Röpke, like Friedman, asserted that he would resign if the dispute was not resolved in a manner he found appropriate. If the removal of Hunold as secretary "would really be carried out," he announced, "I would leave the Mont Pèlerin Society in protest against a grave injustice and in loyalty to a man who has a claim to it."[46]

The society had arrived at an impasse. Friedman and his American colleagues would resign if Hunold was not removed as secretary, and Röpke and his European colleagues would resign if he was. In prior years Hayek had served as the arbitrator between divergent groups within the society; as both economist and political philosopher, free-market advocate and social traditionalist, old-world European and émigré American, he could speak the languages of members who at times perceived one another as alien. But now he was a party to the dispute, and therefore was unable to bring it to a mutually satisfactory close. "What a tiresome affair!" he exclaimed in the summer of 1960. "How I wish I had at the beginning of the difficulties simply proposed the liquidation of the Society and then washed my hands of it as had been my first inclination. But I suppose now it has to be fought through."[47]

For a brief time it appeared that the dispute might be resolved. Ludwig Erhard, then the vice-chancellor of the Federal Republic of Germany, arbitrated an agreement wherein Hayek would be replaced as the society's president by Wilhelm Röpke, and Hunold would resign his position as its secretary in order to become a vice president.[48] The conclusion was announced at the Kassel meeting, where Hayek spoke graciously about the past contributions of Hunold. "I will once more very briefly say that I have no doubt that the Society would never have come into existence and would not have been as successful had it not been for Dr. Hunold's efforts," he told the assembled members. Wilhelm Röpke, the new president, expressed uncertainty about his capacity to fulfill Hayek's role. "I am not a very strong man; I am inexperienced in these affairs; I have other ambitions," he stated, "but I know too well that I have to play this part in this big act of equilibristics, as I think it is called in the music-halls."[49] The suspension of hostilities was brief. Fritz Machlup discovered a set of convenient discrepancies in the transcript of the Kassel meeting prepared by Hunold, and Friedman and Hunold immediately engaged in a sharply worded dispute over the competing versions.[50] Röpke persuaded the parties to arrive at a mutually agreeable version, but the lines of continued resentment had been firmly established.[51] Friedman and his associates believed that Hunold was attempting to manipulate the proceedings of the society by surreptitious means, and Hunold and Röpke believed that Friedman's accusations had plainly violated the spirit of the compromise at Kassel.

During the 1961 meeting in Turin, it became evident that the tensions within the society were unsustainable. Hunold and his American detractors engaged in an aggressive dispute about the location of the next meeting that several times inspired Röpke, when an unfavorable vote appeared imminent, to halt the proceedings with the claim that the tenor of the discussion was dangerous for his weak heart.[52] Friedman intensified the acrimony later in the meeting with a claim that Hunold had reordered the list of vice presidents to position himself, under the terms of an obscure bylaw, to become president in the event of Röpke's resignation. It was, Friedman later wrote, "an attempted coup d'etat" that was intended to bestow the presidency on Hunold by underhanded means.[53] The debate was resolved in Friedman's favor, and Hunold exploded with rage; one unsympathetic member later recounted that Hunold had described the members of the society's board as "rascals," referred to Trygve Hoff as a "useful idiot," declared Bruno Leoni to be "insincere as all the Italians," and told Friedman and Machlup to "go home ugly Americans."[54] Friedman displayed similar vitriol in the days that followed. Hunold, he wrote, "engineered this monstrous attempted fraud" with the intention of becoming "the chief beneficiary of it," demonstrating a "Machiavellianism" that Friedman had made the "fatal mistake" of underestimating.[55] Two months later Hunold's principal adversaries, including Friedman, Stigler, Machlup, and Hayek, signed a letter indicating that the preservation of the society depended on Hunold's resignation.[56]

Hunold's detractors could not understand, in the wake of his more outrageous behavior, how distinguished scholars like Röpke could continue to reinforce him. Some whispered that Röpke's support was attributable to Hunold's access to donors who provided him with significant financial assistance.[57] Hayek, however, continued to attempt to convince Röpke that Hunold's behavior was unwarranted and could be halted if he would only intervene. He told Röpke that Hunold "knows where his bread is buttered": his notoriously difficult personality and minimal professional prestige would leave him with limited capacity to disrupt the society if he was not abetted by more influential friends.[58] But Röpke refused to abandon Hunold, and Hayek grew confused and disillusioned.[59] Hayek knew that the Mont Pèlerin Society had been made possible only through his close collaboration with Röpke.[60] In the current dispute Röpke was allowing himself "to be used as Hunold's tool," Hayek wrote to John Van Sickle after the Turin meeting, and the two of them had become nothing better than "take-over artists."[61] He decided that further collaboration was no longer possible. Röpke had, he believed, "succeeded in destroying in the course of fifteen month [sic] what others have built up in the course of as many years."[62]

Once Hayek determined that Röpke was inseparable from Hunold, he concluded that the society needed a new president. Together with Friedman, he attempted to provoke a resignation by flooding Röpke with minor concerns and complaints.[63] Their effort culminated in a letter that George Stigler sent to the society shortly before Christmas. Stigler adopted an earnest and collegial tone, expressing "embarassment [sic] and distaste" for the society's quarrels concerning "personal manners, which a society of scholars and gentlemen should not even have to consider." He then presented an incongruous ultimatum: "if Roepke does not resign by February 1, 1962, I shall submit my resignation from the Society."[64] Two days later Hunold forwarded to the membership a letter from Röpke's wife indicating that because of the danger the continuing conflict posed to his health, her husband would resign.[65] Before submitting his own resignation Hunold sent out two further issues of the Mont Pèlerin Society Quarterly, which he used as vehicles to expound his perspective, calling the actions of the society's interim president John Jewkes "suspicious," asserting that the "overwhelming majority of the members" preferred his own nominee (Karl Brandt, who declined the nomination and resigned his membership), accusing Hayek of treating the society as "the personal affair of a single man," and insinuating that Hayek's "insecure financial position in Chicago" had led him to perceive Hunold as "an obstacle to be removed."[66] At least ten members had resigned by the end of the summer of 1962, citing either sympathy for Hunold or disapprobation toward the spiteful tenor of the society's internecine disputes.[67] The resignations solidified a transition in the society's balance of power from Europe to the United States, and from its original leaders to a younger generation of scholars affiliated with the Department of Economics at the University of Chicago. The future direction of the Mont Pèlerin Society was to be determined by the individuals who had overseen the successful struggle to expel Albert Hunold.

The vitriol with which Hunold treated his colleagues in the Mont Pèlerin Society was symptomatic of a personal pathology with causes not solely, or even primarily, attributable to their actions. His was increasingly a paranoid style: he saw contrary opinions as hostility, concerted opposition as conspiracy, and formal deliberation as a covert battle for status. But although it can be tempting to reduce the Hunold affair to the psychological vicissitudes of its namesake, his periodic rages were demonstrative of more than a precarious psyche. In justifying his break with the society Hunold expressed a sincere and deeply felt critique of the direction its debates had taken. Its members were increasingly divided, he argued, between those who maintained "a *philosophy* and an *anchored worldview*" and those who sought "in the Marxist sense . . . to construct a philosophy out of the economy" and thereby "'to cure the world from a single point,' namely from pure economics."[68] This was not simply an ex post facto justification. Hunold had long criticized a subset of the society's members for attempting to transform it into an "economic club" instead of addressing "crucial socio-political problems."[69] Röpke shared his concerns, writing in 1955 that the society was subject to "always noticeable" tensions between advocates of "paleoliberalism" and "neoliberalism."[70] He applied the former label to those who sought to reinstitute laissez-faire economic policies reminiscent of the nineteenth century, and the latter to advocates of less rigid and more holistic solutions to contemporary social problems. Röpke's close friend and colleague Alexander Rüstow described the division in still more aggressive terms, arguing that the neoliberals had worked hard to achieve political gains that were now being exploited in "grotesque" and "insolent" fashion by their paleoliberal colleagues.[71] The society had commenced as an attempt to create a new social philosophy, but it was now dominated by economists with narrower proclivities. By the late 1950s polymath members like Jouvenel, Polanyi, and Knight rarely participated in its discussions, and the goal of developing a "new" liberalism that had loomed over its early meetings was rarely mentioned. Hunold, Röpke, and Rüstow felt out of place in debates that were increasingly economistic in style and laissez-faire in inference. The Hunold affair was produced by a potent combination of interpersonal enmity and philosophical despair.

The growing disparity in perspectives was perhaps most apparent in the reactions to the nascent conservative magazine *National Review,* which was founded in 1955 by the young William F. Buckley Jr.[72] Buckley had risen to national prominence four years earlier with the publication of *God and Man at Yale,* which excoriated his alma mater for perceived attempts to persuade its students to become "atheistic socialists." "I myself believe that the duel between Christianity and atheism is the most important in the world," Buckley wrote in his foreword to the first edition. "I further believe that the struggle between individualism and collectivism is the same struggle reproduced on another level."[73] He married an uncompromising antistatism in the economic sphere with a militant anticommunism and a heightened deference to established religious institutions and ways of life. In doing so, he absolved himself of any scholarly pretensions and refrained from providing detailed philosophical justifications of his comprehensive worldview. His rhetoric, however, demonstrated a formidable combination of what one colleague referred to as "elite sensibility and populist power," and Buckley quickly developed a unique fluency as a translator among dissident academics, conservative politicians, and grassroots fomenters of right-wing dissent.[74] His explicit ideological agenda and rhetorical sleights of hand drew audible scorn from the university establishment. The dean of the Faculty of Arts and Sciences at Harvard, McGeorge Bundy, wrote a withering review in the *Atlantic Monthly* that noted the irony of a Catholic calling for a return to religious traditionalism at Yale. Buckley's support for laissez-faire was, Bundy added, far more extreme than that of the academics he and his allies cited for support. Positions that Buckley labeled "radicalism" could be found "in the work of such men as Hayek," and "if Mr. Buckley read Lippmann and Knight, he would be horrified."[75] As Knight had grimly observed, it is difficult to distill challenging ideas into popularly accessible form without doing some violence to their intent. Buckley's success as a polemicist was a product, in part, of his capacity to elide complexities that would detract from his rhetorical force.

With the publication of the *National Review,* Buckley sought to bring to the American political environment the same mode of critical analysis he had previously applied to Yale. In "its maturity," he argued in the magazine's mission statement, "literate America rejected conservatism in favor of radical social experimentation." He blamed this problem both on the "relativism" that had been propounded in universities and on the "ignorance and amorality" of the "well-fed Right." Instead, Buckley cast his lot with the "radical conservatives" who had not yet come to terms with the New Deal, and who were willing to stand with him "athwart history, yelling Stop, at a time when no one is inclined to do so, or to have much patience with those who so urge it."[76] He believed that he was defending a certain idea of the West: one of a society of free individuals who shared certain common and long-established commitments and ideals, and who were willing and eager to fight for that freedom and those ideals when they perceived them to be under assault. The magazine would therefore provide a consistent defense of free markets against the inroads of progressivism and socialism; a militant anticommunism directed at both external and internal threats; and a support for traditional ideas and modes of life in the face of the perceived relativism of the contemporary academy. Like many of his contemporaries in the early Mont Pèlerin Society, Buckley believed that support for free markets would be politically viable only if it were represented as part of a holistic and spiritually grounded worldview. He also shared with the society's early members an extraordinary faith in the power of ideas to effect political change over time. "Our political economy and our high-energy industry run on large, general principles, on ideas—not by day-to-day guess work, expedients and improvisations," he contended in the mission statement.[77] The ideas expressed in the National Review soon attracted public attention and notoriety that far exceeded its sparse initial circulation of 7,500: the editor of Harper's labeled the magazine's readers "extremist" and "the precise opposite of conservatives," and the literary journalist Dwight Macdonald referred to it as a haven for "the lumpen bourgeoisie, the half-educated, half-successful provincials."[78] Over time the National Review attracted allies as ardent as its enemies; after a decade of existence on the edge of financial insolvency, it had accumulated 100,000 subscribers and attained a prominent role in establishing the terms of American political debate.[79]

Röpke saw the National Review's simultaneous embrace of free markets and social traditionalism as an enactment of the revised liberalism that the founders of the Mont Pèlerin Society had originally sought to create. He unequivocally embraced the publication as a "heroic attempt . . . to oppose the all-powerful progressive current in the United States."[80] His admiration for its editorial board was reciprocated: the magazine's prospectus listed Röpke as one of the figures whose ideas it was intended to propagate, belying a tendency that Röpke perceived among many Americans to believe that "les absents ont toujours tort."[81] "This group at the NR is the only one in America where I have found a truly warm-hearted echo for my thoughts," he wrote to one of the magazine's many critics in 1956. Röpke's past endurance of persecution for his political beliefs did not prevent him from defending the magazine's support for Joseph McCarthy. Although he found McCarthy repugnant, Röpke argued that he had been caricatured as a devil by the "communists and crypto-communists" in order "to distract us from the true danger," and that the *National Review* was right to focus on the latter.[82] The publishers of the *National Review,* from his perspective, could do no wrong.

Hayek never perceived Buckley's project as ideologically aligned with his own. The *National Review*'s explicit attempt to "stop" history impressed him as fundamentally reactionary and contrary to an intelligent embrace of social evolution. Although Hayek wanted to prevent government from defining the terms of social progress, he refused to abandon the notion that his social philosophy was itself progressive. The market, after all, was the ultimate instigator of social change, and its spontaneous dictates were a cause for celebration rather than fear. He was a harsh critic of excessive attempts to control social evolution, whether pursued to achieve reformist or regressive ends, and he perceived Buckley as a paradigmatic case of the latter. When Buckley was preparing to publish *God and Man at Yale* in 1951, Hayek declined to write a blurb for it, writing to Henry Regnery that "anything friendly I could say about Buckley's book would have to be hedged about by so many qualifications that it would be useless for your purposes."[83] When Buckley asked to include his name on the masthead of the *National Review* in 1955, Hayek refused, expressing concerns about the divergence between Buckley's conservatism and his own social philosophy.[84] In subsequent years his refined sensibilities were increasingly offended by the magazine's unreconstructed populism. He broke off all association with its editors in 1961, criticizing their lack of "common decency" in publishing comic insinuations that the recently deceased secretary general of the United Nations, Dag Hammarskjöld, cheated at cards.[85]

The most prominent academic to contribute regularly to the *National Review* was the reclusive historian and political theorist Russell Kirk, who wrote a column under the title "From the Academy" for over two decades.[86] Kirk had come to national attention with the appearance of his magnum opus, *The Conservative Mind,* in 1953. The book was accepted by the young conservative publishing house Regnery after it was rejected by Knopf, and Henry Regnery recalled decades later that its "impact was immediate" and "beyond all expectations."[87] *The Conservative Mind* presented an extended plea for a return to the social philosophy of Edmund Burke, whom Kirk saw as an exemplar of "the true school of conservative principle."[88] From a detailed exegesis of a series of seminal texts, Kirk arrived at "six canons of conservative thought": belief in "a transcendent order"; affection for "proliferating variety"; defense of the maintenance of "orders and classes"; a conviction "that freedom and property are closely linked"; a preference for custom, convention, and prescription over "abstract designs"; and support for a "prudent" as opposed to a "hasty" approach to social change.[89] At the suggestion of Whittaker Chambers, *Time* devoted the entire review section of its 6 July issue to the book, concluding that Kirk's philosophy would prove to be of "interest that is not mainly antiquarian" to readers confronting the "shadow of lost illusions" in the wake of two world wars. The crisis of modernity had created space for a philosophy that was founded on its rejection.[90] Kirk became the most visible of a collection of scholars, including Peter Viereck and Robert Nisbet, who were labeled "New Conservatives" for their articulation of a social philosophy that emphasized the maintenance of established communal traditions, social orders, and modes of belief.[91] He remained an influential figure in the conservative movement for over two decades, producing a nationally syndicated column, editing the conservative journal *Modern Age,* and publishing numerous volumes on the sources and implications of his social philosophy. None of his subsequent works, however, attracted a degree of public attention comparable to *The Conservative Mind.* He resigned his academic post in 1959 and became notorious for cultivating an anachronistic personal aesthetic at his residence in rural Michigan. He forsook modern appliances and refused to drive automobiles. His oeuvre included numerous gothic romances and ghost stories and, shortly before his death, an autobiography written in the third person.[92] Even one of Kirk's great admirers, Eugene Genovese, acknowledged that he "seemed like a creature in mothballs."[93] Kirk's conservatism was at once an answer to and a rejection of the social structures of the modern world, and he remained wary of the unpredictable and unmanageable changes that the market interactions at its center necessarily produced.

During the 1950s Röpke and Hayek developed very different impressions of Kirk. For Röpke, the publication of *The Conservative Mind* was both a revelation and an augury of the renaissance of a social philosophy he shared. In an article, "Liberaler Konservatismus in Amerika," published in the *Neue Zürcher Zeitung* in 1955, he argued that Kirk was the major figure in an American movement toward "liberal conservatism," a conservatism that looked for inspiration to figures like Tocqueville, Acton, and Jacob Burckhardt rather than to the reactionary tradition that Europeans often associated with the term. Hayek had cited these same figures as inspirations for the formation of the Mont Pèlerin Society at the outset of its founding meeting. Eight years after that meeting, however, none of the Americans Röpke associated with this emerging movement—including Nisbet, Viereck, and Clinton Rossiter—were involved in the society's activities.[94] And Röpke spoke of Kirk far more generously than his American contemporaries in the society. *The Conservative Mind* was, he said, the "most enthralling" work in both "substance and form" that he had encountered in a long time. It both gave voice to "the most noble American tradition" and had "much to say to us Europeans."[95] He urged his colleagues to read it, and he personally wrote Kirk to remark on the "altogether unusual pleasure, agreement and profit with which I peruse everything you write."[96] Röpke was now establishing his primary transatlantic allegiances outside the society that was intended to foster them.

Hayek's responses to Kirk shifted dramatically with the passage of time. When *The Conservative Mind* was first published, he expressed admiration for the book and qualified enthusiasm for its author. While he thought that the book was "a little uneven," "much too long," and excessively inclined to claim "for conservatism what really were the main contributions of classical liberalism," he told Herbert Cornuelle of the Volker Fund that it was "really excellent in some parts and throughout erudite and readable."[97] He offered a quote to the book's publisher, Henry Regnery, indicating that it would "do much to shift the general discussion."[98] He then wrote directly to the chairman of the Committee on Social Thought at the University of Chicago, John Nef, to urge him to consider adding Kirk to the faculty.[99] Nef shared Hayek's interest, but Kirk indicated that he would be too busy to explore any new employment possibilities for several years.[100] By the time Kirk informed Nef of his availability several years later, he had attained a polarizing degree of notoriety through his activities as a conservative public intellectual. Nef would promise him only three years' affiliation with the committee, under the expectation that his salary would be paid entirely by the Earhart

Foundation and his public activities would be abandoned in favor of serious scholarship.[101] Kirk acknowledged, in his rejection of the unflattering offer, that his adversaries had multiplied in the intervening years.[102]

One of those new adversaries was Friedrich Hayek. Kirk became acutely aware of Hayek's opposition when, at the invitation of Röpke and Hunold, he traveled to St. Moritz to attend the tenth-anniversary meeting of the Mont Pèlerin Society.[103] Hayek used the occasion to deliver a major address, "Why I Am Not a Conservative," in which he repudiated Kirk's worldview without explicitly invoking his name. The address developed a strict differentiation between "liberals," as Hayek considered himself, and "conservatives": liberals maintained a clear and principled philosophy of freedom, embraced the prospect of change despite the unknowable future it conferred, and protected the ability of others to express their views even when they disagreed; conservatives professed no coherent worldview beyond the preservation of the status quo, subjected themselves to authority in order to assuage their fear of social evolution, and sought to impose their opinions on those whom they opposed. Hayek saw a close alignment between socialists and conservatives in their reverence for authority and their common belief that societies should seek to manage the spontaneous interchanges of their constituents. Kirk was an obvious target of Hayek's philippic, and he took it upon himself to deliver an extemporaneous rebuttal.[104] Within the society, however, Hayek's speech also represented a final rejection of the positions that Röpke had long advocated in its debates. In an implicit swipe at the "Third Way" that Röpke had famously advocated in the wake of World War II, Hayek lambasted what he perceived to be the absence of fixed points in a philosophy of compromise. "It has been regularly the conservatives who have compromised with socialism and stolen its thunder," he declared. "Advocates of the Middle Way with no goal of their own, conservatives have been guided by the belief that the truth must lie somewhere between the extremes—with the result that they have shifted their position every time a more extreme movement appeared on either wing." The protection of agricultural interests—a familiar Röpkian theme—was Hayek's foremost example of the conservative capitulation to socialist doctrine.[105] The meeting at St. Moritz firmly established that Hayek's and Röpke's projects were no longer aligned.

Attempts to understand the ramifications of Hayek's rejection of conservatism are complicated by the problem of defining what "conservatism" meant in the American political environment. Two years before Hayek's address, the prominent Harvard political scientist Louis Hartz had argued in *The Liberal Tradition in America* that the "traditionalism of the Americans" bore "marks of antihistorical rationalism" that made it difficult to distinguish between liberalism and conservatism in their politics. He maintained that with no feudal institutions, the Americans had valorized the "new" in a manner that rendered the "war between Burke and Bentham on the score of tradition" meaningless. American conservatives found themselves unable to define their allegiances in a nation with traditions that were themselves revolutionary. "Radicalism and conservatism," Hartz concluded, "have been twisted entirely out of shape by the liberal flow of American history."[106] Hayek acknowledged the points of intersection between liberalism and conservatism in America, asserting in his address that it remained "possible to defend individual liberty by defending long-established institutions" in a nation where "the defense of the existing is often a defense of freedom."[107] To Kirk, this convergence of liberalism and conservatism in the American political arena enabled the establishment of a coalition that held the potential to exert extraordinary political force. It was a source of optimism and a cause for celebration. But to the Hayek who spoke at St. Moritz, this confluence posed a "danger" that merited trepidation.[108] The conservative respect for the status quo, regardless of its content, made its adherents untrustworthy allies. He worried about the nationalist, authoritarian, and reactionary instincts that might lurk within a colleague who advocated liberal policies for reasons other than liberal principles. His was a clarion call for a mode of classical liberalism that made no concessions; he had arrived at the conviction that the time for compromise was past. In a demonstration of his resolve, he successfully argued that Kirk's candidacy for membership in the Mont Pèlerin Society should not be approved.[109]

Kirk bitterly recalled his experience with the Mont Pèlerin Society in the pages of *National Review* five years later, writing that it "might almost have been called 'The John Stuart Mill Club' or 'The Jeremy Bentham Memorial Association,' what with a somewhat rigid adherence to nineteenth-century Liberal dogmas and a rationalistic hostility toward Christianity among a good many members." His scorn was palpable. "By mere dint of repetition, they seemed to believe, they could make an incantation to give dead clichés vitality." He had become more hopeful about the society with Röpke's recent ascension to the presidency, which provided one indication that it might be edging toward "a merging of the best elements in the old conservatism and the old liberalism."[110] When

Röpke, Hunold, and their sympathizers resigned a year later, it had become apparent that the society could no longer sustain such an atmosphere of compromise. Any promise of a redemptive transformation in the tenor of its internal debates had been lost.

In the months before their resignations, Röpke and Hunold had considered the possibility of founding a separate organization that would redress the Mont Pèlerin Society's limitations.[111] Soon after Röpke formally resigned in late 1961, they began discussing the logistics that such an alternative enterprise—which they christened the Forum Atlanticum—would entail. It would seek to abandon the "predominant economism" that rendered the Mont Pèlerin Society "ever more stale," and to overcome the society's persistent failure to develop the coherent "doctrine" or "philosophy" its founding members had sought.[112] Its members would "cede the M.P.S. to its Misesismuns [*sic*] and Hayekismus" and instead "create a forum for the all-encompassing philosophy of the free world" with "the best people" but no "giant apparatus."[113] In Röpke's view, many of the "best people" were the "liberal conservative" Americans he had identified half a decade earlier, and in particular those who traveled within the circles of the *National Review*: William F. Buckley Jr., Richard Weaver, John Courtney Murray, Frank Meyer, and Russell Kirk.[114]

Röpke emphasized that he hoped to create the Forum Atlanticum "without rivalry" and maintained that it could exist in harmony with the Mont Pèlerin Society.[115] Given the lingering resentments created by the Hunold affair and the direct solicitations that the establishment of such an organization required, however, his profession of a noncompetitive stance was disingenuous. Rüstow's attempt to incite a mass resignation from the Mont Pèlerin Society was broadly perceived as an implicit and unseemly declaration of war.[116] Hunold deliberately held on to his membership in the society long after Röpke's resignation in order to publish further polemics in the *Mont Pèlerin Society Quarterly,* which he hoped would inspire further resignations before he folded the publication into its successor organization.[117] The Forum Atlanticum struggled to overcome the impression that it was created primarily in an act of belligerence against the Mont Pèlerin Society, and only secondarily in order to pursue its own independent goals.

The forum's challenges were compounded by a failure in the months after its inception to identify anyone who was willing to accept a leadership role. It is difficult to found an organization without a willingness to assume the primary responsibilities that it entails, but Röpke was very clear that owing to both his health and the lingering trauma of the Hunold affair, he was unable to accept the presidency. He worked, to no avail, to persuade both Karl Brandt and Russell Kirk to accept the proposed position.[118] As time passed, Röpke grew dismayed by the disapprobation his efforts engendered among the remaining members of the Mont Pèlerin Society and disenchanted by his failure to find an individual capable of realizing his vision. Hunold briefly contemplated establishing the Forum Atlanticum with a secondary membership level for those who wanted to remain affiliated with the Mont Pèlerin Society, in order to make it easier for their colleagues who were loath to leave the society to participate.[119] Nothing came of his idea.

It was becoming increasingly clear that the new organization was not viable. Gradually, Röpke's friends in the society began writing him to inquire whether he might consider setting aside any lingering resentments and reenlisting as a member.[120] Röpke called himself the "least resentful man in the world," but he would contemplate rejoining the society only under very specific conditions: he would need to be named an honorary president, and Hunold would need to be reenrolled and officially recognized alongside Röpke and Hayek as one of the "'Mayflower'-Pelerins."[121] These provisions inspired little interest, and Röpke's bitterness only increased. He blamed his lingering heart infarction on the stress the members of the society had inflicted on him. They had, he wrote to Trygve Hoff in 1965, "almost wilfully [sic] . . . come near to killing me."[122] Less than a year after he sent the letter, the same ailment took his life.[123]

The Mont Pèlerin Society Röpke left behind at his death was in many ways unlike the one he had helped establish in the years after World War II. A society originally defined by its elite academic character had become, in the words of one of its members, "a businessmen's sort of trade association meeting."[124] In 1947 only five of its members were active academics born in North America, which gave rise to Hayek's initial concerns that the society was too exclusively oriented toward continental Europe; by the time of Röpke's death one member observed "within the Society an underlying suspicion, mistrust and even fear, of Anglo-Saxon, or more properly, Anglo-American domination."[125] Perhaps most important, the meetings of the society were no longer reflective of a broad atmosphere of consensus within the conservative academic world. Economists who supported free markets were not so eager as in former years—at both the "Colloque Lippmann" in 1938 and the founding of the Mont Pèlerin Society nearly a decade later—to validate certain modes of government intervention and to emphasize the need for philosophical justifications for free markets that extended beyond the material abundance they ostensibly produced. As a result, they no longer appeared to be drawing on a common tradition, or at times even engaging in direct dialogue, with colleagues and peers who remained suspicious toward the application of an unyielding economism. As laissez-faire reemerged as a live possibility, so too did the antagonism between free-market "liberals" and traditionalist "conservatives" that had riven Western societies amid the age of revolution and the early emergence of industry. The Mont Pèlerin Society of the early 1960s, like the American political environment in subsequent decades, cast these divergent groups as uneasy allies. Their interaction was volatile and eventually unsustainable. The foundational tension of postwar American conservatism had begun to emerge.

The challenges posed by this tension are perhaps most evident in the writings of Frank S. Meyer, one of the individuals Röpke had hoped to attract to participate in his planned Forum Atlanticum. After growing up in Newark, New Jersey, and briefly attending Princeton, Meyer had become a prominent Communist organizer as a student at Oxford. His peripatetic career as a party member took him, ironically, through some of the few remaining centers of free-market economics in the 1930s: he was expelled from the London School of Economics in 1934 after recruiting over 500 of its 3,000 students, and later worked—with less success—to enlist graduate students at the University of Chicago.[126] He was a "demonic figure," Edward Shils recalled, who "frequently interrupted . . . fluent if not very solid discourses with Marxist corrections, supplements, and reinterpretations" and "certainly had no interest in learning anthropology."[127] But Meyer began to have doubts about the party while recovering from a foot operation that left him immobilized for eighteen months in the midst of World War II.[128] The experience of reading Hayek's *Road to Serfdom*, he later recalled, "played a decisive part in helping me free myself from Marxist ideology."[129] By 1955 he had followed the well-trodden midcentury path from Communist activism to conservative dissent, and had assumed his lifelong role of columnist and book-review editor at the nascent *National Review*.[130] There he became known as one of the preeminent conservative networkers in the public sphere. He had, as one colleague noted after his sudden death from lung cancer in 1972, "the number of everybody to the right of Clinton Rossiter."[131] Over the years many of the magazine's most prominent contributors journeyed to Meyer's hermitage in Woodstock, New York, where he famously maintained inverted hours, arising at 5:00 p.m. to begin long evenings of work or, when hosting visitors, discussion and drink (a peculiar habit said to have been borne of nights spent bedside, with his rifle, after his break from the party).[132] He became best known, however, for his pursuit of an intellectual project that his contemporaries labeled "fusionism." His goal was to convince his colleagues in the conservative intellectual world that the preservation of economic freedoms and the defense of traditional moral standards were fundamentally aligned. He hoped to reconstitute the atmosphere of consensus and collaboration that had defined the movement in the decades before his rightward turn.

Shortly before the founding of the *National Review* Meyer explained his differences with Russell Kirk, arguing in *The Freeman* that the New Conservatism advocated by Kirk, Peter Viereck, Walter Lippmann, and Clinton Rossiter opposed the concentration of power without identifying "by what standards overconcentration is to be judged."[133] Meyer believed that in the absence of firm guidelines, the New Conservatives had become too skeptical of individualism and too accommodationist in regard to the New Deal. He elaborated on this criticism in 1962 in his principal work, *In Defense of Freedom,* which asserted that the valorization of the status quo had led the New Conservatives to refuse "to recognize the role of reason" and had thereby robbed them of the capacity to apply reasoned principles to question the practices of the present day. Meyer perceived, and rejected, the New Conservatism as a social philosophy in which the individual inquirer was always subordinated to the established logic of the group.[134] At the same time, he was very clear that his criticisms of Kirk did not align him with the growing body of economists who emphasized free markets as a panacea for the problems faced by American society. Of all the disciplines that study human society, he situated economics as the "closest to an exact science" and "the farthest removed from philosophical competence, from the capacity to establish value."[135] Meyer wanted to grant individuals the broadest possible opportunity to choose their actions and beliefs, but he argued that such a system was sustainable only within a social order that firmly grounded its citizens in the "authority of truth" as embodied in Western thought. (Acknowledging that the endeavor might seem "extraordinarily unenlightened and arrogant" in "the relativist atmosphere of the day," Meyer gave his understanding of the social philosophy of the West, and in particular the United States, pride of place in his hierarchical "ranking of nations and cultures.")[136] His goal was to formulate a social environment that preserved the capacity of the individual to choose between "virtue" and "vice" while socializing individuals to take what he perceived to be the virtuous path. *In Defense of Freedom* is loosely theorized and vague in its social prescriptions, but Meyer cited Eric Voegelin, Willmoore Kendall, and in particular Leo Strauss as exemplars of a mode of conservatism that acknowledged the claims of reason against the authority of tradition.[137] Invoking a language familiar to readers of Röpke, he referred to his social vision as a "third way" between the "authority of truth" and the "freedom of men."[138] His contemporaries, however, referred to the project as "fusionism": an attempt to develop a social philosophy that could inspire the allegiance of both laissez-faire economists and conservatives who emphasized the primacy of "virtue" or historically grounded "truths."[139] He was seen as the synthetic philosopher of the increasingly awkward political coalition reflected in the pages of the *National Review*.

On its surface, Meyer's philosophical project bore marked similarities to the program laid out in the "Statement of Aims" that was ratified at the base of Mont Pèlerin in 1947. Like Meyer, the founders of the Mont Pèlerin Society sought to articulate a worldview that would both defend free markets and establish ethical paradigms for a stable and productive social order. As the society's "Statement of Aims" declared, its members would seek to develop a new social philosophy that would combat the "moral and economic origins" of the "present crisis" by defending both "absolute moral standards" and the "competitive market."[140] The differing contemporary environments, however, made Meyer's project dissimilar to the one pursued by the group that gathered for the initial meeting at Mont Pèlerin. In 1947 the prospect of laissez-faire was discredited among economists and marginalized in the political environment, and American advocates of conservative "traditionalism" were difficult to find. By 1962 the postwar Chicago School had revitalized economists' support for laissez-faire, and "New Conservatives" like Russell Kirk had cultivated substantial nonacademic audiences for their ideas. While the early Mont Pèlerin Society manifested a consensus borne of isolation, the writings of Frank Meyer demonstrated a self-conscious attempt to navigate between established, and warring, constituencies. As the trauma of the Hunold affair revealed, the conservative intellectual world had developed divergent subgroups that no longer viewed their respective projects as implicitly aligned. The postwar consensus that made the founding of the Mont Pèlerin Society possible had dissolved.

Hayek was acutely aware of the society's wrenching transition away from its original statement of shared ideals. Even as he ultimately positioned himself in closer alignment with Friedman and Stigler than with Röpke, he continued to share Röpke's belief that the society would be better capable of achieving its vision if it incorporated the broader range of disciplines and social philosophies that had characterized its founding years.[141] Even those most representative of the society's ascendant paradigm recognized that something had been lost. "I confess," George Stigler wrote in his memoirs as his life drew toward its close, "that none of the later meetings I attended equalled for me the interest of the first session."[142] As early as 1957 Milton Friedman was remarking that the society's debates had grown less interesting since that founding meeting, in part because of "the effects of age on organizations as on individuals."[143] If the society's adolescence was a period of experimentation, uncertainty, and open possibilities, the arrival of its maturity was marked by a narrowing of horizons and the accretion of certainties. Decisiveness always entails a process of selection and an act of casting away. In its first fifteen years of existence, the society gradually, and sometimes ungracefully, shed those individuals whose methodologies, assumptions, and goals diverged most explicitly from its emerging paradigm. In 1965 early members in the society, including Raymond Aron, Michael Polanyi, Alexander Rüstow, Wilhelm Röpke, and Bertrand de Jouvenel, were still very much alive but no longer contributing to its debates.

In 1960 Milton Friedman wrote to Jouvenel to obtain his proxy vote in the then-ongoing battle against Albert Hunold. Jouvenel granted the vote, noting both disapproval for Hunold's reactionary tendencies and some concern about the unkindnesses involved in rescinding the secretarial title. But his reply to Friedman's letter demonstrated little sympathy for the direction the society had taken. "I feel very much out of harmony with the Society," he confided, "and should have, consulting intellectual honesty alone, resigned from it." Its members, Jouvenel believed, had "turned increasingly to a Manicheism according to which the State can do no good and private enterprise can do no wrong." They conflated private enterprise and individual liberty, venerated artificial

corporations with "no soul to save and no bottom to be kicked," and
denounced "practically everything which is done in our time, in the
name of a mythical XIXth century." The organization had succumbed,
in short, to "ideological passion," and as a result had transitioned from
"a free company of people who think together with some initial basis of
agreement" into "a team of fighters." He leavened his appreciation for the
courage of its members' convictions with reservations about the philosophical models their certainties wrought. The willingness to "fight
doughtily" is "much to be admired," he acknowledged, but "such people
do harden an intellectual group into a mould."[144]

Jouvenel felt close allegiance to the early Mont Pèlerin Society's mission of defending individual liberties, but could not abide the channeling
of that mission through the vehicle of laissez-faire.[145] It was ironic, then,
that his letter was addressed to the man who, with the publication of
Capitalism and Freedom two years later, would become the society's leading exponent of the very philosophy that he professed to abhor. During
the ensuing decade Milton Friedman would develop a rhetorical mode
and popular profile that supplanted, and exceeded, the Hayekian prece-
dent. The ascent of Friedman would solidify the transformation of the
society that Jouvenel had observed. But while Jouvenel's letter portrayed
that transformation through a narrative of decline that began at the
base of Mont Pèlerin, the life of Milton Friedman resists the declen-
sional mode. His arrival as a major figure in the public sphere does align
with the diminution of a certain sensibility associated with the society's
initial meetings, but it resonates still more audibly as a point of origin
for a process of extraordinary social and political change. The nostalgia
of founding members of the Mont Pèlerin Society like Jouvenel, Röpke,
and Hunold provides, in its manifest regret for changes that increasingly
appeared irreversible, an early intimation that the age of Milton Friedman had begun.

5

THE INVENTION OF MILTON FRIEDMAN

On a warm evening in the late spring of 1962, Milton Friedman rose to address a group of dinner companions at the University of Chicago's Quadrangle Club. They had been summoned by the student members of the Intercollegiate Society of Individualists in order to honor Friedrich Hayek before his impending departure from the university.[1] With superior financial prospects available at the University of Freiburg, Hayek had recently and reluctantly decided to bring his time at Chicago to a close.[2] Friedman, who was in the midst of the final manuscript preparations for his first mass-market book, *Capitalism and Freedom*, took the opportunity to reflect on the challenges that Hayek had long faced and that he was preparing to confront. Hayek was notable, Friedman informed the room, because of "the extent to which he has succeeded in straddling two kinds of worlds"; the act of "spreading ideas among the public at large" was "very seldom combined with thorough, deep, and profound scholarly work that can influence the course of science." The scholarly world was not friendly to those who used positions of academic authority to expound minority views to the public, and Hayek's exemplary performance as both academic and advocate had forced him to endure difficulties that were too rarely acknowledged. Such an observation might easily have been a prelude to expressions of frustration, but Friedman was adept at finding inspiration where others saw grounds for despair. Discouragement from colleagues was "a very good thing," he concluded, "because it means that those of us who hold our views have to be better to get recognized than people who hold the other views. And in the long run, what matters is the quality of people who propose the ideas and not their number and not their position."[3] Friedman maintained a relentless faith in the ability of unpopular ideas to gain recognition and, over the course of decades, to effect political change.

Hayek was a living testimonial to Friedman's confidence. The participants in the dinner recognized him as one of the very few intellectuals whose career had spanned the trajectory between initial expressions of dissent and derivative signs of political change. He was, George Stigler remarked, "one of three or four economic philosophers who have had a noticeable influence on his times." Even Hayek acknowledged that the ideas espoused in *The Road to Serfdom* were on the ascent. "Many who denounced the book without reading it are now beginning to read it," he told the attendees. "The top layer of intellectual leaders, those whose opinions will be effective a generation later, now have a more genuine belief in liberty than they had before."[4] With Hayek's return to Europe, America was losing its most prominent and distinguished public advocate of free markets. He was departing with some lingering frustrations and uncertainties, but no little sense of satisfaction at the increasing public acceptance of his ideas.

This was a moment of transition. Hayek's departure for Freiburg signified that his public career was beginning to draw to a close. He had been disappointed by the sales of his magnum opus, *The Constitution of Liberty*, after its publication in 1960. The book had not been reviewed by *Time* or *Life*, and *Reader's Digest* had resisted his entreaties to condense it.[5] He was nearing a conventional age for retirement, and his retreat across the Atlantic consigned him to a peripheral role in the American academic and political spheres. By the end of the decade he was wrestling with personal depression and diminished productivity that further distanced him from the intellectual communities he had helped create. Friedman, on the other hand, was on the verge of a rapid personal and professional ascent. In the half decade after his remarks at the Quadrangle Club dinner, his reputation as an economist would be solidified with the publication of *A Monetary History of the United States, 1867–1960* (cowritten with Anna Schwartz) and election to the presidency of the American Economic Association, and his popular profile would dramatically expand with the publication of a best-selling book and a prominent advisory role in the Goldwater campaign. He had grown into a leadership position within the Mont Pèlerin Society as well. In 1957 he and his wife Rose ended a decade of inactivity and began regularly attending meetings; after the Hunold affair one of the society's financial supporters told Friedman that the society had been saved "largely due to your interposition . . . and your leadership"; and by the mid-1960s his colleagues were urging him to consider accepting the society's presidency.[6] Even as Hayek allied himself with Friedman on many matters of economic policy, he maintained some unease about Friedman's methodology and political philosophy.[7] But as Friedman addressed the crowd at the Quadrangle Club on the occasion of Hayek's departure, it was clear that the mantle of the leading advocate of free markets in the American public sphere was being passed.

The transfer of leadership from Hayek to Friedman was emblematic of a generational change. With rare exceptions, the careers of academics tend to center on the set of problems that are deemed most pressing by their colleagues in the period when they begin to reach the height of their intellectual and professional powers. For the first generation of leaders of the Mont Pèlerin Society, that period was the Great Depression, and the problems they grappled with were the grim conundrums of Depression economics. The scope of governmental activities was rapidly and massively increasing, and their goal was correspondingly modest: to convince their colleagues that there was some limited space within which, or some degree to which, the government should not intervene. Milton Friedman, in contrast, came of age during the early stages of the Cold War, and the task of his generation would be to determine the economic approach taken by the United States in the face of an extranational other.[8] While his predecessors' work was ingrained with a sense of caution at the knife's edge of catastrophe, Friedman's was infused with Cold War dualisms. If pure communism was defined by the government's total subsumption of the market mechanism, its most perfect contrast would be defined by a refusal to interfere with the market's invisible decrees. Friedman's philosophical models brooked no concessions to communism, and the America of his time found a ready audience for a philosophy that did not allow itself to be measured in degrees.

While previous members of the Mont Pèlerin Society had labored to develop philosophical models that would prove palatable to their more moderate contemporaries, Friedman did not hesitate to emphasize those points where his perspective diverged from established views. "I believe that people are unduly deterred by the prospect of publicly taking an unpopular position," he asserted in a retrospective at the end of his career. "As someone who has repeatedly done so over a very long period, I believe that doing so seldom involves high costs."[9] Friedman built his professional and public career on the advocacy of positions that ran contrary to received opinion, and he endured the resulting controversies to find himself regaled with private wealth, academic honors, and lasting political recognition. Most important, in the process he persuaded substantial portions of the public to adopt an approach to government policy that resembled his own. Even John Kenneth Galbraith would eventually admit that in "the history of economics the age of John Maynard Keynes gave way to the age of Milton Friedman."[10] To write the history of Milton Friedman is to attempt to situate a point of origin for a dramatic process of social and ideological change.

Given Friedman's indisputable influence on the political thought of both his time and the present day, he has received remarkably little scholarly attention outside the economics profession.[11] He has been the subject of one short popular biography, several books of ideological analysis and synthetic condensation published well over a decade ago, a scattered collection of isolated articles, occasional polemics from his political foes, and countless cursory mentions in popular newspapers and journals.[12] Milton Friedman's rise to public prominence, despite its world-historical force, has yet to be historicized. This failure is in part a reflection of the academic abandonment of the history of economic thought, which has been marginalized by economics departments focused wholly on the development of contemporary analytics, ignored by historians of science who maintain a restrictive understanding of the parameters of their field, and bypassed by historians wary of the relationship between abstract academic debate and processes of social and political change. The hybrid nature of Friedman's career poses a further discouragement to research, because he blurred the lines between popular politics, forays into political philosophy, and work in technical economics that can prove difficult for nonspecialists to comprehend. The irony is that scholars have abandoned inquiry into these modes of analysis even as their importance to our public life has grown. For better or for worse, we now live in an era in which economists have become our most influential philosophers, and when decisions made or advised by economistic technocrats have broad and palpable influence on the practice of our everyday lives. No figure is more representative of this development than Milton Friedman.

An understanding of Friedman's life and work requires an engagement with precisely the hybrid aspects of his career that have deterred scholars in the past, because the unique nature of his contribution is most apparent in those instances when his role as an economist, a political philosopher, and a popular polemicist were entwined. And an examination of the intersection of Friedman's various roles is particularly revealing of the manner in which institutional structures can affect the careers of influential individuals and thereby contribute subtly, but decisively, to changes in the public policy arena. At various stages in his professional development, Friedman made pivotal decisions that would not have been possible without the availability of the network of peers assembled by the Mont Pèlerin Society or the existence of the early-stage funding institutions that sustained it. The intellectual environment provided by these institutions provoked a cascading effect, creating opportunities that snowballed until they fundamentally altered the nature and structure of Friedman's public career. The influence of organizations like the Mont Pèlerin Society and the Volker Fund can largely be reduced to their effects on the ideas and activities of their constituents. In the case of Milton Friedman those effects were substantial, with social ramifications that exceeded the ambitions that even their founders espoused.

Milton Friedman was born in Brooklyn in 1912. Shortly after his first birthday, his parents—who had immigrated as teenagers from Carpathian Ruthenia, which was then part of Hungary—moved to the commuter town of Rahway, New Jersey. After an unsuccessful attempt to sustain a small clothing factory, his mother ran a dry-goods store beneath their apartment, and his father worked as a jobber in New York City. "I do not know what that meant," Friedman frankly acknowledged in his memoirs. "The one thing I do know is that he never made much money." Rahway had a small Jewish community of about a hundred families that defined his family's social circle. Friedman's struggles with religion in the context of a Jewish upbringing demonstrated an early proclivity for earnest conviction. "Until not long before my bar mitzvah, I was fanatically religious," he recalled, but by "the age of twelve or so, I decided that there was no valid basis for my religious beliefs or for the rigid customs that I had followed, and I shifted to complete agnosticism." In 1928 he arrived at Rutgers, where he demonstrated a proclivity for math that inspired him to anticipate a career as an actuary, the "only paying occupation I had heard about that used mathematics." After two years of work in the mathematics department, he switched his major to economics. There he came under the influence of two young faculty members: Arthur F. Burns, the future chairman of the Federal Reserve, who was working to finish a doctoral dissertation at Columbia; and Homer Jones, a former student of Frank Knight at the University of Iowa and the University of Chicago. Friedman remembered Jones as putting "major stress on individual freedom" and expressing skepticism toward "attempts to inter-

fere with the exercise of individual freedom in the name of social planning or collective values," a set of perspectives that in his recollection
"even then was known as the Chicago view."[13] With the endorsement of
Jones, Friedman declined a graduate position in applied mathematics at
Brown to accept a tuition scholarship in the Department of Economics at
Chicago. "Put yourself in 1932 with a quarter of the population unem-
ployed," he recalled over seventy years later. "What was the important
urgent problem?"[14] He had decided, in the depths of the Great Depression, to embark on a career as an economist.

A set of highly contingent factors brought Friedman to the University
of Chicago when Jacob Viner and Frank Knight were at the height of
their careers, but it did not take him long to realize that the department
would have a decisive influence on his intellectual development. Jacob
Viner's introductory course on price theory, in particular, came as "a
revelation" that opened his eyes to a world he "had not realized existed."
Viner had the capacity to represent economic theory as a source of
"beauty" and "power" and to assemble a series of apparently discrete insights into "a coherent and logical whole."[15] Friedman was less explicit
about Frank Knight's influence, which he admitted was "certainly not on
particular points" but rather "on general outlook or general philosophy,
general feeling of the limitations of economics and of what economic
theory could do."[16] He attributed the greatest degree of importance, however, to a close-knit circle of graduate students that developed in Knight's
orbit in the fall of 1934, including George Stigler, Aaron Director, and
Allen Wallis.[17] Their friendship was formed in regular gatherings at
Knight's or Director's residence in which they spent hours engaged in cor-
dial but heated debate.[18] All four would later serve as professors at the
University of Chicago, and would play decisive roles in developing the
institutional orientation and practices that became known as the hall-
marks of the Chicago "school."[19] Collectively, the Department of Economics impressed Friedman as a place where the "general atmosphere"
imparted an appreciation for price theory and encouraged students to
adopt a skeptical approach to socialist economics.[20] Friedman came away
from Chicago with a sense of the scope and coherence of economic theory and an increasing conviction that its tenets were incompatible with
socialism.

Despite the manifest influence of Chicago on the trajectory of Friedman's career, it is crucial to understand that his economic methodology
did not develop organically out of his studies with Viner and Knight. In

his second year of graduate school, at the urging of the Chicago statistical economist Henry Schultz, Friedman accepted a generous stipend of $1,500 to study with Harold Hotelling at Columbia.[21] Under Hotelling, whom he admired as a uniquely capable figure, he engaged in an intensive study of statistics and mathematical economics. "Hotelling did for mathematical statistics what Jacob Viner had done for economic theory," he later recalled, by revealing "it to be an integrated logical whole, not a set of cook-book recipes."[22] In his remaining time Friedman attended courses taught by the other major figures in the Economics Department at Columbia, including John M. Clark and Wesley C. Mitchell.[23] Under Mitchell and Clark, Columbia had become known for its orientation toward institutionalist economics.[24] Mitchell, in particular, emphasized the primacy of careful empirical work: as was evident in his magisterial research into business cycles, he believed that the accumulation of data should precede the construction of interpretive theories.[25] Friedman's initial reaction was to be "contemptuous of what was going on at Columbia in the theoretical area," concluding that Mitchell "really wasn't a theorist and didn't understand economic theory" (which, he added, "was probably true").[26] But over time Friedman's perspective was decisively influenced by his studies at Columbia and his later work under Mitchell at the National Bureau of Economic Research (NBER).[27] His subsequent attentiveness to clear and coherent language derived in part from a harsh scolding he received from Mitchell about carelessness with words.[28] He attributed his well-known emphasis on frank and open debate in part to Mitchell's (and his student Arthur F. Burns's) willingness to engage forthrightly with all criticism, "asking only the question is it right and not from whom does it come or does it threaten me."[29] Economists oriented toward empirical research, Friedman concluded, tended to be more open to learning from disagreements than economists who were beholden to particular abstract theories. Mitchell constantly reiterated the importance of empirical analysis, referring frequently to John Neville Keynes's distinction between positive and normative economics.[30] "Repeatedly I recall his asserting that we cannot know what we want to do unless we know what the consequences of doing one thing or another are," Friedman later recalled. "Thus positive economics is an essential foundation for normative statements."[31] Friedman left Columbia with a new respect for the virtues of empiricism and a belief that attention to historical evidence could do far more to resolve differences in opinion than normative assertions.[32]

As Friedman attempted to articulate his methodology during the subsequent decades, he envisioned it as adopting the virtues of both Chicago and Columbia while discarding the vices engendered by their respective excesses. It was simply impossible, he believed, to pursue empirical research without filtering it through the lens of an interpretive theory. Facts, he repeatedly asserted, "are simply those theories that are currently being accepted for the purpose of discussion or for the purpose of the particular investigation."[33] Mitchell's consistent refusal to rely explicitly on economic theory to derive hypotheses was, he argued, not a defensible methodology so much as an indicator that he was "not a good theorist and not really interested in theory."[34] But at the same time, theory was both practically and rhetorically impotent if it was not tested against and refined by the available data. A good economist would use economic theory to derive a hypothesis and then evaluate the hypothesis by its ability to explain and predict actual marketplace behavior. Friedman believed that in this manner economics could become known—to adopt his terminology—as a "serious" subject that helped people solve "real" problems.

Friedman did not begin to develop a coherent articulation of his methodology until over a decade after his year at Columbia.[35] Elements of his emerging position were evident in a harshly critical 1946 review of Oskar Lange's *Price Flexibility and Employment*. Lange, a prominent socialist who had served on the economics faculty of the University of Chicago in the late 1930s and early 1940s, had recently returned to his native Poland to work for its newly formed Communist government. Friedman began his review by complimenting Lange as a preeminent and highly skilled practitioner of a particular form of economic logic, and then excoriated that mode of analysis as "sterile," "unreal," and "artificial."[36] By focusing on "the formal structure of the theory, the logical interrelations of the parts," to the exclusion of virtually everything else, Lange "in the main reaches conclusions no observed facts can contradict." He created highly formalized representations of imaginary worlds that held no capacity to predict in the "real" world.[37] Without being able to judge the theories' predictive capacities, scientists were left with no ability to evaluate the legitimacy of Lange's arguments.

It is no surprise, then, that Friedman viewed Karl Popper as a kindred spirit when he first met him at the inaugural Mont Pèlerin Society meeting in 1947. After authoring *Logik der Forschung* and *The Open Society and Its Enemies*, Popper had recently assumed, with Hayek's assistance, a position at the London School of Economics. *Logik der Forschung* had rejected an account of scientific research as a mode of inductive logic, arguing that such accounts failed to provide a suitable *"criterion of demarcation"* between the empirical sciences, on the one hand, and mathematics, logic, and metaphysics, on the other.[38] Instead, Popper argued that scientists should proceed through a *"deductive method of testing"* that enabled them to arrive at conclusions that could be *"intersubjectively tested"* and, potentially, falsified.[39] Friedman quickly realized that Popper had articulated and systematized a methodological predisposition that he had independently adopted during his time in graduate school.[40] He was particularly struck by Popper's insight that scientific observations need to be falsifiable but can never be finally or conclusively verified.[41] Their productive interchange across both disciplines and national boundaries modeled the precise mode of interaction the Mont Pèlerin Society had been intended to foster.

A half decade later Friedman published a detailed overview of his approach to economic analysis in his essay "The Methodology of Positive Economics" (1953). Drawing on Popper, he argued that the only relevant test of the validity of a hypothesis was a comparison of its predictions and experience, adding that "evidence can never 'prove' a hypothesis; it can only fail to disprove it." Hypotheses that had "survived many opportunities for contradiction" were accorded "great confidence"; those that were contradicted more often than alternative hypotheses were discarded.[42] Crucially, the validity of a hypothesis was to be determined solely by its predictive capacity, and not by the conformity of its assumptions with our understanding of reality.[43] The most elegant and valuable theories would present a simplistic mechanism to generate consistently successful predictions for the behavior of vastly more complicated sets of data. Friedman appropriated John Neville Keynes's designation "positive economics" to describe this approach, and announced that it was "in principle independent of any particular ethical position or normative judgments" and could be "an 'objective' science, in precisely the same sense as any of the physical sciences."[44] In Western societies, he asserted, "differences about economic policy among disinterested citizens derive predominantly from different predictions about the economic consequences of taking action—differences that in principle can be eliminated by the progress of positive economics—rather than from fundamental differences in basic values, differences about which men can ultimately only fight."[45] Despite the severity of its implicit criticism of prevalent modes of economic analysis, "The Methodology of Positive Economics" was a fundamentally optimistic text. In Friedman's view economists could overcome the particular challenges of the social sciences to achieve an "objective" perspective and in doing so could build a reasoned consensus in the population at large. Friedman put forward a highly controversial methodological claim while at the same time arguing that the role of the economist should largely be one of identifying and broadening points of common ground.

The publication of "The Methodology of Positive Economics" was a pivotal moment in the history of free-market advocacy for two reasons. First, Friedman's emphasis on the necessary descriptive simplification entailed in the act of generating hypotheses reinvigorated the embattled theory of perfect competition. Economists had long struggled against the descriptive inaccuracies of the *homo economicus*; as Frank Knight had often observed, its atomistic and coldly calculating vision of human activity utterly failed to explain many self-evident aspects of intersocial behavior. To Friedman, the individual falsities were beside the point, because the only criterion to use in evaluating the theory that individuals "single-mindedly" seek to maximize their "money income" was its relative capacity to predict successfully when confronted with aggregated data.[46] Friedman's distinction between a theory's descriptive and predictive capacities helped justify economists' use of an abstract theory that appeared, when applied to individual cases, to be manifestly untrue. The defense of simplified hypotheses in "The Methodology of Positive Economics" was, implicitly if not overtly, a defense of the model of perfect competition. Friedman's critics insinuated that the entire dispute over methodology was a displaced substitute for a debate over the legitimacy of that model.[47] Friedman had opened a formidable new front in an argument that many in the prior generation of free-market economists had abandoned as lost.[48]

Second, Friedman's treatise put forward a dramatically different understanding of economic methodology than had conventionally been associated with advocates of laissez-faire. Since the late nineteenth-century *Methodenstreit* between the Austrian economist Carl Menger and the German economist Gustav von Schmoller, opponents of state intervention had been associated in the public mind with a belief that economic theory could be deduced from a priori principles.[49] Menger's methodological views were more complex than such representations allowed; but Ludwig von Mises, the preeminent exemplar of "Austrian" economics in the interwar years, argued that economics was unique among the sciences precisely because its theories were "not open to any verification or falsification on the ground of experience."[50] Friedman worried that Mises's mode of economics provided no means for the adjudication of conflicting claims. He explained his reservations in a private letter to Hayek after a discussion of methodology at Hillsdale College. "Needless to say," he wrote, "there was sharp disagreement between the enthusiastic Austrians, who follow Mises on the praxeological method, and myself as a believer with Popper in the testing of scientific hypotheses by attempted disproof or inconsistency of observations with implications." He asked Hayek to imagine an individual who asserts that a particular theory is true but untestable. "Suppose another individual disagrees with him," he posited. "How is the difference to be resolved? In the praxeological context, only by either conversion or force." Friedman's methodological approach, in contrast, offered a mechanism for adjudication: "You believe a particular theory to be true; I believe that theory to be false or a different theory true. We do not argue for the moment the issues. Rather we agreed between us on what set of facts if observed would lead you to accept my theory and what set of facts if observed would lead me to accept your theory. We thus have a peaceful method of reconciling disagreements between us."[51] Friedman believed that the practitioners of praxeology were incapable of engaging in productive and open interchange with their colleagues. He told an interviewer that in admitting "no role whatsoever for empirical evidence," its practitioners developed "an attitude of human intolerance."[52] He repeatedly stressed that his goal was to maintain "humility": to practice a mode of economic reasoning that avoided any claims to absolute truth or certainty, and that provided an objective basis for settling differences of opinion.[53]

Many of Friedman's most powerful and distinctive rhetorical tools in the public policy arena derived from his methodological innovations. His belief in the persuasive capacities of empirical evidence inspired his consistent attempts to shift public discussions away from debates over divergent normative ends and toward the means of achieving ends that were broadly shared. Whenever possible, he would concede that he shared the goals of his ideological opponents and then argue that they were misguided about how those goals would best be attained. He foresaw little success in the endeavor to change government policy by attempting to indoctrinate other people with his values. Instead, he sought to convince them that he had assembled material evidence that demonstrated that their own values could best be met through implementation of the policies he recommended. His methodology further undergirded his constant emphasis on toleration of opposing views, openness to new ideas, and willingness to debate anyone whose perspective differed from his own. These qualities lent his ideas a degree of populism and an aura of reasonableness that are crucial to the early public life of positions supported by a radical minority. The relative efficacy of Friedman's approach was demonstrated in the divergent trajectories of Mises's followers and his own: while economists in the Austrian tradition have been ghettoized in a small subset of sympathetic institutions and academic departments, Chicago economists have pervaded the profession and assumed positions of broad political influence.[54]

"The Methodology of Positive Economics" is sometimes cited as Friedman's most influential work.[55] It played a central role in his research program and public rhetoric, and has long served as a primary point of disputation for his ideological opponents. Its prominent role in Friedman's canon draws attention to his steadfast refusal to engage in any further discussion of its contents. Friedman believed that he would be more persuasive if he performed positive economics and refrained from further discussions of its normative underpinnings.[56] He was very attentive to his areas of comparative advantage as an economist and likely recognized that establishing the philosophical foundations of the discipline was not one of them. "I don't recall ever having read much philosophy," he acknowledged at the end of his career. "Certainly, about the only methodology philosophy I've read is Popper."[57] As a debater, he was skilled at shifting discussions away from points of potential weakness in his argument and toward evident flaws in the ideas expressed by his opponents. He may have recognized that his methodology appeared more efficacious when it was practiced than when it was elaborated. And he was canny enough to realize that some essays attract more attention when they are left to stand alone. "The Methodology of Positive Economics" was by no means "the most important thing I've ever done," he told *Reason* magazine in 1995, but it "has probably been reprinted more often and referred to more often than anything else I've written." He explained the disparity: "I made a distinct point of not replying to any criticism of that essay. And I think that's why it's so commented on."[58] Milton Friedman was not known for his love of ambiguity, but in this case he acknowledged that it too could have rhetorical force.

Friedman's career as an economist was made possible, in a minor irony that he readily acknowledged, by the economic programs of the New Deal. As his second year at the University of Chicago drew to a close in the spring of 1935, he had limited prospects for academic employment. "Absent the New Deal, it is far from clear that we could have gotten jobs as economists," he recounted in his autobiography. "Academic posts were few. Anti-Semitism was widespread in the academy." In the midst of this grim professional environment, the "new government programs created a boom market for economists, especially in Washington," which proved to be "a lifesaver for us personally."[59] He benefited from the extraordinary expansion of economists' influence on public policy during the 1930s, which itself was precipitated by the challenges of economic dislocation and the novel interventions it inspired.[60] With the assistance of his fellow Chicago graduate student Allen Wallis, he obtained a position at the National Resources Committee, where he worked to calculate a cost-of-living index.[61] It was the first of a series of government posts that he held through the mid-1940s: working closely with Simon Kuznets and under Wesley Mitchell at the NBER from 1937 to 1940, under Hans Morgenthau in the Treasury Department from 1941 to 1943, and in the Statistical Research Group from 1943 to 1945. His academic experience before his return to Chicago in 1946 was sparse: he served as a visiting professor at the University of Wisconsin during the 1940–1941 academic year, ultimately receiving notice that the university had declined to offer him tenure; and he joined George Stigler at the University of Minnesota for the first year after the war.[62]

During his time in government service, Friedman did not align himself with any explicit political ideology. He had arrived in 1932 at graduate school in Chicago as what one colleague described—citing the prominent socialist presidential candidate—as a "Norman Thomas–type socialist."[63] In Friedman's recollection, he "wasn't very politically oriented," and although it was "obvious I was not a Marxist or a Socialist or anything like that," he was also not an ardent opponent of their views.[64] He recalled objecting to the price- and wage-fixing components of the New Deal but joining his colleagues at Chicago in support of the Works Progress Administration, the Public Works Administration, and the Civilian Conservation Corps as "appropriate responses to the critical situation."[65] He vaguely remembered voting for Roosevelt over Alf Landon in the presidential election of 1936.[66] And he devoted the majority of his time at the Treasury Department to work with a small team tasked with the development of a federal withholding tax, which he and his colleagues and followers subsequently excoriated as a mechanism to disguise the cost of taxation from its subjects. Friedman later expressed "no apologies," citing the fact that at the time they "were concentrating on the war."[67] The withholding tax entered his pantheon of government programs that were useful when implemented but problematic once entrenched.[68]

In these initial stages in his career, Friedman presented himself as a statistician rather than a macroeconomist and registered little interest in questions of public policy.[69] His political identity formed slowly during the two decades after his arrival in Washington. Its emergence was unquestionably related to developments in his economic thought. His graduate dissertation, *Income from Independent Professional Practice* (coauthored with Simon Kuznets for the NBER), demonstrated a proclivity to advocate the extension of markets to areas where restrictions were well entrenched and widely assumed to be beneficial. In the densely statistical format common to the NBER, Friedman and Kuznets argued that the high wages of medical doctors relative to dentists was attributable largely to the restrictions on entry to the profession entailed in the licensing requirements enforced by the American Medical Association.[70] The manuscript inspired a bureaucratic controversy that delayed its approval and, correspondingly, Friedman's ability to receive an official doctoral degree until after its publication in 1945.[71] But Friedman did not begin to conceive of himself as a political figure or to write tracts accessible to popular readers until he came into contact with a series of institutions developed to advocate for free markets. His emergence as a public intellectual was a product of his interactions in the years after the war with the Foundation for Economic Education, the Mont Pèlerin Society, and the William Volker Charities Fund. Together, these institutions brought Friedman into contact with like-minded intellectuals who led him to reconceive his professional ideas in political terms, and commissioned him to write popular articles and lectures that eventually changed the trajectory of his career.

Friedman's first major popular tract was a pamphlet on rent control commissioned by the Foundation for Economic Education (FEE) in

1946. The FEE had been founded by Leonard Read, a former executive vice president of the National Industrial Conference Board who had rapidly grown frustrated with the business advocacy organization's policy of presenting "both sides" of political and economic issues covered in its educational activities. With funding from the retired oil magnate H. B. Earhart and a number of major corporations, Read established his new organization in a decaying mansion in Irvington-on-Hudson, New York, with the goal of educating the public on the virtues of free-market economics. By mid-1947 he had accumulated $254,000 in donations.[72] As one of its earliest activities the foundation offered Friedman and George Stigler $650 to write a pamphlet outlining economic reasons to oppose rent controls. It planned to provide 500,000 abbreviated copies of the pamphlet to the National Association of Real Estate Boards, which was in the midst of a concerted lobbying effort to reverse existing rent control policies.[73]

The resulting pamphlet, entitled "Roofs or Ceilings?," argued that the pressing shortage of housing in the immediate postwar period was attributable to distortions in the market structure caused by rent controls. Friedman and Stigler exhibited their argument through a striking analogy, comparing the housing market in San Francisco after the massive destruction of the 1906 earthquake with its housing market in 1946. The housing situation quickly normalized in the period after the earthquake, they wrote, because of the ability to ration the available units through higher rents and the strong incentives those higher rents created to build more units as quickly as possible. In 1946, despite the absence of a comparable catastrophe, the housing situation was dire, a product, they concluded, of the disincentives fostered by rent control. They called for the abandonment of rent control and the restoration of normal market conditions.[74] The publication of the pamphlet was an important moment in Friedman's career. The clarity and concision of its argument and the vividness of its examples revealed his capabilities as a popular writer. It was, as Paul Krugman has acknowledged, "beautifully and cunningly written."[75] It also established Friedman's reputation as a political extremist and popular polemicist within the cadre of academic economists. The pamphlet, Paul Samuelson recalled, "outraged the profession."[76] Robert Bangs referred to it in the *American Economic Review* as "a political tract, of the same species as, *e.g.*, *The Road to Serfdom*, though even more timely and specific."[77] He was less forgiving in the *Washington Post*, referring to it as "an insidious little pamphlet" published by "a propaganda front for reactionary interests," and concluding that economists "who sign their names to drivel of this sort do no service to the profession they represent."[78] The central figures in Friedman's and Stigler's education at the University of Chicago—Jacob Viner and Frank Knight—had avoided public rhetoric whenever possible, and had adopted a tone of exaggerated equanimity when they were thrust into political discussion. The publication of "Roofs or Ceilings?" provided a preliminary, but unequivocal, indication that Friedman and Stigler would follow a different path.

Even as Friedman's "Roofs or Ceilings?" revealed his proclivity for, and inclination toward, engagement in public debate, it also introduced him to the challenges of working with ideologically motivated institutions. In the month before the publication of the pamphlet, Friedman and Stigler engaged in a fierce dispute with FEE administrators that nearly led them to withdraw it from publication and decline the attendant compensation. The issue centered on a paragraph professing the authors' support for economic equality:

> The fact that, under free market conditions, better quarters go to those who have larger incomes or more wealth is, if anything, simply a reason for taking long-term measures to reduce the inequality of income and wealth. For those, like us, who would like even more equality than there is at present, not alone for housing but for all products, it is surely better to attack directly existing inequalities in income and wealth at their source than to ration each of the hundreds of commodities and services that compose our standard of living. It is the height of folly to permit individuals to receive unequal money incomes and then to take elaborate and costly measures to prevent them from using their incomes.[79]

As the publication date neared, the FEE expressed concern about the implications of the paragraph and attempted to edit it to remove the phrase "like us." Stigler protested vigorously. "We have sought to keep more of the original tone of dispassionate evaluation, whereas your suggestions accentuate its polemical character," he wrote to V. O. Watts at the foundation. In contrast to the contentions in the authors' version of the article that inequality was undesirable but not a reason for continuing rent controls, Stigler observed that the foundation's version implied that inequality was a blessing. He concluded that the moderating phrases in the essay were "indispensable in giving the tone of objectivity we seek" and helped them "to convince the open-minded, not those who already favor our position."[80] He wrote privately to Friedman of his concern that

they would suffer "the complete loss of our reputations if we started suppressing our own views" for "a little dubious fame."[81] The staff of the
FEE, however, remained concerned that the passage would appear to be
"an endorsement by the Foundation of certain collectivist ideas which
are repugnant to us" and would violate their pact to avoid "compromising with what we considered to be error."[82] They finally reached a compromise wherein the pamphlet included an editor's footnote indicating
that the "long-term measures" might include nothing more than the abolition of special privileges granted by the government.

The brief controversy preceding the publication of "Roofs or Ceilings?" revealed that Friedman and Stigler were fiercely protective of
their public reputations and unwilling to alter their arguments to suit
the desires of funding institutions. The FEE could, and did, influence their
output by convincing them to write for a popular audience and determining the subject matter they would address—in itself a substantial
concession in a professional context that viewed public advocacy with
considerably more skepticism than is conventional among economists
today—but they would not alter the nature or the rhetorical structure
of their arguments. Stigler was frankly appalled at what he perceived to
be the myopic dogmatism of their funders at the FEE.[83] He warned Watts
that his ideological strictures would have prevented him from publishing "the articles of Hayek or Henry Simons, or, for that matter, of Ricardo or Adam Smith."[84] Both Stigler and Friedman refused to maintain
relations with affiliates of the FEE for years after the publication of the
pamphlet.[85]

Even at this early stage of his career, Friedman was eager to emphasize
that he shared many goals with his colleagues on the left. "I believe it
essential to make it clear wherein we are criticizing means and wherein
ends," he wired to Leonard Read, adding that the failure "of liberals to
emphasize their objectives seems to me one of [the] reasons they are so
often labelled reactionaries."[86] Whereas many of the foundations and
polemicists on the right devoted their propaganda to the converted,
Friedman strenuously sought to engage those with whom he disagreed.
He adopted a tone of reasonable moderation while forwarding policies
that would otherwise have appeared uncompromising and extremist.
The young Friedman, however, was willing to make more substantial
concessions to progressives than would subsequently be the case. The im-
plication that inequality was "bad," and that measures should be taken
to reduce it, would fall away from Friedman's popular writings later in
his career. The contrast between the controversial paragraph in "Roofs

or Ceilings?" and his later work indicates that he may have perceived his postwar audience to be more redistributionist than in subsequent years, and demonstrates that his political leanings were still in the midst of an evolutionary process.

The first Mont Pèlerin Society meeting in 1947 was a crucial moment in the development of Friedman's approach to public policy. His brother-in-law and longtime colleague Aaron Director, who had previously spent a year at the London School of Economics, asked Hayek to include Friedman on the list of invitees. To Friedman, who was still a young scholar and had never journeyed outside the United States, the opportunity to travel, with all expenses paid, across the Atlantic on an ocean liner to visit war-ravaged Europe seemed extraordinary. "Here I was, a young, naive provincial American," he later recalled, "meeting people from all over the world, all dedicated to the same liberal principles as we were; all beleaguered in their own countries, yet among them scholars, some already internationally famous, others destined to be."[87] He credited the gathering in Switzerland as "what really got me started in policy and what led to *Capitalism and Freedom*." The society was important less for the particular ideas that arose in its discussions than for the community of supporters it was able to establish. "If you have a person isolated in an environment unfriendly to his ideas and thoughts, he tends to turn bitter and self-directed," he explained. "But the same person with three or four other people around—it doesn't have to be a lot of people—will be in a wholly different position since he will receive support from the others." When Friedman expressed his ideas to fellow economists or to the public at large in the years after the war, he, like many of his colleagues, felt the need to temper statements that might be perceived as extreme with demonstrations of his moderation. The Mont Pèlerin Society provided a culture in which it was possible to express an appreciation for free markets that was undiluted by acts of rhetorical moderation. "Its great contribution," he maintained, "was that it provided a week when people like that could get together and open their hearts and minds and not have to worry about whether somebody was going to stick a knife in their back."[88] Within the confines of the meeting halls at Mont Pèlerin, the institutional incentives were briefly but crucially reversed: whereas elsewhere constant pressures existed to push the society's members to conform with the vital center, the society welcomed and even admired its members' statements of ideological dissent.

During his time at Mont Pèlerin, Friedman was introduced to a number of colleagues who would play crucial roles in his political activities over the next two decades. One of them was Trygve Hoff, the outspoken editor of the Norwegian business journal *Farmand*. At Hoff's request, Friedman provided the journal with an essay outlining his political views under the title "Neoliberalism and Its Prospects" in 1951. The essay provides a comprehensive introduction to his perspectives at this stage in his career and demonstrates their unmistakable differences from his later positions. More than four years into his tenure in Chicago, Friedman continued to hold political views that were closely aligned to those of his predecessors at Chicago and the founding members of the Mont Pèlerin Society. He affiliated himself with a position that he termed "neoliberalism," which had attracted "a strong cross-current of opinion" and offered "a real hope of a better future." Neoliberalism was unambiguously critical of laissez-faire, which relied on "basic error" that had been exposed by the failures of "19th century individualist philosophy": "it underestimated the danger that private individuals could through agreement and combination usurp power and effectively limit the freedom of other individuals; it failed to see that there were some functions the price system could not perform and that unless these other functions were somehow provided for, the price system could not discharge effectively the tasks for which it is admirably fitted." Friedman looked to his mentor Henry Simons as an exemplar of a neoliberal "new faith" that would avoid both the errors of statism and the manifest failures of laissez-faire. While severely restricting government activities, neoliberalism would "explicitly recognize that there are important positive functions that must be performed by the state." As examples, Friedman cited the Sherman Antitrust Act and the "function of relieving misery and distress," which could not be left "to private charity or local responsibility" in a world that was "complicated and intertwined."[89] "Neoliberalism and Its Prospects" demonstrated that Friedman now included political engagement among his activities as a professional economist. The Mont Pèlerin Society had inspired him to conceive of himself as part of a concerted attempt to generate long-term political change. It is equally clear that Friedman's political thought was, at this point, in close conformity with that expressed by the leading members of the society during the initial meeting at Mont Pèlerin. The basic assumptions reflected in the essay—including the need to overcome the dogmas of nineteenth-century liberalism, the hazards of monopoly, the benefits of corporate regulations, and the desirability of government-sponsored relief for the poor—were parroted from Hayek's and Röpke's descriptions of their mutual goals. Friedman had aligned himself with an ideological program, but he had not yet elaborated the characteristics that would mark his political philosophy as a distinctive departure from that of his predecessors in Chicago and forebears at Mont Pèlerin.

Friedman's views hardened during the 1950s in conjunction with a network of colleagues at the University of Chicago who had also attended the 1947 meeting at Mont Pèlerin. The society's representation on the faculty at Chicago was enabled in part by the Volker Fund, which underwrote Hayek's salary and funded the Free Market Study that drew Aaron Director to a position at the Law School in 1946.[90] Hayek only occasionally interacted with Friedman during his time in Chicago because of his separate position on the Committee on Social Thought and his growing interest in problems that were peripheral to the postwar economics profession. Director's close connections to Friedman through both family and graduate school, however, led his presence on the faculty to have a powerful influence on his colleague's social and intellectual world. After shedding the leftist instincts of his youth, Director had come to view himself as a more rigorous defender of the free market than Friedman; before they received their doctorates, he was already joking about his brother-in-law's "very strong New Deal leanings," and he continued to tease him over ideological lapses for the remainder of his career.[91] By the early 1950s Director's assaults on regulatory bodies in the Law School's antitrust course were becoming increasingly notorious. Although he published little, his relentless logic and urbane sensibility exerted a powerful hold over generations of students and earned him broad influence among the faculty; as the founding editor of the *Journal of Law and Economics,* he eventually helped shape an emerging subfield as well.[92] During the decade Friedman abandoned the sympathy for the Sherman Antitrust Act that he had expressed in "Neoliberalism and Its Prospects" and increasingly concurred with Director's hardened skepticism about government regulation.

George Stigler, who had traveled with Friedman to attend the initial meeting at Mont Pèlerin, left Columbia to accept a position in the business school at Chicago in 1958. He was lured by a professorship endowed by the Walgreen Foundation, which, under the advice of Leonard Read of the Foundation for Economic Education, had found a number of candidates unacceptable before finally acceding to Stigler's appointment.[93] Like Friedman, Stigler had expressed some enthusiasm about trust-busting in the years after the publication of "Roofs or Ceilings?" and had gone so far as to recommend the "dissolution" of all companies that demonstrated "monopoly power" in 1952.[94] But under the influence of public choice theory, Ronald Coase's work on transaction costs, and his new colleagues, Stigler began work not long after his arrival at Chicago on a series of articles that reexamined the economic effects of regulation. He emerged with the conclusion that regulators usually failed to achieve their goals and often provided competitive advantages to the very organizations they were intended to oversee.[95] His work provided a formal validation of his colleagues' incipient concerns and would later play a decisive role in the early stages of the deregulation movement.[96]

Together, Friedman, Director, and Stigler formed a nexus that connected the graduate program in economics and the professional schools. Over time the interpersonal relationships that drew these programs together were reinforced by a distinctive institutional culture. In the early 1950s Friedman and several of his colleagues used funding from both the Ford Foundation and a Chilean fellowship program to pioneer the development of a novel system of workshops. In an attempt to model social-scientific research after scientific labs, professors and advanced graduate students began meeting regularly to discuss their emerging work in a shared field of interest. Presenters distributed mimeographed papers before the meetings, and the discussions that ensued became notorious for dispensing with the culture of politeness that characterized much of the American academic world. The most distinguished of these workshops, which included Friedman's on money and banking, Stigler's on industrial organization, and the Law School's on law and economics, helped drill students in their professors' distinctive modes of analysis. The culture of these research communities accounted for much of the shared identity and methodological influence of the postwar Chicago School.[97]

Although Director and Stigler did much to shape the research program of their colleagues and students, they largely avoided public engagement. Director rarely published, and Stigler remained unconvinced of the merits of public advocacy, arguing that popularity and influence were usually "rivals, not partners."[98] Friedman became the public rhetorician of the jaundiced view of government intervention that increasingly characterized Chicago economics. Here, too, the Volker Fund played an integral role. Its program officers carefully monitored the participants in the events they sponsored and sought to engage them in its other related activities whenever synergies were apparent. Beginning in 1952, it assembled a comprehensive directory of liberal intellectuals who were affiliated directly with its programs, or whose participation they sought; by 1956 the list had grown to include over 1,841 names.[99] In the mid-1950s the fund determined that the time had arrived for it to begin transitioning from "a program centered on the discovery and encouragement of individual scholarship" to one "with an emphasis on effective dissemination."[100] To that end, it devoted $100,000 per annum to the development of a summer conference program that by 1956 included eight conferences on subjects ranging from economics and political science to history and sociology.[101] As a general model, the conferences involved three or four presenters and twenty or thirty junior academics.[102] Along with Ludwig von Mises, Friedrich Hayek, and Frank Knight, among others, Friedman participated in the early stages of planning for conference activities in his area of expertise.[103] He went on to participate in Volker conferences at Wabash College, Claremont College, the University of North Carolina, and Oklahoma State University. In each of the meetings he devoted some time to a statement of the foundational principles of his approach to political economy and then proceeded to apply those principles to different aspects of public policy.[104] "Those seminars forced me to systematize my thoughts and present them in a coherent way," Friedman recalled decades later.[105] Eventually the organizers from the Volker Fund applied "friendly pressures to write them up in tentative form."[106] Rose Friedman assembled the transcribed tapes of his presentations and consolidated them into the manuscript of *Capitalism and Freedom*.[107]

Capitalism and Freedom codified a political philosophy that departed significantly from Friedman's description of his positions in the early 1950s. He now referred to himself as a "consistent liberal" but was adamant that the label was not commensurate with anarchism. There was, he admitted, a role for government that maintained law and order, preserved property rights, adjudicated disputes, enforced contracts, provided a monetary framework, protected the incompetent, and mitigated "technical monopolies" and neighborhood effects. Despite this acknowledgment of an appropriate sphere for government action, Friedman was beginning to retreat from his earlier opposition to monopolies and support for poor relief. He argued that private unregulated monopolies were far less troubling than private monopolies regulated by the state or government operations, because they were "generally unstable and of brief duration unless they can call government to their assistance."[108] And he emphasized that although a liberal "may approve state action toward ameliorating poverty," he would do so "with regret . . . at having to substitute compulsory for voluntary action."[109] The book then went on to advocate an extension of market principles that was breathtaking in its audacity. Among many other policy proposals, Friedman called for the elimination of agricultural price supports, tariffs and export restrictions, the minimum wage, the regulatory activities of the Interstate Commerce Commission and the Federal Communications Commission, social security, public housing, the military draft, all systems of professional licensure, and all national parks.[110] The popular success of *Capitalism and Freedom* was limited at first, in part because it went largely unnoticed in both general-interest magazines and professional journals; but over time the pace of its sales began to increase, and eventually well over half a million copies were printed.[111] If *The Road to Serfdom* had presented a defensive manifesto for an ideology in a state of retreat and disarray, *Capitalism and Freedom* provided a platform for a movement that was prepared for an aggressive offense. As was readily apparent to the book's growing readership, the era of apologetic moderation had passed.

Friedman's career as a public intellectual was initiated, cultivated, and promoted by a series of institutions designed to further the cause of free-market ideas. His first foray into popular pamphleteering had been precipitated by a generously funded commission from the Foundation for Economic Education; his political awakening had arrived under the auspices of the Mont Pèlerin Society and been nurtured and enriched by its members; and the systematization and popularization of his incipient ideas had been inspired and enabled by the ambitious summer conference program arranged and underwritten by the Volker Fund. His personal narrative provides an example of the cascading effect that minor institutional influences can have on the structure of an intellectual career, and an implicit validation of the long-term approach to ideological change that Hayek expounded and the administrators of the Volker Fund deliberately employed. These organizations did not create Friedman's ideology; he was uncowed by public controversy and fiercely protective of his independence as a scholar, and in many cases his positions represented a departure from his predecessors' ideas and his funders' expectations. Instead, they created an environment in which he was inspired to perceive his career in a political context and encouraged to share his perspective in a language that a general population could understand. To adopt terms that Milton Friedman would appreciate, institutions like the Volker Fund and the Mont Pèlerin Society are the venture capitalists of the intellectual world, allocating a broad dispersion of small investments with an extended time horizon and an understanding that one spectacular success can compensate for the toll of many minor failures. Friedman was the beneficiary of a network of organizations established by individuals who were uniquely reconciled to the assumption that the nature of their impact would not be revealed until long after their ability to appreciate it had passed.

In an implicit recognition of the changing framework of his social philosophy, Milton Friedman had stopped referring to himself as a "neoliberal" by the late 1950s. But he, too, suffered from the terminological challenge that had been discussed ad nauseam among free-market sympathizers since they first assembled at the "Colloque Lippmann" in Paris in 1938. During his career in the public arena, Friedman never settled on a consistent term to define his point of view. The word "libertarian" might have seemed a natural choice, but as early as 1957 he had determined to avoid it whenever possible. His problem with the term was purely "semantic": "It seems to me to lend itself greatly to confusion with the word 'libertine' and gives the impression of an anarchistic kind of a view."[112] Friedman sympathized with anarchism and admitted that he "would like to be a zero-government libertarian," but he believed that a society with no government whatsoever was not "a feasible social structure."[113] He was also highly conscious of a need to distance himself from anarchism in order to maintain credibility in public debates, and was constantly forced to defend himself against respectable opponents—like Senator Joseph Clark of Pennsylvania—who dismissed him as a "neo-anarchist" who would be "a fine candidate for president of the John Birch Society."[114] Although he sometimes acknowledged that popular parlance would label him a "conservative," Friedman expressed dissatisfaction with that term as well.[115] He could not identify himself with a social philosophy that implied a respect for the status quo. He told an interviewer in 1967 that "conservatism" is equivalent to a blind acceptance of the past, "including all the foolish legislation put in place from the New Deal forward."[116] When he was asked whether he was a conservative a decade later, he responded: "Good God, don't call me that. The conservatives are the New Dealers like Galbraith who want to keep things the way they are. They want to conserve the programs of the

New Deal."[117] As he had explained in *Capitalism and Freedom,* the problem with conservatism lay in its implied rejection of radicalism.[118] He later clarified that "radical" meant to him "going to the root of the matter," and that he viewed himself "as a radical in the same sense in which John Stuart Mill, Jeremy Bentham and others in 19th-century England regarded themselves as philosophical radicals."[119] He believed that the "rightful and proper" description for this social philosophy was "liberalism," but invoked a famous predecessor's explanation of the difficulties posed by the term. In his *History of Economic Analysis* Joseph Schumpeter wrote that it "has acquired a different—in fact almost the opposite—meaning since about 1900 and especially since about 1930: as a supreme, if unintended, compliment, the enemies of the system of private enterprise have thought it wise to appropriate its label."[120] The only term Friedman could find to describe himself had come to hold a contradictory connotation in the public mind. In this single area, for once in his life, he was at a loss for words.

Friedman's approach to the problem of terminology distinguished him from his predecessors in the Mont Pèlerin Society in significant ways. His concerns about the term "liberalism" were wholly semantic and not at all substantive. An earlier generation at Chicago and in the Mont Pèlerin Society had expressed explicit dissatisfactions with the "Manchester liberalism" of their ostensible predecessors and a desire to replace it with a novel worldview. In contrast, Friedman explained that he thought he "was going back to some fundamentals rather than creating anything new"; to him, the word "liberalism" was inadequate only because of the loss of the meaning it had once held.[121] His unequivocal representation of himself as a "radical" and his professed abhorrence of the term "conservative" revealed a sensibility that was unafraid of rapid and transformative social change. Hayek, Röpke, and Knight had emphasized the importance of continuity, and had centered their criticisms of the New Deal on the unprecedented pace and scope of the social transformations it entailed. Even in "Why I Am Not a Conservative," Hayek allowed that conservatism was "a legitimate, probably necessary, and certainly widespread attitude of opposition to drastic change," and he joined many conservatives in expressing respect for the benefits of gradual and organic social evolution.[122] With sensibilities formed in reaction to the dramatic political and economic upheavals of the first half of the twentieth century, the founders of the Mont Pèlerin Society perceived the maintenance of social stability as a foundational goal. Friedman, in contrast, advocated for the immediate implementation of his policy suggestions regardless of the difficulties entailed in a process of transition. He deliberately cultivated and carefully protected the persona of a contrarian gadfly in the venues of public debate. When he received an inquiry about joining Eisenhower's Council of Economic Advisers, he worried that in such a position it would seem "right and natural to compromise" and turned it down. "I think society needs a few kooks, a few extremists," he explained. He adopted a similar persona in his academic career. "To keep the fish that they carried on long journeys lively and fresh, sea captains used to introduce an eel into the barrel," his frequent sparring partner Paul Samuelson said. "In the economic profession, Milton Friedman is that eel."[123]

In his capacity as a "radical liberal," Friedman created a social philosophy that was much less conflicted than those of the leading figures in the early Mont Pèlerin Society. Whereas they tied themselves in philosophical and rhetorical knots attempting to escape failings of nineteenth-century liberalism that they readily acknowledged, Friedman simply argued that those ostensible failures were mythical creations of his ideological opponents. "The closest approach that the United States has had to true free enterprise capitalism was in the nineteenth century," he said. "Anybody was free to put up an enterprise, anybody was free to come to this country: it was a period when the motto on the Statue of Liberty meant what it said. It was a period in which the ordinary man experienced the greatest rise in his standard of life that was probably ever experienced in a comparable period in any country at any time." Against the contemporary historical profession's contention that nineteenth-century America was not a land of unencumbered capitalism, as well as the widely shared belief that the extremes of wealth and poverty in the nineteenth century had fostered social instability and discontent, Friedman sought to rehabilitate the classic narrative of the American frontier.[124] He then held that vision of a vibrant frontier capitalism against a depiction of a contemporary America overwrought by misguided bureaucracies.

The turning point in his narrative came in the 1930s, when socialist ideas that had long been germinating among the intellectual classes finally gained traction in the midst of a global economic catastrophe.[125] In his understanding of world history, there was an unproblematic correlation between government intervention and national decline: "Whether we look at the Golden Age of Ancient Greece, or the early centuries of the Roman era, or at the Renaissance, we see that widening individual freedom and quickening of economic growth went hand-in-hand—and that when freedom was destroyed, economic decline was not far behind."[126] With all the bureaucratic accretions of the decades after the implementation of the New Deal, America was approaching "a real dividing point, a real crossing point in our national development." In the near future, he ominously predicted, the scales would tip, and the country would lose the spoils it had reaped in its less encumbered years.[127] Friedman valorized an idealized vision of the nineteenth century and then leveraged that vision to lambast the administrative practices of the present day. Through the sheer force of certainty he sought to turn what his predecessors viewed as a potentially insurmountable weakness for advocates of free markets—the example of the nineteenth century—into a source of rhetorical strength. Its factual merits aside, the endeavor was not without success. As one colleague ruefully allowed, "I wish I was as sure of one thing as Milton Friedman is of all things."[128]

Friedman's consistent preference for unconstrained markets combined with his methodological orientation toward empiricism to inspire him to propose an astonishing range of specific alterations to governmental practice. With few exceptions, the previous generation of academics in the Mont Pèlerin Society had limited their engagement in public questions, and their discourse tended overwhelmingly to unfold at the level of the general rather than the specific. Friedman, in striking contrast, filled his speeches with detailed suggestions about the myriad ways in which his philosophical orientation could be reflected in legislation. In the decades after the publication of *Capitalism and Freedom* in 1962, he advocated a range of ideas that restructured the terms of public debate about issues of fundamental importance.

Friedman's popular rhetoric drew heavily on his academic work from the 1950s and early 1960s, which launched a multipronged assault on the Keynesian consensus. In *A Theory of the Consumption Function* Friedman challenged the belief that households would rapidly shift their consumption habits to incorporate new infusions of capital, arguing instead that they made such decisions on the basis of longer-term estimates of their "permanent income." This contested the assumption that temporary shifts in income would have a significant effect on aggregate demand and raised new questions about the capacity of fiscal policy to counteract an economic downturn.[129] Meanwhile, in *A Monetary History of the United States* and a collection of articles from his workshop at Chicago, he also brought renewed attention to the importance of money.[130] Along with his collaborator, Anna Schwartz, he pored over historical data to argue for a close relationship between movements in the stock of money and changes in income and prices.[131] They assailed the historical record of monetary authorities, describing the Great Depression as the "Great Contraction" and blaming its severity on the deflationary policies of the Federal Reserve.[132] Elsewhere, Friedman attacked the international monetary framework, criticizing both the Bretton Woods system and the gold standard in order to make a case for the feasibility of flexible exchange rates.[133] And in a presidential address before the American Economic Association, he criticized the widespread assumption that there was a long-term trade-off between inflation and unemployment. Unanticipated inflation, he acknowledged, would lead real wages to go down and thereby precipitate a temporary increase in employment. But employees would rapidly account for this new inflation and begin bargaining for commensurate increases in their nominal wages. As a result, inflation could stave off unemployment only as long as it grew at an accelerating rate. Such a path was self-evidently unsustainable: in attempting to inflate their way to full employment, governments were courting disaster.[134]

Friedman readily acknowledged that it was "difficult" to relay these views in a form that was "accessible to the general reader," but such concerns did not stop him from trying.[135] He devoted two early chapters in *Capitalism and Freedom* to monetary policy and international finance, his first collection of popular essays focused almost exclusively on these issues, and he dwelled on them more frequently than any other topic in his columns for *Newsweek*.[136] His most persistent theme was the need to establish a rule forcing the monetary authority to keep the growth of the stock of money within a specified range.[137] He missed few opportunities in the late 1960s to contrast what he saw as the lurching behavior of the Federal Reserve with the apparent consistency and predictability of his rule-based approach. A series of prescient predictions in the late 1960s, followed by the onset in the 1970s of precisely the kind of inflationary recession he had anticipated in his presidential address, led Friedman's suggestions on monetary policy to achieve broad influence. In 1979 Paul Volcker set aside his reservations and embraced a central tenet of Friedman's advice, inducing the Federal Reserve to begin targeting the money supply rather than interest rates. It soon became clear that the proliferation of new financial vehicles muddied the estimates that this approach required, and Volcker's monetarist experiment was abandoned.[138] Its adoption in the midst of an employment crisis and runaway inflation, however, signified the degree to which Friedman's popular and professional writings had shifted prevailing views on monetary policy.

In conjunction with his peers at Chicago, Friedman also came to adopt a much more audacious and aggressive stance against antitrust activities than his mentors. One of the simplest ways to restore the competitive landscape of the nineteenth century, he argued, was to abandon the ongoing attempts to restrict private monopoly. He called for the repeal of all aspects of the Sherman Antitrust Act excluding those that involved the nonenforcement of certain contracts. In justification, he argued that "there has hardly ever been a private monopoly that has been able to maintain its monopoly position without assistance from the government."[139] He asserted that with the removal of tariffs, significant revisions to the corporate tax code, and the elimination of special governmental support, all serious problems related to monopoly would be solved.[140] The very notion of "pure monopoly" was troubling to him because "everything has substitutes," even if those substitutes take a very different form.[141]

He also targeted the system of federal taxation. In contrast to the current system in which he thought taxes were much too high and much too complex, he advocated a single flat rate on income with none of the "loopholes and deductions that enable so many persons to avoid paying their fair share of the taxes and that require so many more to take tax considerations into account in their every economic decision." To address the needs of poorer citizens who would thereby need to pay higher rates, he proposed a doubling of the "disgracefully low" personal exemption.[142] He would eliminate the tax exemption for charities, which he believed had "no justification," left nonprofits beholden to the state, and encouraged their institutional constituents to advocate higher taxes since it "cost them nothing" and increased "the value of the tax exempt privilege."[143] He argued against the taxation of corporations, suggesting that any earnings above dividends should be attributed to the individual stockholders and taxed appropriately.[144] He also sought to abolish the estate tax. "There is no such thing as an effective inheritance tax," he stated. "People will always find a way around it."[145] Counterarguments on ethical grounds failed to move him. "This distinction is untenable," he wrote. "Is there any greater ethical justification for the high returns to the individual who inherits from his parents a peculiar voice for which there is a great demand than for the high returns to the individual who inherits property?"[146] Friedman also identified areas of the tax code that advantaged "living in sin" and argued that they should be restructured either to become neutral or to encourage marriage.[147] He was a tireless advocate for "constitutional measures that set a limit to total government spending both at the state level and at the federal level," often participating in advocacy tours on their behalf.[148] Many of these policy proposals became central components of the Republican platform in the final quarter of the twentieth and the beginning of the twenty-first century.

Friedman's most famous, and perhaps most influential, proposal in the area of taxation was his scheme for a "negative income tax." In *Capitalism and Freedom* he argued that if the government was going to provide aid to the poor, it could do so more efficiently in the form of an income-tax credit than in the existing network of welfare benefits and target programs. He proposed a graduated subsidy for individuals who earned an income below a preestablished floor. Such a system, he asserted, would eliminate much of the waste entailed in administering conventional welfare and substantially ameliorate its market-distorting effects.[149] It had the further virtue, he added in an article in 1968, of treating its recipients "as responsible individuals, not as incompetent wards of the state."[150] The idea was one of Friedman's most popular with the political Left; he told the Chamber of Commerce of the United States in 1966 that it had "been greeted with considerable (though far from unanimous) enthusiasm on the left and with considerable (though again far from unanimous) hostility on the right."[151] He viewed the program as clearly beneficial to advocates of limited government and was puzzled by both parties' responses. Nevertheless, he embraced the issue as a demonstration that market-friendly policies could manifest compassion, and over time he succeeded in generating significant political interest in his proposal. Although a negative income tax has never been pursued in the mode Friedman suggested, his arguments helped inspire the reappraisal of welfare that led to the Earned Income Tax Credit programs that were first implemented in 1975, made permanent in 1978, and dramatically expanded between 1986 and 1993, as well as the subsequent welfare-to-work programs implemented in the Personal Responsibility and Work Opportunity Reconciliation Act of 1996.[152]

Friedman brought an equally prolific policy imagination to areas of governmental management and regulation. He was uniformly skeptical of regulatory agencies and argued that many of them should be shuttered altogether. One of his most frequent targets was the Federal Communications Commission; he proposed "abolishing the FCC and having a truly free radio and TV to parallel a free press" by auctioning "off to the highest bidders the rights to specified channels now embodied in licenses."[153] He argued that the Food and Drug Administration (FDA) "should be abolished" as well, because the harm caused by its excessively cautious delays in approving drugs outweighed the dangers entailed in making those same drugs available on an open market.[154] The failures of the FDA, in his opinion, were irremediable: "The way the FDA now behaves, and the adverse consequences, are not an accident, not a result of some easily corrected human mistake, but a consequence of its constitution in precisely the same way that a meow is related to the constitution of a cat."[155] Friedman was also an implacable opponent of the minimum wage, which he provocatively described as "the most anti-Negro law on our statute books—in its effect not its intent."[156] Agricultural subsidies should, he argued, be abolished altogether.[157] If the public wanted to regulate environmental pollution, he was adamant that it should do so through effluent taxes rather than regulatory standards.[158] And in the wake of Hurricane Agnes in 1972, he implied that the federal government should not provide aid after a natural disaster. Such aid encouraged the inhabitation of unsafe areas, he asserted, and would inevitably lead to a situation in which the government needed to regulate where one could and could not live. Here, as elsewhere, he urged a devolution of responsibility to private individuals and organizations. "Surely," he wrote, "nothing has done so much over the years to destroy a sense of human community, of individual responsibility for assisting the less fortunate, as the bureaucratizing of charity."[159]

Often to the dismay of his Republican admirers, Friedman was equally iconoclastic in his approach to foreign policy. He was an ardent opponent of the military draft and vigorously lobbied Nixon for its abolishment. Nixon appointed him to the Advisory Commission on an All-Volunteer Armed Force, which precipitated the official elimination of the draft in 1973.[160] Friedman later recalled the event as his "most important" policy accomplishment.[161] He believed that the country's borders should be completely open and unrestricted to immigrants, although he stipulated that this would only be practicable if accompanied by a complete rollback of government welfare.[162] He was a consistent critic of the Marshall Plan and disapproved of all foreign aid, which he said tended "to strengthen governments in the foreign countries relative to the private sector, to promote centralized planning and socialist methods of control, and to reduce the strength and the force of the free enterprise sector, political democracy and freedom."[163] And he favored the unilateral imposition of free trade, arguing that reciprocal negotiations would be "lengthy, time-consuming, and ineffective."[164] Cumulatively, these proposals reveal the uniformity with which Friedman argued that markets should remain free from coercive incursions, and demonstrate the disagreements with the Republican Party that his consistency sometimes inspired.

Despite having spent his life in a university environment, Friedman was sharply critical of government aid to institutions of higher learning. He excoriated state-financed universities for imposing "costs on low-income people to provide subsidies to high-income people."[165] Taxing poor citizens to help finance the education of middle- and upper-class citizens was, he dramatically asserted, the "great scandal of our times."[166] He recognized that emphasizing the portion of tax revenue that came from the poor could make cultural institutions appear frivolous, and he leveraged that rhetorical insight in his assaults on state financing of the Corporation for Public Broadcasting and the National Endowments for the Arts and the Humanities as well. Such uses of government funds were "particularly indefensible," he asserted, because they targeted programs that "have traditionally been supported by private funds" and imposed "taxes on low-income people to finance luxuries for high-income people."[167] He was also deeply suspicious of government involvement in the earlier stages of schooling, but was willing to consider alternatives that fell short of the complete termination of financial support. In *Capitalism and Freedom* he suggested a voucher system: "Parents who choose to send their children to private schools would be paid a sum equal to the estimated cost of educating a child in a public school, provided that at least this sum was spent on education in an approved school." Such an approach "would permit competition to develop. The development and improvement of all schools would thus be stimulated."[168] This proposal inaugurated decades of intensive public policy debates, and remained one of Friedman's primary interests; in 1996 he and his wife Rose jointly established the Friedman Foundation for Educational Choice to continue advocating for voucher proposals in the public sphere.

Milton Friedman had arrived at a philosophy of capitalism and a program for political action that differentiated him from all of his mentors and most of his peers. In contrast to their deliberate moderation and rhetorical restraint, he expressed an uncompromising belief that markets would engender better social outcomes than programs administered by the government. This unapologetic support for laissez-faire made him an unprecedented anomaly among respectable academics in the postwar

American public sphere and in itself generated substantial interest in his ideas. Friedman's scientific reputation and radical self-presentation alone would have made him a formidable figure in the conservative intellectual world, but he multiplied his influence by combining these attributes with an extraordinarily inventive approach to public policy. The unorthodoxy of his perspective enabled him to apply a single set of analytic tools to generate a profusion of novel ideas, and he presented his readers with an abundance of explicit proposals that were clearly derived from and representative of a singular worldview. Over time and in combination, these qualities enabled him to shift the parameters of public debate.

Friedman's career has been patterned by Paul Krugman on the model of a counterreformation: a return to the status quo before Keynes. "If Keynes was Luther," Krugman quipped, "Friedman was Ignatius of Loyola."[169] But the narrative of Friedman's influence cannot be traced through such a clean reversal of the lines his predecessor traced. For one thing, Krugman's imputation of the hegemony of neoclassicism and laissez-faire in the years preceding Keynes's *General Theory* was misplaced; economists at the time relied heavily on institutionalist methodologies with an implicit leftist valence that were discarded by most of the profession, with the notable exception of Galbraith, in subsequent years.[170] Perhaps more important, the positions advocated by the conservative economists of the previous generation bore little resemblance to those espoused by Friedman in the years after the publication of *Capitalism and Freedom*. By the early 1940s Frank Knight, Jacob Viner, and Henry Simons in the United States, Wilhelm Röpke in Geneva, and Friedrich Hayek and Lionel Robbins in London all recognized a broad scope for the government to intervene, with beneficial effects, in the workings of the economy and the distribution of goods. All of them manifested reservations about the effects of unhindered competition and increasing skepticism toward the social and political viability of laissez-faire. In the case of Friedman, as Krugman accurately observed, it is "extremely hard" to find places where he "acknowledged the possibility that markets could go wrong, or that government intervention could serve a useful purpose."[171] The universality of Friedman's belief in the efficacy of free markets exceeded even that of the nineteenth-century theorists whose legacy Hayek had spent the postwar years working to overcome. His was not a Spencerian or Sumnerian world in which free markets dealt crushing blows to some in order to contribute to the greater advancement of humanity. Rather, it was one in which incontrovertible benefits redounded, in a display of spectacular bounty, to people of all kinds and in all situations. He represented markets as an unremitting good.

When Hayek first spoke before the members of the Mont Pèlerin Society, he explained that his goal was to consolidate the efforts of those who sought "to reconstruct a liberal philosophy which can fully meet the objections which in the eyes of most of our contemporaries have defeated the promise the earlier liberalism offered."[172] The rise of Milton Friedman represents both the realization of Hayek's dream of inspiring broad popular support for the benefits free markets have to offer, and the final failure of his ambition to create a new social philosophy that would moderate the excesses of prior modes of market advocacy. The irony of the Mont Pèlerin Society is that it achieved its goal of generating social change at the expense of the new philosophy that its members had assumed any such change would require. Friedman served as both the society's greatest engine of influence and its most forceful exponent of an uncompromising adherence to the market mechanism. To Hayek and the other founders of the Mont Pèlerin Society, Friedman's ascent within its orbit reflected the collapse of its attempt to integrate a restrained defense of free markets into a traditionalist worldview. In the broader social environment Friedman's rise portended, and precipitated, the triumphant return of laissez-faire.

6

MORAL CAPITAL

Shortly before Hayek's departure from the University of Chicago, Milton Friedman was scheduled to give a presentation on his political ideas to a weekly convocation at Haverford College. The *Haverford News* recounted that "most students, upon hearing that Mr. Friedman was an economist, calmly settled back for the usual espousal of big government and the welfare state that all intelligent people—especially intelligent economists—are known to support." Friedman, however, was intent on defying their expectations. He had already informed the college president of his dissatisfactions about expounding his concept of freedom to a compulsory audience. As he rose to the podium, he asked the faculty and staff in the balcony to finish filling out their attendance records. He then informed the students that they were free to leave if they wished, and sat down in his chair to wait. Friedman later recalled that "the students hadn't really thought that I was going to do it and when I did, about one or two people got up to leave and the rest of them booed them because obviously, I was talking on their level." He then proceeded to deliver a speech titled "The Road to Hell," assailing government-provided health care, public housing, foreign aid, and agricultural subsidies. The *Haverford News* recounted that as they heard him condemn "every institution dear to the modern liberal" in "colorful and provocative" language, the students were quickly "shaken out of their lethargy." Friedman recalled his audacious opening to the speech with evident pride, observing that he had "seldom had a student audience who were so completely on my side as that group, even though the political atmosphere at Haverford was very much to the left."[1] He had disarmed a potentially unsympathetic audience with a combination of bold self-presentation and unconventional ideas.

Although Friedman remembered the dramatics of his Haverford presentation as a uniquely impressive "coup," its underlying narrative was repeated throughout his public career. As an economist, he was uniquely— perhaps unprecedentedly—skilled as a rhetorician. He had mastered the difficult art of persuading diverse audiences to take seriously an unconventional point of view. "No other American economist of the first rank can match Friedman's forensic skills and persuasive powers," the *Washington Post* wrote in 1963. Those intrepid enough to serve as his public sparring partners often found themselves "torn to shreds," as the *New York Times* said of a former chairman of the Council of Economic Advisers, Walter Heller, in 1970. His performances before Congress left some of its members spellbound; one said, using terms rarely applied to an economist, that Friedman could "thrill me as nobody has since Teddy Roosevelt." Paul Samuelson backhandedly remarked that Friedman's personal powers of persuasion were so formidable that his ideas, if he suddenly passed away, would disappear with him.[2] To the continuing benefit of his like-minded colleagues in the economics profession and his allies in popular politics, Friedman demonstrated an extraordinary facility at the emerging practice of messaging.

During the 1960s Friedman became a forceful advocate for laissez-faire on the public stage, developing an argumentative framework that would provide the foundation for much of the Republican Party's policy platform in the decades that followed. He transfixed audiences, both in frequent public lectures and in increasingly ubiquitous appearances on the printed page, with his formidable rhetorical capabilities and the relentless consistency of his message. While his predecessors in the Mont Pèlerin Society had approached their public roles with explicit reservations, Friedman embraced his with relish. Within months of the publication of *Capitalism and Freedom* he had commenced a rapid transition from academic economist to public policy advocate, and he enthusiastically devoted his full attention and energy to the cultivation of his emerging role. "Milton is back but Chicago is only a base," George Stigler wrote in 1963; "the public is gradually discovering that he is the leading conservative intellectual in the country, and he takes to lecturing as he does to economics."[3]

Friedman's predecessors in the Mont Pèlerin Society had largely aligned themselves with a rhetoric of deliberate moderation, attempting to pull their mainstream colleagues closer to their positions by ceding ground wherever possible. His approach was different: he was a controversialist who attempted to generate agreement by restructuring the very terms of the debate. He worked to convince his audiences that he shared their most humane ends—the well-being of the poor and the establishment of a broad-based prosperity—and then labored to demonstrate that they were misguided about the means to achieve them. He amplified this rhetoric with an unapologetic populism that belied the elitism and detachment of previous free-market economists. Markets, he argued, constituted the only truly progressive social order, and the negative freedom they enabled would generate the best possible outcome for America's most humble residents. Cumulatively, Friedman's new polemical mode heralded both a return to the market advocacy of the nineteenth century and the arrival of something wholly new. In his efforts to expound his approach to political economy to the public, Friedman developed the rhetorical architecture of an unapologetically market-centered world.

Friedman framed his market advocacy around a distinctive rendering of the morals of capitalism. Previous members of the Mont Pèlerin Society had adopted complex and conflicted approaches to the relationship between markets and moral ideals. Frank Knight, for example, saw little or no connection between morality and production for the marketplace. Society appears "to search in vain for any really ethical basis of approval for competition as a basis for an ideal type of human relations," he wrote. "Its only justification is that it is effective in getting things done," he continued, "but any candid answer to the question, 'what things,' compels the admission that they leave much to be desired."[4] Friedrich Hayek's assessment of the moral landscape of capitalism was less bleak than Knight's, but he did not believe that markets necessarily rewarded merit. Instead, his market advocacy was premised on the more restrained claim that markets provided an ethically neutral arbiter, and that this was preferable to any system that tried to determine outcomes on the basis of a preconceived notion of the good.[5] Friedman abandoned these qualifications and complications, arguing instead that markets elegantly and reliably promoted virtuous behavior. In adopting this approach, he was able to connect his market advocacy to a simple, holistic, and rhetorically compelling worldview. Markets, according to Friedman, provided an ideal system for directing compensation to the deserving, and any attempt to interfere with them on ethical grounds should therefore be subject to doubt.

Friedman did not share Knight's concerns that unmoderated capitalism might give rise to moral degradations. Instead, he saw markets as a mode of social organization that incentivized virtue. "I would say that a free enterprise system tends to promote a higher standard of morality and a greater relation between values and actions than almost any other," he wrote in private correspondence in 1978. "The reason is because it emphasizes individual responsibility. It therefore tends to promote values of self-reliance, of commitment. By ruling out in principle at least coercion it requires emphasis on mutual benefit which is a far more ennobling creed than the use of force. Of course this is an idealization."[6] Friedman's emphasis on making claims that could be subjected to empirical tests, and his reluctance to impose his own ethical standards on the choices made by others, left him with no criterion to evaluate the success of a system apart from the capacity it engendered to satisfy the wants that people appeared to have. But in making the individual "responsible for and to himself," he believed that capitalism would inherently "lead to a higher and more desirable moral climate." In his worldview there was no social trade-off between hedonism and virtue. Capitalism tended "to develop an atmosphere which is more favorable to the development on the one hand of a higher moral climate of responsibility and on the other to greater achievements in every realm of human activity."[7] In the unremitting magic of the market exchange, it was possible to have one's cake and eat it too.

Friedman conceded that in the case of particular individuals, actions attributable to motives other than—and possibly contradictory to—the price mechanism were legitimate and at times even laudable. But he categorically asserted that no motive apart from enlightened self-interest (which was equated, in the case of the business corporation, with the bottom line) was valid for entities consisting of more than one individual. He provided a brief but clear articulation of this perspective in *Capitalism and Freedom*, and several years later presented a more detailed justification of his view to a seminar at the Institute for Religious and Social Studies.[8] If businesses were asked to serve any entity other than their shareholders, he argued, they would merely create openings for leaner businesses to supplant them. Further, he ominously predicted that ceding ground in this area would open the back door to government-run enterprises and thereby prove "subversive of a free society." "If these businessmen and labor leaders are 'public' servants who are exercising a 'public' function, then it is inevitable that sooner or later they be selected through an explicitly political process and their powers be circumscribed and their responsibilities delineated by a political mechanism," he told the attendees.[9] He presented a paper on the topic at the Mont Pèlerin Society in 1970, and shortly thereafter published a version in the *New York Times Magazine* under the audacious title "The Social Responsibility of Business Is to Increase Its Profits."[10] "What does it mean to say that 'business' has responsibilities?" he asked. The answer, he concluded, was nothing: "Only people can have responsibilities." He then presented a simple binary: either his readers supported shareholder income as the sole mission of a corporate entity, or they did not support the price mechanism at all. The doctrine of social responsibility "does not differ in philosophy from the most explicitly collectivist doctrine," he concluded. "It differs only by professing to believe that collectivist ends can be attained without collectivist means."[11]

In developing this argument, Friedman drew on Frank Knight's aphorism that "business is business," which Knight had defined as meaning that "business is one thing, and 'charity' another." Knight, however, had accompanied that statement with a series of characteristic caveats: it assumed mutual free consent, which precluded the modes of persuasion often adopted in advertising; public engagement and oversight would be necessary to avoid externalities; and the pursuit of profits "must be sometimes seasoned with mercy."[12] The extent of Friedman's departure from Knight's position was evident in his comments in a 1972 interview in the *Business and Society Review*. "If a chemist feels it is immoral to make napalm, he can solve his problem by getting a job where he doesn't have to," he told the interviewer. "He will pay a price. But the ultimate effect will be that if many, many people feel that way, the cost of hiring people to make napalm will be high, napalm will be expensive, and less of it will be used. This is another way in which the free market does provide a much more sensitive and subtle voting mechanism than does the political system."[13] Friedman's comments here strongly implied that any social harms brought about by a transaction could be redressed through the effect of the qualms of unique individuals on the marketplace price. He did not concede the existence of a collective-action problem even in matters involving a weapon of extraordinary force. The best approach, he insisted, lay in the complete devolution of responsibility to individual agents.

Friedman's writings and speeches frequently relied on, but never substantively addressed, an embedded theory of agency. He relegated group agency to the realm of conceptual impossibility and redirected all questions of morality to the level of the individual. "I think only people can be altruists," he told the congressional Joint Economic Committee in 1971.[14] "Government can't have a responsibility any more than [a] business can," he elaborated the following year. "The only entities which can have responsibilities are people."[15] "What would it mean to say that a system is moral?" he asked a businessman in private correspondence in 1978. "Isn't morality a characteristic of people rather than of rocks or buildings or systems?"[16] Entities involving multiple individuals existed, he believed, solely to adjudicate and apply their discrete interests. In the vast majority of cases, he determined that the efficient achievement of that goal relied on the faithful application of the price mechanism.

The choice between resorting to government and relying on the market was, in Friedman's terms, one between "bureaucratic democracy" and "participatory democracy."[17] The act of participation required choices that, he believed, were lost to the individual who consigned final authority to a politician rather than the market. Friedman's preference for adjudication through market prices rather than political structures was based, in part, on arguments developed by two colleagues in the Mont Pèlerin Society who also received graduate educations at the University of Chicago. Relying on recent scholarship from James Buchanan and George Stigler, Friedman concluded that politicians are led, through the pursuit of their own interests, to advocate policies that are injurious to the public good.[18] In *The Calculus of Consent* Buchanan and his colleague Gordon Tullock had employed an assumption of methodological individualism and the tools of basic game theory to arrive at the conclusion that "majority voting will tend to cause overinvestment in the public sector relative to the private sector."[19] In his work on regulatory agencies, Stigler had determined that industries in democratic societies tended to capture the entities created to regulate them.[20] Both analyses depicted politicians as actors who pursued their rational self-interest, and both found that the inherent logic of the political process led them to implement policies that were against the best interests of the broader public. Friedman frequently referred to this insight as the "invisible hand in politics," which he defined on the bicentennial of *The Wealth of Nations* as "the precise reverse of the invisible hand in the market": politicians seeking to promote the public interest are "led by an invisible hand to promote an end which was no part of their intention." As a result, they sacrifice "the public interest to the special interest, the interest of the consumers to that of producers, of the masses who never go to college to that of those who attend college, of the poor working-class saddled with employment taxes to the middle class who get disproportionate benefits from social security, and so down the line."[21] In a rejoinder to the common assumption that market advocates were allies of big business and the wealthy, Friedman was careful to emphasize the injurious effects of the political process on consumers, the uneducated, and the poor. The implicit conclusion was that more or less everyone—even those commonly criticized by the Right for benefiting at the expense of others—was harmed when the government intervened.

The strength of Friedman's conviction that the government worked to the detriment of its constituents at times led him to express a desire for it to perform poorly in its intended tasks. "The most important single cause for hope, beyond any doubt, is the incredible inefficiency of government," he told students at the University of Pittsburgh. "People are always complaining about government waste. I don't complain about government waste; I welcome it. . . . Efficiency is a vice if it is devoted to doing the wrong thing. If the government were spending the forty per cent of our income that it now spends efficiently, we would long since have lost our freedom."[22] Friedman implied that the individual harms caused by government inefficiencies were, in both their obstruction of politicians' goals and their erosion of public confidence in government action, perversely beneficial. He believed that individuals who sought the nation's best interest should in many cases root for its government to fail.

Despite advocating for ideas that had long been associated with those in positions of privilege, Friedman was able to present himself as a genuine and emphatic populist. His appearance helped him assume the role; standing about five feet tall, he projected the unaffected aura, as the patrician *New York Times* observed, of a "pushy Jewish kid from New Jersey."[23] His abhorrence of all modes of exclusivity extended even into the realm of private conversation, in which he frequently cited the personal mantra: "What I say to one person, I say to everyone."[24] This claim, which is validated in the papers maintained in Friedman's archives, made him a uniquely controversial public figure and a singularly unsurprising private correspondent. He attempted to treat all people equally regardless of their rank or position, and his personal files are filled with multi-page responses to the peculiar questions of obscure individuals. He also expressed a willingness to consult with any political figure who actively sought his input. "I am willing to advise anyone who asks me," he told the *San Francisco Examiner and Chronicle* in 1976. "I have no partisan scruples about giving advice."[25] This maxim provided Friedman with a compelling, if to many unsatisfying, justification of his relations with the Chilean government during his visit in 1975. More important, it provided an appearance of legitimacy to his assertions that his economic philosophy was constructed with the well-being of average individuals—and even the destitute—as a paramount goal. Despite their considerable efforts, it was difficult for members of the American Left to brand Friedman as a deliberate enemy of the working class. One could argue that Friedman was wrong, but his public persona made it very hard to represent him as maliciously so.

Friedman studiously represented his free-market philosophy as a manifestation of respect for the perspectives and preferences of average individuals, and worked to convince his sympathizers to adopt a similar approach. In a 1960 meeting of the Mont Pèlerin Society, he excoriated his colleagues for demonstrating a "lack of respect for the masses of the people" in frequent statements that "depreciate[d]" them and assumed that they were "ignorant." He continued: "I think, if we look at the fact, we will come to the conclusion that the situation is almost the reverse. If by and large we ask why has freedom been preserved in our society, it is largely because the masses of the people has [*sic*] stubbornly stuck to basic values. . . . If the masses of the people would change and were as easily moved as the intellectual classes, I do not think, we would be living in a free society. (laughter) (applause)." He asserted that the fundamental plea of the society's members should be that "people are people and there were no such things as masses and classes" but rather simply "individuals."[26] Friedman's constant emphasis on choice was a reflection of his approach; he sought to represent free-market economists as possessors of respect for the manifest preferences of average consumers, and supporters of government intervention as paternalists imposing their beliefs on those less enlightened than themselves. He told *Playboy* that "what the critics really complain about" is "that under capitalism, consumers get what they want rather than what the critics think they should have."[27] Intellectuals were sympathetic to collectivism, he asserted, because it presented a social model in which they would have more power than they would under free enterprise.[28] His deprecation of a language of "classes" drew on an insight that advocates of free markets should represent themselves as guardians of government neutrality, in contrast to a perceived left-wing tendency to divide societies into oppositional groups. He hoped to turn his political allies into defenders of equality and the ordinary individual, and interventionists into practitioners of social differentiation and paternalist elites. Characteristically, Friedman solved a rhetorical problem by restructuring the terms of the debate.

Recognizing that advocates of free markets had long been considered apologists for the depredations of big business, Friedman particularly emphasized his differences with corporate executives. He expressed continued frustration with a "failure to distinguish between being pro–free enterprise and pro-business," arguing that the misunderstanding has "led persons opposed to particular existing businesses to oppose free enterprise."[29] Businessmen, Friedman argued, were constantly in search of special privileges. They worked relentlessly, and in democratic societies often with success, to obtain competitive advantage from the government. The result, he believed, was a cavalcade of special-interest legislation that ultimately redounded to everyone's harm. "Over and over again you have the big businessman who talks very effectively about the great virtues of free enterprise and, at the same time, he is off on a plane to Washington to push for special legislation or some special measures for his own benefit," he recounted. "I don't blame him from the point of view of his business, but I do blame him because very often he is shortsighted and ultimately does himself more harm than good."[30] In an invocation of the dual villains of populism, Friedman repeatedly argued that "the two groups that threaten the free market most are businessmen and intellectuals."[31] The one exception he carved out was for "small businessmen," whose interests, he argued, consistently aligned with his own economic vision.[32] Small businessmen shared the corporate executives' understanding of the virtues of a free-enterprise system without the latter's capacity to acquire special advantages from the federal government. Friedman wisely refused to situate himself against the popular discontent with corporate America. Instead, he attempted to leverage that discontent through arguments that the most troubling aspects of business enterprises were wholly attributable to government interventions on their behalf.

Friedman's populism was complemented by a relentless emphasis on the optimism of his outlook. He had derived a crucial lesson from the nadir of laissez-faire economics in the 1930s that subsequently defined his approach to the public discussion of economic ideas. At the London School of Economics in the 1930s, when Hayek and Robbins were together on the faculty and Austrian business-cycle theory was prevalent, "the dominant view was that the depression was an inevitable result of the prior boom" and that "the only sound policy was to let the depression run its course, bring down money costs, and eliminate weak and unsound firms." Such fatalist rhetoric, Friedman believed, was unsalable in a world searching for dynamic solutions. In contrast, the news of Keynes's interpretation of the Depression "must have come like a flash of light on a dark night. It offered a far less hopeless diagnosis of the disease. More important, it offered a more immediate, less painful, and more effective cure in the form of budget deficits. It is easy to see how a young, vigorous, and generous mind would have been attracted to it."[33] Ironically, it was Friedman's observation of the ascent of Keynesianism that demonstrated to him the importance of providing the public with policy proposals that offered practical solutions to the felt problems of the day. Free-market economists needed to couch their ideas in a language that appealed to the public's intrinsic desire to act. His critique of existing policies was therefore always paired with his confidence that the major contemporary social and economic problems could be redressed.

From the very first meeting of the Mont Pèlerin Society, he pleaded with his colleagues to abandon a rhetoric of stasis and resignation. "Liberalism is in a curious position, and on the downgrade," he told them in a preliminary discussion of the society's statement of aims. "It is at times used as a defence of the status quo, instead of being dynamic and progressive. We want to make sure that our manifesto is concerned in the progress of man's welfare. We have to distinguish between the negative and the positive approach. Broad statements on which we can very easily agree are negative in nature. We ought to agree on the necessity for a positive approach."[34] He urged them to include in the statement "the idea that liberalism has a humanitarian aim and is a progressive philosophy."[35] Although he had little success at persuading his early colleagues in the Mont Pèlerin Society to alter their rhetorical mode, his work exemplified the importance of a positive tone. He rarely enumerated the failures of government intervention to achieve its intended goals without presenting a contrary argument that free-market policies could meet those goals more successfully and at little cost. Friedman could channel the opposing languages of the critic and the visionary, the realist and the utopian. He appealed simultaneously to dissatisfaction with the status quo and the desire for a deus ex machina, and he ensured that his gloom about his ideological opponents' policies was always tempered by a visceral excitement at the alternatives he proposed.

Another rhetorical maneuver in Friedman's repertoire entailed the simultaneous invocation of abstract ideals and immediately achievable goals. He endorsed a conception of government that was vanishingly small, and occasionally articulated a social ideal that closely resembled that of a radical libertarian fringe. Despite these affinities, he informed members of the International Society for Individual Liberty in 1990 that utopian visions should be only one component of their contributions to the public debate. "It is of course desirable to have a vision of the ideal, of Utopia," he said. "Far be it from me to denigrate that. But we can't stop there. If we do, we become a cult or a religion, and not a living, vital force." Instead, it was necessary to come up with solutions that would help inaugurate an extended process of transition: "You cannot simply describe the utopian solution, and leave it to somebody else how we get from here to there. . . . It is irresponsible, immoral I would say, simply to say, 'Oh well, somehow or other we'll overnight drop the whole thing.' You have to have some mechanism of going from here to there." Friedman was attempting to overcome the perceived failures of his generational predecessors. Some early members of the Mont Pèlerin Society had been so focused on presenting ideas that were palatable to their contemporaries that he believed their critique of existing practices had lost its critical edge. He worried that without frequent reference to foundational ideals, debates would regress to a reactive mean. Others, however, had clung so tightly to their ideals that they found themselves unable to engage in dialogue with people in positions of political power or even, in some cases, their peers. (Friedman noted Ludwig von Mises and Ayn Rand as prominent examples of this shortcoming.)[36] He perceived the challenge faced by advocates of free markets as one of maintaining reference to a utopian ideal while presenting partial solutions that were politically feasible in the present day. In adopting this approach, Friedman gave himself the capacity to address libertarian audiences as one of their own while at the same time participating as more than a fringe player in broader venues of public debate.

Many of Friedman's most influential policy suggestions were explicitly formed in this spirit of incremental compromise. Most notably, he argued vociferously in favor of school vouchers and a negative income tax while acknowledging that both were way stations on the road toward the abandonment of government involvement in education and welfare that he ultimately sought. "We are talking at cross purposes because of what I regard as the important necessity of keeping clearly separate the long-run ideal goal and tactical steps that may be appropriate in moving toward it," he told Patrick Buchanan. "I have long supported and pushed the voucher plan for schooling as well as the negative income tax in welfare. In both cases I do so not because these are necessarily part of my ideal utopian society but because they seem to me the most effective steps, given where we are, in moving toward where we want to go." The voucher system was a trojan horse that would enable the gradual extinction of government-run schools: "By permitting parents to supplement the voucher, it is possible to conceive of the system developing into one where the government contribution becomes less and less." Similarly, the negative income tax would allow for the gradual diminution of welfare benefits until they disappeared altogether. "Exactly the same logic underlies my belief in a negative income tax," he told Buchanan. "I see no other way in which we can go from our present situation toward the ultimate situation you and I would like."[37] Friedman was vocal about these long-term goals when he engaged in discussion with ideological sympathizers, but he only rarely mentioned them when addressing a general audience. He was a radical idealist who constructed his public policy proposals with a deep and perceptive attention to strategy. Few public figures in modern history have matched a utopian social philosophy with such close attention to the maintenance of practical goals.

During the years surrounding World War II, the leading market advocates in the United States had generally remained distant from public discussion and wary of popular audiences. In their occasional public appearances Hayek and Mises were received as exotic specimens from the Viennese intellectual world. Wilhelm Röpke was too sensitive to engage in dispute with fellow intellectuals—much less general audiences—without descending into an introverted gloom. The only thing Frank Knight abhorred more than an audience of his fellow academics was one of nonacademics, and he correspondingly refused to share his ideas outside a university environment. The early Mont Pèlerin Society was so dubious about public interaction that it risked attaining, as Hayek regretfully acknowledged, the reputation of a "secret society."[38] The public reserve of free-market advocates provided implicit support for the notion that it was a philosophy cultivated by and for elites, in contradiction to the compassion of their redistributionist foes. In contrast, Friedman's extraordinary skills as a rhetorician were augmented by his unflagging energy and constant willingness to expound his public policy suggestions to anyone who was willing to listen. After the publication of *Capitalism and Freedom* he used every available media venue to try to popularize his ideas, including university lectures, political stump speeches, newspaper editorials, magazine columns, audiotaped discussions, mass-market paperbacks, and even a Public Broadcasting System documentary. Between the early 1960s and the end of the Reagan presidency, he was an omnipresent generator of ideas in the American public sphere.

As Friedman matured as an economist, he gradually began shifting his focus away from his technical work and toward his pursuits as a popular proselytizer. Beginning with Barry Goldwater's presidential run in 1964, he accepted advisory positions on political campaigns; and after an invitation in 1966 to write a column in every third edition of *Newsweek,* he started to produce short articles for popular consumption on a regular schedule. "I really had two lives," he recalled. "One was as a scientist—as an economist—and one was as a public intellectual. And everybody more or less does his major scientific work at a relatively early age. And it's kind of natural, I think, that people switch from the one area to the other."[39] He shared elsewhere his belief that "almost all important contributions of a scientist are made in the first 10 years after he enters the discipline," and he frankly acknowledged that he did his "most important economic work" between the 1940s and the 1960s.[40] There came a point in his professional life when he decided that his energies could most effectively be directed toward expounding rather than developing his economic ideas.

Unlike predecessors who insisted that the vocation of an academic entailed restrictions on public engagement, Friedman believed that his position as an academic uniquely enabled him to participate in policy debates without feeling beholden to a higher authority that could censor or influence his perspective. "My connections in Washington are entirely informal and personal," he told an interviewer in 1971. "I speak only for myself and I find it very pleasing to be able to speak only for myself."[41] He urged those interested in policy to follow a similar path. "If you really want to engage in policy activity, don't make that your vocation," he said late in his career. "Make it your avocation. Get a job. Get a secure base of income. Otherwise, you're going to get corrupted and destroyed." In contrast, "By having a good firm position in the academic world, I was perfectly free to be my own person in the world of policy."[42] Friedman even went so far as to assert that academics, and in particular economists, had an obligation to engage in discussions of public policy when they felt that their insights would be valuable. He told *Fortune* in 1967 that "economists cannot just stand aside and lose themselves in indifference curves. Their ideas do have practical consequences and when things are going wrong they should speak up."[43] He saw his ability to contribute as an independent intellectual to public policy debates as both a privilege and a duty.

By the end of the Eisenhower presidency, Friedman had grown disillusioned with the Republican Party. In 1962 he asserted, in a statement that he provided to a committee assigned to outline the principles of the Republican Party in advance of the congressional elections, that Republicans and Democrats had essentially converged on a set of common policy perspectives: "As of now, rhetoric aside, it is difficult to distinguish any difference between the philosophy reflected in Republican policy and the philosophy of the Democrat party. Both are committed to wide ranging government intervention into the personal and economic affairs of the citizens of this country; both are committed to a foreign economic policy that will inevitably strengthen the government sector of the underdeveloped countries relative to the private sector, and so ultimately redound to the disadvantage of the free world." Friedman urged the Republicans to adopt a new approach that would clearly differentiate their perspectives from those of the Democrats. Recent experiences of the "bankruptcy of the philosophy of government intervention" had, he believed, presented the Republican Party with a "great opportunity" to stop following trends and to "take the offensive."[44] He then presented his vision for its future economic message: "The Republican party could have much to offer as an alternative. It could stand for freeing men from the stifling restrictions that have accumulated in one area of our life after another as a result of government intervention. It could offer the reduction of heavy tax burdens that now go to support inefficient and unnecessary government action." He wanted the Republicans to abandon a shortsighted strategy of moderation and to embrace a more radical emphasis on economic freedoms. "A consistent philosophy of freedom may not win the Republican party the next election," he wrote. "But it would appeal to basic values and beliefs of the American people that are lying dormant."[45] Friedman emphasized that such an approach would capture the imagination of the young, and expressed his conviction that encouraging changes were already under way.

When Friedman wrote this letter, there was one prominent politician whom he believed to share his ideals. He had first contacted Barry Goldwater in December 1960 after encountering an article on Goldwater's approach to the balance-of-payments deficit in the *Wall Street Journal* that disturbed him. The *Journal* had reported that Goldwater was calling for restrictions on the amount of money tourists were allowed to take abroad.[46] Friedman urged Goldwater to rethink his position, saying that he provided this advice "as one of your admirers, as a fellow believer in a free society based on free enterprise, and as a professional economist." He then asked Goldwater whether he would be willing to meet with him and his colleagues at the University of Chicago to discuss economic policy. "As you probably know," he told Goldwater, "Chicago has for decades been the stronghold in the economics profession of believers in free enterprise—for a long time just about all by itself. This is why I believe such a meeting might further the aims we share."[47] Goldwater profusely thanked Friedman for his views on floating exchange rates, asserting that he found them "to be in complete keeping with my thinking" and adding that "if we could only present this in a reasonable way to all the members of Congress, I feel sure we could influence many of them." He proposed a meeting during his planned visit to Chicago in September 1961.[48] The two subsequently maintained close contact through periodic meetings at the house of Bill Baroody, the director of the American Enterprise Institute (Friedman served on its academic advisory board).[49] Friedman was unreserved in his admiration and support. "You cannot know how heartening it is for all of us to have a Senator who is willing to take a stand on the principles of freedom and to fight on the public hustings for what we believe in," he wrote to Goldwater in 1962. "More power to you."[50] Goldwater shared Friedman's sentiments and was effusive in his praise of *Capitalism and Freedom* when he read the manuscript before its publication.[51] Friedman had finally found a charismatic politician whose popular rhetoric and economic positions very closely aligned with his own.[52]

When Goldwater announced his candidacy for the presidency, it was widely expected within the community of professional economists that Friedman would serve as his primary adviser.[53] With Bill Baroody's encouragement, Friedman agreed to construct an economic platform for the campaign.[54] He became the center of a committee of economic advisers that drew heavily on the membership of the Mont Pèlerin Society, including Warren Nutter, Karl Brandt, W. Glenn Campbell, and Yale Brozen. The group attracted significant public attention because of a perceived disregard for orthodoxy in its members' approach to economic policy. "Professor Friedman, a monetary expert, may be more extreme on many issues than Senator Goldwater himself," an article in the *New York Times* reported. Newspapers interpreted the absence of a number of prominent members of Eisenhower's Council of Economic Advisers—including Paul McCracken, Henry Wallach, and the chairman, Arthur F. Burns—as a sign that the Goldwater team's radicalism had generated little academic support.[55] Friedman was represented as the leader of a dissident band of policy intellectuals who were generating proposals that fell far outside the economic mainstream.

Friedman did not want to abandon his academic work to participate actively in the day-to-day campaign, and Goldwater liked to maintain some distance between himself and his advisers.[56] Nevertheless, Friedman's prominent affiliation led him to become a widely known public figure for the first time in his career. He arrived at Columbia as a visiting professor at the height of the campaign in the fall of 1964, and found that he was just about the only "respectable intellectual in New York who was willing to defend Goldwater." He then entered into a "blur of one meeting or interview or talk after another, leaving barely enough time for me to meet my professorial obligations."[57] Economists were describing Goldwater's positions as "pure Friedman," and the media were increasingly referencing him as an ideological architect of the campaign.[58] It was a dubious entrance into the public sphere. "In academic circles, admitting to Goldwater leanings has come close to wearing the scarlet letter," the *Wall Street Journal* reported. "Even many parts of the more-Republican business and professional community have tended to look down their noses at Goldwater fans."[59] A half decade later the *Journal* wrote that Friedman probably remained "best known as the 'ultraconservative' economics professor who served as an adviser to Barry Goldwater in the Senator's disastrous effort to unseat Lyndon Johnson in the 1964 Presidential race."[60] Regardless of the campaign's ignominious end, Friedman expressed no regrets about his participation. "Despite the subsequent election results," he wrote in his autobiography, "the defeat of the hitherto dominant Rockefeller Republicans was a crucial step in the gradual shift of public opinion away from liberalism as popularly understood and toward free-market conservatism."[61]

When he was asked about the campaign three years after its conclusion, Friedman expressed only two criticisms of Goldwater's performance. The first was that Goldwater failed to hold his ground on the idea that social security was best obtained by voluntary or charitable means. Second, he believed that Goldwater should have given his speech on civil rights earlier than he did.[62] Goldwater had argued in *The Conscience of a Conservative* in 1960 that although he was "in agreement with the *objectives* of the Supreme Court as stated in the *Brown* decision," he was not prepared "to impose that judgment of mine on the people of Mississippi or South Carolina." Asserting that the Constitution did not permit any federal interference in the field of education, he had concluded that the issue was "their business, not mine."[63] Goldwater built on that argument when he prominently announced his opposition to the civil rights bill of 1964. At the time Friedman expressed a belief that Goldwater's perspective was "excellent" and a true manifestation of the concept of "equal treatment of all, regardless of race."[64] Three years later his only revision to this evaluation was to argue that Goldwater had not expressed his position soon enough.

Friedman's perspective on civil rights was complex. His correspondence from the early 1950s demonstrated a genuine concern with civil rights and a preference for politicians who emphasized the issue.[65] By the time he wrote *Capitalism and Freedom,* however, he had developed a strong opposition to civil rights legislation. He categorized the problem of segregated schools as one more example of why government-administered education was an unwise idea, arguing that much of the social conflict over desegregation was caused by the absence of institutional alternatives. In Friedman's view, a world with competing private institutions would be likely to integrate much faster than one with a government-run monopoly. His views on schooling aligned with his argument that market costs would provide the most effective impetus to resolve the social problems that racism imposed. "The man who objects to buying from or working alongside a Negro, for example, thereby limits his range of choice," he explained. "He will generally have to pay a higher price for what he buys or receive a lower return for his work. Or, put the other way, those of us who regard color of skin or religion as irrelevant can buy some things more cheaply as a result." He believed that the market, over time and aided by continued public discussion,

would eventually lead people to act as the advocates of civil rights legislation wished.[66] His views were indicative of the degree to which he
trusted markets to solve even the most apparently intractable and morally abhorrent social problems. His unqualified confidence in the ame-
liorative capacities of the market was not shared by Hayek, who, despite
some reservations about the coercive aspects of the fair-employment
clause and the public accommodation clause, expressed sympathy for
what he otherwise regarded as a "highly desirable" civil rights bill.[67]

Friedman's position on civil rights put him in some regressive company, and he was eager to differentiate himself from the radical fringes
of the American Right. He publicly condemned the views of the John
Birch Society as "fundamentally wrong" and privately wrote to William
F. Buckley Jr. to congratulate him on an editorial denouncing its leadership.[68] He also openly criticized the "intellectual shabbiness" of a group
Buckley had helped establish, Young Americans for Freedom, comment-
ing that it "resorts to the same exaggerated approach and smear type of
attack that you find in the Daily Worker."[69] Friedman was positioning
himself in a strained category: as a free-market intellectual who expressed radical ideas in numerous public forums of debate, but maintained no connection to the unsavory fringe groups of the radical Right
and some credibility within the academic establishment. To the extent
that he was successful in doing so, he became an extraordinarily valuable commodity for media establishments that were eager to solicit sophisticated representations of a conservative point of view. John Fischer,
the editor of *Harper's*, wrote to Friedman in 1961 to express his enthusiasm at the possibility of receiving a manuscript from him, given "the
difficulty of extracting good manuscripts from conservative writers."[70]
William F. Buckley Jr. particularly treasured Friedman as "among the
pleasantest people in the whole world," from whom one could learn "at
a positively obscene rate," and the two of them went skiing together for
nineteen consecutive years.[71] Friedman provided a combination of intellectual legitimacy, creative ideas, and cogent and provocative writing
that was unparalleled in the conservative intellectual world, and its leading publicists recognized him as a unique and irreplaceable asset. With
the inception of his *Newsweek* column in 1967, he obtained an ideal
venue to bring his dissident perspective to a mainstream audience.

By the early 1970s he was beginning to attract recognition as a major
force in the American public sphere. His warnings—both in his 1967
presidential address before the American Economic Association and in

popular columns—of the possibility of what became known as "stagfla-tion" seemed prophetic amid a repetitive series of inflationary reces-sions.[72] His longtime public and professional advocacy of floating ex-change rates both presaged and abetted the unfolding collapse of the Bretton Woods system.[73] His acknowledged influence over Nixon's eco-nomic advisers and occasional provision of advice to Nixon himself gave him a direct channel to influence federal economic policy.[74] And his public break with Nixon over the latter's institution of wage and price controls in the summer of 1971 drew still more controversy and atten-tion to his ideas.[75] Commentators have noted that Friedman "blunted his lance" with inaccurate predictions and prognostications during the 1980s.[76] Between the late 1960s and the mid-1970s, however, his ideas seemed irresistibly prescient, and those of his more numerous opponents repeatedly wrong. He had accumulated disciples in the general public whom some referred to as "Friedmanics," and one fellow economist told the *Wall Street Journal* that he "may well go down as the most influential economist of our time."[77] The picketers who began to appear outside his lectures provided the generational imprimatur of political influence.[78] Despite his relative youth, the *New York Times* reported that he was a leading contender for the economics profession's inaugural Nobel Prize.[79]

Friedman's path to the Nobel was not as seamless as some expected it to be, and he was forced to wait until its eighth conferral in 1976 before receiving the award. The protracted delay was widely perceived to be a product, in part, of the selection committee's disapproval of his political advocacy of free markets. It is a plausible explanation; the Nobel Prize in Economic Sciences has always served in part as a barometer of the conventional wisdom of the economics profession. Its establishment im-measurably increased the prestige of the discipline's leading practitio-ners and commensurately heightened the difficulty of supplanting their established views. But if Friedman's initial wait revealed lingering op-position to Chicago economics and laissez-faire approaches to political economy, the subsequent generation of recipients manifested an aston-ishing reversal: between 1974 and 1991, seven of the awardees were members of the Mont Pèlerin Society.[80] The creators of the Nobel Prize in Economic Sciences may at first have wielded it as an expression of implicit disapprobation of Friedman's political views, but in the longer term it proved to be an invaluable lever of support.

Friedman's acceptance of the Nobel was marred by a growing public controversy surrounding his visit to Chile a year earlier. Friedman and his colleague Arnold Harberger traveled to Chile for six days in March 1975, during which they delivered a series of public lectures evaluating its economic and political policies and on one occasion met personally with its military dictator, Augusto Pinochet.[81] Pinochet had entrusted economic policy to a group of radical economists, many of whom had attended the University of Chicago between 1956 and 1964 under the auspices of a program sponsored by the Agency for International Development.[82] At the time of Friedman's visit they were in the midst of implementing a rapid series of free-market reforms, including deregulation, privatization, elimination of price controls, cuts in government spending, and an expansion of free trade. Critics have argued that the implementation of the economic policies that Friedman advocated required the use of the junta's repressive measures, and have strongly implied the existence of sinister motives on the part of Friedman and his colleagues. They have raised enduring questions about the human costs of the "shock treatment" Friedman recommended and the wisdom of providing personal advice to terroristic regimes.[83] But Friedman was also severely critical of the Chilean government's repressive measures before, during, and after his visit, and refused receipt of two honorary degrees in order to avoid an implicit endorsement he did not want to bestow.[84] Regardless of any ambiguities, he became a consistent target of protesters, and his lectures were plagued by deliberate disruptions. When an audience member interrupted his presentation during a 1978 lecture in Glasgow, Scotland, Friedman immediately drew the audience's attention to the distinction between their respective modes of debate. "I thought a university was a place for intellectual discussion," he said. "We're getting our roles a little mixed, there will be plenty of room for discussion and question [sic] after and I should welcome them."[85] He was a natural target for expressions of anticapitalist discontent, but his earnest populism posed a problem to those who relied on blunt instruments to expose the hypocrisy of elites.

Several weeks after he received the Nobel Prize, Friedman left the University of Chicago to accept an appointment as a senior research fellow at the Hoover Institution, where he would remain for the final decades of his career. The Hoover Institution, a research institute that had been founded on the Stanford University campus by Herbert Hoover in 1919, had entered into a crisis of purpose amid disagreements between the former president and the university administration during the 1950s. By 1958 Hoover had become increasingly concerned that "leftwingers" had "taken over" the institution that bore his name.[86] The following year he personally appointed a young economist who had recently received his doctorate from Harvard, W. Glenn Campbell, to serve as the institution's director. Under Campbell it was reinvented as a think tank that sought to provide a conservative counterpart to the Brookings Institution.[87] Over the subsequent two decades its staff grew rapidly from 35 to 135, and its programs became increasingly ambitious. "Whereas in the past its fellows were frequently dismissed as rabidly anti-Communist cranks," the *New York Times* reported in 1978, "now they include such well-known and widely respected scholars as philosopher Sidney Hook, sociologist Seymour Martin Lipset and the Nobel Prize–winning economist Milton Friedman." The article asserted that through its "ties with the right wing of the Republican Party, the Hoover Institution is exerting increasing political influence. It is the brightest star in a small constellation of conservative think tanks that serve as workshops where out-of-office intellectuals can fabricate the underpinnings of domestic- and foreign-policy positions for the Republicans." This was a grim contrast, it concluded, with the status of the "liberal think tanks," some of which were "nearly defunct."[88] The world of conservative think tanks had traveled a great distance since the early days of the Volker Fund and the Earhart Foundation, and Friedman's arrival on the permanent staff of the Hoover Institution was a powerful signal of their ascendance. The late 1970s were a heady time in the Republican policy world: the Institute for Humane Studies was reaching its maturity, the American Enterprise Institute was growing in size and influence, and new venues were rapidly appearing with the establishment of the Heritage Foundation in 1973 and the Cato Institute in 1977. In stark contrast to the early postwar years, Friedman would conclude near the end of his career that "there are too damn many think tanks now," adding that they simply "don't have the talent for it."[89]

The rise of Friedman's ideas was marked by Ronald Reagan's election to the presidency in 1980.[90] Friedman first met Reagan when he was a visiting professor at UCLA in the winter of 1967. Reagan had read *Capitalism and Freedom* before his campaign for the governorship, and the two of them had a "long and thoroughly enjoyable" conversation that served as a foundation for their mutual admiration. In 1973 Friedman joined Reagan for a vigorous series of stump speeches across California in support of Proposition 1—which would limit the size of the California state budget—and announced at a rally that he planned to support

Reagan for the presidency in 1976.[91] He saw Reagan and Goldwater as ideological twins, describing them as "two men with essentially the same program and the same message."[92] Reagan's election was therefore a symbol to him of the "big change in public opinion" since the early postwar years.[93] Martin Anderson, a prominent economic adviser to Reagan, recalled Friedman's particular influence. "Reagan was especially taken with Milton Friedman," he wrote in 1988. "He just could not resist Friedman's infectious enthusiasm and Reagan's eyes sparkled with delight every time he engaged in a dialogue with him."[94] In retrospect, Friedman was disappointed that although Reagan "talked about cutting down the size of government, he did not succeed."[95] Nevertheless, the very fact of Reagan's presidency served as an indicator of the journey the Republican Party had taken since Friedman vocalized his disillusionment in the years before Goldwater's presidential campaign. The rhetorical strategy that Friedman advocated then—with its emphasis on human freedom, its disparagement of government intervention, and its relentlessly optimistic valence—had become, via Reagan, the message of the party itself. It was an extraordinary demonstration of the capacity of radical opinion to become, over time and in concert with circumstance, accepted as the norm.

Shortly after assuming the presidency of the Mont Pèlerin Society in 1970, Friedman reopened an issue that Hayek had advanced a decade earlier. In a circular distributed to the society's full membership, he indicated that the institution might have outlived its usefulness. "Our basic problems," he wrote, "arise out of our success." In particular, the society's membership had grown ever larger. The 1968 meeting in Aviemore, Scotland, had included 295 members and guests; the 1970 meeting in Munich had encompassed 330.[96] By 1972 the membership rolls listed 372 people from thirty-two countries.[97] Its ability to inspire broad-based interest and support was a cause for celebration, but also led to an inevitable drain on the quality of the conversations it had been created to foster. The gatherings were undermined by two potentially insurmountable problems: "First, our meetings are such pleasant occasions . . . that, to an increasing number of participants, I fear they have become tourist attractions during a vacation period rather than exciting intellectual experiences. Second, the sessions have become large formal meetings at which the papers given have necessarily only skimmed the surface of important issues and the discussion has been discursive rather than penetrating."[98]

As one of the few remaining participants who had been present at the founding meeting in 1947, Friedman was acutely aware of the differences between the society in its early years and in its maturity. What had once been a venue for "vigorous and wide-ranging discussions" had begun "to take on the character of presentations to an audience." Increasing public receptivity to the society's ideas had diminished the importance of the atmosphere of collegiality that had infused its earliest gatherings with meaning. Friedman convened an assembly of the society's surviving founding members and former officers to discuss these problems in Montreux, Swizerland, in 1971. In a reminder of the qualities that the society had lost, the smaller size of this congregation recreated "to some extent the feeling of the first."[99] Friedman pressed forward with a suggestion that the society's challenges were insurmountable and that it should celebrate its achievements at its twenty-fifth anniversary the following year before permanently shuttering its doors.[100] The attendees rejected the proposal that the society's activities should cease, arguing that it remained an invaluable source of networking and intellectual exchange. Instead, they decided to institute certain limitations on the addition of new members and to experiment with new formats for the society's debates. "Those measures," Friedman concluded decades later, "have not been very effective."[101]

If the Mont Pèlerin Society was—against Friedman's better judgment—to survive, he wanted it to address a problem in the dissemination of free-market ideas that he found particularly troubling. He outlined the challenge in a presidential lecture, "Capitalism and the Jews," before the society's members at its twenty-fifth-anniversary meeting in 1972. Friedman indicated that he and other Jewish members of the Mont Pèlerin Society found themselves "embattled, being regarded not only as intellectual deviants but also as traitors to a supposed cultural and national tradition." He attributed this to what he perceived as a paradox in the response to capitalism among Jewish intellectuals: "Two propositions can be readily demonstrated: first, the Jews owe an enormous debt to free enterprise and competitive capitalism; second, for at least the past century the Jews have been consistently opposed to capitalism and have done much on an ideological level to undermine it." Friedman saw this as an emblematic case of a broader problem: "Why have we been so unsuccessful in persuading intellectuals everywhere of our views?" After a protracted analysis he attributed the Jewish "paradox" to a set of inter-connected factors, including certain contingencies in nineteenth-century European politics, a cultural sensitivity to injustice and commitment to charity, what he perceived to be a "subconscious attempt by Jews to demonstrate to themselves and the world the fallacy of the anti-semitic stereotype," and, finally, "whatever the forces are that predispose intel-lectuals toward the Left." The primary impression left by Friedman's analysis, however, is one of bafflement. He simply could not muster any compelling or justifiable reasons for the continuing distrust of capitalism manifested by many Jewish intellectuals. His conclusion demonstrated his utter lack of sympathy: "On a much more subtle and sophisticated level, they were in the position of the rich parlor socialists—of all ethnic and religious backgrounds—who bask in self-righteous virtue by con-demning capitalism while enjoying the luxuries paid for by their capitalist inheritance."[102] Friedman's inability to understand or sympathize with an anticapitalist mentality led him to adopt notes of frustration and dis-gust that he otherwise strenuously avoided. He had arrived at an insolu-ble problem: if he was right about the manifest benefits of markets and the long-term rationality of crowds, he simply could not understand a group that consistently rejected a social philosophy that he perceived to be in their self-interest.

Others were less puzzled by the problem. At the 1970 meeting John Davenport, a *Fortune* journalist who had written an extended profile of Friedman three years earlier, attempted to explain why the society's members continued to experience resistance to their ideas. He called for his colleagues to "stretch our minds to encompass issues not dreamt of in utilitarian economics," and "to re-examine our own political and philosophical premises." The problem, he argued, was that in the soci-ety's relentless emphasis on the superior efficiency of laissez-faire, its members had abandoned a language of values. "Economics, we say, is neutral," he said. "On the other hand, in seeking to maximize human choice and options, we have, I submit, been far from neutral. We have, to some degree, smuggled in ends or values, and we have to this extent tried to define the political and human good. My suggestion is that the smuggling process should stop and that our choice of values be made explicit." He then explained his prescription for the society in greater detail: "At the least in the matter of morality I suggest that the libertar-ian should move over a bit to make room for what some of our conser-vative friends have been long urging—namely that the end of man is not just the pursuit of pleasure but of something quite different—the pursuit of excellence, the pursuit, let us say it, of *virtue*."[103] Although he did not frame his suggestions in these terms, Davenport was calling for the society to return to its original statement of aims. In its founding meeting the society's leading members had expressed a conviction that free markets would be compelling to the public only if they were presented as part of a comprehensive moral worldview. They attributed the final abandonment of nineteenth-century liberalism to its formal abstraction, unqualified prioritization of laissez-faire efficiencies, and occasional orientation toward a reductive language of pleasures and pains. Davenport saw a society that had again adopted the abstract modes of analysis that it had ostensibly been founded to overcome. Admittedly, it had achieved more rapid popular success than the founders of the society had ever presumed to imagine, but Davenport maintained that it would need to return to its original purpose in order to precipitate an enduring transformation in the public mind.

Friedman had little sympathy for this argument, but he recognized that it was the kind of discussion the society should inspire. In an attempt to foster further debates of this nature, he renewed Hayek's longtime efforts to attract academic noneconomists as participants in the society's debates. Friedman's challenge, however, was even more formidable than Hayek's. After his arrival at the Committee on Social Thought and his work on the philosophy of social science, Hayek had developed a reputation as an interdisciplinary scholar, and during his early presidency the society had incorporated a substantive body of prominent noneconomists and members with openly conflicting political views. By the time Friedman ascended to the society's presidency, its academic membership had become overwhelmingly oriented toward technical economics, and its public policy perspective was unambiguously libertarian. Noneconomists and social traditionalists were wary of participating in a group defined by positions and methodologies that diverged from their own. The nature of the problem became apparent to Friedman when he asked Irving Kristol to join the society for its twenty-fifth-anniversary meeting in 1972. Kristol's political history did not accord with that of most members of the Mont Pèlerin Society. He had been a member of the Young People's Socialist League when he attended City College in the late 1930s, and more recently he had advocated aspects of Lyndon Johnson's Great Society and had provided support to Hubert Humphrey's presidential ambitions. Since founding the journal *Public*

Interest in 1965, Kristol had gradually dispensed with his technocratic sympathies, becoming known as both a harsh critic of the New Left and an exponent of the benefits of the market mechanism. By 1972 he was an ally of Richard Nixon and, as of September, an inaugural member of the Board of Contributors to the editorial page of the *Wall Street Journal,* which Friedman frequently appeared in and unequivocally admired.[104] But Kristol coupled his concerns about the excesses of contemporary social policy with a warning, as he wrote in a collection of essays that year, that capitalism was living off the "accumulated moral capital" of social philosophies that it had since supplanted.[105] He worried that the relentless materialism of market advocates rendered them incapable of combating the forces behind the nation's cultural decline.[106] In refusing Friedman's request, Kristol indicated that the Mont Pèlerin Society suffered from an excessive emphasis on economics, which led its members to adopt "libertarian," as opposed to "traditionalist," ideals. Friedman argued that the society was not at fault for any apparent uniformities, writing that the "only reason that the professional emphasis is on economics is because economists have been somewhat more immune to the socialist-liberal bug than non-economists."[107]

After much determined cajoling from Friedman, Kristol agreed to attend the twenty-fifth-anniversary gathering in 1972. But instead of attempting to identify shared projects or common ground, he focused his attention directly on the points of divergence between his ideas and those advocated by the society's members. The problem, he believed, was that they were still fighting a battle that they had already effectively won. "To think economically has come to mean thinking along lines established by the so-called 'Chicago School,'" he told the meeting participants. "So I think one can say that this ideological battle is over, and the dispute over the relative economic merits of central planning vis-à-vis the market has been settled." This was a cause for congratulation, and Kristol expressed his appreciation and admiration profusely. The "sum and substance" of his report, however, was "that what we might call the Mont Pelerin Movement has been winning an impressive series of battles but is in grave danger of losing the war." While the members of the Mont Pèlerin Society were still engaging in debates that focused on economic efficiency, the Left had largely abandoned an argument of efficiency in favor of an analysis centering on values. The "identifying marks of the New Left," Kristol asserted, "are its refusal to think economically and its contempt for bourgeois society precisely because this is a society that does think economically." John Kenneth Galbraith was "not really an economist," he added, but rather a "reluctant rabbi." Indeed, Kristol saw the emerging critique of capitalism not as progressive, as it claimed to be, but rather as "utterly regressive," adopting the logic of the Old Right that "never did accept the liberal-bourgeois revolutions of the 18th and 19th centuries." The members of the Mont Pèlerin Society were using the presuppositions of modernity to argue against a critique that rejected modernity itself.

Kristol positioned Friedman as the emblematic figure of an emboldened libertarianism that refused to engage with any substantive criticisms of the cultural perils of capitalism:

> Though Milton Friedman's writings on this matter are not entirely clear—itself an odd and interesting fact, since he is usually the most pellucid of thinkers—one gathers that he is, in the name of "libertarianism," reluctant to impose any prohibition or inhibition on the libertine tendencies of modern bourgeois society. He seems to assume, as I read him, that one must not interfere with the dynamics of "self-realization" in a free society. He further seems to assume that these dynamics cannot, in the nature of things, be self-destructive—that "self-realization" in a free society can only lead to the creation of a self that is compatible with such a society.

These assumptions relied on a secular, libertarian social philosophy that, Kristol concluded, "simply had too limited an imagination when it came to vice." Such a philosophy assumed that individuals were not irredeemably corrupted in the process of private vices becoming public virtues: "It never really could believe that vice, when unconstrained by religion, morality, and law, might lead to viciousness."[108] Kristol believed that the members of the Mont Pèlerin Society needed to situate their economic insights within a comprehensive moral framework that preserved a place for virtue and correspondingly delineated boundaries of human interaction where the marketplace should be curtailed. Otherwise, they risked undermining their substantial achievements by elevating a partial truth to the status of the absolute.

For many reasons, the path that Kristol proposed was one that Milton Friedman was unwilling to follow. Friedman had little patience for discussions of norms, which he perceived as a distraction from the empirical mode of disputation he relied on for persuasive force. Even in those moments when he turned his attention to normative concerns, he resolutely disagreed with Kristol's evaluation; in his representation capitalism remained a generator of self-sufficient virtue rather than materialistic vice. And Friedman had little interest in restraining his advocacy of markets in order to reward certain character traits and discourage others. His entire social philosophy rested on a stance of self-effacing deference to the preferences of discrete individuals. The only determinative norms that he was willing to allow, if not to recognize, were those that were silently instituted through the distributive authority of the market mechanism itself. In his presentation before the Mont Pèlerin Society, Kristol was asking its members to forgo precisely the positions that made Friedman's political perspective unique: it was a plea, between the lines, for the leading advocates of capitalism to abandon their earnest embrace of the logic of Friedmanism.

Milton Friedman never disparaged Hayek, whose insights and influence he consistently extolled, and drew no attention to his own differences from the other participants in the founding meeting at Mont Pèlerin. Nevertheless, he had, since inheriting Hayek's role as the preeminent scholar in the society and the leading advocate of free markets in the public sphere, quietly precipitated a dramatic transformation in the membership's worldview. Methodologically, he redirected the members' focus away from abstract theory and toward empirical modes of analysis, in a transition that entailed the abandonment of the very inquiries into questions of value that Hayek had established the society to address. Economically, he cast aside a cautious and conservative policy of moderation and rehabilitated the advocacy of an unmediated laissez-faire. Strategically, he tore down the barriers his predecessors had constructed between economists and public policy debates, and he both encouraged and enacted aggressive new rhetorical modes. John Davenport and Irving Kristol were not critics of the society in its inherent or historical form. Rather, they were expressing dissatisfaction with what—under Friedman's formidable influence—it had become.

CONCLUSION
The Spirit of an Age

As a global financial crisis approached its apex in the fall of 2008, commentators on both sides of the political aisle declared that a long era in American political history was drawing to a close. According to their narrative, the rise of deregulation in the 1970s and the subsequent election of Ronald Reagan had ushered in nearly thirty years during which the primacy of free markets was largely assumed. Advocates of government intervention had adopted a defensive rhetoric and approached economic legislation in a spirit of accession and compromise, while the invocation of free-market doctrines among those in positions of political power had become ever more strident and self-assured. Now—in the wake of income stagnation, rising inequality, an unprecedentedly unpopular president, conspicuous market imperfections, and an economic collapse widely attributed to failures of regulation—a tectonic shift had begun. The conservative era, a staff writer for the *New Yorker* proclaimed, "rose amid the ashes of the New Deal coalition in the late sixties, consolidated its power with the election of Ronald Reagan, in 1980, and immolated itself during the Presidency of George W. Bush." In the midst of the financial crisis the need for "new machinery" was "painfully obvious" as "the old assumptions of free-market fundamentalism have, like a charlatan's incantations, failed to work."[1] We had, in other words, arrived again at the end of laissez-faire.

Economists, politicians, and journalists on the left greeted the arrival of this perceived transformation with a combination of earnest anticipation and retrospective admonition. The events of the financial crisis, in their interpretation, had validated their long-ignored warnings about the excesses of their ideological opponents. The economist Jeffrey Sachs announced in *Fortune* that Reaganomics, which "began with a wrong

214

diagnosis and a great lie" that "played into the fantasies of a free-market, go-it-alone America," was now "over—even the moderate, triangulating version of the Clinton years."[2] British prime minister Gordon Brown argued that "laissez-faire has had its day" and encouraged his colleagues to assert with confidence that "the old idea that markets were by definition efficient and could work things out themselves is gone."[3] A writer in the *Nation* surveyed the landscape and concluded, with evident satisfaction, "The Friedmanite myth of the perfect market lies in ruins."[4] He was joined by a senior editor of the *New Republic,* who announced that the nation was no longer "America the conservative" and, pending further developments, might well be on the path to becoming "America the liberal."[5] The question of what new economic philosophy would take the place of the Friedmanite doctrine remained a subject of contestation, but the assumption that it was in the process of being displaced was broadly shared.

Imputations of a generational shift in the American political environment were not solely the province of the Left. David Brooks wrote in the *New York Times* that "we're in for a Keynesian renaissance," predicting the onset of a "Gingrich revolution in reverse and on steroids."[6] Peggy Noonan, a former speechwriter for Ronald Reagan, observed in the *Wall Street Journal* that "something new is happening in America" and foresaw "the imminent arrival of a new liberal moment."[7] Her newspaper's editorial page grimly anticipated "the restoration of the activist government that fell out of public favor in the 1970s" and "a period of unchecked left-wing ascendancy."[8] Economists long known for their orientation toward laissez-faire economic policies called for vigorous stimulus policies to counteract the downturn.[9] In an iconic moment, Alan Greenspan delivered a prepared statement before the House Committee on Government Oversight and Reform acknowledging that "those of us who have looked to the self-interest of lending institutions to protect shareholders' equity, myself especially, are in a state of shocked disbelief." Under intense questioning from Henry Waxman, Greenspan admitted that he had "made a mistake in presuming that the self-interest of organizations, specifically banks and others, were such as that they were best capable of protecting their own shareholders and their equity in the firms." Asked whether his ideology had led him to make erroneous decisions, Greenspan said: "What I'm saying to you is, yes, I've found a flaw. I don't know how significant or permanent it is. But I have been very distressed by that fact." The flaw had destabilized "the model that I perceived is the critical functioning structure that defines how the world works, so to speak." Waxman continued: "In other words, you found that your view of the world, your ideology was not right, it was not working." "Absolutely, precisely," Greenspan replied.[10] Even the public icons of the free market seemed to be renouncing their established convictions before the nation's eyes.

For a brief period it seemed that the developed world was reenacting the collapse of market advocacy that had unfolded in the wake of the Great Depression. Much, however, had changed since Keynes first delivered his lecture "The End of Laissez-Faire." In the intervening decades market advocates developed an elaborate intellectual and rhetorical apparatus in support of their worldview, a substantial base of supporters in the academic and public policy worlds, and extensive institutional structures that were adept at incentivizing and propagating their ideas. Radical alternatives to capitalist modes of social organization found little traction in the global public sphere, and assumptions about the benefits and organizational necessity of a market framework became much more broadly shared. Although opinion polls in the wake of the crisis registered increased uncertainty about the benefits of free markets, the hold of market advocacy on the popular imagination has remained far stronger than in the early 1930s. Even the rhetoric of Milton Friedman's critics is now often infused with his celebrations of competition and choice. Capitalism may be in crisis, but the horizon of alternatives has narrowed.

Historians have long argued that a critical engagement with the assumptions of the present day requires an understanding of the contingency of their development. Keynes held this view, expressing the belief that history was a means of precipitating, and not merely recording, processes of ideological change. "A study of the history of opinion," he told his audience in Oxford, "is a necessary preliminary to the emancipation of the mind."[11] Hayek, too, cast his work in this vein, appropriating Lord Acton's assertion that "few discoveries are more irritating than those which expose the pedigree of ideas" as an epigraph in *The Road to Serfdom*.[12] The assumptions of an era seem less firm when they are placed in a context that includes their formation, degeneration, and reformation again. The partial triumph shared by the founders of the Mont Pèlerin Society reveals, if nothing else, that the beliefs held at any given time are in the midst of supersession even at the moment when their ascendance seems most complete. The successes of market advocates in the later years of the twentieth century were made possible by the challenges they confronted in earlier years. Those who set themselves against the prevailing opinions of today can take comfort in the knowledge that discursive constraints are never absolute, and often help create the conditions of their own decline.

When Hayek was preparing to found the Mont Pèlerin Society, he turned to Keynes's representation of the relationship between ideas and historical change. Keynes had famously commented at the end of *The General Theory* that "practical men, who believe themselves to be quite exempt from any intellectual influences, are usually the slaves of some defunct economist." As Hayek observed, that was an assertion that Keynes was uniquely qualified to posit. But he went on to quote Keynes's subsequent, less often cited words: "I am sure that the power of vested interests is vastly exaggerated compared with the gradual encroachment of ideas. Not, indeed, immediately, but after a certain interval; for in the field of economic and political philosophy there are not many who are influenced by new theories after they are twenty-five or thirty years of age, so that the ideas which civil servants and politicians and even agitators apply to current events are not likely to be the newest. But, soon or late, it is ideas, not vested interests, which are dangerous for good or evil."[13] In this regard Hayek and Keynes agreed. People doubt that "human ideas and beliefs are the main mover of history," Hayek asserted, because "we all find it so difficult to imagine that our belief [*sic*] might be different from what they in fact are." He attributed a certain merit to this perception of intractability: the "interval between the time when ideas are given currency and the time when they govern action" can, he acknowledged, be long. "It is usually a generation," he said, "or even more, and that is one reason why on the one hand our present thinking seems so powerless to influence events, and why on the other so much well meant effort at political education and propaganda is mispent [*sic*], because it is almost invariably aimed at a short run effect." Hayek's goal was to imitate the socialists, who had long emphasized the primacy of ideas and maintained "the courage to be 'utopian.'"[14] The Mont Pèlerin Society was, above all else, an expression of faith in the power of philosophical abstractions to instigate long-term political change. Hayek had no explicit theory of transmission and little interest in cultivating or supporting modes of propagation; his sole concern was to create a space that would foster the generative capacity of ideas.

Milton Friedman disagreed in many ways with Hayek and still more so with Keynes, but he, too, shared their belief in the long-term political impact of economic ideas. An article in *Time* in 1969 compared Friedman to "a Paris designer whose haute couture is bought by a select few, but who nonetheless influences almost all popular fashions."[15] A year later, he explained to the magazine the process through which his ideas entered the political mainstream:

> Act I: The views of crackpots like myself are avoided.
>
> Act II: The defenders of the orthodox faith become uncomfortable because the ideas seem to have an element of truth.
>
> Act III: People say, "We all know that this is an impractical and theoretically extreme view—but of course we have to look at more moderate ways to move in this direction."
>
> Act IV: [They] convert my ideas into untenable caricatures so that they can move over and occupy the ground where I formerly stood.[16]

He was confident that contemporary resistance to his ideas would gradually give way as the arguments in favor of their legitimacy accumulated. At times invoking the historian of science Thomas Kuhn, he expressed a belief that economic opinion followed certain broad paradigms that were eventually discarded when new theories did a better job of describing the available evidence.[17] Although a change in perspectives often required the passage from influence of an entrenched generation, Friedman was confident that when it was merited, it would eventually occur. In 1988 he and his wife Rose explained their three-part historical typology of Anglo-American political economy: first, "The Rise of Laissez-Faire (the Adam Smith Tide)," running from the second half of the eighteenth century to the 1880s; second, "The Rise of the Welfare State (the Fabian Tide)," running from the 1880s to the postwar period; and finally, "The Resurgence of Free Markets (the Hayek Tide)," which was "approaching middle age" in public opinion and "still in its infancy" in its effects on public policy. All these "tides" provoked ideological countercurrents at precisely the moment their influence on public policy matured. "Promise tends to be utopian," the Friedmans wrote. "Performance never is and therefore disappoints."[18]

In explaining his understanding of the relationship between ideas and historical change, Milton Friedman often cited a collection of lectures by the turn-of-the-century British constitutional lawyer Albert Venn Dicey.[19]

Dicey originally delivered his *Lectures on the Relation between Law and Public Opinion* to an audience of Harvard Law School students in 1898; after further refinement in Oxford, they were published in 1905.[20] Dicey's goal was to tell the story of English law via its complex relationship with public opinion, which engaged in a volatile journey during the nineteenth century through both laissez-faire and collectivism.[21] The result, Friedman said, was an "enormously insightful and prophetic" book, and one of a small collection of texts that had played a formative role in the development of his approach to social policy.[22] He read Dicey as a how-to manual for the practice of generating ideological change, and extensively appropriated the lectures' analysis in explanations of his intended political role.

In his second lecture Dicey argued that political change tends to begin not with a conviction growing up "spontaneously among the multitude," but rather through the concerted efforts of "some single thinker or school of thinkers." He then described how the process would typically unfold: "A new and, let us assume, a true idea presents itself to some one man of originality or genius; the discoverer of the new conception, or some follower who has embraced it with enthusiasm, preaches it to his friends or disciples, they in their turn become impressed with its importance and its truth, and gradually a whole school accept the new creed." Eventually "the preachers of truth make an impression, either directly upon the general public or upon some person of eminence, say a leading statesman, who stands in a position to impress ordinary people and thus to win the support of the nation."[23] He saw ideas as spreading from one individual to a group of sympathizers, to those in positions of influence, and finally to a broad mass of public constituents. This was not a rapid process but rather "gradual, or slow, and continuous," often taking twenty or thirty years to unfold.[24] It required the political ascension of those who had "picked up their convictions, and, what is of more consequence, their prepossessions, in early manhood, which is the one period of life when men are easily impressed with new ideas."[25] As a result, the governmental practices of one period were often attributable to the ideologies of their generational predecessors, and countervailing opinions would be gaining influence within the intellectual classes even as politicians put the new conventional wisdom into practice.

Friedman took from this a strong conviction that marginalized individuals had the capacity to effect political change, and an understanding that public assumptions about political economy were malleable only over very long periods. "All important movements in the history of mankind have come from tiny minorities," he said at a commencement ceremony in 1969. "They are made by a few creative individuals who see ahead of the masses and who lay the path for the future."[26] He never showed signs of being disheartened at those stages of his career when his ideas were rejected by most of his colleagues in the academy and his politics were widely derided as far outside the mainstream. Instead, he resolutely sought to affect the views of the young, whom he saw as the only demographic group open minded enough to develop new perspectives based on their encounters with his or his colleagues' ideas. The "people now running the country reflect the intellectual atmosphere of some two decades ago when they were in college," he told an audience of executives in 1977. "Most men's basic ideas are formed in their teens. Very few people change their fundamental values and ideas in later life." As a result, "the old theories still dominate what happens in the political world."[27] His goal was to present his minority perspective in a manner that would compel members of the younger generation to adopt it as their own. He believed that this process of generational transfer, rather than any more immediate forms of advocacy, would prove the most effective means of engendering political change.

Friedman also took from Dicey a belief that transformations in public opinion could not be brought about through the force of argument alone; something needed to happen that compelled the public to confront the fundamental failure of its previous approach. Dicey wrote that a "change of belief arises, in the main, from the occurrence of circumstances which incline the majority of the world to hear with favour theories which, at one time, men of common sense derided as absurdities, or distrusted as paradoxes."[28] Transformations in public opinion required the availability of new ideas, but the acceptance of the new ideas required that a part be played by external events. Friedman devoted his efforts to the first part of this equation: the provision of ideas to a public that might adopt them when circumstances turned in his favor. He explained this approach in a preface to the 1982 edition of *Capitalism and Freedom* that posited two purposes for the book. First, he modestly suggested that it could "provide subject matter for bull sessions." His second purpose was more ambitious: the book would help "to keep options open until circumstances make change necessary. There is enormous inertia—a tyranny of the status quo—in private and especially governmental arrangements. Only a crisis—actual or perceived—produces real change. When that crisis occurs, the actions that are taken depend on the ideas that are lying around." Friedman believed that his "basic function" was "to develop alternatives to existing policies, to keep them alive and available until the politically impossible becomes politically inevitable."[29] Floating exchange rates were considered a live possibility, he argued, because the intellectual work had already been done. They would not have been adopted in the absence of a crisis; but when the collapse arrived, it proved crucial that an alternative was readily available.[30] Friedman believed that sooner or later events arise that lead people to consider other possibilities, and he took it upon himself to bring a prolific range of unconventional proposals into the public sphere.

Dicey had expressed little confidence in the capacity of the general public to adjudicate among complex ideas. The very nature of popular rhetoric, he argued in his twelfth and final lecture, was not conducive to nuance or sophistication in the presentation of economic opinion. "Absolute precepts may command absolute belief and obedience," he wrote. "But a rule originally supposed to be without exception true, is certain, when qualified by even the fairest of exceptions, to lose far more of weight with the general public than ought in reason to be taken from it."[31] Friedman acknowledged that in matters of economic policy "the patient is incompetent to choose the physician," but he saw "no alternative in a free society." In an environment structured around uninformed opinions, he assumed "the writings that demand least in the way of hard thought and that appeal most to emotion and prejudice are likely to command the widest readership."[32] Friedman shared Hayek's understanding of the importance of ideas and the long horizons of ideological change, but they parted ways on the question of rhetoric. Friedman's public utterances, unlike those of his predecessor, are marked by their near-total instantiation of Dicey's warning against qualifications in the presentation of an economic philosophy. While Hayek remained aloof from politics and confident in the influence of his ideas unaided by his public persona, Friedman embraced the reductive language of the American public sphere as one more lever in the provocation of ideological change. He recognized the absence of limitations in his advocacy of laissez-faire as a primary source of its polemical strength.

For all their differences, Hayek and Friedman are both exemplars of a Diceyan insight: the importance of a belief in the generative capacity of ideas. Both of them built their public lives on an abiding faith that intellectual arguments could transform political practice. The efficacy of their modes of analysis and advocacy was a product less of chance than of deliberate strategy. Their confidence in their ideological agency enabled them to exert it on a world-historical stage. Ambitions for the actions of others are not often perfectly fulfilled, and Hayek and Friedman were acutely aware of the innumerable ways in which their ideas failed to transform the practice of their times. Politics transpire on many registers united only by the uncertainty with which each of them unfolds. But Hayek and Friedman, along with their colleagues in the Mont Pèlerin Society, incontrovertibly played a role in the formation of that network of presuppositions that Dicey referred to as the "spirit of an age." Their narrative, however exceptional, provides an implicit rebuke to the fatalism engendered by encounters with the real. Ideological changes require individuals who can continue to believe, against good evidence, that actions will at some point catch up with their ideas.

Even as the members of the Mont Pèlerin Society experienced greater public and professional influence in its later years, many of its founders remained distinctly ambivalent about its trajectory. Some stopped attending meetings, sending notes to Hayek in which they indicated that the tenor of its arguments no longer reflected their perspectives; others continued to participate while expressing private dismay at the direction its membership had taken. Their frustrations were not related to the society's impact: its membership continued to expand rapidly, its leading figures advised politicians who were well positioned to enact their ideas, and the institutional apparatus in support of free-market principles was growing ever more intricate and extensive. Rather, the early members worried that the ideas the society now represented were quite different from those that had dominated the initial meetings at Mont Pèlerin. Friedman's persuasive capacity had proved to be far more potent than their own, but they expressed concern that it was leveraged in the service of a very different social philosophy. Members who had come of age reminding socialists of unwelcome complexities could not wholly embrace the simpler logic that now shaped the public understanding of their worldview.

The participants in the "Colloque Lippmann" and the inaugural meeting at Mont Pèlerin shared a sense that capitalism was in a state of crisis, and they responded by questioning the moral implications of exchange and debating constraints on the workings of the market. Over time the conditions that inspired these lines of inquiry slowly fell away. Economic depression and its attendant anxieties gave way to an era of unprece-dented and broad-based prosperity. Economists, in the midst of a heady period of disciplinary specialization, lost interest in broad-based dia-logue with practitioners in other fields. The geopolitical flux of the early 1930s was replaced by the static dualisms of the Cold War. Market ad-vocates who had once struggled to find institutions supportive of their views now enjoyed a growing array of policy institutes interested in funding actionable ideas. Milton Friedman's social philosophy invoked an optimistic language, ideological coherence, disciplinary prestige, and policy imagination that suited the needs of this new age. Combating representations of the market as a volatile engine that required both veneration and constraint, he reimagined it as an infinite resource that yielded social benefits in proportion to the extent it was set free. Al-though Friedman often failed to convert the public to his specific views, over time his rhetorical audacity succeeded in restructuring the terms of popular debate.

Of course, the history of the Mont Pèlerin Society and its members is only one of many discrete subnarratives of the wrenching ideological transformation of the United States between the presidencies of Franklin Roosevelt and Ronald Reagan. Here, as everywhere, the relationship be-tween abstract ideas and processes of political change is difficult to cali-brate and challenging to represent. The modes of transmission that the society's members employed were varied and diffuse, and public manifes-tations of their policy ideas always followed processes of mediation and contestation that rendered them irrevocably transformed. One might ex-pect that of all historical figures, Milton Friedman would have looked back with some satisfaction at the public influence of his ideas, but even he was disquieted by the thickness inherent in the political process. Shortly after George W. Bush was elected to a second term, Friedman explained the sources of his discontent: "After World War II, opinion was socialist while practice was free market; currently, opinion is free market while practice is heavily socialist. We have largely won the battle of ideas (though no such battle is ever won permanently); we have succeeded in stalling the progress of socialism, but we have not succeeded in reversing its course. We are still far from bringing practice into conformity with opinion."[33] The programs that Friedman wanted to see dismantled had remained largely, although by no means entirely, intact. He worried, as he approached the hundredth anniversary of his birth, that he had helped transform the ideas but far less so the practices of his time.[34]

The history of the Mont Pèlerin Society can, and to some extent should, be read as an extended plea for the relevance of the history of ideas to the history of politics. Prior representations of the rise of modern American conservatism have tended to depict it as a domestic, popular, political movement, rooted in a set of sometimes pathological anxieties about the changing structure of the social environment. When ideas appear, they are invoked as strategic weapons or static tools, and only rarely as sites of contestation that are themselves subject to reformulation and change. The relationship between theory and praxis is richer than this narrative implies. The members of the Mont Pèlerin Society reveal the dynamic nature of a historical transformation that has too often been portrayed in unilinear terms.

The emergence of the conservative movement was enabled by the growing interconnectivity of the late twentieth-century world. The Mont Pèlerin Society demonstrates the degree to which the collapse of barriers to international communication has facilitated the incubation of dissent. Its earliest participants, despite their diverse personal experiences and regional backgrounds, described its formation in remarkably similar terms: individuals who were secluded within their national environments became, through the acts of congregation and communication, participants in a purposive community. A Russian proverb holds that one person on a battlefield is no warrior; similarly, isolated individuals do not constitute a movement. The members of the Mont Pèlerin Society were able to find traction for their ideas only through continued acts of interpersonal transmission, engagement, and support. The arguments employed by parochial politicians in the present day were formed within—and made possible by—a global community of ideas.

The rise of modern American conservatism was heavily inflected but not overdetermined by its populism. Even anti-intellectual movements draw on assumptions that are not wholly untouched by the philosopher's hand. The members of the Mont Pèlerin Society performed a number of roles that were essential to the conservative ascent over the long postwar era: they developed and refined academic theories that validated the predispositions of market advocates and persuaded others to reformulate their views; they popularized their perspectives in magazine articles and mass-market books; they provided guidance to the politicians and rhetoricians who more readily controlled the levers of legislative power; they lectured broadly in support of the policies they proposed and the ideas those policies embodied; they molded and trained subsequent generations of theoreticians and proselytizers; and they leveraged their academic reputations to legitimize the social philosophies their followers came to espouse. We may not be the slaves of defunct economists, but we cannot inhabit a world uncolonized by their ideas.

As one would expect—but as is not always implied—each gathering of the Mont Pèlerin Society unfolded as a dialogue rather than a chorus. No two individuals who are worthy of attention have ever manifested complete agreement in their respective views, and the society's coherence emerged only through the continued disputation of its members. Too often, histories of conservatism have fallen prey to the social-scientific impulse to harden ideas into rigid blocs, but it should tell us something that the figures often invoked as the ideological founders of "conservatism" or "neoliberalism" only rarely acceded to the use of either term as a description of their ideas. Amid their evident sympathies and points of convergence, they, like members of all ideological communities, devoted much closer attention to the problems that separated them than to those that brought them together. And the points of differentiation were substantial: they sharply diverged over the appropriate nature of their political role, the ethical foundations and implications of capitalism, and the desirability and practicability of laissez-faire. If the society is viewed synchronically, there were moments of coherence; if it is viewed diachronically, the overwhelming impression is one of change. The evolution of the society's membership resulted in a transformation of its shared assumptions, and in recent years the advocates of capitalism have been much more sanguine in their description of its benefits and much less convinced of its limitations than was the case when this book began.

The one commonality shared by all members of the Mont Pèlerin Society was a conviction that capitalist modes of social organization should be encouraged and preserved. In 1947, against the persistent specter of communism and amid the global detritus of ideological war, that was distinction enough. The question the members then sought to address, and about which they continually disagreed, was what kind of capitalism they would like to inhabit, or where and why the price mechanism should be implemented or restrained. In subsequent decades assumptions about the benefits of markets came to be much more broadly shared. The members of the Mont Pèlerin Society moved rightward with their surroundings, and their advocacy transitioned from the generic category of capitalism to the much more specific category of a capitalism unencumbered by substantial constraints. As we enter a new age of uncertainty, the global community again confronts the question with which the society's founding members began: To what extent do we wish to make ours a market-centered world? This remains a source of discontent. We have accepted the virtues of markets but failed to determine how to integrate them into life as we wish it to be.

NOTES

ACKNOWLEDGMENTS

INDEX

NOTES

Introduction

1. For further background on Keynes, see the three-volume biography by Robert Skidelsky: *John Maynard Keynes,* vol. 1, *Hopes Betrayed, 1883–1920* (London: Macmillan, 1983); vol. 2, *The Economist as Savior, 1920–1937* (London: Macmillan, 1992); vol. 3, *Fighting for Freedom, 1937–1946* (London: Macmillan, 2000). Also see R. F. Harrod, *The Life of John Maynard Keynes* (London: Macmillan, 1951); and Peter Clarke, *The Keynesian Revolution in the Making, 1924–1936* (Oxford: Clarendon Press, 1988).

2. John Maynard Keynes, *The End of Laissez-Faire* (London: Hogarth, 1927), 5. The lecture was first delivered as the Sidney Ball Lecture at Oxford in 1924 and subsequently at the University of Berlin in 1926.

3. Ibid., 17, 20.

4. Ibid., 32.

5. Ibid., 33.

6. John Elliott Cairnes, *Essays in Political Economy: Theoretical and Applied* (London: Macmillan, 1873), 244.

7. Keynes, *End of Laissez-Faire,* 32–33.

8. Ibid., 34–35.

9. Ibid., 36.

10. Ibid., 44.

11. Ibid., 38.

12. Skidelsky, *John Maynard Keynes,* vol. 2, *Economist as Saviour,* 225–229.

13. Keynes, *End of Laissez-Faire,* 52–53.

14. Ibid., 46–47.

15. Ibid., 50.

16. "Review: *The End of Laissez Faire,*" *Journal of Political Economy* 36, no. 1 (1928): 179–180; Sidney Webb, "The End of Laissez-Faire," *Economic Journal* 36, no. 143 (1926): 434–441.

17. Eric Hobsbawm, *The Age of Extremes: A History of the World, 1914–1991* (London: Michael Joseph and Pelham, 1994; reprint, New York: Vintage, 1996), 94–95 (page citations are to the reprint edition).

18. Michael Bernstein, *A Perilous Progress: Economists and Public Purpose in Twentieth-Century America* (Princeton: Princeton University Press, 2001), 64.

19. Frank Knight to Charles Tippetts, 7 July 1933, box 62, folder 10, Frank H. Knight Papers, Regenstein Library, University of Chicago (hereafter Knight Papers); Frank Knight to Dr. Edward Theiss, 9 December 1933, box 62, folder 9, Knight Papers.

20. In a speech before the Conservative Political Action Conference in 1981, Ronald Reagan stated, "Intellectual leaders like Russell Kirk, Friedrich Hayek, Henry Hazlitt, Milton Friedman, James Burnham, Ludwig von Mises—they shaped so much of our thoughts." Ronald Reagan, "Remarks at the Conservative Political Action Conference," in *Speaking My Mind* (New York: Simon and Schuster, 1989), 96. On a visit to the Conservative Research Department in 1975, Margaret Thatcher interrupted a discourse on the virtues of the "middle way" to throw a copy of Friedrich Hayek's *Constitution of Liberty* on a table and say, "This is what we believe." Richard Cockett, *Thinking the Unthinkable: Think-Tanks and the Economic Counter-revolution, 1931–1983* (London: HarperCollins, 1994), 174.

21. Alan Brinkley, "The Problem of American Conservatism," *American Historical Review* 99, no. 2 (1994): 409; Michael Kazin, "The Grass-Roots Right: New Histories of U.S. Conservatism in the Twentieth Century," *American Historical Review* 97, no. 1 (1992): 136.

22. Thomas Frank, *What's the Matter with Kansas? How Conservatives Won the Heart of America* (New York: Henry Holt, 2004). On the populist strains in conservative rhetoric, see Jonathan Rieder, "The Rise of the 'Silent Majority,'" in *The Rise and Fall of the New Deal Order,* ed. Steve Fraser and Gary Gerstle (Princeton: Princeton University Press, 1989), 243–268; Rick Perlstein, *Before the Storm: Barry Goldwater and the Unmaking of the American Consensus* (New York: Hill and Wang, 2001); and Dan T. Carter, *The Politics of Rage: George Wallace, the Origins of the New Conservatism, and the Transformation of American Politics* (New York: Simon and Schuster, 1995).

23. Lisa McGirr, *Suburban Warriors: The Origins of the New American Right* (Princeton: Princeton University Press, 2001), 163; Jerome L. Himmelstein, *To the Right: The Transformation of American Conservatism* (Berkeley: University of California Press, 1990), 45. For other representations of modern conservatism as an assemblage of allied but not integrated views, see Jonathan Schoenwald, *A Time for Choosing: The Rise of Modern American Conservatism* (Oxford: Oxford University Press, 2001), 8; and Sara Diamond, *Roads to Dominion: Right-Wing Movements and Political Power in the United States* (New York: Guilford, 1995), 6–7.

24. On status anxiety, see Richard Hofstadter, "The Pseudo-conservative Revolt," in *The New American Right*, ed. Daniel Bell (New York: Criterion, 1955), 42. Michael Rogin criticizes Hofstadter's emphasis on the irrational nature of mass political movements in *The Intellectuals and McCarthy: The Radical Specter* (Cambridge, Mass.: M.I.T. Press, 1967). On the racial politics of the conservative movement, see Joseph Crespino, *In Search of Another Country: Mississippi and the Conservative Counterrevolution* (Princeton: Princeton University Press, 2007); Thomas Byrne Edsall and Mary D. Edsall, *Chain Reaction: The Impact of Race, Rights, and Taxes on American Politics* (New York: W. W. Norton, 1992); Thomas Byrne Edsall, "The Changing Shape of Power: A Realignment in Public Policy," in Fraser and Gerstle, *Rise and Fall of the New Deal Order*, 269–293; Matthew Lassiter, *The Silent Majority: Suburban Politics in the Sunbelt South* (Princeton: Princeton University Press, 2006).

25. Steven B. Smith, *Reading Leo Strauss: Politics, Philosophy, Judaism* (Chicago: University of Chicago Press, 2006); Catherine Zuckert and Michael Zuckert, *The Truth about Leo Strauss: Political Philosophy and American Democracy* (Chicago: University of Chicago Press, 2006); Bruce Caldwell, *Hayek's Challenge: An Intellectual Biography of F. A. Hayek* (Chicago: University of Chicago Press, 2004); Michael Kimmage, *The Conservative Turn: Lionel Trilling, Whittaker Chambers, and the Lessons of Anti-communism* (Cambridge, Mass.: Harvard University Press, 2009); Jennifer Burns, *Goddess of the Market: Ayn Rand and the American Right* (Oxford: Oxford University Press, 2009). One valuable contribution to the literature arrived at an earlier date: Robert Devigne, *Recasting Conservatism: Oakeshott, Strauss, and the Response to Postmodernism* (New Haven: Yale University Press, 1994). Significant studies have begun to emerge on the major figures in the French and German political environments as well. See Olivier Dard, *Bertrand de Jouvenel* (Paris: Perrin, 2008); and Hans Jörg Hennecke, *Wilhelm Röpke: Ein Leben in der Brandung* (Stuttgart: Schäffer-Poeschel, 2005).

26. Kevin M. Kruse, *White Flight: Atlanta and the Making of Modern Conservatism* (Princeton: Princeton University Press, 2005).

27. Darren Dochuk, *From Bible Belt to Sun Belt: Plain-Folk Religion, Grassroots Politics, and the Rise of Evangelical Conservatism* (New York: W. W. Norton, 2011); Bethany Moreton, *To Serve God and Wal-Mart: The Making of Christian Free Enterprise* (Cambridge, Mass.: Harvard University Press, 2009).

28. On the relationship between financial markets and advocacy of laissez-faire in the early years of the twentieth century, see Julia C. Ott, "'The People's Market,'" chap. 9 in *When Wall Street Met Main Street: The Quest for an Investors' Democracy* (Cambridge, Mass.: Harvard University Press, 2011); and Beverly Gage, *The Day Wall Street Exploded: A Story of America in Its First Age of Terror* (Oxford: Oxford University Press, 2008). On the relationship between business organizations and free-market advocacy, see Kim Phillips-Fein, *Invisible*

Hands: The Making of the Conservative Movement from the New Deal to Reagan (New York: W. W. Norton, 2009); Phillips-Fein, "Business Conservatives and the Mont Pèlerin Society," in The Road from Mont Pèlerin: The Making of the Neoliberal Thought Collective, ed. Philip Mirowski and Dieter Plehwe (Cambridge, Mass.: Harvard University Press, 2009), 280–301; Moreton, To Serve God and Wal-Mart; and Eduardo Canedo, "The Rise of the Deregulation Movement in Modern America, 1957–1980" (PhD diss., Columbia University, 2008).

29. S. M. Amadae, Rationalizing Capitalist Democracy (Chicago: University of Chicago Press, 2003).

30. Steven M. Teles, The Rise of the Conservative Legal Movement: The Battle for Control of the Law (Princeton: Princeton University Press, 2008).

31. Jeffrey Hart, The Making of the American Conservative Mind: "National Review" and Its Times (Wilmington, Del.: ISI, 2005).

32. Kim Phillips-Fein surveys much of this emerging literature in "Conservatism: A State of the Field," Journal of American History 98, no. 3 (2011): 723–743.

33. Keynes, End of Laissez-Faire, 50.

34. On Hayek's selection criteria for members, see "Address by Prof. Hayek on Aims and Organisation of the Conference," 4, box 5, folder 13, Mont Pèlerin Society Records, Hoover Institution Archives, Stanford, Calif.

35. The most thorough scholarly treatment of the Mont Pèlerin Society is Bernhard Walpen's Die offenen Feinde und ihre Gesellschaft: Eine hegemonietheoretische Studie zur Mont Pèlerin Society (Hamburg: VSA, 2004). Philip Plickert provides a more sympathetic reconstruction in Wandlungen des Neoliberalismus: Eine Studie zu Entwicklung und Ausstrahlung der "Mont Pèlerin Society" (Stuttgart: Lucius & Lucius, 2008). R. M. Hartwell's A History of the Mont Pelerin Society (Indianapolis: Liberty Fund, 1995) provides a celebratory account of the society's activities. Ben Jackson examines the establishment of the society in the context of interwar debates over neoliberalism in "At the Origins of Neo-liberalism: The Free Economy and the Strong State, 1930–1947," Historical Journal 53, no. 1 (2010): 129–151. For discussion of the role of the Mont Pèlerin Society in the development of institutional supports for libertarian ideas, see Cockett, Thinking the Unthinkable, 100–121; and John L. Kelley, "The Revitalization of Market Liberalism," chap. 2 in Bringing the Market Back In: The Political Revitalization of Market Liberalism (Basingstoke: Macmillan, 1997).

36. Friedrich Hayek, "Individualism: True and False," in Individualism and Economic Order (Chicago: University of Chicago Press, 1948), 2–3.

37. Taylor Boas and Jordan Gans-Morse discuss this divergence in "Neoliberalism: From a New Liberal Philosophy to Anti-liberal Slogan," Studies in Comparative International Development 44, no. 2 (2009): 137–161.

38. George H. Nash surveys this milieu in *The Conservative Intellectual Movement in America: Since 1945* (New York: Basic Books, 1976).

39. Roger E. Backhouse, "The Rise of Free Market Economics: Economists and the Role of the State since 1970," in "Economists and the Role of Government," ed. Peter Boettke and Steven Medema, *History of Political Economy* 37 (2005): S355–S392.

1. Market Advocacy in a Time of Crisis

1. A. W. Coats, "The Distinctive LSE Ethos in the Inter-war Years," *Atlantic Economic Journal* 10, no. 1 (1982): 19; Lionel Robbins, *Autobiography of an Economist* (London: Macmillan, 1971), 72.

2. Aubrey Jones, in *My LSE*, ed. Joan Abse (London: Robson, 1977), 36.

3. Friedrich Hayek, "The Trend of Economic Thinking," *Economica* 40 (1933): 121. The title of Hayek's lecture was likely a reference to a recent volume edited by Rexford Tugwell, *The Trend of Economics* (New York: F. S. Crofts and Co., 1930).

4. Lionel Robbins, "The Present Position of Economic Science," *Economica* 28 (1930): 23.

5. Frank Knight to Adelphi Company, 9 May 1934, box 58, folder 2, Frank H. Knight Papers, Regenstein Library, University of Chicago (hereafter Knight Papers).

6. Wilhelm Röpke, "Fascist Economics," *Economica,* n.s., 2, no. 5 (1935): 85.

7. Robert Collins, *The Business Response to Keynes, 1929–1964* (New York: Columbia University Press, 1981), 30–31.

8. Yuval P. Yonay, *The Struggle over the Soul of Economics: Institutionalist and Neoclassical Economists in America between the Wars* (Princeton: Princeton University Press, 1998); Malcolm Rutherford, *The Institutionalist Movement in American Economics, 1918–1947* (Cambridge: Cambridge University Press, 2011); Wayne Parsons, *The Power of the Financial Press: Journalism and Economic Opinion in Britain and America* (Aldershot, U.K.: Edward Elgar, 1989).

9. Collins, *Business Response to Keynes,* 50.

10. Hayek, "Trend of Economic Thinking," 121.

11. George Bernard Shaw, "Sixty Years of Fabianism: A Postscript," in *Fabian Essays,* 6th ed., ed. George Bernard Shaw (London: George Allen and Unwin, 1962), 314.

12. Sidney Webb, "Introduction to the 1920 Reprint," in Shaw, *Fabian Essays,* 280.

13. Asa Briggs, "Introduction" (from an unpublished speech given to a Labor Party Conference in 1923), in Shaw, *Fabian Essays,* 15.

14. Shaw, "Preface to the 1931 Reprint," in Shaw, *Fabian Essays,* 257–258.

15. Coats, "Distinctive LSE Ethos in the Inter-war Years," 19–20.

16. Bernard Crick, in Abse, *My LSE,* 146.

17. Ralf Dahrendorf, *LSE: A History of the London School of Economics and Political Science, 1895–1995* (Oxford: Oxford University Press, 1995), 11.

18. Beatrice Webb diaries, 17 December 1931 (vol. 45), 28 February 1932 (vol. 46), 12 March 1934 (vol. 48), 19 January 1935 (vol. 49), and 1 May 1937 (vol. 51), in Passfield Papers, LSE Archives; emphasis in original.

19. Edwin Cannan, *The Economic Outlook* (London: P. S. King and Son, 1922), 11.

20. Edwin Cannan, *An Economist's Protest* (London: P. S. King and Son, 1927), vi–vii.

21. Donald Winch, *Economics and Policy: A Historical Study* (London: Hodder and Stoughton, 1969), 148; Joseph Dorfman, *The Economic Mind in American Civilization,* vol. 4 (New York: Viking, 1959), 171.

22. Edwin Cannan, "The Need for Simpler Economics," *Economic Journal* 43, no. 171 (1933): 370.

23. C. R. Fay, "Edwin Cannan: The Tribute of a Friend," *Economic Record* 13 (1937): 16.

24. Robbins, *Autobiography of an Economist,* 85; Friedrich Hayek, interview by Nadim Shehadi, 1983, Nadim Shehadi Papers, LSE Archives (hereafter Shehadi Papers).

25. Susan Howson, *Lionel Robbins* (New York: Cambridge University Press, 2011), 82.

26. Robbins, *Autobiography of an Economist,* 83.

27. T. E. Gregory, "Edwin Cannan: A Personal Impression," *Economica* 2, no. 8 (1935): 365.

28. Robbins, *Autobiography of an Economist,* 83.

29. Friedrich Hayek, "The London School of Economics, 1895–1945," *Economica* 13, no. 49 (1946): 23.

30. John Hicks, "Introductory: LSE and the Robbins Circle," in *Money, Interest and Wages* (Cambridge, Mass.: Harvard University Press, 1982), 4; Friedrich Hayek, interview by Nadim Shehadi, 1983, Shehadi Papers.

31. See, for example, Friedrich Hayek, interview by James Buchanan, 28 October 1978, Center for Oral History Research, UCLA Library.

32. Coats, "Distinctive LSE Ethos in the Inter-war Years," 25.

33. Erik Grimmer-Solem, *The Rise of Historical Economics and Social Reform in Germany, 1864–1894* (Oxford: Clarendon Press, 2003), 254.

34. Ludwig von Mises, "Economic Calculation in the Socialist Commonwealth," trans. S. Adler, in Friedrich Hayek, ed., *Collectivist Economic Planning: Critical Studies on the Possibilities of Socialism* (London: George Routledge and Sons, 1935; reprint, London: George Routledge and Sons, 1938), 110 (page citations are to the reprint edition).

35. Ludwig von Mises, *Socialism: An Economic and Sociological Analysis*, trans. J. Kahane (Indianapolis: Liberty Fund, 1981).

36. Howson, *Lionel Robbins*, 135.

37. Lionel Robbins, *An Essay on the Nature and Significance of Economic Science* (London: Macmillan, 1932), 72–76.

38. Robert Skidelsky, *John Maynard Keynes*, vol. 2, *The Economist as Savior, 1920–1937* (London: Macmillan, 1992), 334.

39. Susan Howson and Donald Winch, *The Economic Advisory Council, 1930–1939* (Cambridge: Cambridge University Press, 1977), 58.

40. Robbins, *Autobiography of an Economist*, 151.

41. Friedrich Hayek, interview by Armen Alchian, 11 November 1978, Center for Oral History Research, UCLA Library; Friedrich Hayek, interview by Nadim Shehadi, 1983, Shehadi Papers. Robbins's other suggestions included Jacob Viner, Wilhelm Röpke, and Bertil Ohlin. Howson, *Lionel Robbins*, 180.

42. Howson and Winch, *Economic Advisory Council*, 60–61.

43. For an overview, see Howson and Winch, *Economic Advisory Council*, 30–81; and Bruce Caldwell, "Introduction," in *The Collected Works of F. A. Hayek*, vol. 9, *Contra Keynes and Cambridge: Essays, Correspondence*, ed. Bruce Caldwell (Indianapolis: Liberty Fund, 1995), 20.

44. Howson, *Lionel Robbins*, 178.

45. Joan Robinson, "The Second Crisis of Economic Theory," in *Contributions to Modern Economics* (New York: Academic Press, 1978), 2.

46. J. C. Gilbert, interview by Nadim Shehadi, 4 March 1983, Shehadi Papers; Sir Roy Allen, interview by Nadim Shehadi, undated, Shehadi Papers; Aubrey Jones, in Abse, *My LSE*, 36.

47. For a synthesis of Hayek's theory of the business cycle, see Caldwell, "Introduction," 14–18.

48. Friedrich Hayek, *Prices and Production*, 2nd ed. (London: Routledge and Kegan Paul, 1935), 99.

49. Ibid., 127.

50. Robbins, *Autobiography of an Economist*, 127; Howson, *Lionel Robbins*, 200.

51. Friedrich Hayek, interview by Earlene Craver, 1978, Center for Oral History Research, UCLA Library.

52. Friedrich Hayek, interview by Armen Alchian, 11 November 1978, Center for Oral History Research, UCLA Library.

53. F. A. Hayek, *Hayek on Hayek: An Autobiographical Dialogue*, ed. Stephen Kresge and Leif Wenar (Chicago: University of Chicago Press, 1994), 100.

54. John Maynard Keynes, "The Pure Theory of Money: A Reply to Dr. Hayek," in Caldwell, *Contra Keynes and Cambridge*, 153.

55. John Maynard Keynes to Friedrich Hayek, 29 March 1932, in Caldwell, *Contra Keynes and Cambridge*, 173.

56. Piero Sraffa, "Dr. Hayek on Money and Capital," in Caldwell, *Contra Keynes and Cambridge*, 200, 205.

57. Keynes, "Pure Theory of Money," 154; Sraffa, "Dr. Hayek on Money and Capital," 201.

58. Robbins, *Autobiography of an Economist*, 132; Friedrich Hayek, interview by Nadim Shehadi, 1983, Shehadi Papers; Howson, *Lionel Robbins*, 200.

59. Friedrich Hayek, interview by Nadim Shehadi, 1983, Shehadi Papers; Howson, *Lionel Robbins*, 206.

60. Nicholas Kaldor, *Essays on Value and Distribution*, 2nd ed. (London: Duckworth, 1980), xi.

61. Robbins, *The Great Depression* (London: Macmillan and Co., 1934), 60.

62. Ibid., 125.

63. Ibid., 172, 183, 189, 190.

64. Ibid., 60.

65. Ibid., 194.

66. Hayek, "Trend of Economic Thinking," 123.

67. Lionel Robbins, letter to the editor, *Economist*, 28 May 1932, 1189.

68. John Maynard Keynes, *The General Theory of Employment, Interest, and Money* (London: Macmillan, 1936; reprint, San Diego: Harvest, 1964), 23–34 (page citations are to the reprint edition). For a contextual overview of the contributions of *The General Theory*, see Skidelsky, *John Maynard Keynes*, vol. 2, *Economist as Saviour*, 537–571.

69. Frank Knight to Jacob Viner, 6 August 1940, box 16, folder 24, Jacob Viner Papers, Mudd Library, Princeton (hereafter Viner Papers).

70. Jacob Viner, "Mr. Keynes on the Causes of Unemployment," *Quarterly Journal of Economics* 51 (1936): 147.

71. Jacob Viner to Lionel Robbins, 21 January 1938, box 22, folder 14, Viner Papers.

72. Albert Hirschman, "How the Keynesian Revolution Was Exported from the United States, and Other Comments," in *The Political Power of Economic Ideas*, ed. Peter A. Hall (Princeton: Princeton University Press, 1989), 349.

73. Paul Samuelson, "Lord Keynes and the General Theory," *Econometrica* 14 (1946): 187.

74. Joseph Schumpeter, "Review: *The General Theory of Employment, Interest and Money*," *Journal of the American Statistical Association* 31, no. 196 (1936): 791.

75. Tibor Scitovsky, interview by Nadim Shehadi, 15 November 1983, Shehadi Papers.

76. Nicholas Kaldor, interview by Nadim Shehadi, undated, Shehadi Papers; Howson, *Lionel Robbins*, 253.

77. Alvin Hansen, "Mr. Keynes on Underemployment Equilibrium," *Journal of Political Economy* 44, no. 5 (1936): 669.

78. Keynes, *General Theory of Employment, Interest, and Money*, 322.

79. Nicholas Kaldor, interview by Nadim Shehadi, undated, Shehadi Papers; Howson, *Lionel Robbins*, 252. On the notoriety of Kaldor's interjections, see Jack Fisher, interview by Nadim Shehadi, 1984, Shehadi Papers.

80. See, for example, Friedrich Hayek to Tim Groseclose, 9 June 1985, box 22, folder 27, Friedrich Hayek Papers, Hoover Institution Archives, Stanford, Calif. (hereafter Hayek Papers); Friedrich Hayek to Philippe Beaugrand, 19 January 1982, box 11, folder 40, Hayek Papers.

81. John Hicks, "The Hayek Story," in *Critical Essays in Monetary Theory* (Oxford: Oxford University Press, 1967), 214.

82. Ibid., 205.

83. Tibor Scitovsky, interview by Nadim Shehadi, 15 November 1983, Shehadi Papers.

84. Milton Friedman, "Mr. Market: A Nobelist Views Today's Fed, Currencies, Social Security, Regulation," interview by Gene Epstein, *Barron's,* 24 August 1998, 34.

85. Ludwig M. Lachmann, interview by W. W. Bartley III, January 1984, Shehadi Papers.

86. Dorothy Hahn, interview by author, Cambridge, U.K., November 2006.

87. Friedrich Hayek, interview by Jack High, 1978, Center for Oral History Research, UCLA Library.

88. Friedrich Hayek, interview by Nadim Shehadi, 1983, Shehadi Papers.

89. Lionel Robbins, *The Economic Problem in Peace and War* (London: Macmillan, 1947), 8, 14, 17, 75.

90. Ibid., 67; emphasis in original.

91. Robbins, *Autobiography of an Economist,* 109.

92. Robbins, *Economic Problem in Peace and War,* 67.

93. Ibid., 68.

94. Robbins, *Autobiography of an Economist,* 154.

95. Hayek, "Trend of Economic Thinking," 134.

96. Robbins, *Autobiography of an Economist,* 132.

97. Jacob Viner to Frances Viner, 28 October 1927, from the Jacob Viner correspondence files in the possession of Ellen Viner Seiler, Montgomery Township, N.J.

98. Lionel Robbins, *Jacob Viner: A Tribute* (Princeton: Princeton University Press, 1970), 2; emphasis in original.

99. Friedrich Hayek, "The Mythology of Capital," *Quarterly Journal of Economics* 50 (1936): 201.

100. Friedrich Hayek, interview by Leo Rosten, 15 November 1978, and interview by Jack High (undated), Center for Oral History Research, UCLA Library; Frank Knight, *The Ethics of Competition* (New York: Harper and Brothers,

1935; reprint, with an introduction by Richard Boyd, New Brunswick, N.J.: Transaction, 1997), 1 (page citations are to the reprint edition).

101. Lionel Robbins to Jacob Viner, 21 December 1937, box 22, folder 14, Viner Papers.

102. See, for example, Frank Knight, "Intellectual Confusion on Morals and Economics," *International Journal of Ethics* 45 (January 1935): 200–220. On the Chicago economists' movement away from institutionalism and Knight's conflicted stance on institutionalist economics, see Rutherford, *Institutionalist Movement in American Economics*, 145–150.

103. For a sharply critical review, see Frank Knight, "Unemployment: And Mr. Keynes's Revolution in Economic Theory," *Canadian Journal of Economics and Political Science* 3 (February 1937): 100–123. For a more generous (if still critical) assessment, see Viner, "Mr. Keynes on the Causes of Unemployment," 147–167.

104. Milton Friedman, interview by J. Daniel Hammond, 24 July 1989, unpublished.

105. Narratives emphasizing the continuity of the prewar and postwar Chicago economists include Louis A. Dow and Lewis M. Abernathy, "The Chicago School on Economic Methodology and Monopolistic Competition," *American Journal of Economics and Sociology* 22, no. 2 (1963): 235–249; H. Laurence Miller Jr., "On the 'Chicago School of Economics,'" *Journal of Political Economy* 70, no. 1 (1962): 64–69; Johan Van Overtveldt, *The Chicago School: How the University of Chicago Assembled the Thinkers Who Revolutionized Economics and Business* (Chicago: Agate, 2007); and, to a lesser extent, Melvin W. Reder, "Chicago Economics: Permanence and Change," *Journal of Economic Literature* 20, no. 1 (1982): 1–38. Some scholars have highlighted the unique positions held by the earlier Chicago economists, including Martin Bronfenbrenner, "Observations on the 'Chicago School(s),'" *Journal of Political Economy* 70, no. 1 (1962): 72–75; J. Ronnie Davis, "Chicago Economists, Deficit Budgets, and the Early 1930s," *American Economic Review* 58, no. 3 (1968): 476–481; and, most forcefully, Rob Van Horn and Philip Mirowski, "The Rise of the Chicago School of Economics and the Birth of Neoliberalism," in *The Road from Mont Pèlerin: The Making of the Neoliberal Thought Collective,* ed. Philip Mirowski and Dieter Plehwe (Cambridge, Mass.: Harvard University Press, 2009), 139–178.

106. Frank Knight, "Review: *Economic Planning and International Order,*" *Journal of Political Economy* 46 (April 1938): 259–260.

107. Henry Simons to Walter Lippmann, 5 October 1937, box 4, folder 18, Henry C. Simons Papers, Regenstein Library, University of Chicago (hereafter Simons Papers).

108. Jacob Viner to John Hicks, 3 April 1935, box 14, folder 7, Viner Papers.

109. Frank Knight, "Professor Mises and the Theory of Capital," *Economica* 8, no. 32 (November 1941): 409–410.

110. Jacob Viner to Paul Douglas, 3 June 1945, box 9, folder 5, Viner Papers; Frank Knight to General Editor and Committee on Publication, University of Chicago Press, 10 December 1943, box 40, folder 17, Knight Papers.

111. Reder, "Chicago Economics," 6. James Buchanan describes Knight's dominant personality within the department in "Frank H. Knight," in *Remembering the University of Chicago: Teachers, Scientists, and Scholars,* ed. Edward Shils (Chicago: University of Chicago Press, 1991), 244–252. On Knight as the progenitor of Chicago economics, see William Breit and Roger L. Ransom, *The Academic Scribblers,* rev. ed. (Chicago: Dryden, 1982), 193–204; Sherryl Davis Kasper, "Frank Hyneman Knight, the Moral Philosopher," chap. 2 in *The Revival of Laissez-Faire in American Macroeconomic Theory: A Case Study of the Pioneers* (Cheltenham, U.K.: Edward Elgar, 2002); and Johan Van Overtveldt, "Chicago's Pioneers: The Founding Fathers," chap. 2 in Van Overtveldt, *Chicago School.*

112. The quote is attributed to James Creighton in Alvin Johnson, *Pioneer's Progress* (New York: Viking, 1952), 227.

113. Buchanan, "Frank H. Knight," 244.

114. "By Degrees," *Daily Maroon* (University of Chicago), 18 March 1938, 1, box 137, Viner Papers.

115. James Buchanan, "Better than Plowing," in *Economics from the Outside In: "Better than Plowing" and Beyond* (College Station: Texas A&M University Press, 2007), 5.

116. George Stigler, *Memoirs of an Unregulated Economist* (New York: Basic, 1988), 16; Milton Friedman to the editor of *Challenge,* July 1964, box 1, folder 3, Milton Friedman Papers, Hoover Institution Archives, Stanford, Calif.; Milton Friedman, in Milton Friedman and Rose D. Friedman, *Two Lucky People: Memoirs* (Chicago: University of Chicago Press, 1998), 35; Paul Samuelson, "Economics in a Golden Age: A Personal Memoir," in *The Twentieth-Century Sciences: Studies in the Biography of Ideas,* ed. Gerald Holton (New York: W. W. Norton, 1972), 161.

117. Frank Knight to Jacob Viner, 9 September 1925, box 16, folder 24, Viner Papers. Dorothy Ross emphasizes this quality in a perceptive overview of Knight's economic and political thought in *The Origins of American Social Science* (Cambridge: Cambridge University Press, 1991), 420–427.

118. Frank Knight, *Risk, Uncertainty and Profit* (Boston: Houghton Mifflin, 1921; reprint, with prefaces by the author from the 1933, 1948, and 1957 editions, Mineola, N.Y.: Dover, 2006), 313 (page citations are to the reprint edition).

119. When simplifications were unavoidable, Knight would tell his students to employ them only through the use of a "relatively absolute absolute," that is, a temporary assumption that remained open to subsequent critique. See James Buchanan, "Born-Again Economist," in Buchanan, *Economics from the Outside In,* 78–79.

120. Frank Knight, "The Rôle of Principles in Economics and Politics," *American Economic Review* 41, no. 1 (1951): 6.

121. Knight, *Risk, Uncertainty and Profit,* 360.

122. Knight, "Ethics and the Economic Interpretation" (1922), in Knight, *Ethics of Competition,* 30.

123. Knight, "The Ethics of Competition" (1923), in Knight, *Ethics of Competition,* 58.

124. Frank Knight, "World Justice, Socialism, and the Intellectuals," *University of Chicago Law Review* 16, no. 3 (1949): 441.

125. Frank Knight to Walter Smith, 29 November 1933, box 62, folder 2, Knight Papers.

126. Frank Knight to Herbert Joseph Muller, 6 November 1957, box 61, folder 8, Knight Papers.

127. Paul Samuelson, "Jacob Viner, 1892–1970," *Journal of Political Economy* 80, no. 1 (1972): 6.

128. "By Degrees," *Daily Maroon,* 18 March 1938, 1.

129. Samuelson, "Economics in a Golden Age," 161.

130. Milton Friedman, interview by J. Daniel Hammond, 24 July 1989; Robert McQueen, "Viner: An Economist," *Winnipeg Free Press,* 18 March 1936; Buchanan, "Born-Again Economist," 75.

131. Viner's major work was *Studies in the Theory of International Trade* (New York: Harper and Brothers, 1937), and many of his essays are collected in *The Long View and the Short* (Glencoe, Ill.: Free Press, 1958). For further background, see Arthur I. Bloomfield, "On the Centenary of Jacob Viner's Birth: A Retrospective View of the Man and His Work," *Journal of Economic Literature* 30, no. 4 (1992): 2052–2085; Douglas A. Irwin, introduction to *Essays on the Intellectual History of Economics,* by Jacob Viner (Princeton: Princeton University Press, 1991), 3–35; and Donald Winch, "Jacob Viner as Intellectual Historian," in *Research in the History of Economic Thought and Methodology,* vol. 1, ed. Warren J. Samuels (Greenwich, Conn.: JAI, 1983), 1–17.

132. Lemuel Parton, "Who's News Today," *Baltimore Evening Sun,* 10 February 1936. Parton's representation of Viner's conservatism was not consistent; in a column two years earlier he had wondered why Viner was regarded as "the white hope of the conservatives," given that he was "a liberal economist" who had been "pretty thoroughly in agreement with the Administration fiscal program." See Lemuel Parton, "Who's News" (syndicated column), 4 October 1934, box 1, folder 3, Viner Papers.

133. Jacob Viner, interview by Wendell H. Link, Princeton, N.J., 11 February 1953, 36, Oral History Research Office, Columbia University Library.

134. Louis Stark, "Say 'Big Business' Fails in Humanity," *New York Times,* 21 August 1931, 22.

135. Jacob Viner to Laird Bell, 16 November 1937, box 3, folder 33, Viner Papers; emphasis in original.

136. Vermont Royster, "Politics and Economics," *Wall Street Journal,* 12 April 1951.

137. Jacob Viner to Lionel Robbins, 30 January 1940, box 22, folder 14, Viner Papers.

138. Robbins, *Jacob Viner,* 10.

139. "Banker's Objections," *Architectural Forum,* February 1935.

140. A. Wilfred May, "Conclusion from an 'All-Stars' Conference," *Commercial and Financial Chronicle,* 12 April 1951, 5; "Viner's Naming Supports Talk of Money Pact," unidentified press clipping from March 1934, box 137, Viner Papers.

141. Edmund W. Kitch, ed., "The Fire of Truth: A Remembrance of Law and Economics at Chicago, 1932–1970," *Journal of Law and Economics* 26 (1983): 176–177.

142. Simons's wife informed the coroner that he had been taking pills for severe insomnia in increasing doses in the months before his death, and that she did not believe that he had taken an overdose willfully. See "Coroner's Office Studies U. of C. Man's Death," *Chicago Daily News,* in box 10, folder 10, Simons Papers.

143. Don Patinkin, ed., *Essays on and in the Chicago Tradition* (Durham, N.C.: Duke University Press, 1981), 5.

144. Kitch, "Fire of Truth," 179.

145. On Henry Simons, see John Davenport, "The Testament of Henry Simons," *University of Chicago Law Review* 14 (1946): 5–14; Gregory T. Eow, "Henry Simons and the Chicago School of Economics," chap. 2 in "Fighting a New Deal: Intellectual Origins of the Reagan Revolution, 1932–1952" (PhD diss., Rice University, 2007); and Charles Oscar Hardy, "Liberalism in the Modern State: The Philosophy of Henry Simons," *Journal of Political Economy* 56, no. 4 (1948): 305–314.

146. Simons adopted the term "libertarian" in *Economic Policy for a Free Society* (Chicago: University of Chicago Press, 1948), 1. His binary worldview is apparent in his speech on the peace in box 9, folder 4, Simons Papers.

147. Henry Simons to Arthur Dahlberg, 6 October 1938, box 2, folder 31, Simons Papers.

148. Stigler, *Memoirs of an Unregulated Economist,* 20.

149. Henry Simons, "Address to 'Republicans,'" 3 August 1938, box 9, folder 2, Simons Papers.

150. Simons, *Economic Policy for a Free Society,* 43, 51, 58.

151. Henry Simons, box 9, folder 3, Simons Papers; emphasis in original.

152. Henry Simons to Trygve Hoff, 7 February 1939, box 3, folder 48, Simons Papers.

153. Aaron Director to Leonard Read, 24 November 1947, box 58, folder 16, Hayek Papers.

154. William F. Buckley Jr., *God and Man at Yale: The Superstitions of "Academic Freedom"* (Chicago: Henry Regnery, 1951; reprint, with an introduction by the author, South Bend, Ind.: Gateway, 1986), 94 (page citations are to the reprint edition).

155. Kitch, "Fire of Truth," 178.

156. Eduardo Canedo, "Ralph Nader and the Rise of Deregulation" (paper presented at the annual meeting of the American Historical Association, Atlanta, Ga., 6 January 2007).

157. J. Ronnie Davis, "Three Days with Knight: A Personal Reminiscence," *Nebraska Journal of Economics and Business* 13 (1974): 26; Patinkin, *Essays on and in the Chicago Tradition,* 266.

158. Stigler, *Memoirs of an Unregulated Economist,* 148–149.

159. Jacob Viner to Frank Knight, 8 November 1920, box 16, folder 24, Viner Papers; Frank Knight to Jacob Viner, 18 November 1920, box 16, folder 24, Viner Papers.

160. Jacob Viner to Frank Knight, 19 January 1926, box 16, folder 24, Viner Papers.

161. Jacob Viner to Frank W. Taussig, 13 June 1927, box 26, folder 1, Viner Papers.

162. Frank Knight to Jacob Viner, 15 June 1926, box 16, folder 24, Viner Papers.

163. Frank Knight to Jacob Viner, 9 December 1932, box 16, folder 24, Viner Papers.

164. Simeon E. Leland, "Jacob Viner: Teacher, Colleague, Friend," box 1, folder 4, Viner Papers.

165. Jacob Viner to Frank Knight, 31 July 1925, box 16, folder 24, Viner Papers.

166. Jacob Viner to J. M. Clark, 22 May 1935, box 6, folder 28, Viner Papers.

167. Jacob Viner to H. A. Millis, 7 June 1937, box 35, folder 22, Viner Papers.

168. Paul Douglas to Frank Knight, 5 January 1935, box 59, folder 16, Knight Papers.

169. Henry Simons to Carl Friedrich, 20 February 1935, box 2, folder 76, Simons Papers.

170. Henry Simons to C. W. Wright, 20 February 1939, box 8, folder 10, Simons Papers; emphasis in original.

171. Buchanan, "Better than Plowing," 5.

172. Milton Friedman, interview by J. Daniel Hammond, 24 July 1989.

173. Paul Samuelson, "Frank Knight, 1885–1972," *Newsweek,* 31 July 1972, 55.

174. Kitch, "Fire of Truth," 178–179.

175. See, for example, Barton Bernstein, "The New Deal: The Conservative Achievements of Liberal Reform," in *Towards a New Past: Dissenting Essays in American History,* ed. Barton Bernstein (New York: Vintage, 1969), 263–288; Skidelsky, *John Maynard Keynes,* vol. 2, *Economist as Savior,* 521.

176. Robbins, *Essay on the Nature and Significance of Economic Science,* 15.

177. Ibid., 31.

178. Ibid., 23.

179. Mark Blaug, *The Methodology of Economics; or, How Economists Explain* (Cambridge: Cambridge University Press, 1980), 87; D. P. O'Brien, *Lionel Robbins* (Houndmills, U.K.: Macmillan, 1988), 24.

180. Robbins, "Present Position of Economic Science," 23–24.

181. Frank Knight, "The Nature of Economic Science in Some Recent Discussion," *American Economic Review* 24, no. 2 (1934): 229n8.

182. See, for example, Frank Knight, "The Passing of Liberalism," 11, box 17, folder 25, Knight Papers; and Knight, "World Justice, Socialism, and the Intellectuals," 437–438.

183. Knight, *Risk, Uncertainty and Profit,* xxxv–xxxvi.

184. Knight, "Economic Theory and Nationalism," in Knight, *Ethics of Competition,* 348n.

185. Frank Knight to Paul Douglas, 27 December 1933, box 59, folder 16, Knight Papers.

186. Frank Knight to George L. Burr, 24 August 1934, box 58, folder 10, Knight Papers.

187. Angus Burgin, "The Radical Conservatism of Frank H. Knight," *Modern Intellectual History* 6, no. 3 (2009): 513–538.

188. Jacob Viner to J. Blaustein, 6 May 1943, box 3, folder 7, Viner Papers.

189. Jacob Viner to Lionel Robbins, 7 January 1935, box 22, folder 14, Viner Papers.

190. Hayek, "Trend of Economic Thinking," 123–124.

191. Frank Knight, for example, wrote several articles questioning the coherence of Austrian capital theory, including "Professor Hayek and the Theory of Investment," *Economic Journal* 45, no. 177 (1935): 77–94.

192. Friedrich Hayek, *Individualism and Economic Order* (Chicago: University of Chicago Press, 1948), 33n1, 35; Hayek, interview by Earlene Craver, 1978, Center for Oral History Research, UCLA Library.

193. Hayek, *Individualism and Economic Order,* 50–55.

194. Friedrich Hayek to David Theroux, 13 April 1980, box 42, folder 13, Hayek Papers; interview by Armen Alchian, 11 November 1978, Center for Oral History Research, UCLA Library; Friedrich Hayek to Israel M. Kirzner, 30 March 1985, box 30, folder 27, Hayek Papers.

195. Hayek, *Individualism and Economic Order,* 54.

196. Henry Simons to Charles D. Anderson, 29 November 1943, box 4, folder 29, Simons Papers.

197. Henry Simons to Irving Fisher, 1940, box 2, folder 66, Simons Papers.

198. Henry Simons to Frank Knox, 27 July 1939, box 3, folder 74, Simons Papers.

199. Henry Simons to Trygve Hoff, 7 February 1939, box 3, folder 48, Simons Papers.

200. Henry Simons to Malcolm H. Bryan, box 1, folder 57, Simons Papers.

201. Van Horn and Mirowski discuss Simons's proposal in "Rise of the Chicago School of Economics," 145–146.

202. Henry Simons, "Memorandum I," box 8, folder 9, Simons Papers.

203. Fay, "Edwin Cannan," 11.

204. Friedrich Hayek to Jacob Viner, 3 June 1947 and 13 July 1947, box 13, folder 26, Viner Papers.

205. Frank Knight to Warren Nutter, 16 April 1965, box 61, folder 12, Knight Papers.

2. Entrepreneurial Ideas

1. Barry Riccio, *Walter Lippmann: Odyssey of a Liberal* (New Brunswick, N.J.: Transaction, 1994), 98; Charles Merriam, "Review: *The Good Society,*" *Political Science Quarterly* 53, no. 1 (March 1938): 134.

2. William Rappard to Walter Lippmann, 11 September 1937, box 31, folder 61, William E. Rappard Papers, Bundesarchiv, Bern, Switzerland (hereafter Rappard Papers).

3. Henry Simons to Walter Lippmann, 5 October 1937, folder 1949, Walter Lippmann Papers, microfilm, Yale University Library (hereafter Lippmann Papers).

4. Friedrich Hayek to Walter Lippmann, 18 December 1959, folder 1011, Lippmann Papers.

5. Walter Lippmann, *An Inquiry into the Principles of the Good Society* (Boston: Little, Brown, 1937), vii.

6. The most extensive treatments of this topic are Serge Audier, *Le Colloque Lippmann: Aux origines du néo-libéralisme* (Lormont: Le Bord de l'Eau, 2008); Bernhard Walpen, "'Rue Montpensier 2' in Paris: Erste Adressanzeige des Neoliberalismus," chap. 1 in *Die offenen Feinde und ihre Gesellschaft: Eine hegemonietheoretische Studie zur Mont Pèlerin Society* (Hamburg: VSA, 2004); François Denord, *Néo-libéralisme version française: Histoire d'une idéologie politique* (Paris: Demopolis, 2007); François Denord, "French Neoliberalism and Its Divisions: From the Colloque Walter Lippmann to the Fifth Republic," in *The Road from Mont Pèlerin: The Making of the Neoliberal Thought Collective,* ed. Philip Mirowski and Dieter Plehwe (Cambridge, Mass.: Harvard Uni-

versity Press, 2009), 45–67; and Ben Jackson, "At the Origins of Neo-liberalism: The Free Economy and the Strong State, 1930–1947," *Historical Journal* 53, no. 1 (2010): 129–151.

7. For two recent typologies of the term, see Philip Mirowski, "Postface: Defining Neoliberalism," in Mirowski and Plehwe, *Road from Mont Pèlerin*, 417–458; and Johanna Bockman, *Markets in the Name of Socialism: The Left-Wing Origins of Neoliberalism* (Stanford, Calif.: Stanford University Press, 2011), 4.

8. Jamie Peck, "Remaking Laissez-Faire," *Progress in Human Geography* 32, no. 1 (2008): 3–43.

9. See David Harvey, *A Brief History of Neoliberalism* (Oxford: Oxford University Press, 2005); and Monica Prasad, *The Politics of Free Markets: The Rise of Neoliberal Economic Policies in Britain, France, Germany, and the United States* (Chicago: University of Chicago Press, 2006).

10. Michel Foucault, *The Birth of Biopolitics: Lectures at the Collège de France, 1978–1979,* ed. Michael Senellart and trans. Graham Burchell (Basingstoke, U.K.: Palgrave Macmillan, 2008), 217–219.

11. Audier, *Colloque Lippmann;* Jackson, "At the Origins of Neo-liberalism"; Philip Plickert, *Wandlungen des Neoliberalismus: Eine Studie zu Entwicklung und Ausstrahlung der "Mont Pèlerin Society"* (Stuttgart: Lucius & Lucius, 2008); Jamie Peck, *Constructions of Neoliberal Reason* (New York: Oxford University Press, 2010); Taylor Boas and Jordan Gans-Morse, "Neoliberalism: From New Liberal Philosophy to Anti-liberal Slogan," *Studies in Comparative International Development* 44, no. 2 (2009): 137–161.

12. On abeyance structures, see Verta Taylor, "Social Movement Continuity: The Women's Movement in Abeyance," *American Sociological Review* 54, no. 5 (1989): 761–775.

13. Ronald Steel, *Walter Lippmann and the American Century* (Boston: Little, Brown, 1980), 306.

14. Ibid., 300.

15. Riccio, *Walter Lippmann,* 97.

16. Ibid., 98.

17. Walter Lippmann, *The Method of Freedom* (New York: Macmillan, 1934), 14–15.

18. Ibid., vii.

19. Ibid., 69.

20. Ibid., 46; emphasis in original.

21. David Ciepley discusses Lippmann's shifting perspectives in this period in "The Retreat from Cooperation to Fiscal Compensation," chap. 7 in *Liberalism in the Shadow of Totalitarianism* (Cambridge, Mass.: Harvard University Press, 2006).

22. Lippmann, *Inquiry into the Principles of the Good Society,* vii; Friedrich Hayek, ed., *Collectivist Economic Planning: Critical Studies on the Possibilities*

of Socialism (London: George Routledge and Sons, 1935; reprint, London: George Routledge and Sons, 1938).

23. Walter Lippmann to Friedrich Hayek, 12 March 1937, folder 1011, Lippmann Papers.

24. Walter Lippmann to Henry Simons, 8 February 1937, folder 1949, Lippmann Papers.

25. Brian Van De Mark, "Beard on Lippmann: The Scholar vs. the Critic," *New England Quarterly* 59, no. 3 (September 1986): 402–405.

26. Friedrich Hayek to Walter Lippmann, 11 August 1937, folder 1011, Lippmann Papers.

27. Lippmann, *Inquiry into the Principles of the Good Society,* 4.

28. Ibid., 49.

29. John Dewey, "Liberalism in a Vacuum: A Critique of Walter Lippmann's Social Philosophy," *Common Sense,* December 1937, 9.

30. Lewis Mumford, "Mr. Lippmann's Heresy Hunt," *New Republic,* 29 September 1937, 220.

31. Merriam, "Review: *The Good Society,*" 133.

32. Lippmann, *Inquiry into the Principles of the Good Society,* 180, 208.

33. Henry Steele Commager, *The American Mind: An Interpretation of American Thought and Character since the 1880s* (New Haven: Yale University Press, 1950), 223.

34. W. H. Hutt, "Pressure Groups and *Laissez-Faire,*" *South African Journal of Economics* 6, no. 1 (1938): 5; emphasis in original.

35. Ralph Barton Perry, "The Liberal State," *Yale Review* 27, no. 2 (1937): 402.

36. Henry Simons to Walter Lippmann, 5 October 1937, folder 1949, Lippmann Papers.

37. Frank Knight, "Lippmann's *The Good Society,*" *Journal of Political Economy* 46, no. 6 (1938): 866.

38. Henry Simons to Walter Lippmann, 5 October 1937, folder 1949, Lippmann Papers.

39. Knight, "Lippmann's *The Good Society,*" 867–869.

40. Lippmann, *Inquiry into the Principles of the Good Society,* 31–32.

41. It should be noted here that Lippmann believed that the "common law" was grounded in an ambiguously defined "higher law." This argument puzzled his contemporaries but—as John Diggins has argued in "From Pragmatism to Natural Law," *Political Theory* 19, no. 4 (November 1991): 519–553—presaged his primary emphasis on natural law in *Essays in the Public Philosophy* (Boston: Little, Brown, 1955).

42. Friedrich Hayek to Walter Lippmann, 11 August 1937, folder 1011, Lippmann Papers.

43. See, for example, William Rappard to Walter Lippmann, 11 September 1937, box 31, folder 61, Rappard Papers; and Wilhelm Röpke to Walter Lippmann,

14 September 1937, Secured Files, Wilhelm Röpke Papers, Institut für Wirtschafts-politik, Cologne, Germany (hereafter Röpke Papers). The Secured Files in the Röpke Papers include portions of his correspondence with prominent individuals and are preserved in a safe separate from the remainder of his papers.

44. Van De Mark, "Beard on Lippmann," 403.

45. Wilhelm Röpke to Lionel Robbins, 13 February 1937; Wilhelm Röpke to Karl Brandt, 7 May 1936; and Wilhelm Röpke to Friedrich Hayek, 13 April 1936; all in Secured Files, Röpke Papers.

46. A. J. Nicholls, *Freedom with Responsibility: The Social Market Economy in Germany, 1918–1963* (Oxford: Clarendon Press, 1994), 39–41, 57–58.

47. Lippmann, *Inquiry into the Principles of the Good Society*, 240.

48. Wilhelm Röpke to Walter Lippmann, 14 September 1937, Secured Files, Röpke Papers.

49. Wilhelm Röpke to Karl Brandt, 7 May 1936, Secured Files, Röpke Papers; translated from the German.

50. Friedrich Hayek to Walter Lippmann, 6 April 1937, folder 1011, Lippmann Papers.

51. Walter Lippmann to Friedrich Hayek, 28 April 1937, folder 1011, Lippmann Papers.

52. Friedrich Hayek to Walter Lippmann, 11 June 1937, folder 1011, Lippmann Papers.

53. Friedrich Hayek to Walter Lippmann, 11 August 1937, and Friedrich Hayek to Walter Lippmann, 11 June 1937, folder 1011, Lippmann Papers.

54. Wilhelm Röpke to Lionel Robbins, 17 November 1937, Secured Files, Röpke Papers.

55. Wilhelm Röpke to Walter Lippmann, 14 September 1937, Secured Files, Röpke Papers.

56. Friedrich Hayek to Walter Lippmann, 10 July 1937, folder 1011, Lippmann Papers.

57. Louis Rougier, *La scolastique et le thomisme* (Paris: Gauthier-Villars, 1925). For a useful overview of Rougier's early career, see Jean-Claude Pont, "Coup d'œil sur l'œuvre de Louis Rougier," *Philosophia Scientiae*, Cahier spécial 7 (2007): 9–18.

58. Mathieu Marion, "Louis Rougier, the Vienna Circle and the Unity of Science," in *Paris-Wien: Enzyklopädien im Vergleich*, ed. Elisabeth Nemeth and Nicolas Roudet (Vienna: Springer, 2005), 151–157; Maurice Allais, *Louis Rougier: Prince de la pensée* (Lourmarin: Fondation de Lourmarin, 1990), 11.

59. Louis Rougier, *Les mystiques politiques contemporaines et leurs incidences internationales* (Paris: Librairie du Recueil Sirey, 1935), 11; translated from the French.

60. Serge Audier discusses the development of Rougier's ideas in *Colloque Lippmann*, 44–58.

61. Rougier, *Mystiques politiques contemporaines*, 121; translated from the French; emphasis in original.

62. François Denord, "Aux origins du néo-libéralisme en France: Louis Rougier et le Colloque Walter Lippmann de 1938," *Le Mouvement Social* 194 (2001): 18.

63. Louis Rougier to Walter Lippmann, 8 July 1937, folder 1848, Lippmann Papers.

64. The overtly propagandistic nature of the series inspired some concern among Rougier's colleagues. See, for example, William Rappard to Louis Rougier, 9 September 1937, box 42, folder 84, Rappard Papers.

65. Louis Rougier, "Retour au libéralisme," *Revue de Paris* 45, no. 1 (1 January 1938): 182.

66. Ibid., 187; translated from the French.

67. Louis Rougier, *Les mystiques économiques: Comment l'on passe des démocraties libérales aux états totalitaires* (Paris: Librairie de Médicis, 1938), 70–88.

68. See Walter Lippmann, *Public Opinion* (New York: Harcourt, Brace, 1922).

69. Rougier, "Retour au libéralisme," 189; translated from the French.

70. Rougier, *Mystiques économiques*, 7; translated from the French.

71. Rougier, "Retour au libéralisme," 196–197.

72. Walter Lippmann to Louis Rougier, 12 July 1937, folder 1848, Lippmann Papers.

73. Walter Lippmann to Louis Rougier, 4 May 1938, folder 1848, Lippmann Papers.

74. Louis Rougier to William Rappard, 21 June 1938 and 24 June 1938, box 42, folder 84, Rappard Papers; translated from the French.

75. Walter Lippmann to William Rappard, 23 June 1938, and William Rappard to Walter Lippmann, 24 June 1938, box 31, folder 61, Rappard Papers; and Wilhelm Röpke to Walter Lippmann, 24 June 1938, folder 1837, Lippmann Papers.

76. Walter Lippmann to Louis Rougier, 1 July 1938, folder 1848, Lippmann Papers.

77. Walter Lippmann to William Rappard, 1 July 1938, box 31, folder 61, Rappard Papers.

78. "Conférence Walter Lippmann," 12 July 1938, box 42, folder 84, Rappard Papers; translated from the French.

79. *Compte-Rendu des Séances du Colloque Walter Lippmann* (Paris: Librairie de Médicis, 1938), 13, 16; translated from the French; emphasis in original; Lippmann, *Inquiry into the Principles of the Good Society*, 284.

80. *Compte-Rendu des Séances du Colloque Walter Lippmann*, 99; translated from the French.

81. Louis Baudin, in *Compte-Rendu des Séances du Colloque Walter Lippmann*, 29; translated from the French.

82. *Compte-Rendu des Séances du Colloque Walter Lippmann,* 7; translated from the French.

83. Although he did not attend the conference, Frank Knight also disparaged the term "neoliberalism." His understanding of the term, however, was quite different; he believed that it referred to democratic governments that attempted to "organize and control modern economic life and remain democratic" (a goal that he believed was "impossible"). Frank Knight, "Economic Theory and Nationalism," in *The Ethics of Competition* (New York: Harper and Brothers, 1935; reprint, with an introduction by Richard Boyd, New Brunswick, N.J.: Transaction, 1997), 312 (page citations are to the reprint edition).

84. *Compte-Rendu des Séances du Colloque Walter Lippmann,* 31–34, 101; translated from the French.

85. For a further discussion of these two perspectives, see T. Lecoq, "Louis Rougier et le néo-libéralisme de l'entre-deux-guerres," *Revue de Synthèse* 4, no. 2 (April–June 1989), 241–255.

86. *Compte-Rendu des Séances du Colloque Walter Lippmann,* 91; translated from the French.

87. Nicholls, *Freedom with Responsibility,* 41–49.

88. *Compte-Rendu des Séances du Colloque Walter Lippmann,* 78; translated from the French.

89. Ibid., 83; translated from the French.

90. Ibid., 100, 105.

91. Ibid., 91; translated from the French.

92. Ibid., 69, 71, 75.

93. Ibid., 31; translated from the French.

94. For further discussion of Mises's relationship with the other participants in the "Colloque Lippmann," see Jörg Guido Hülsmann, *Mises: The Last Knight of Liberalism* (Auburn, Ala.: Ludwig von Mises Institute, 2007), 737–738.

95. Friedrich Hayek to Walter Lippmann, 11 June 1937, folder 1011, Lippmann Papers.

96. Fritz Machlup to Friedrich Hayek, 12 November 1940, box 36, folder 17, Friedrich Hayek Papers, Hoover Institution Archives, Stanford, Calif. (hereafter Hayek Papers).

97. Fritz Machlup to Friedrich Hayek, 14 March 1941, box 36, folder 17, Hayek Papers.

98. *Compte-Rendu des Séances du Colloque Walter Lippmann,* 109.

99. Ibid., 110.

100. Walter Lippmann to Louis Rougier, 28 October 1938 and 17 October 1939, folder 1848, Lippmann Papers.

101. Louis Rougier, "Centre International d'Études pour la Rénovation du Libéralisme," box R1, Louis Rougier Papers, Château de Lourmarin, Lourmarin,

France (hereafter Rougier Papers); translated from the French; emphasis in original.

102. Louis Rougier, "Manifeste du Centre International d'Études sur le Libéralisme," box R1, Rougier Papers.

103. Louis Rougier to Friedrich Hayek, 29 January 1940, box 42, folder 84, Rappard Papers; translated from the French.

104. Louis Rougier, "Centre International d'Études sur le Libéralisme," box R1, Rougier Papers; translated from the French.

105. Louis Rougier to Walter Lippmann, 3 March 1939, folder 1848, Lippmann Papers.

106. Louis Rougier to William Rappard, 2 July 1939, box 42, folder 84, Rappard Papers; Ludwig von Mises to Friedrich Hayek, 19 July 1939, box 38, folder 24, Hayek Papers.

107. Friedrich Hayek, introduction to *The Genius of the West,* by Louis Rougier (Los Angeles: Nash, 1971), xvi.

108. The best English-language overview of this incident is provided in Jeffrey Mehlman, "Louis Rougier and the 'Pétain-Churchill Agreement,'" chap. 7 in *Émigré New York: French Intellectuals in Wartime Manhattan, 1940–1944* (Baltimore: Johns Hopkins University Press, 2000).

109. Friedrich Hayek to Wilhelm Röpke, 17 August 1941, in "Briefe 1940–1942," Röpke Papers.

110. Wilhelm Röpke to Friedrich Hayek, 13 November 1941, box 79, folder 1, Hayek Papers.

111. Rougier told Maurice Allais that he was prevented from participating in the society by Lionel Robbins, who had reportedly said to Ludwig von Mises, "We English, we don't want to work with Rougier because he has criticized Churchill!" See Louis Rougier to Maurice Allais, 13 May 1947, in Allais, *Louis Rougier,* 34; translated from the French.

112. Olivier Dard, "Louis Rougier: Itinéraire intellectuel et politique, des années vingt à nouvelle *école," Philosophia Scientiae,* Cahier spécial 7 (2007): 50.

113. See Gaétan Pirou, *Néo-libéralisme, néo-corporatisme, néo-socialisme* (Paris: Gallimard, 1939), 36.

114. Hayek, introduction to Rougier, *Genius of the West,* xvi.

115. Walter Lippmann to Louis Rougier, 28 October 1938, folder 1848, Lippmann Papers.

116. The Soviet army found Mises's files on a train in Bohemia at the conclusion of the war; they were considered lost until their rediscovery in a secret archive in Moscow in 1991. See Hülsmann, *Mises,* 726–727.

117. Ibid., 756.

118. Ibid., 847.

119. William Rappard to Alvin Johnson, 9 January 1941, box 27, folder 53, Rappard Papers.

120. Friedrich Hayek to Wilhelm Röpke, 17 August 1941, in "Briefe 1940–1942," Röpke Papers.

121. Friedrich Hayek to Wilhelm Röpke, 12 April 1941, in "Briefe 1940–1942," Röpke Papers.

122. See Friedrich Hayek to William Rappard, 10 May 1942, and William Rappard to Friedrich Hayek, 26 August 1942, box 23, folder 46, Rappard Papers.

123. Friedrich Hayek to William Rappard, 25 March 1942, box 23, folder 46, Rappard Papers.

124. Wilhelm Röpke to Allan G. B. Fisher, 24 February 1939, Secured Files, Röpke Papers.

125. Ludwig von Mises to Friedrich Hayek, 1 December 1944, box 38, folder 24, Hayek Papers; Fritz Machlup to Friedrich Hayek, 23 October 1942, box 36, folder 17, Hayek Papers.

126. Ludwig von Mises to Friedrich Hayek, 18 June 1941, box 38, folder 24, Hayek Papers.

127. Friedrich Hayek, *The Road to Serfdom* (Chicago: University of Chicago Press, 1944; reprint, with an introduction by Milton Friedman and prefaces by the author from the 1956 and 1976 editions, Chicago: University of Chicago Press, 1994), 24 (page citations are to the reprint edition).

128. The most thorough examination of Röpke's life and career is Hans Jörg Hennecke, *Wilhelm Röpke: Ein Leben in der Brandung* (Stuttgart: Schäffer-Poeschel, 2005). For an English-language treatment of Röpke's ideas, see John Zmirak, *Wilhelm Röpke: Swiss Localist, Global Economist* (Wilmington, Del.: ISI, 2001). Nicholls discusses Röpke's role in the development of the social market economy in *Freedom with Responsibility*.

129. Wilhelm Röpke, *The Social Crisis of Our Time,* trans. Annette Jacobsohn and Peter Schiffer Jacobsohn (London: William Hodge, 1950), 6.

130. Ibid., 9.

131. Wilhelm Röpke to Friedrich Hayek, 29 May 1942, box 79, folder 1, Hayek Papers. The circulation of *Reader's Digest* in the mid-1940s exceeded eight million, and it distributed over 600,000 copies of its condensed version of *The Road to Serfdom* to the Book-of-the-Month Club alone. Milton Friedman, introduction to Hayek, *Road to Serfdom,* xix.

132. Röpke, *Social Crisis of Our Time,* 22–23.

133. Friedrich Hayek to Wilhelm Röpke, 6 June 1942, in "Briefe 1940–1942," Röpke Papers; Wilhelm Röpke to Philip Cortnoy, 31 January 1951, in "1951–1952," Röpke Papers.

134. Wilhelm Röpke, comments at the "Colloque d'Avignon" on 1 April 1948, as recorded in Néo-Libéralisme Annexe 2B, Rougier Papers; translated from the French. This is part of an extensive but incomplete transcript of the discussion.

135. Wilhelm Röpke to Lionel Robbins, 6 May 1936, Secured Files, Röpke Papers.

136. Röpke, *Social Crisis of Our Time*, 21.

137. Ibid., 220.

138. Ibid., 182.

139. Friedrich Hayek to Wilhelm Röpke, 6 June 1942, in "Briefe 1940–1942," Röpke Papers.

140. Wilhelm Röpke to Friedrich Hayek, 2 January 1945, Secured Files, Röpke Papers.

141. Röpke indicated that the following individuals had accepted positions as contributing editors: William Rappard (Geneva), Hans Barth (Zurich), Benedetto Croce (Rome), Luigi Einaudi (Italy), Salvador de Madariaga (Oxford), Harry Gideonse (Brooklyn), Howard S. Ellis (Washington), Allan G. B. Fisher (London), Verrijn Stuart (Utrecht), Walter Eucken (Freiburg), Alexander Rüstow (Istanbul), Friedrich Hayek (London), John Jewkes (Manchester), André Siegfried (Paris), and E. Heckscher (Stockholm). Wilhelm Röpke to William S. Schlamm, 8 July 1946, vol. 5, Röpke Papers.

142. Wilhelm Röpke to William S. Schlamm, 8 July 1946, vol. 5, Röpke Papers.

143. Wilhelm Röpke to Walter Eucken, 14 November 1945, Secured Files, Röpke Papers.

144. Wilhelm Röpke, "Plan for an International Periodical," box 79, folder 1, Hayek Papers; emphasis in original.

145. Ludwig von Mises to Friedrich Hayek, 31 December 1946, box 38, folder 24, Hayek Papers; translated from the German.

146. Albert Hunold to William Rappard, 6 March 1946, box 25, folder 50, Rappard Papers; Wilhelm Röpke to William S. Schlamm, 8 July 1947, vol. 5, Röpke Papers.

147. Wilhelm Röpke to Friedrich Hayek, 26 February 1946, box 79, folder 1, Hayek Papers; translated from the German.

148. Albert Hunold to Friedrich Hayek, 28 February 1946, Albert Hunold Papers, Institut für Wirtschaftspolitik, Cologne, Germany; translated from the German. The majority of Hunold's papers associated with the society were bequeathed to the Hoover Institution, where they formed the foundation of the Mont Pèlerin Society Records. Three binders of significant material, however, were instead added to the Röpke Papers in the Institut für Wirtschaftspolitik.

149. Nicholls, *Freedom with Responsibility*, 145–146.

150. Wilhelm Röpke to Friedrich Hayek, 22 June 1945, Secured Files, Röpke Papers.

151. Walter Lippmann to Friedrich Hayek, 14 February 1947, box 77, folder 15, Hayek Papers.

152. Friedrich Hayek to Wilhelm Röpke, 5 December 1945, box 79, folder 1, Hayek Papers.

153. Friedrich Hayek to Wilhelm Röpke, 5 December 1945, box 79, folder 1, Hayek Papers; Wilhelm Röpke to Friedrich Hayek, 25 October 1945, box 79, folder 1, Hayek Papers; translated from the German; and Wilhelm Röpke to Hans Kohn, 24 November 1948, vol. 6, Röpke Papers; translated from the German.

3. Planning against Planning

1. Friedrich Hayek, *Hayek on Hayek: An Autobiographical Dialogue,* ed. Stephen Kresge and Leif Wenar (Chicago: University of Chicago Press, 1994), 103.

2. Jeremy Shearmur, "Hayek, *The Road to Serfdom,* and the British Conservatives," *Journal of the History of Economic Thought* 28, no. 3 (September 2006): 310.

3. Hayek, *Hayek on Hayek,* 101.

4. Friedrich Hayek, "Planning and 'The Road to Serfdom,'" *Chicago Sun Book Week,* 6 May 1945, 1.

5. Bruce Caldwell, introduction to *The Collected Works of F. A. Hayek,* vol. 2, *The Road to Serfdom: Text and Documents,* by Friedrich Hayek (Chicago: University of Chicago Press, 2007), 19.

6. Lawrence Dame, "An Interview with Prof. Hayek: Economist Stresses Peril of Deficit Gov't Spending," *Boston Traveler,* 17 April 1945; Croswell Bowen, "How Big Business Raised the Battle Cry of 'Serfdom,'" *PM,* 14 October 1945.

7. Hayek, *Hayek on Hayek,* 105.

8. Friedrich Hayek, *The Road to Serfdom* (Chicago: University of Chicago Press, 1944; reprint, with an introduction by Milton Friedman and prefaces by the author from the 1956 and 1976 editions, Chicago: University of Chicago Press, 1994), 6, 16, 48 (page citations are to the reprint edition).

9. Bowen, "How Big Business Raised the Battle Cry of 'Serfdom.'"

10. John Heidenry, *Theirs Was the Kingdom: Lila and DeWitt Wallace and the Story of the "Reader's Digest"* (New York: W. W. Norton, 1993), 21.

11. Louis Gottschalk, "Some Recent Countersocialistic Literature," *Journal of Modern History* 17, no. 3 (1945): 222n11.

12. Bowen, "How Big Business Raised the Battle Cry of 'Serfdom.'"

13. Friedrich Hayek, "The Road to Serfdom," *Reader's Digest,* April 1945, 5.

14. Bowen, "How Big Business Raised the Battle Cry of 'Serfdom.'"

15. C. Hartley Grattan, "Hayek's Hayride; or, Have You Read a Good Book Lately?," *Harper's Magazine,* July 1945, 49.

16. Lawrence Frank, "The Rising Stock of Dr. Hayek," *Saturday Review of Literature,* 12 May 1945, 5; Harold Fleming, "Does Growth of Federal Powers

Point toward Totalitarianism?," *Christian Science Monitor,* 26 April 1945, 15; Henry Steele Commager, "Democracy and Planning," *American Mercury,* 1 June 1946, 113.

17. Herman Finer, *The Road to Reaction* (Boston: Little, Brown, 1946), xii, 15.

18. Friedrich Hayek, *Law, Legislation and Liberty,* vol. 1 (Chicago: University of Chicago Press, 1973), 58; Hayek, *Road to Serfdom,* xxiv; Friedrich Hayek to Paul Samuelson, 18 December 1980, box 48, folder 5, Friedrich Hayek Papers, Hoover Institution Archives, Stanford, Calif. (hereafter Hayek Papers).

19. Hayek, *Road to Serfdom,* 3, 21.

20. Ibid., 22, 43, 44, 133–135, 217.

21. Ibid., 41.

22. A. C. Pigou, "Review: The Road to Serfdom," *Economic Journal* 54, no. 214 (1944): 217; John Davenport, "A Great Restatement of Liberal Principles Comes out of Britain," *Fortune,* November 1944, 221; Louis Hacker, "The State vs. Liberty," *American Mercury,* 1 June 1946, 108; Antonin Basch, "Review: The Road to Serfdom," *Political Science Quarterly* 60, no. 3 (1945): 450.

23. "Road to Serfdom?," *Economist,* 13 May 1944, 639.

24. John Maynard Keynes to Friedrich Hayek, 28 June 1944, in John Maynard Keynes, *The Collected Writings of John Maynard Keynes,* vol. 27, *Activities 1940–1946,* ed. Don Moggridge (Cambridge: Cambridge University Press, 1980), 385.

25. Lawrence Dame, "An Interview with Prof. Hayek: Noted Economist Offers Plan to Salvage Germany," *Boston Traveler,* 19 April 1945; Dame, "An Interview with Prof. Hayek: British Economist Urges Free Trade for Prosperity," *Boston Traveler,* 18 April 1945.

26. Hayek, *Road to Serfdom,* 48.

27. John Maynard Keynes to Friedrich Hayek, 28 June 1944, in Keynes, *Collected Writings,* vol. 27, *Activities 1940–1946,* 386.

28. Victor S. Yarros, "Social Workers v. Hayekism," *Social Service Review* 20, no. 1 (1946): 106; Abba P. Lerner, "Planning and Freedom: Is Free Competition Essential to Efficiency?," *New Leader* 28 (20 January 1945): 7; Joseph Mayer, "Review: The Road to Serfdom," *Annals of the American Academy of Political and Social Science* 239 (1945): 202.

29. Eric C. Kollman, "Review: *The Road to Serfdom,*" *Mississippi Valley Historical Review* 32, no. 2 (1945): 265.

30. Grattan, "Hayek's Hayride," 47.

31. Hayek, "Planning and 'The Road to Serfdom,'" 1.

32. Hayek, *Hayek on Hayek,* 103.

33. Friedrich Hayek to William Rappard, 17 May 1945, box 23, folder 46, William E. Rappard Papers, Bundesarchiv, Bern, Switzerland (hereafter Rappard Papers).

34. Ludwig von Mises to Friedrich Hayek, 23 February 1945 and 29 September 1945, box 38, folder 24, Hayek Papers.

35. See Henry Simons to Friedrich Hayek, 2 July 1945, box 58, folder 16, Hayek Papers; and Friedrich Hayek to Wilhelm Röpke, 15 August 1945, box 79, folder 1, Hayek Papers.

36. "Memorandum on the Proposed Foundation of an International Academy for Political Philosophy Tentatively Called 'the Acton-Tocqueville Society,'" 1, August 1945, Albert Hunold Papers, Institut für Wirtschaftspolitik, Cologne, Germany (hereafter Hunold Papers). The earlier draft that Hayek sent to Luhnow is not known to have been preserved.

37. Ludwig von Mises to Friedrich Hayek, 1 December 1944, box 38, folder 24, Hayek Papers.

38. Hayek, "The Prospects of Freedom," 1, box 5, folder 12, Mont Pèlerin Society Records, Hoover Institution Archives, Stanford, Calif. (hereafter MPS Records).

39. "Memorandum on the Proposed Foundation," 1, 4, Hunold Papers.

40. "Memorandum on the Proposed Foundation," 6, Hunold Papers; Friedrich Hayek to Harold Luhnow, 17 January 1947, box 58, folder 16, Hayek Papers.

41. Friedrich Hayek, "The Prospects of Freedom," 10, box 5, folder 12, MPS Records.

42. Ibid., 12–13.

43. Karl Popper to Friedrich Hayek, 11 January 1947, box 305, folder 13, Karl Popper Papers, Hoover Institution Archives, Stanford, Calif.

44. Hayek, *The Constitution of Liberty* (Chicago: University of Chicago Press, 1960), 63.

45. Ludwig von Mises, "Observations on Professor Hayek's Plan," box 38, folder 24, Hayek Papers.

46. Ludwig von Mises to Salvador de Madariaga, 18 February 1953, and Ludwig von Mises to Salvador de Madariaga, 1 April 1953, box 31, folder 62, Rappard Papers.

47. William Rappard to Salvador de Madariaga, 7 July 1953, box 31, folder 62, Rappard Papers; translated from the French.

48. Bertrand de Jouvenel to Wilhelm Röpke, undated, vol. 5, Wilhelm Röpke Papers, Institut für Wirtschaftspolitik, Cologne, Germany (hereafter Röpke Papers).

49. Bertrand de Jouvenel to Wilhelm Röpke, undated, vol. 5, Röpke Papers.

50. Friedrich Hayek to Jasper Crane, 31 January 1949, box 73, folder 1, Hayek Papers.

51. Friedrich Hayek to Albert Hunold, 9 October 1946, box 5, folder 4, MPS Records.

52. Albert Hunold to Friedrich Hayek, 22 October 1946, box 5, folder 4, MPS Records.

53. Friedrich Hayek to Albert Hunold, 13 November 1946, box 5, folder 4, MPS Records.

54. Friedrich Hayek to Joseph Willits of the Rockefeller Foundation, 10 December 1950, box 59, folder 3, Hayek Papers.

55. Alan Ebenstein, *Friedrich Hayek: A Biography* (Chicago: University of Chicago Press, 2001), 298.

56. Friedrich Hayek to Wilhelm Röpke, 8 February 1946, box 79, folder 1, Hayek Papers.

57. Wilhelm Röpke to Friedrich Hayek, 12 July 1946, box 79, folder 1, Hayek Papers; translated from the German.

58. "The William Volker Fund: A Brief Statement of Policy," draft, 1955, William Volker Fund file, Felix Morley Papers, Herbert Hoover Presidential Library, West Branch, Iowa. I am indebted to Steven Teles for sharing these materials. For the story of William Volker's life, see the biography by the early Volker Fund administrator Herbert C. Cornuelle, *Mr. Anonymous: The Story of William Volker* (Chicago: Gateway, 1951).

59. Background on the Volker Fund was gathered during interviews by the author with Richard Cornuelle (New York City, 15 December 2006) and Ken Templeton (Indianapolis, 13 September 2007). Cornuelle and Templeton were both program officers at the Volker Fund in the 1950s.

60. Hayek, *Hayek on Hayek*, 126–127.

61. Friedrich Hayek to Harold Luhnow, 3 May 1945, box 58, folder 16, Hayek Papers.

62. Friedrich Hayek to Harold Luhnow, 27 September 1945, box 58, folder 16, Hayek Papers; Harold Luhnow to Friedrich Hayek, 27 January 1947, box 58, folder 16, Hayek Papers.

63. Cornuelle, interview.

64. Friedrich Hayek to William Rappard, 23 November 1946, box 45, folder 6, Hayek Papers.

65. Harold Luhnow to Friedrich Hayek, 6 January 1947, box 58, folder 16, Hayek Papers.

66. Friedrich Hayek to Harold Luhnow, 17 January 1947, box 58, folder 16, Hayek Papers.

67. Friedrich Hayek to Harold Luhnow, 17 January 1947, box 58, folder 16, Hayek Papers.

68. "Memorandum on the Proposed Foundation," 4–5, Hunold Papers.

69. Milton Friedman, in Milton Friedman and Rose D. Friedman, *Two Lucky People: Memoirs* (Chicago: University of Chicago Press, 1998), 159.

70. Jennifer Van Vleck, "No Distant Places: Aviation and the Global American Century" (PhD diss., Yale University, 2009), 301.

71. Tony Judt, *Postwar: A History of Europe since 1945* (New York: Penguin, 2005), 84–86.

72. Friedrich Hayek, "Address by Prof. Hayek on Aims and Organisation of the Conference," 1–2, 8, box 5, folder 13, MPS Records.

73. Henry Hazlitt, in "Discussion on Agenda, Etc.," box 5, folder 13, MPS Records. Members' comments during sessions of the 1947 conference were recorded in an abbreviated transcript by Friedrich Hayek's secretary, Dorothy Hahn. Hahn's notes are extensive and well organized, but her transcriptions of the members' comments are approximate. Although these notes provide a critical tool in the reconstruction of the conversations held at the initial meeting, the individuals cited from its discussions should not be held responsible for the exact words they are reported to have employed. "Minutes of Discussion at Mont Pelerin Conference," box 5, folder 13, MPS Records.

74. "Statement of Aims," 7 April 1947, box 5, folder 12, MPS Records. This draft is also available in R. M. Hartwell, *A History of the Mont Pelerin Society* (Indianapolis: Liberty Fund, 1995), 49–50.

75. "Statement of Aims," box 5, folder 12, MPS Records.

76. The full statement of aims is reprinted in Hartwell, *History of the Mont Pelerin Society,* 41–42.

77. Lionel Robbins, in "The Present Political Crisis," 9 April 1947, 8, box 5, folder 12, MPS Records; emphasis in original.

78. Melvyn Leffler, *The Specter of Communism: The United States and the Origins of the Cold War, 1917–1953* (New York: Hill and Wang, 1994), 58.

79. Michael Polanyi, in "The Present Political Crisis," 2, box 5, folder 12, MPS Records.

80. Bertrand de Jouvenel to Friedrich Hayek, 9 March 1948, box 76, folder 15, Hayek Papers.

81. Joseph Schumpeter, *Capitalism, Socialism and Democracy,* 3rd ed. (New York: Harper, 1950; reprint, with an introduction by Thomas McCraw, New York: Harper, 2008), 146 (page citations are to the reprint edition).

82. Bertrand de Jouvenel to Friedrich Hayek, 28 October 1947, box 76, folder 15, Hayek Papers.

83. Ludwig von Mises, "On the Study of the Cultural and Sociological Consequences of Capitalism," in *In Remembrance of the Congress of the Mont Pèlerin Society* (1950), 5, box 6, folder 8, MPS Records.

84. Ludwig von Mises, transcribed comments at the 1956 meeting of the Mont Pèlerin Society, Berlin, box 9, folder 8, MPS Records.

85. Maurice Allais to Friedrich Hayek, 12 May 1947, box 72, folder 6, Hayek Papers; Maurice Allais to Louis Rougier, 18 April 1947, Louis Rougier Papers, Château de Lourmarin, Lourmarin, France; translated from the French. Allais was a critic of private property in land; his views are elaborated in

Maurice Allais, *Traité d'économie pure* (Paris: Imprimerie Nationale, 1952), 804–852. This is the more widely available second edition of *À la recherche d'une discipline économique* (1943).

86. Raymond Aron, "Du prejuge favorable à l'égard de l'Union Sovietique," 10, box 7, folder 6, MPS Records; translated from the French.

87. Raymond Aron, *The Opium of the Intellectuals*, trans. Terence Kilmartin (Garden City, N.Y.: Doubleday, 1957), 209–210.

88. Friedrich Hayek, "The Intellectuals and Socialism," in *The Collected Works of F. A. Hayek*, vol. 10, *Socialism and War: Essays, Documents, Reviews*, ed. Bruce Caldwell (London: Routledge, 1997), 237.

89. Milton Friedman, in "Discussion on Agenda, etc," 4 April 1947, 5, box 5, folder 13, MPS Records.

90. On the decline of social Darwinism, see Richard Hofstadter, *Social Darwinism in American Thought* (Boston: Beacon, 1944; reprint with a new introduction by Eric Foner, Boston: Beacon, 1992), 201–204 (page citations are to the reprint edition).

91. Friedrich Hayek, "Individualism: True and False," in *Individualism and Economic Order* (Chicago: University of Chicago Press, 1948), 8.

92. Ibid., 9.

93. Ibid., 16.

94. Michael Polanyi, *The Logic of Liberty* (Chicago: University of Chicago Press, 1951; reprint, with a foreword by Stuart Warner, Indianapolis: Liberty Fund, 1998), 191 (page citations are to the reprint edition).

95. Ibid., 196.

96. Michael Polanyi, *Personal Knowledge: Towards a Post-critical Philosophy*, corr. ed. (Chicago: Chicago University Press, 1962), 64.

97. Ibid., 53.

98. Ibid., 264.

99. Ibid., 62.

100. Oakeshott acknowledges Polanyi in Michael Oakeshott, "Rationalism in Politics," in *Rationalism in Politics and Other Essays* (New York: Methuen, 1962; reprint, with a foreword by Timothy Fuller, Indianapolis: Liberty Fund, 1991), 13n (page citations are to the reprint edition).

101. Guy Griffith and Michael Oakeshott, *A Guide to the Classics; or, How to Pick the Derby Winner* (London: Faber and Faber, 1936).

102. C. P. Ives, "Harold Laski's Successor," *The Freeman*, 15 December 1952, 204.

103. Michael Oakeshott, "Political Education," in Oakeshott, *Rationalism in Politics*, 44, 60.

104. Ibid., 65.

105. A. E. Cherryman, "The Legend of LSE," *Truth*, 5 November 1954, 1363.

106. Oakeshott, "Rationalism in Politics," 26.

107. "Meeting on Organisation," 9 April 1947, box 5, folder 13, MPS Records.

108. Hayek, *Constitution of Liberty,* 420n9. Hannes H. Gissurarson, *Hayek's Conservative Liberalism* (New York: Garland, 1987), 20–24; Chandran Kukathas, *Hayek and Modern Liberalism* (Oxford: Clarendon Press, 1989), 20–31; and Christina Petsoulas, *Hayek's Liberalism and Its Origins* (London: Routledge, 2001), 107–145, all identify significant but limited commonalities between Hayek and Hume. For a defense of the coherence of Hayek's Humean inheritance, see Donald W. Livingston, "Hayek as Humean," *Critical Studies* 5, no. 2 (1991): 159–177.

109. David Hume, "Idea of a Perfect Commonwealth," in *Essays Moral, Political, and Literary* (Indianapolis: Liberty Fund, 1985), 512–513. For an introduction to Hume's political thought, see Duncan Forbes, *Hume's Philosophical Politics* (Cambridge: Cambridge University Press, 1975).

110. David Hume, "Of Commerce," in Hume, *Essays Moral, Political, and Literary,* 262.

111. Hayek, *Constitution of Liberty,* 25, 30, 38.

112. Frank Knight, "The Ethics of Competition," in *The Ethics of Competition* (New York: Harper and Brothers, 1935; reprint, with an introduction by Richard Boyd, New Brunswick, N.J.: Transaction, 1997), 49 (page citations are to the reprint edition).

113. Friedrich Hayek, "Equality, Value, and Merit," chap. 6 in Hayek, *Constitution of Liberty.*

114. Frank Knight, "Laissez-Faire: Pro and Con," *Journal of Political Economy* 75, no. 6 (1967): 792.

115. Knight, "Ethics of Competition," 38.

116. Bertrand de Jouvenel, *On Power: The Natural History of Its Growth* (New York: Viking, 1948; reprint, Indianapolis: Liberty Fund, 1993), 409–410 (page citations are to the reprint edition).

117. Bertrand de Jouvenel to Friedrich Hayek, undated, box 76, folder 15, Hayek Papers. Subsequent correspondence indicates that this letter was written in 1950.

118. Friedrich Hayek to Bertrand de Jouvenel, 4 October 1950, box 76, folder 15, Hayek Papers.

119. The anecdote about Mises is provided, without a source, in Richard Cockett, *Thinking the Unthinkable: Think-Tanks and the Economic Counterrevolution, 1931–1983* (London: HarperCollins, 1994), 114. Milton Friedman recalled the incident in "Best of Both Worlds," interview by Brian Doherty, *Reason* 27, no. 2 (1995): 37.

120. Ludwig von Mises, "On the Study of the Cultural and Sociological Consequences of Capitalism," 8–9, box 6, folder 8, MPS Records.

121. Wilhelm Röpke, "Progressive Ideologies," 4–5, box 6, folder 11, MPS Records.

122. Wilhelm Röpke, *A Humane Economy: The Social Framework of the Free Market,* trans. Elizabeth Henderson, 3rd ed. (Wilmington, Del.: ISI Books, 1998), 4, 8.

123. Wilhelm Röpke, in "Agricultural Policy," 9 April 1947, 4, box 5, folder 13, MPS Records.

124. William A. Orton to Friedrich Hayek, 8 January 1947, box 78, folder 25, Hayek Papers.

125. Karl Brandt, "Economic Strategy of Agricultural Development," 2, box 8, folder 8, MPS Records.

126. Oakeshott, "Rationalism in Politics," 26.

127. Michael Oakeshott to Friedrich Hayek, 18 April 1949, box 40, folder 24, Hayek Papers.

128. Michael Polanyi to Friedrich Hayek, 9 November 1955, box 43, folder 35, Hayek Papers.

129. Frank Knight, "Economic Theory and Nationalism," in Knight, *Ethics of Competition,* 292.

130. Ludwig von Mises, "A Program for Freedom," 2, box 81, folder 4, Hayek Papers.

131. Wilhelm Röpke, in "Modern Historiography and Political Education," 2 April 1947, 11, box 5, folder 13, MPS Records.

132. William Henry Chamberlin, "The Pragmatic Value of Liberty," 1, box 11, folder 3, MPS Records.

133. Knight, "Economic Theory and Nationalism," 342.

134. James Buchanan, "Economic Policy, Free Institutions, and Democratic Process," 10, box 8, folder 9, MPS Records.

135. James Buchanan and Gordon Tullock, *The Calculus of Consent* (Ann Arbor: University of Michigan Press, 1962), 96.

136. Ibid., 306.

137. Wilhelm Röpke, *The Social Crisis of Our Time,* trans. Annette Jacobsohn and Peter Schiffer Jacobsohn (London: William Hodge, 1950), 85, 95.

138. Hayek, "Individualism," 29–30.

139. Hayek, *Constitution of Liberty,* 106.

140. A. A. Shenfield, "Democracy, Socialism, and the Rule of Law," 5, box 8, folder 8, MPS Records.

141. A. A. Shenfield, "Liberalism and Colonialism," 1–2, box 11, folder 3, MPS Records.

142. Edmond Giscard d'Estaing, "Liberalisme et Colonialisme," 2, box 11, folder 3, MPS Records; translated from the French.

143. Karl Brandt, "Liberal Alternatives in Western Policies toward Colonial Areas," 8, 10, box 11, folder 3, MPS Records.

144. John MacCallum Scott, transcribed comments at the 1956 meeting of the Mont Pèlerin Society, Berlin, box 9, folder 8, MPS Records. On MacCallum

Scott's involvement in the Liberal International, see Julie Smith, "Liberals Unite: The Origins of Liberal International," *Journal of Liberal Democrat History,* no. 17 (1998): 3–4.

145. Lionel Trilling, *The Liberal Imagination* (New York: Viking, 1950; reprint, with an introduction by Louis Menand, New York: New York Review of Books, 2008), xv (page citations are to the reprint edition).

146. Richard Hofstadter, "The Pseudo-conservative Revolt," in *The New American Right,* ed. Daniel Bell (New York: Criterion, 1955), 35.

147. See Lisa McGirr, *Suburban Warriors: The Origins of the New American Right* (Princeton: Princeton University Press, 2001), 163; Jerome Himmelstein, *To the Right: The Transformation of American Conservatism* (Berkeley: University of California Press, 1990), 45; and Jonathan Schoenwald, *A Time for Choosing: The Rise of Modern American Conservatism* (Oxford: Oxford University Press, 2001), 8.

4. New Conservatisms

1. Friedrich Hayek to Albert Hunold, 5 February 1956, Albert Hunold Papers, Institut für Wirtschaftspolitik, Cologne, Germany (hereafter Hunold Papers); translated from the German.

2. Friedrich Hayek to Richard Ware, 5 May 1956, box 17, folder 37, Friedrich Hayek Papers, Hoover Institution Archives, Stanford, Calif. (hereafter Hayek Papers).

3. Friedrich Hayek to Michael Polanyi, 20 November 1955, box 43, folder 35, Hayek Papers.

4. Friedrich Hayek to Albert Hunold, 5 February 1956, Hunold Papers; Friedrich Hayek to Fritz Machlup, 18 February 1956, box 36, folder 17, Hayek Papers; Friedrich Hayek to Richard Ware, 5 May 1956, box 17, folder 37, Hayek Papers.

5. The events of the Hunold affair are recounted in Bernhard Walpen, *Die offenen Feinde und ihre Gesellschaft: Eine hegemonietheoretische Studie zur Mont Pèlerin Society* (Hamburg: VSA, 2004), 118–159; and R. M. Hartwell, *A History of the Mont Pelerin Society* (Indianapolis: Liberty Fund, 1995), 100–133.

6. Friedrich Hayek, "Address by Prof. Hayek on Aims and Organisation of the Conference," 1–2, box 5, folder 13, Mont Pèlerin Society Records, Hoover Institution Archives, Stanford, Calif. (hereafter MPS Records).

7. Friedrich Hayek, "A Rebirth of Liberalism," *The Freeman,* 28 July 1952, 731. This is an English-language version of an essay first published as "Die Überlieferung der Ideale der Wirtschaftsfreiheit," *Schweizer Monatshefte* 31, no. 6 (1951): 333–338.

8. In the society's early years the annual membership dues were $4.00.

9. Albert Hunold, "How the Mont Pèlerin Society Lost Its Soul" (1962), 13–14, box 3, R. M. Hartwell Papers, Hoover Institution Archives, Stanford, Calif. For the financing of the Kassel meeting, see "Rechnung über Einnahmen und Ausgaben der Jahrestagung der Mont Pèlerin Society," box 15, folder 3, MPS Records.

10. Harold Luhnow to Friedrich Hayek, 15 November 1956, box 58, folder 19, Hayek Papers.

11. Richard Cornuelle, interview by the author, New York City, 15 December 2006; Ken Templeton, interview by the author, Indianapolis, 13 September 2007.

12. Cornuelle, interview.

13. Harold Luhnow, "A Review and Recommendations," 5 September 1956, 46–48, private papers of Ken Templeton.

14. On the history of conservative think tanks in an American context, see James Allen Smith, *The Idea Brokers: Think Tanks and the Rise of the New Policy Elite* (New York: Free Press, 1991); Alice O'Connor, "Financing the Counterrevolution," in *Rightward Bound: Making America Conservative in the 1970s,* ed. Bruce Schulman and Julian Zelizer (Cambridge, Mass.: Harvard University Press, 2008), 148–168; and Jason Michael Stahl, "Selling Conservatism: Think Tanks, Conservative Ideology, and the Undermining of Liberalism, 1945–Present" (PhD diss., University of Minnesota, June 2008).

15. Hartwell, *History of the Mont Pelerin Society,* 26, 89, 91.

16. "Minutes of the Proceedings of the Meeting of the Council," 10 September 1959, box 13, folder 8, MPS Records.

17. Fritz Machlup to Trygve Hoff, 2 February 1961, box 86, folder 3, Milton Friedman Papers, Hoover Institution Archives, Stanford, Calif. (hereafter Friedman Papers).

18. Milton Friedman to Arthur Seldon, 10 October 1961, box 33, folder 2, Friedman Papers.

19. "Minutes of the Proceedings of the Meeting of the Council," 10 September 1959, box 13, folder 8, MPS Records. The minutes include a synthesis of participants' remarks, and do not reflect their exact words.

20. Lawrence Fertig, "This Year at Mont Pelerin," *National Review,* 23 October 1962, 311.

21. Arthur Seldon to Milton Friedman, 21 September 1961, box 33, folder 2, Friedman Papers.

22. Milton Friedman to Arthur Seldon, 10 October 1961, box 33, folder 2, Friedman Papers.

23. Milton Friedman to Richard Cornuelle, 23 September 1957, box 24, folder 9, Friedman Papers.

24. Friedrich Hayek, interview by W. W. Bartley III, Freiburg, Germany, 10 February 1983; partial transcript provided to the author by Bruce Caldwell.

25. Hayek, interview.

26. Friedrich Hayek, draft of valedictory address (unsent), February 1962, 6–8, box 71, folder 8, Hayek Papers.

27. Hunold later estimated these expenses at $20,000 between 1947 and 1953. Between 1953 and 1961 the expenses, which he estimated at $30,000, were absorbed by the Swiss Institute of International Studies, of which Hunold was director. Albert Hunold to Henry Regnery, 6 October 1961, box 43, folder 4, MPS Records; Hunold, "How the Mont Pèlerin Society Lost Its Soul," 12.

28. Friedrich Lutz to Milton Friedman, 19 May 1960, box 86, folder 2, Friedman Papers.

29. Trygve J. B. Hoff to Milton Friedman, 27 September 1961, box 86, folder 4, Friedman Papers.

30. Wilhelm Röpke, transcribed article sent to the members of the Mont Pèlerin Society, 10 August 1959, box 39, folder 11, MPS Records.

31. Albert Hunold to Felix Morley, 13 January 1948, box 29, folder 4, MPS Records; Albert Hunold to Felix Morley, 31 October 1947, box 29, folder 4, MPS Records.

32. Albert Hunold, editorial, *Mont Pèlerin Society Quarterly* 1, no. 3 (1959): 3; Albert Hunold to Wilhelm Röpke, 4 November 1959, in "1957–1958," Wilhelm Röpke Papers, Institut für Wirtschaftspolitik, Cologne, Germany (hereafter Röpke Papers); translated from the German.

33. Hayek, "Introduction," 1 April 1959, Hunold Papers. Hayek sent this statement to Hunold for inclusion in the first issue of the *Mont Pèlerin Society Quarterly*.

34. Albert Hunold to Alice Widener, 15 April 1959, box 39, folder 8, MPS Records.

35. Fritz Machlup to H. Berger-Lieser, 27 May 1959, box 39, folder 6, MPS Records; Albert Hunold to Fritz Machlup, 1 June 1959, box 39, folder 6, MPS Records. Several months earlier he wrote that "it is for the first time that the platform is not being arranged by Hayek and myself but is entirely in the hands of Jewkes and his commissars." Albert Hunold to Alice Widener, 16 March 1959, box 39, folder 8, MPS Records.

36. Albert Hunold to the members of the British Organising Committee, 14 August 1959, box 40, folder 2, MPS Records.

37. Albert Hunold to the Directors of the Mont Pèlerin Society, 30 December 1959, box 42, folder 8, MPS Records; Albert Hunold to Trygve Hoff, 2 February 1960, box 41, folder 6, MPS Records.

38. Friedrich Hayek to Wilhelm Röpke, 19 January 1960, box 79, folder 1, Hayek Papers; translated from the German.

39. Friedrich Hayek to the members of the Mont Pèlerin Society, 3 August 1960, box 86, folder 2, Friedman Papers.

40. Friedrich Hayek to H. Barth, W. Bretscher, W. Kägi, E. Bieri, F. A. Lutz, C. Mötteli, M. Silberschmidt, G. Winterberger, and R. Ottinger, 3 July 1960, box

14, folder 3, MPS Records; Friedrich Hayek to the Directors of the Mont Pèlerin Society Meeting at Kassel, 13 August 1960, box 14, folder 3, MPS Records.

41. William Rappard to Friedrich Hayek, 4 December 1947, box 23, folder 46, William E. Rappard Papers, Bundesarchiv, Bern, Switzerland.

42. Milton Friedman to Harry Gideonse, 8 August 1960, box 86, folder 2, Friedman Papers.

43. Milton Friedman to Frank Knight, 8 August 1960, box 86, folder 2, Friedman Papers.

44. Milton Friedman to Harry Gideonse, 8 August 1960, box 86, folder 2, Friedman Papers.

45. Louis Baudin, Franz Böhm, Wilhelm Röpke, and Albert Hunold to the members of the Mont Pèlerin Society, 18 July 1960, box 14, folder 3, MPS Records.

46. Wilhelm Röpke to the members of the Mont Pèlerin Society, 18 August 1960, box 14, folder 3, MPS Records.

47. Friedrich Hayek to Fritz Machlup, 20 July 1960, box 86, folder 2, Friedman Papers.

48. Wilhelm Röpke to the members of the Mont Pèlerin Society, December 1961, box 14, folder 3, MPS Records.

49. Transcript of the General Meeting, 9 September 1960, box 16, folder 4, MPS Records.

50. Fritz Machlup to Milton Friedman, Friedrich Hayek, Bruno Leoni, Clarence Philbrook, and George Stigler, 27 January 1961, box 86, folder 3, Friedman Papers; Albert Hunold to Milton Friedman, 15 February 1961, box 86, folder 3, Friedman Papers.

51. Wilhelm Röpke to Milton Friedman, 16 February 1961, box 86, folder 3, Friedman Papers.

52. Wilhelm Röpke to the members of the society, 6 December 1961, box 86, folder 4, Friedman Papers; Jacques Van Offelen to Wilhelm Röpke, 9 December 1961, box 88, folder 6, Friedman Papers; Wilhelm Röpke to the members of the society, December 1961, box 14, MPS Records; Friedrich Hayek, draft of valedictory address (unsent), February 1962, 30, box 71, folder 8, Hayek Papers.

53. Milton Friedman to the members of the Council of the Mont Pèlerin Society, 10 September 1961, box 86, folder 3, Friedman Papers.

54. Draft minutes of newly elected board of directors of the MPS, 9 September 1961, box 86, folder 3, Friedman Papers; Bruno Leoni, "From a Confidential Letter to George Koether," 14 October 1961, box 86, folder 4, Friedman Papers.

55. Milton Friedman to the members of the Council of the Mont Pèlerin Society, 10 September 1961, box 86, folder 3, Friedman Papers; Milton Friedman to Bruno Leoni, 12 September 1961, box 86, folder 3, Friedman Papers.

56. Letter from Milton Friedman, Friedrich Hayek, and George Stigler to Trygve Hoff, Hans Ilau, John Jewkes, Bruno Leoni, Fritz Machlup, Clarence Philbrook, and Arthur Shenfield, November 1961, box 86, folder 4, Friedman Papers.

57. Friedrich Lutz to Milton Friedman, 19 May 1960, box 86, folder 2, Friedman Papers.

58. Friedrich Hayek to Wilhelm Röpke, 11 November 1961, box 79, folder 1, Hayek Papers; translated from the German.

59. Friedrich Hayek to Alfred Müller-Armack, 6 January 1962, box 39, folder 13, Hayek Papers.

60. Hayek, "Rebirth of Liberalism," 731.

61. Friedrich Hayek to John Van Sickle, 10 November 1961, box 79, folder 32, Hayek Papers; Friedrich Hayek to John Van Sickle, 16 November 1961, box 79, folder 32, Hayek Papers.

62. Friedrich Hayek, draft of valedictory address (unsent), February 1962, 35, box 71, folder 8, Hayek Papers.

63. This intention is discussed in Friedrich Hayek to Bruno Leoni, 5 October 1961, box 86, folder 4, Friedman Papers; and Bruno Leoni to Milton Friedman, 15 November 1961, box 86, folder 4, Friedman Papers. For examples, see Friedrich Hayek to Wilhelm Röpke, 5 October 1961, box 86, folder 4, Friedman Papers; and Milton Friedman to Wilhelm Röpke, 31 October 1961, box 86, folder 4, Friedman Papers.

64. George Stigler to the members of the Mont Pèlerin Society, 19 December 1961, box 86, folder 4, Friedman Papers.

65. Eva Röpke to the members of the Mont Pèlerin Society, 21 December 1961, box 88, folder 6, Friedman Papers.

66. Albert Hunold, editorial, *Mont Pèlerin Society Quarterly* 3, no. 4 (1962): 2; Hunold, "How the Mont Pèlerin Society Lost Its Soul," 32–34.

67. Hartwell, *History of the Mont Pelerin Society*, 138. The resignations were coordinated by Alexander Rüstow, who forwarded a joint resignation letter to forty-eight members of the society for their consideration. Friedrich Hayek to John Jewkes, Milton Friedman, Bruno Leoni, Fritz Machlup, Daniel Villey, and Karl Brandt, 23 August 1962, box 86, folder 5, Friedman Papers.

68. Albert Hunold, "Kurzer Abriss über die Hintergründe des Zwistes in der Mont Pèlerin Society," 23 February 1962, Secured Files, Röpke Papers; translated from the German; emphasis in original.

69. Albert Hunold to Salvador de Madariaga, 4 November 1959, box 40, folder 1, MPS Records.

70. Wilhelm Röpke to Helmut Schoeck, 2 December 1955, in "1955–1957," Röpke Papers; translated from the German.

71. Alexander Rüstow to Hans Otto Wesemann, 17 December 1955, in "Rüstow II: 1946–1963," Röpke Papers; translated from the German.

72. The early years of the *National Review* are reconstructed by two staff members of the magazine in Linda Bridges and John R. Coyne Jr., *Strictly Right: William F. Buckley Jr. and the American Conservative Movement* (Hoboken, N.J.: John Wiley and Sons, 2007), 39–65.

73. William F. Buckley Jr., *God and Man at Yale: The Superstitions of "Academic Freedom"* (Chicago: Henry Regnery, 1951; reprint, with an introduction by the author, South Bend, Ind.: Gateway, 1986), lx–lxi (page citations are to the reprint edition). Buckley discusses the creation of and response to the book in *Miles Gone By: A Literary Autobiography* (Washington, D.C.: Regnery, 2004), 57–94.

74. Jeffrey Hart, *The Making of the American Conservative Mind: "National Review" and Its Times* (Wilmington, Del.: ISI, 2005), 8.

75. McGeorge Bundy, "The Attack on Yale," *Atlantic Monthly*, November 1951, 51.

76. William F. Buckley Jr., "Publisher's Statement," *National Review*, 19 November 1955, 5.

77. Ibid.

78. John Fischer, "Why Is the Conservative Voice So Hoarse?," *Harper's*, March 1956, 22; Dwight Macdonald, "Scrambled Eggheads on the Right," *Commentary* 21, no. 4 (1956): 367; emphasis in original.

79. Hart, *Making of the American Conservative Mind*, 9.

80. Wilhelm Röpke to F. Ernest Spat, 10 February 1956, in "1955–1957," Röpke Papers; translated from the German.

81. Florence Norton to Wilhelm Röpke, 8 August 1954, in "Letters 1953–1955," Röpke Papers; Wilhelm Röpke to Philip Cortnoy, 7 May 1955, in "1953–1955," Röpke Papers.

82. Wilhelm Röpke to Kurt L. Hanslowe, 20 February 1956, in "1955–1957," Röpke Papers; translated from the German. On the *National Review* and McCarthy also see Wilhelm Röpke to F. Ernest Spat, 28 February 1956, in "1955–1957," Röpke Papers.

83. Friedrich Hayek to Henry Regnery, 25 November 1951, box 24, folder 19, Hayek Papers.

84. John Judis to Friedrich Hayek, 15 May 1984, box 29, folder 47, Hayek Papers; Friedrich Hayek to John Judis, 27 May 1984, box 29, folder 47, Hayek Papers.

85. Friedrich Hayek to William F. Buckley Jr., 22 November 1961, in "1962–1963," Röpke Papers.

86. For additional background on Kirk, see Gerald J. Russello, *The Postmodern Imagination of Russell Kirk* (Columbia: University of Missouri Press, 2007); and W. Wesley McDonald, *Russell Kirk and the Age of Ideology* (Columbia: University of Missouri Press, 2004).

87. Henry Regnery, "A Conservative Publisher in a Liberal World," *Alternative*, October 1971, 15.

88. Russell Kirk, *The Conservative Mind: From Burke to Eliot* (Chicago: Henry Regnery, 1953; reprint, with an essay by Henry Regnery and a foreword by the author, Washington, D.C.: Regnery, 1985), 5 (page citations are to the reprint edition).

89. Ibid., 8–9.

90. "Generation to Generation," *Time*, 6 July 1953.

91. See Peter Viereck, *Conservatism Revisited: The Revolt against Ideology* (New York: Charles Scribner's Sons, 1949; reprint, with an author's note and introductory essays, New Brunswick, N.J.: Transaction, 2005); and Robert Nisbet, *The Quest for Community: A Study in the Ethics of Order and Freedom* (New York: Oxford University Press, 1953).

92. Russell Kirk, *The Sword of Imagination: Memoirs of a Half-Century of Literary Conflict* (Grand Rapids, Mich.: William B. Eerdmans, 1995).

93. Eugene Genovese, "Captain Kirk," *New Republic*, 11 December 1955, 35.

94. Clinton Rossiter, a political scientist at Cornell, was best known within the conservative movement as the author of *Conservatism in America* (New York: Knopf, 1955).

95. Wilhelm Röpke, "Liberaler Konservatismus in Amerika," *Neue Zürcher Zeitung*, 15 May 1955, 5; translated from the German.

96. Wilhelm Röpke to Russell Kirk, 14 March 1957, in "1955–1957," Röpke Papers.

97. Friedrich Hayek to Herbert Cornuelle, 28 March 1953, box 58, folder 18, Hayek Papers.

98. Friedrich Hayek to Henry Regnery, 14 April 1953, box 24, folder 19, Hayek Papers.

99. Friedrich Hayek to John Nef, 21 May 1953, box 39, folder 39, Hayek Papers.

100. John Nef to Friedrich Hayek, 30 May 1953, box 39, folder 39, Hayek Papers; Russell Kirk to John Nef, 22 October 1953, box 25, folder 24, John U. Nef Papers, Regenstein Library, University of Chicago (hereafter Nef Papers).

101. John Nef to Russell Kirk, 7 May 1956, box 25, folder 24, Nef Papers.

102. Russell Kirk to John Nef, 12 May 1956, box 25, folder 24, Nef Papers.

103. Wilhelm Röpke to Albert Hunold, 14 November 1956, in "1955–1957," Röpke Papers; Hayek, interview.

104. Henry Regnery, "The Making of *The Conservative Mind*," in Kirk, *Conservative Mind*, x.

105. Friedrich Hayek, *The Constitution of Liberty* (Chicago: University of Chicago Press, 1960), 398–399.

106. Louis Hartz, *The Liberal Tradition in America* (New York: Harcourt, Brace, 1955; reprint, with an introduction by Tom Wicker, San Diego: Harvest, 1991), 48–50 (page citations are to the reprint edition).

107. Hayek, *Constitution of Liberty*, 399, 410.

108. Ibid., 397.

109. Hunold, "How the Mont Pèlerin Society Lost Its Soul," 34; Wilhelm Röpke to Russell Kirk, 19 May 1960, in "1960–1962," Röpke Papers.

110. Russell Kirk, "The Mt. Pelerin Society," *National Review,* 21 October 1961, 270. His bleak assessment elicited an aggressive refutation from Aaron Director, Milton Friedman, and George Stigler in "The Mont Pelerin Society," *National Review,* 2 December 1961, 390.

111. Albert Hunold to Alexander Rüstow, 19 April 1960, in "1960–1962," Röpke Papers.

112. Wilhelm Röpke to Alexander Rüstow, 23 February 1962, in "Rüstow II: 1946–1963," Röpke Papers; translated from the German.

113. Wilhelm Röpke to Karl Brandt, 3 December 1962, in "1962–1963," Röpke Papers; translated from the German.

114. William F. Buckley Jr. to Wilhelm Röpke, undated, in "1962–1963," Röpke Papers.

115. Wilhelm Röpke to Karl Brandt, 3 December 1962, in "1962–1963," Röpke Papers; translated from the German.

116. Friedrich Hayek to Milton Friedman, John Jewkes, Bruno Leoni, Franz Böhm, Arthur Shenfield, and Fritz Machlup, 26 July 1962, in box 86, folder 5, Friedman Papers; Wilhelm Röpke to Albert Hunold, 18 August 1962, in "1962–1963," Röpke Papers; Wilhelm Röpke to Albert Hunold, 27 August 1962, in "1962–1963," Röpke Papers.

117. Albert Hunold to Wilhelm Röpke, 15 February 1962, in "1962–1963," Röpke Papers.

118. Wilhelm Röpke to Karl Brandt, 3 December 1962, in "1962–1963," Röpke Papers; Wilhelm Röpke to Russell Kirk, 14 February 1963, in "1963–1964," Röpke Papers; Wilhelm Röpke to Karl Brandt, 26 April 1963, in "1963–1964," Röpke Papers.

119. Albert Hunold to Wilhelm Röpke, 28 August 1963, in "1963–1964," Röpke Papers.

120. Wilhelm Röpke to Albert Hunold, 15 September 1964, in "1964–1965," Röpke Papers; Wilhelm Röpke to Karl Brandt, 31 December 1964, in "1964–1965," Röpke Papers.

121. Wilhelm Röpke to Karl Brandt, 31 December 1964, in "1964–1965," Röpke Papers; translated from the German.

122. Wilhelm Röpke to Trygve Hoff, 5 May 1965, in "1965," Röpke Papers.

123. On Röpke's death, see Hans Jörg Hennecke, *Wilhelm Röpke: Ein Leben in der Brandung* (Stuttgart: Schäffer-Poeschel, 2005), 239–246.

124. The comment is attributed to Harry Gideonse in a letter from Karl Brandt to Wilhelm Röpke, 8 December 1964, in "1964–1965," Röpke Papers.

125. Friedrich Hayek to George E. Shambough, 25 November 1951, box 49, folder 36, Hayek Papers. The comment on Anglo-American domination is attributed to a letter written by Arthur Kemp in 1963 in Hartwell, *History of the Mont Pelerin Society*, 141.

126. Kevin J. Smant, *Principles and Heresies: Frank S. Meyer and the Shaping of the American Conservative Movement* (Wilmington, Del.: ISI Books, 2002), 1–18.

127. Edward Shils, "Totalitarians and Antinomians," in *Political Passages: Journeys of Change Through Two Decades, 1968–1988*, ed. John H. Bunzel (New York: Free Press, 1988), 11.

128. Smant, *Principles and Heresies*, 13.

129. Frank S. Meyer, "Champion of Freedom," *National Review*, 7 May 1960, 305; Peter P. Witonski, "The Political Philosopher," *National Review*, 28 April 1972, 467.

130. Several prominent case studies of the intellectual transition from left to right in this period are examined in John Patrick Diggins, *Up from Communism: Conservative Odysseys in American Intellectual Development* (New York: Columbia University Press, 1994).

131. C. H. Simonds, "At Home," *National Review*, 28 April 1972, 468.

132. Smant, *Principles and Heresies*, 20.

133. Frank S. Meyer, "Collectivism Rebaptized" (1955), in *In Defense of Freedom and Related Essays* (Indianapolis: Liberty Fund, 1996), 9.

134. Meyer, *In Defense of Freedom*, 35, 64.

135. Ibid., 137.

136. Ibid., 131, 38.

137. Ibid., 60, 62n.

138. Ibid., 131–132.

139. The label "fusionist" was first adopted by L. Brent Bozell in "Freedom or Virtue?," *National Review*, 11 September 1962, 181. Meyer rejected the term, arguing that instead of creating a "fusion" he was trying "to help articulate" the "instinctive consensus" of the conservative movement, in "Why Freedom," *National Review*, 25 September 1962, 223.

140. Hartwell, *History of the Mont Pelerin Society*, 41.

141. Friedrich Hayek to John Davenport, 12 March 1970, box 16, folder 56, Hayek Papers.

142. George Stigler, *Memoirs of an Unregulated Economist* (New York: Basic, 1988), 145.

143. Milton Friedman to Richard Cornuelle, 23 September 1957, box 24, folder 9, Friedman Papers.

144. Bertrand de Jouvenel to Milton Friedman, 30 July 1960, box 86, folder 2, Friedman Papers.

145. Jouvenel's growing distance from the society and the decline of French influence in its debates are briefly discussed in Olivier Dard, *Bertrand de Jouvenel* (Paris: Perrin, 2008), 278–285.

5. The Invention of Milton Friedman

1. Alan Ebenstein, *Friedrich Hayek: A Biography* (Chicago: University of Chicago Press, 2001), 213.

2. The financial proposal offered by the University of Chicago and its inadequacy in relation to the Freiburg offer are detailed in D. Gale Johnson to John U. Nef, 16 April 1962, box 29, folder 33, Friedrich Hayek Papers, Hoover Institution Archives, Stanford, Calif. (hereafter Hayek Papers).

3. Milton Friedman, remarks at 1962 testimonial dinner for Hayek, in Alan Ebenstein, *Hayek's Journey* (New York: Palgrave Macmillan, 2003), 168–169.

4. Chesly Manly, "Hayek Feted as He Plans to Leave U. C.," *Chicago Daily Tribune*, 25 May 1962, 15.

5. Alan Ebenstein, *Friedrich Hayek*, 203.

6. Rose Friedman, in Milton Friedman and Rose D. Friedman, *Two Lucky People: Memoirs* (Chicago: University of Chicago Press, 1998), 334; Jasper Crane to Milton Friedman, 9 February 1962, box 86, folder 5, Milton Friedman Papers, Hoover Institution Archives, Stanford, Calif. (hereafter Friedman Papers); R. M. Hartwell, *A History of the Mont Pelerin Society* (Indianapolis: Liberty Fund, 1995), 151; Trygve Hoff to Milton Friedman, 14 August 1964, box 28, folder 14, Friedman Papers.

7. Friedrich Hayek to Morris Wilhelm, 22 February 1965, box 58, folder 13, Hayek Papers.

8. Warren J. Samuels discusses the Cold War context of Friedman's economic thought in "Rose Friedman and Milton Friedman's *Two Lucky People*," in *Research in the History of Economic Thought and Methodology*, vol. 18, ed. Warren J. Samuels (Greenwich, Conn.: JAI, 2000), 245.

9. Milton Friedman, in Friedman and Friedman, *Two Lucky People*, 362.

10. John Kenneth Galbraith, *Economics in Perspective: A Critical History* (Boston: Houghton Mifflin, 1987), 274.

11. Friedman's scientific work has attracted a vast literature within the economics profession. A selection of major articles is available in John Cunningham Wood and Ronald J. Woods, eds., *Milton Friedman: Critical Assessments*, 4 vols. (New York: Routledge, 1990). A subset of articles related to Friedman's monetarism is available in Robert Leeson, ed., *Keynes, Chicago and Friedman*, 2 vols. (London: Pickering and Chatto, 2003).

12. Two articles that situate Friedman's career within a broader political framework are Béatrice Cherrier, "The Lucky Consistency of Milton Friedman's Science and Politics, 1933–1963," in *Building Chicago Economics: New Per-*

spectives on the History of America's Most Powerful Economics Program, ed. Robert Van Horn, Philip Mirowski, and Thomas Stapleford (Cambridge: Cambridge University Press, 2011), 335–367; and Jamie Peck, "Finding the Chicago School," in *Constructions of Neoliberal Reason* (Oxford: Oxford University Press, 2010), 82–132. The only extended historical overview of Friedman's life is Lanny Ebenstein, *Milton Friedman: A Biography* (New York: Palgrave Macmillan, 2007). For an introduction to Friedman's economic and political writings, see Eamonn Butler, *Milton Friedman: A Guide to His Economic Thought* (New York: Universe, 1985). Briefer overviews of Friedman's intellectual career are available in Leonard Silk, *The Economists* (New York: Basic Books, 1974), 47–93; and William Breit and Roger L. Ransom, "Milton Friedman—Classical Liberal as Economic Scientist," chap. 14 in *The Academic Scribblers,* rev. ed. (Chicago: Dryden, 1982). William Frazer discusses the genesis and influence of Friedman's ideas in *Power and Ideas: Milton Friedman and the Big U-Turn,* 2 vols. (Gainesville, Fla.: Gulf/Atlantic, 1988).

13. Milton Friedman, in Friedman and Friedman, *Two Lucky People,* 21–32.

14. Milton Friedman, quoted in Lanny Ebenstein, *Milton Friedman,* 18.

15. Milton Friedman to William Breit, 22 June 1967, box 26, folder 1, Friedman Papers; Milton Friedman to Abraham Hirsch, 5 December 1983, box 8, George J. Stigler Papers, Regenstein Library, University of Chicago (hereafter Stigler Papers).

16. Milton Friedman, interview by J. Daniel Hammond, 24 July 1989, unpublished.

17. Milton Friedman to William Breit, 22 June 1967, box 26, folder 1, Friedman Papers.

18. Milton Friedman, interview by J. Daniel Hammond, 24 July 1989.

19. The most extensive single-author treatment of the formation of the Chicago School is Johan Van Overtveldt, *The Chicago School: How the University of Chicago Assembled the Thinkers Who Revolutionized Economics and Business* (Chicago: Agate, 2007). Rob Van Horn and Philip Mirowski provide an archival history of the foundations of the Chicago School in "The Rise of the Chicago School of Economics and the Birth of Neoliberalism," in *The Road from Mont Pèlerin: The Making of the Neoliberal Thought Collective,* ed. Philip Mirowski and Dieter Plehwe (Cambridge, Mass.: Harvard University Press, 2009), 139–180. Robert Leeson presents a sociological analysis of the Chicago School's attempts to engender intellectual and policy transformations in "The Chicago Counter-revolution and the Sociology of Economic Knowledge," chap. 3 in *The Eclipse of Keynesianism: The Political Economy of the Chicago Counter-revolution* (Houndmills, U.K.: Palgrave, 2000). The essays in Warren J. Samuels, ed., *The Chicago School of Political Economy* (University Park, Pa.: Association for Evolutionary Economics, 1976), continue to provide a useful introduction to the major debates surrounding Chicago economics. The contributions of Aaron

Director and the development of law and economics at Chicago are discussed in Steven M. Teles, "Law and Economics I: Out of the Wilderness," chap. 4 in *The Rise of the Conservative Legal Movement: The Battle for Control of the Law* (Princeton: Princeton University Press, 2008); and Rob Van Horn, "Reinventing Monopoly and the Role of Corporations: The Roots of Chicago Law and Economics," in Mirowski and Plehwe, *Road from Mont Pèlerin,* 204–237.

20. Milton Friedman, interview by J. Daniel Hammond, 24 July 1989.

21. Lanny Ebenstein, *Milton Friedman,* 25. Friedman recalled that the fellowship was "generous by the standards of the time," and that Columbia had "more of that kind of money at that time than any place." Milton Friedman, interview by J. Daniel Hammond, 24 July 1989.

22. Lanny Ebenstein, *Milton Friedman,* 26.

23. Milton Friedman, interview by J. Daniel Hammond, 24 July 1989.

24. Malcolm Rutherford, "Institutionalism at Columbia University," chap. 8 in *The Institutionalist Movement in American Economics, 1918–1947* (Cambridge: Cambridge University Press, 2011); Yuval P. Yonay, *The Struggle over the Soul of Economics: Institutionalist and Neoclassical Economists in America between the Wars* (Princeton: Princeton University Press, 1998), 56.

25. See Wesley Clair Mitchell, *Business Cycles* (Berkeley: University of California Press, 1913). Portions of this work were later published in revised editions.

26. Milton Friedman, interview by J. Daniel Hammond, 24 July 1989.

27. On Friedman's inheritances from Columbia, see Thomas Stapleford, "Positive Economics for Democratic Policy: Milton Friedman, Institutionalism, and the Science of History," in Van Horn, Mirowski, and Stapleford, *Building Chicago Economics,* 3–35.

28. Milton Friedman to Abraham Hirsch, 5 December 1983, box 8, Stigler Papers.

29. Milton Friedman to William Breit, 22 June 1967, box 26, folder 1, Friedman Papers.

30. See John Neville Keynes, *The Scope and Method of Political Economy,* 2nd rev. ed. (London: Macmillan, 1897), 35–36.

31. Milton Friedman to Abraham Hirsch, 5 December 1983, box 8, Stigler Papers.

32. Mitchell's influence on Friedman's methodology is discussed in Abraham Hirsch and Neil de Marchi, "Friedman's Unorthodox Position," chap. 2 in *Milton Friedman: Economics in Theory and Practice* (Ann Arbor: University of Michigan Press, 1990).

33. See Milton Friedman to Ronald Coase, 7 January 1982, box 7, Stigler Papers; Milton Friedman, in J. Daniel Hammond, "An Interview with Milton Friedman on Methodology," in *Research in the History of Economic Thought and Methodology,* vol. 10, ed. Warren J. Samuels (Greenwich, Conn.: JAI Press, 1992), 92.

34. Milton Friedman to Abraham Hirsch, 5 December 1983, box 8, Stigler Papers.

35. J. Daniel Hammond outlines the gradual emergence of Friedman's methodology in "Friedman's Methodology Essay in Context," in *The Anti-Keynesian Tradition*, ed. Robert Leeson (New York: Palgrave, 2008), 78–93.

36. Milton Friedman, "Lange on Price Flexibility and Employment: A Methodological Criticism," *American Economic Review* 36, no. 4 (1946): 613.

37. Ibid., 618.

38. Karl Popper, *The Logic of Scientific Discovery* (London: Hutchinson, 1959; reprint, London: Routledge Classics, 2002), 11 (page citations are to the reprint edition); emphasis in original.

39. Ibid.; emphasis in original.

40. Hammond, "Interview with Milton Friedman on Methodology," 100.

41. Milton Friedman to Abraham Hirsch, 5 December 1983, box 8, Stigler Papers.

42. Milton Friedman, "The Methodology of Positive Economics," in *Essays in Positive Economics* (Chicago: University of Chicago Press, 1953), 9.

43. Ibid., 14.

44. Ibid., 4.

45. Ibid., 5.

46. Milton Friedman, quoted in John McDonald, "The Economists," *Fortune*, December 1950, 111.

47. See Eugene Rotwein, "On 'The Methodology of Positive Economics,' " *Quarterly Journal of Economics* 73, no. 4 (1959): 554–575; and Paul Samuelson, in "Discussion," *American Economic Review* 53, no. 2 (1963): 231–236.

48. The most extensive treatment of Friedman's methodology is Uskali Mäki, ed., *The Methodology of Positive Economics: Reflections on the Milton Friedman Legacy* (New York: Cambridge University Press, 2009). Also see Bruce Caldwell, *Beyond Positivism: Economic Methodology in the Twentieth Century* (London: George Allen and Unwin, 1982), 173–188. Marion Fourcade observes the relationship between Friedman's instrumentalist epistemology and his defense of laissez-faire in *Economists and Societies: Discipline and Profession in the United States, Britain, and France, 1890s to 1990s* (Princeton: Princeton University Press, 2009), 93–96.

49. Erik Grimmer-Solem provides a nuanced overview of the *Methodenstreit* in *The Rise of Historical Economics and Social Reform in Germany, 1864–1894* (Oxford: Clarendon Press, 2003), 246–279.

50. Ludwig von Mises, *Human Action: A Treatise on Economics* (New Haven: Yale University Press, 1949), 862. On the distinction between Menger and Mises, see Karen Vaughn, *Austrian Economics in America: The Migration of a Tradition* (Cambridge: Cambridge University Press, 1994), 68–78.

51. Milton Friedman to Friedrich Hayek, 11 September 1975, box 20, folder 19, Hayek Papers.

52. Friedman later added, "You'll notice that Mises himself was a highly intolerant person. Ayn Rand was a highly intolerant person." See Milton Friedman, in Hammond, "Interview with Milton Friedman on Methodology," 101–102.

53. Milton Friedman to Jacqueline Blake, 25 October 1979, box 20, folder 53, Friedman Papers; Milton Friedman to Friedrich Hayek, 11 September 1975, box 20, folder 19, Hayek Papers.

54. Karen Vaughn provides a useful history of the trajectory of Austrian economics since the 1950s in *Austrian Economics in America*, 92–178. For a comparative analysis of "Austrian" and "Chicago" economics by an economist trained in the Austrian tradition, see Mark Skousen, *Vienna and Chicago: Friends or Foes?* (Washington, D.C.: Capital, 2005).

55. Milton Friedman to Ronald Coase, 7 January 1982, box 7, Stigler Papers.

56. Milton Friedman, in Hammond, "Interview with Milton Friedman on Methodology," 107.

57. Ibid., 99.

58. Milton Friedman, in "Best of Both Worlds," interview by Brian Doherty, *Reason* 27, no. 2 (1995): 38.

59. Milton Friedman, in Friedman and Friedman, *Two Lucky People,* 58.

60. Michael Bernstein, *A Perilous Progress: Economists and Public Purpose in Twentieth-Century America* (Princeton: Princeton University Press, 2001), 76.

61. Lanny Ebenstein, *Milton Friedman,* 36.

62. Ibid., 41, 47.

63. Ibid., 34.

64. Milton Friedman, interview by J. Daniel Hammond, 24 July 1989.

65. Milton Friedman, in Friedman and Friedman, *Two Lucky People,* 59.

66. Lanny Ebenstein, *Milton Friedman,* 34.

67. Milton Friedman, in "Best of Both Worlds," 33.

68. Milton Friedman, in Friedman and Friedman, *Two Lucky People,* 123.

69. Silk, *Economists,* 57–58; Frazer, *Power and Ideas,* vol. 1, 151.

70. See Milton Friedman and Simon Kuznets, *Income from Independent Professional Practice* (New York: National Bureau of Economic Research, 1945), 8–30, 135–137.

71. For minor administrative reasons related to the expense of submission, Friedman submitted his dissertation for a degree from Columbia rather than Chicago. Columbia had a requirement that doctoral dissertations be published before receipt of the degree. Milton Friedman, interview by J. Daniel Hammond, 24 July 1989.

72. Brian Doherty, *Radicals for Capitalism: A Freewheeling History of the Modern American Libertarian Movement* (New York: PublicAffairs, 2007), 155–157. Kim Phillips-Fein provides an extensive overview of Read's activities

and the early history of the FEE in *Invisible Hands: The Making of the Conservative Movement from the New Deal to Reagan* (New York: W. W. Norton, 2009), 3–86.

73. George Stigler to Milton Friedman, early August 1946, and George Stigler to Milton Friedman, 27 August 1946, in *Making Chicago Price Theory*, ed. J. Daniel Hammond (New York: Routledge, 1980), 20, 32.

74. Milton Friedman and George J. Stigler, "Roofs or Ceilings? The Current Housing Problem," *Popular Essays on Current Problems* 1, no. 2 (1946): 7–22.

75. Paul Krugman, "Who Was Milton Friedman?," *New York Review of Books*, 15 February 2007, 29.

76. Silk, *Economists*, 71.

77. Robert Bangs, "Review: *Roofs or Ceilings? The Current Housing Problem*," *American Economic Review* 37, no. 3 (1947): 482.

78. Robert Bangs, "Rent Relaxation Propaganda," *Washington Post*, 14 January 1947, 8.

79. Friedman and Stigler, "Roofs or Ceilings?," 10.

80. George Stigler to V. O. Watts, 7 August 1946, in Hammond, *Making Chicago Price Theory*, 19–20.

81. George Stigler to Milton Friedman, 27 August 1946, in Hammond, *Making Chicago Price Theory*, 32.

82. V. O. Watts to George Stigler, 28 August 1946, in Hammond, *Making Chicago Price Theory*, 34–35.

83. George Stigler to Milton Friedman, 27 August 1946, in Hammond, *Making Chicago Price Theory*, 32.

84. George Stigler to V. O. Watts, 3 September 1946, in Hammond, *Making Chicago Price Theory*, 38.

85. Milton Friedman, in Friedman and Friedman, *Two Lucky People*, 151.

86. Milton Friedman, citation of a wire transcript from 9 August 1946 in a letter to Leonard Read, 10 August 1946, in Hammond, *Making Chicago Price Theory*, 21.

87. Milton Friedman, in Friedman and Friedman, *Two Lucky People*, 159.

88. Milton Friedman, in "Best of Both Worlds," 34, 36.

89. Milton Friedman, "Neoliberalism and Its Prospects," 4–7, box 42, folder 8, Friedman Papers. A version of this essay was translated into Norwegian and published as "Nyliberalismen og dens Muligheter," *Farmand*, 17 February 1951, 89–93.

90. On the Free Market Study, see Van Horn and Mirowski, "Rise of the Chicago School of Economics and the Birth of Neoliberalism."

91. Aaron Director, quoted by Rose Friedman, in Friedman and Friedman, *Two Lucky People*, 81; Arlene Hershman and Susan Antilla, "The Men Who Sell the Free Market," *Dun's Review*, June 1979.

92. Steven G. Medema, "Chicago Price Theory and Chicago Law and Economics: A Tale of Two Transitions," in Van Horn, Mirowski, and Stapleford, *Building Chicago Economics,* 164–166.

93. Edward Nik-Khah, "George Stigler, the Graduate School of Business, and the Pillars of the Chicago School," in Van Horn, Mirowski, and Stapleford, *Building Chicago Economics,* 124.

94. George Stigler, "The Case against Big Business," *Fortune,* May 1952, 167.

95. George Stigler, "What Can Regulators Regulate? The Case of Electricity," *Journal of Law and Economics* 5 (1962): 1–16; Stigler, "Public Regulation of the Securities Markets," *Journal of Business* 37, no. 2 (1964): 117–142; Stigler, "The Theory of Economic Regulation," *Bell Journal of Economics and Management Science* 2, no. 1 (1971): 3–21.

96. Eduardo Canedo, "The Rise of the Deregulation Movement in Modern America, 1957–1980" (PhD diss., Columbia University, 2008), 98–133.

97. Ross Emmett, "Sharpening Tools in the Workshop: The Workshop System and the Chicago School's Success," in Van Horn, Mirowski, and Stapleford, *Building Chicago Economics,* 93–115.

98. George Stigler, "Do Economists Matter?," in *The Economist as Preacher and Other Essays* (Chicago: University of Chicago Press, 1982), 67.

99. William Volker Fund, "Review and Recommendations," 1956, 16, private papers of Ken Templeton.

100. Harold Luhnow to Felix Morley, 25 January 1956, William Volker Fund file, Felix Morley Papers, Herbert Hoover Presidential Library, West Branch, Iowa (hereafter Morley Papers).

101. William Volker Fund, "Review and Recommendations," 1956, 8, private papers of Ken Templeton; Harold Luhnow to Felix Morley, 25 January 1956, Morley Papers.

102. Milton Friedman, in Friedman and Friedman, *Two Lucky People,* 339.

103. Form letter, 9 December 1954, box 34, folder 29, Friedman Papers.

104. Milton Friedman, *Capitalism and Freedom* (Chicago: University of Chicago Press, 1962; reprint, with a preface by the author, Chicago: University of Chicago Press, 1982), x (page citations are to the reprint edition).

105. Milton Friedman, in "Best of Both Worlds," 34.

106. Friedman, *Capitalism and Freedom,* x.

107. Milton Friedman, in "Best of Both Worlds," 35.

108. Friedman, *Capitalism and Freedom,* 34, 131.

109. Ibid., 195.

110. Ibid., 35–36.

111. Milton Friedman, "An Interview with Milton Friedman," interview by Russell Roberts, *Library of Economics and Liberty,* 4 September 2006, http://www.econlib.org/library/Columns/y2006/Friedmantranscript.html; Milton Friedman, interview by J. Daniel Hammond, 24 July 1989.

112. Milton Friedman to Roland Holmes, 21 November 1957, box 28, folder 16, Friedman Papers.

113. Milton Friedman, in "Best of Both Worlds," 35.

114. Excerpted from the *Philadelphia Daily News,* 4 May 1961, box 1, folder 1, Friedman Papers.

115. For examples of Friedman's occasional use of the word "conservative" in relation to his ideas, see Milton Friedman to Raymond Kirby, 14 January 1949, box 27, folder 22, Friedman Papers; and Milton Friedman to Samuel Brooks, 2 July 1969, box 10, folder 7, Friedman Papers.

116. John Davenport, "The Radical Economics of Milton Friedman," *Fortune,* 1 June 1967, 131.

117. Robert Edward Brown, "Milton Friedman," *Human Behavior,* November 1978, 30.

118. Friedman, *Capitalism and Freedom,* 6.

119. "The American Economist Milton Friedman, in Conversation with Robert McKenzie, Gives His View of How Our Economic Problems Could Be Solved," *Listener,* 11 February 1971, 169. On philosophical radicalism, see Elie Halévy, *The Growth of Philosophic Radicalism,* trans. Mary Morris (London: Faber and Gwyer, 1928; reprint, Boston: Beacon, 1955).

120. Joseph A. Schumpeter, *History of Economic Analysis,* ed. Elizabeth Boody Schumpeter (New York: Oxford University Press, 1954), 394.

121. Milton Friedman, in "Best of Both Worlds," 35.

122. Friedrich Hayek, *The Constitution of Liberty* (Chicago: University of Chicago Press, 1960), 397.

123. "Whatever Happened to Free Enterprise?," *Vision,* April 1972, 43.

124. Friedman's conception of an unencumbered and individualistic frontier lifestyle drew on a narrative of western history that was common among historians in the early twentieth century. An exemplary text is Frederic Paxson, *History of the American Frontier, 1763–1893* (Boston: Houghton Mifflin, 1924). Long before Friedman delivered his speech, this narrative had been subjected to devastating criticisms; see, for, example, Benjamin Wright, "American Democracy and the Frontier," *Yale Review* 20 (1931): 349–365.

125. Milton Friedman, "The Future of Capitalism," from the Student Conference on National Affairs, Texas A&M University, Twentieth Proceedings, 1975, 8, box 55, folder 15, Friedman Papers.

126. Milton Friedman, "Individuality and the New Society: The Market vs. the Bureaucrat," 16 March 1968, box 50, folder 2, Friedman Papers.

127. Milton Friedman, "The Future of the American Economy," Bicentennial Lecture, American Experience Program, University of Pittsburgh, 5 February 1976, box 55, folder 18, Friedman Papers.

128. "American Economist Milton Friedman, in Conversation with Robert McKenzie," 170.

129. Milton Friedman, *A Theory of the Consumption Function* (Princeton: Princeton University Press, 1957), 238.

130. Milton Friedman, ed., *Studies in the Quantity Theory of Money* (Chicago: University of Chicago Press, 1956); Milton Friedman and Anna Jacobson Schwartz, *A Monetary History of the United States, 1867–1960* (Princeton: Princeton University Press, 1963).

131. Friedman and Schwartz, *Monetary History of the United States*, 678.

132. Milton Friedman and Anna Jacobson Schwartz, "The Great Contraction, 1929–1933," chap. 7 in Friedman and Schwartz, *Monetary History of the United States*.

133. Milton Friedman, "The Case for Flexible Exchange Rates," in Friedman, *Essays in Positive Economics*, 157–203.

134. Milton Friedman, "The Role of Monetary Policy," *American Economic Review* 58, no. 1 (1968): 1–17.

135. Milton Friedman, *There's No Such Thing as a Free Lunch* (La Salle, Ill.: Open Court, 1975), 56.

136. The collection of popular essays is Milton Friedman, *Dollars and Deficits: Living with America's Economic Problems* (Englewood Cliffs, N.J.: Prentice-Hall, 1968).

137. See, for example, Friedman, *Capitalism and Freedom*, 54.

138. Greta Krippner, *Capitalizing on Crisis: The Political Origins of the Rise of Finance* (Cambridge, Mass.: Harvard University Press, 2011), 114–120; Daniel Rodgers, *Age of Fracture* (Cambridge, Mass.: Harvard University Press, 2011), 54–55.

139. "Milton Friedman Speaks," *World Research Ink* 1, no. 3 (December 1976): 2.

140. Milton Friedman to Lawrence F. Cavenaugh Jr., 1 March 1966, box 11, folder 2, Friedman Papers; Milton Friedman, *An Economist's Protest: Columns in Political Economy* (Glen Ridge, N.J.: Thomas Horton, 1972), 197.

141. Milton Friedman, "Playboy Interview" (1973), in Friedman, *There's No Such Thing as a Free Lunch*, 15.

142. Milton Friedman, "Regressive Income Tax," 22 April 1968, in Friedman, *Economist's Protest*, 76–77.

143. Milton Friedman to Patrick Buchanan, 2 October 1973, box 22, folder 11, Friedman Papers.

144. Friedman, *Capitalism and Freedom*, 132.

145. Friedman, "Playboy Interview," 22.

146. Friedman, *Capitalism and Freedom*, 164.

147. Milton Friedman, "A Family Matter," 10 April 1972, in Friedman, *Economist's Protest*, 87–89.

148. Milton Friedman to Earl E. Chapman, 14 June 1978, box 11, folder 3, Friedman Papers.

149. Friedman, *Capitalism and Freedom*, 191–195.

150. Milton Friedman, "Negative Income Tax—II," 7 October 1968, in Friedman, *Economist's Protest*, 134.

151. Milton Friedman, "The Case for the Negative Income Tax: A View from the Right," 9 December 1966, box 49, folder 5, Friedman Papers.

152. Steve Holt, "The Earned Income Tax Credit at Age 30: What We Know" (Brookings Institution Research Brief, February 2006).

153. Milton Friedman, "Individuality and the New Society: The Market vs. the Bureaucrat," 16 March 1968, box 50, folder 2, Friedman Papers.

154. Milton Friedman, "Frustrating Drug Advancement," 8 January 1973, in Friedman, *There's No Such Thing as a Free Lunch*, 232.

155. Milton Friedman, "Barking Cats," 19 February 1973, in Friedman, *There's No Such Thing as a Free Lunch*, 232.

156. Milton Friedman, "Minimum-Wage Rates," 26 September 1966, in Friedman, *Economist's Protest*, 144.

157. "Professor's Budget Cut Would Be Perilous," *Commercial and Financial Chronicle*, 9 May 1957, box 1, folder 1, Friedman Papers.

158. Milton Friedman, in *The Legal and Economic Aspects of Pollution: A Discussion by University of Chicago Faculty Members George Anastaplo, R. Stephen Berry, Ronald H. Coase, Harold Demsetz, Milton Friedman* (Chicago: University of Chicago, Center for Policy Study, 1970), 14, box 2, folder 2, Friedman Papers; Friedman, "Playboy Interview," 16.

159. Milton Friedman, "Federal Flood Relief," 4 September 1972, in Friedman, *There's No Such Thing as a Free Lunch*, 304.

160. Lanny Ebenstein, *Milton Friedman*, 186–187.

161. Milton Friedman, in "Best of Both Worlds," 38.

162. Milton Friedman to Donald Bishop, 29 January 1965, box 10, folder 1, Friedman Papers.

163. Milton Friedman, "An Alternative to Aid: An Economist Urges U.S. to Free Trade, End Grants of Money," *Wall Street Journal*, 30 April 1962, 12.

164. Milton Friedman to Senator Jacob Javits, 29 June 1966, box 28, folder 31, Friedman Papers.

165. Milton Friedman, "Government and Education," in Friedman, *Economist's Protest*, 185.

166. Friedman, "Economic Myths and Public Opinion," January 1976, in *Bright Promises, Dismal Performance: An Economist's Protest* (San Diego: Harcourt Brace Jovanovich, 1983), 74.

167. Milton Friedman, "Whose Money Is It Anyway?," 4 May 1981, in Friedman, *Bright Promises, Dismal Performance*, 304.

168. Friedman, *Capitalism and Freedom*, 93.

169. Paul Krugman, "Who Was Milton Friedman?," 27. Representations of Friedman's ideas as a cyclical reversion have an extended history: Harry Johnson

described monetarism as a "counter-revolution" in "The Keynesian Revolution and the Monetarist Counter-revolution," *American Economic Review* 61, no. 2 (1971): 1–14.

170. Yonay, *Struggle over the Soul of Economics,* 4.

171. Paul Krugman, "Who Was Milton Friedman?," 30.

172. Friedrich Hayek, "Address by Prof. Hayek on Aims and Organisation of the Conference," 1, box 5, folder 13, Mont Pèlerin Society Records, Hoover Institution Archives, Stanford, Calif.

6. Moral Capital

1. Don Moore, "Economist Friedman Speaks at Collection: 'The Road to Hell,'" *Haverford News,* 13 April 1962; Milton Friedman, in "Best of Both Worlds," interview by Brian Doherty, *Reason* 27, no. 2 (1995): 36.

2. Milton Viorst, "Friedmanism, *n.* Doctrine of Most Audacious U.S. Economist; Esp., Theory 'Only Money Matters,'" *New York Times Magazine,* 25 January 1970; Harvey H. Segal, "Economic Front: Back to a Beggar-My-Neighbor Policy?," *Washington Post,* 18 November 1963, B6.

3. George Stigler to Lionel Robbins, 6 January 1963, box 12, George J. Stigler Papers, Regenstein Library, University of Chicago (hereafter Stigler Papers).

4. Frank Knight, "The Ethics of Competition," in *The Ethics of Competition* (New York: Harper and Brothers, 1935; reprint, with an introduction by Richard Boyd, New Brunswick, N.J.: Transaction, 1997), 66 (page citations are to the reprint edition).

5. Hayek, *The Constitution of Liberty* (Chicago: University of Chicago Press, 1960), 94.

6. Milton Friedman to Norman Axelrad, 27 March 1978, box 19, folder 31, Milton Friedman Papers, Hoover Institution Archives, Stanford, Calif. (hereafter Friedman Papers).

7. Milton Friedman, "Is Capitalism Humane?," in *Bright Promises, Dismal Performance: An Economist's Protest* (San Diego: Harcourt Brace Jovanovich, 1983), 87, 90.

8. Milton Friedman, *Capitalism and Freedom* (Chicago: University of Chicago Press, 1962; reprint, with a preface by the author, Chicago: University of Chicago Press, 1982), 133 (page citations are to the reprint edition).

9. Milton Friedman, "Responsibility: Insights from Economics," Faculty Seminar I, Institute for Religious and Social Studies, 8 March 1965, box 48, folder 15, Friedman Papers.

10. F. A. Harper notes the topic of Friedman's Mont Pèlerin Society presentation in "Milton Friedman at Mont Pelerin Society," *Register* (Santa Ana, Calif.), 12 September 1970, A12.

11. Milton Friedman, "A Friedman Doctrine—The Social Responsibility of Business Is to Increase Its Profits," *New York Times Magazine*, 13 September 1970, 33, 126.

12. Frank Knight, "Ethics and Economic Reform," in *Freedom and Reform: Essays in Economics and Social Philosophy* (New York: Harper and Brothers, 1947; reprint, with a foreword by James M. Buchanan, Indianapolis: Liberty Fund, 1982), 69–74 (page citations are to the reprint edition).

13. Milton Friedman, in "A *Business and Society Review* Interview," in *There's No Such Thing as a Free Lunch* (La Salle, Ill.: Open Court, 1975), 245.

14. "Excerpt from Testimony of Milton Friedman before Joint Economic Committee," 23 September 1971, box 33, folder 15, Friedman Papers.

15. Friedman, *There's No Such Thing as a Free Lunch*, 247.

16. Milton Friedman to Norman Axelrad, 27 March 1978, box 19, folder 31, Friedman Papers.

17. Milton Friedman, "Individuality and the New Society: The Market vs. the Bureaucrat," 16 March 1968, box 50, folder 2, Friedman Papers.

18. Friedman acknowledges the influence of Buchanan and Stigler on his approach to the analysis of political entities in his "Comment on Leland Yeager's Paper on the Keynesian Heritage," Mont Pèlerin Society, September 1984, box 8, Stigler Papers.

19. Buchanan and Tullock made this claim on the basis of a criterion of Pareto optimality, which they acknowledged was "severely limited in certain important respects." James M. Buchanan and Gordon Tullock, *The Calculus of Consent: Logical Foundations of Constitutional Democracy* (Ann Arbor: University of Michigan Press, 1962; reprint, Ann Arbor: University of Michigan Press, Ann Arbor Paperbacks, 1965), 202 (page citations are to the reprint edition).

20. George J. Stigler, "The Theory of Economic Regulation," *Bell Journal of Economics and Management Science* 2, no. 1 (1971): 3–21.

21. Milton Friedman, "Adam Smith's Relevance for 1776," Mont Pèlerin Society, 27 August 1976, box 55, folder 21, Friedman Papers. For other uses of the phrase "invisible hand in politics," see Milton Friedman, *An Economist's Protest: Columns in Political Economy* (Glen Ridge, N.J.: Thomas Horton, 1972), 142–143; Friedman, *There's No Such Thing as a Free Lunch*, 253; and Friedman, *The Invisible Hand in Economics and Politics* (Singapore: Institute of Southeast Asian Studies, 1981).

22. Milton Friedman, "The Future of the American Economy," delivered to the American Experience Program, University of Pittsburgh, 5 February 1976, box 55, folder 18, Friedman Papers.

23. Viorst, "Friedmanism, *n.*"

24. Lanny Ebenstein, *Milton Friedman: A Biography* (New York: Palgrave Macmillan, 2007), x.

25. "Friedman to Live Here, Looks Back on His Career," *San Francisco Sunday Examiner and Chronicle,* 5 December 1977, C11. Friedman demonstrated this inclination as early as 1952, when he provided detailed advice to the cochairman of the National Stevenson for President Committee despite the fact that "I shall almost certainly vote against you." Milton Friedman to Walter Johnson, 16 August 1952, box 14, folder 3, Friedman Papers.

26. Milton Friedman, transcription of discussion from 17:00 to 19:00, 7 September 1960, box 16, folder 5, Mont Pèlerin Society Records, Hoover Institution Archives, Stanford, Calif. (hereafter MPS Records). These quotes are excerpted from a transcript of Friedman's comments, and any grammatical errors should not be attributed to him.

27. Friedman, *There's No Such Thing as a Free Lunch,* 32.

28. Ibid., 256.

29. Milton Friedman, "Regulatory Schizophrenia," 29 July 1981, in *Bright Promises, Dismal Performance,* 131.

30. Milton Friedman, "The Source of Strength," Presidents' Club of Michigan General Corporation, New Orleans, 2 April 1977, box 56, folder 1, Friedman Papers.

31. Friedman, *Economist's Protest,* 203. Also see Milton Friedman to Sir John Clark, 9 May 1977, box 11, folder 5, Friedman Papers.

32. Milton Friedman, "The Source of Strength," Presidents' Club of Michigan General Corporation, New Orleans, 2 April 1977, box 56, folder 1, Friedman Papers.

33. Milton Friedman, "Comments on the Critics," in *Milton Friedman's Monetary Framework: A Debate with his Critics,* ed. Robert J. Gordon (Chicago: University of Chicago Press, 1974), 162–163.

34. Milton Friedman, in "Discussion on Agenda, Etc.," 4 April 1947, 5, box 5, folder 13, MPS Records.

35. Milton Friedman, in "Statement of Aims," 7 April 1947, 4, box 5, folder 12, MPS Records.

36. Milton Friedman, "Say 'No' to Intolerance," *Liberty* 4, no. 6 (1991): 17–20. This is an edited transcript of a talk that was delivered in 1990.

37. Milton Friedman to Patrick Buchanan, 25 October 1973, box 22, folder 11, Friedman Papers.

38. Friedrich Hayek to Shinzo Koizumi, 26 February 1965, box 31, folder 15, Friedrich Hayek Papers, Hoover Institution Archives, Stanford, Calif. (hereafter Hayek Papers).

39. Milton Friedman, "An Interview with Milton Friedman," interview by Russell Roberts, *Library of Economics and Liberty,* 4 September 2006, http://www.econlib.org/library/Columns/y2006/Friedmantranscript.html.

40. Milton Friedman, in "Best of Both Worlds," 38.

41. Milton Friedman, in "The American Economist Milton Friedman, in Conversation with Robert McKenzie, Gives His View of How Our Economic Problems Could Be Solved," *Listener*, 11 February 1971, 171.

42. Milton Friedman, in "Best of Both Worlds," 34.

43. John Davenport, "The Radical Economics of Milton Friedman," *Fortune*, 1 June 1967, 148.

44. Milton Friedman to Melvin R. Laird, 28 March 1962, box 29, folder 31, Friedman Papers. Friedman expressed similar positions in 1959, emphasizing in a letter to the chairman of the Republican Committee on Program and Progress that the Republicans needed to adopt a leadership position rather than "trailing afterwards by a long lag," and criticizing them for their "implicit acceptance of the central thesis of the left-wing democratic position, namely, that 'welfare' rather than 'freedom' should be the major direct aim of government, as well as their minor thesis that a free economy is inherently unstable and requires sensitive and continual control by the central government." Milton Friedman to Charles H. Percy, 2 August 1959, box 31, folder 27, Friedman Papers.

45. Friedman said that the contents of his letter were copied from "a brief statement that I wrote for another purpose a year ago." Milton Friedman to Melvin R. Laird, Chairman, Joint Committee on Republican Principles, 28 March 1962, box 29, folder 31, Friedman Papers.

46. "Goldwater Urges Halt to U.S. Economic Aid, Limit on Tourist Funds," *Wall Street Journal*, 9 December 1960, 7.

47. Milton Friedman to Barry Goldwater, 12 December 1960, box 27, folder 24, Friedman Papers.

48. Barry Goldwater to Milton Friedman, 16 July 1961, box 27, folder 24, Friedman Papers.

49. Milton Friedman, in "Best of Both Worlds," 33.

50. Milton Friedman to Barry Goldwater, 12 January 1962, box 27, folder 24, Friedman Papers.

51. Barry Goldwater to Milton Friedman, 13 July 1962, box 27, folder 24, Friedman Papers.

52. Rick Perlstein describes the initial contacts between Friedman and Goldwater in *Before the Storm: Barry Goldwater and the Unmaking of the American Consensus* (New York: Hill and Wang, 2001), 420–423.

53. "Theorizing for Goldwater?," *Business Week*, 23 November 1963, 106.

54. Milton Friedman, in Milton Friedman and Rose Friedman, *Two Lucky People: Memoirs* (Chicago: University of Chicago Press, 1998), 367–368.

55. M. J. Rossant, "Republican Economists Split on Goldwater," *New York Times*, 31 July 1964, 31; "Goldwater's Economists," *Newsweek*, 31 August 1964, 63.

56. Milton Friedman, in Friedman and Friedman, *Two Lucky People,* 368; Charles Mohr, "Goldwater Gets Ideas from Many," *New York Times,* 31 March 1964, 20.

57. Milton Friedman, in Friedman and Friedman, *Two Lucky People,* 370.

58. Chesly Manly, "U.C. Economic Experts Advise Goldwater," *Chicago Tribune,* 12 April 1964, 8.

59. Alan L. Otten, "Barry's Boys," *Wall Street Journal,* 17 July 1964, 6.

60. Alfred L. Malabre Jr., "Influential Economist," *Wall Street Journal,* 4 November 1969, 1.

61. Milton Friedman, in Friedman and Friedman, *Two Lucky People,* 369.

62. Davenport, "Radical Economics of Milton Friedman," 150.

63. Barry Goldwater, *The Conscience of a Conservative* (Shepherdsville, Ky.: Victor, 1960; reprint, with a foreword by George F. Will and an afterword by Robert F. Kennedy Jr., Princeton: Princeton University Press, 2007), 31 (page citations are to the reprint edition); emphasis in original.

64. Manly, "U.C. Economic Experts Advise Goldwater," 8.

65. See Milton Friedman to Fritz Machlup, 26 October 1952, box 38, folder 25, Fritz Machlup Papers, Hoover Institution Archives, Stanford, Calif.

66. Friedman, *Capitalism and Freedom,* 110. Friedman continued to write on civil rights legislation through the early 1970s; see Milton Friedman, "The Negro in America," 11 December 1967, in Friedman, *Economist's Protest,* 150–152; "3 Profs Cite Good, Bad in Riot Report," *Chicago Tribune,* 3 March 1968, 1; Friedman, "Playboy Interview" (1973), in Friedman, *There's No Such Thing as a Free Lunch,* 34–35; Friedman, "The Voucher Idea," 23 September 1973, in Friedman, *There's No Such Thing as a Free Lunch,* 277–278; Friedman, "Whose Intolerance?," 6 October 1975, in Friedman, *Bright Promises, Dismal Performance,* 169–171.

67. Friedrich Hayek to Edward R. Dunn, 28 July 1964, box 17, folder 32, Hayek Papers.

68. Excerpt from *Philadelphia Daily News,* 4 May 1961, in box 1, folder 1, Friedman Papers; Milton Friedman to William F. Buckley Jr., 13 February 1962, box 22, folder 13, Friedman Papers. The editorial that Friedman referenced was "The Question of Robert Welch," *National Review,* 13 February 1962, 83–88.

69. Chesly Manly, "Conservatism Trend Makes Gains at University of Chicago," *Chicago Daily Tribune,* 20 May 1962, 10.

70. John Fischer to Milton Friedman, 28 June 1961, box 27, folder 41, Friedman Papers.

71. William F. Buckley Jr. to Milton Friedman, 15 January 1968, box 22, folder 13, Friedman Papers; William F. Buckley Jr., "One of a Kind," *Hoover Digest,* no. 4 (2006): 40. For an extended description of their shared skiing vacations, see William F. Buckley Jr., *Miles Gone By: A Literary Autobiography* (Washington, D.C.: Regnery, 2004), 197–205.

72. Milton Friedman, "The Role of Monetary Policy," *American Economic Review* 58, no. 1 (1968): 1–17; Friedman, "Inflationary Recession," 17 October 1966, in Friedman, *Economist's Protest*, 40–42.

73. Milton Friedman, "The Case for Flexible Exchange Rates," in *Essays in Positive Economics* (Chicago: University of Chicago Press, 1953), 157–203.

74. Allen J. Matusow, "Nixon and the Fed," chap. 1 in *Nixon's Economy: Booms, Busts, Dollars, and Votes* (Lawrence: University Press of Kansas, 1998).

75. Friedman, "Why the Freeze Is a Mistake," 30 August 1971, in Friedman, *There's No Such Thing as a Free Lunch,* 125–127.

76. David Warsh, "Milton Friedman's Surprising Secret," *Boston Globe,* 17 May 1992, 37.

77. H. Erich Heinemann, "The Money Squeeze," *New York Times,* 20 August 1969, 66; Alfred L. Malabre Jr., "Influential Economist," *Wall Street Journal,* 4 November 1969, 1.

78. Davenport, "Radical Economics of Milton Friedman," 131.

79. Heinemann, "Money Squeeze," 61.

80. The awardees were Friedrich Hayek (1974), Milton Friedman (1976), George Stigler (1982), James Buchanan (1986), Maurice Allais (1988), Ronald Coase (1991), and Gary Becker (1992). R. M. Hartwell, *A History of the Mont Pelerin Society* (Indianapolis: Liberty Fund, 1995), 160. Tom Karier provides synopses of the careers of many of them in the context of other Nobel recipients in *Intellectual Capital: Forty Years of the Nobel Prize in Economics* (Cambridge: Cambridge University Press, 2010), 14–57.

81. Arnold Harberger, "Setting the Record Straight on Chile," *Wall Street Journal,* 10 December 1976, 12; Milton Friedman, in Friedman and Friedman, *Two Lucky People,* 399–400.

82. For further background on the "Chicago Boys," see Juan Gabriel Valdés, *Pinochet's Economists: The Chicago School in Chile* (Cambridge: Cambridge University Press, 1995).

83. See Orlando Letelier, "The 'Chicago Boys' in Chile: Economic 'Freedom's' Awful Toll," *Nation,* 28 August 1976, 137–142; Naomi Klein, *The Shock Doctrine: The Rise of Disaster Capitalism* (New York: Metropolitan, 2007), 59–159.

84. Harberger, "Setting the Record Straight on Chile," 12.

85. Milton Friedman, Hoover Foundation Inaugural Lecture, Strathclyde Business School, Glasgow, Scotland, recorded 21 April 1978 for "The Money Programme: Has the Tide Turned?" (BBC), box 56, folder 20, Friedman Papers.

86. George Nash, *Herbert Hoover and Stanford University* (Stanford, Calif.: Hoover Institution Press, 1988), 143.

87. James Allen Smith, *The Idea Brokers: Think Tanks and the Rise of the New Policy Elite* (New York: Free Press, 1991), 184–189.

88. Kenneth Lamott, "Right-Thinking Think Tank," *New York Times Magazine,* 23 July 1978, 16, 45. The foremost history of the growth of conservative

think tanks focuses on the British policy arena: see Richard Cockett, *Thinking the Unthinkable: Think-Tanks and the Economic Counter-revolution, 1931–1983* (London: HarperCollins, 1994).

89. Milton Friedman, in "Best of Both Worlds," 37.

90. The relationship between Friedman's proposals and Reagan's policies is discussed at length in Elton Rayack, *Not So Free to Choose: The Political Economy of Milton Friedman and Ronald Reagan* (New York: Praeger, 1987).

91. Milton Friedman, in Friedman and Friedman, *Two Lucky People*, 209, 388–389.

92. Milton Friedman, "Preface, 1982," in Friedman, *Capitalism and Freedom*, viii.

93. Friedman, "Interview with Milton Friedman."

94. Martin Anderson, *Revolution* (San Diego: Harcourt Brace Jovanovich, 1988), 172.

95. Milton Friedman, in "Best of Both Worlds," 33.

96. Milton Friedman, Presidential Circular, October 1970, box 86, folder 12, Friedman Papers.

97. Edwin McDowell, "A Mountain Where Thinkers Dwell," *Wall Street Journal*, 20 September 1972, 16.

98. Milton Friedman, Presidential Circular, October 1970, box 86, folder 12, Friedman Papers. Many of the members agreed with Friedman's assessment; see "Extracts from Letters on the Future of MPS," box 87, folder 1, Friedman Papers.

99. Milton Friedman, in Friedman and Friedman, *Two Lucky People*, 334.

100. Milton Friedman, Presidential Circular, October 1971, box 87, folder 1, Friedman Papers.

101. Milton Friedman, in Friedman and Friedman, *Two Lucky People*, 334.

102. Milton Friedman, "Capitalism and the Jews," 1972, box R7, Louis Rougier Papers, Château de Lourmarin, Lourmarin, France (hereafter Rougier Papers). For an extended discussion of Friedman's "paradox," see Jerry Muller, "The Jewish Response to Capitalism: Milton Friedman's Paradox Reconsidered," in *Capitalism and the Jews* (Princeton: Princeton University Press, 2010), 72–132.

103. John Davenport, "The Long Pilgrimage," September 1970, box R7, Rougier Papers; emphasis in original.

104. Peter Steinfels, "Irving Kristol, Standard-Bearer," chap. 5 in *The Neoconservatives: Men Who Are Changing America's Politics* (New York: Simon and Schuster, 1979); Murray Friedman, "The Rise of the Neoconservatives," chap. 7 in *The Neoconservative Revolution: Jewish Intellectuals and the Shaping of Public Policy* (Cambridge: Cambridge University Press, 2005); "Board of Contributors," *Wall Street Journal*, 14 September 1972, 18.

105. Irving Kristol, *On the Democratic Idea in America* (New York: Harper and Row, 1972).

106. Justin Vaïsse, *Neoconservatism: The Biography of a Movement* (Cambridge, Mass.: Belknap Press of Harvard University Press, 2010), 55.

107. Milton Friedman to Irving Kristol, 1 November 1972, box 85, folder 8, Friedman Papers.

108. Irving Kristol, "Socialism, Capitalism, Nihilism" (1972), box R7, Rougier Papers.

Conclusion

1. George Packer, "The New Liberalism: How the Economic Crisis Can Help Obama Redefine the Democrats," *New Yorker,* 17 November 2008, 84.

2. Jeffrey D. Sachs, "The New New Deal," *Fortune,* 27 October 2008, 112–113.

3. Patrick Wintour and Nicholas Watt, " 'Only We Have the Answers,' Insists Brown," *Guardian,* 17 March 2009, 14.

4. André Schiffrin, "Socialism Is No Longer a Dirty Word: European Countries Have Shown There Is a Practical Case for Public Ownership," *Nation,* 29 December 2008, 21.

5. John B. Judis, "America the Liberal," *New Republic,* 19 November 2008, 20.

6. David Brooks, "Big Government Ahead," *New York Times,* 14 October 2008, 29.

7. Peggy Noonan, "Obama and the Runaway Train," *Wall Street Journal,* 1 November 2008, A11.

8. "A Liberal Supermajority," *Wall Street Journal,* 17 October 2008, A12.

9. Martin Feldstein told the House Committee on Financial Services, "I am, as you know, a fiscal conservative. I generally oppose increased government spending and increased fiscal deficit. But I am afraid that is now the only way to increase overall national spending and to reverse the country's economic downturn." See House Committee on Financial Services, *Oversight of Implementation of the Emergency Economic Stabilization Act of 2008 and of Government Lending and Insurance Facilities: Impact on the Economy and Credit Availability,* 110th Cong., 2d sess., 2008, serial no. 110-145, 70.

10. House Committee on Oversight and Government Reform, *The Financial Crisis and the Role of Federal Regulators,* 110th Cong., 2d sess., 23 October 2008, Federal News Service, in LexisNexis Congressional.

11. John Maynard Keynes, *The End of Laissez-Faire* (London: Hogarth, 1927), 16.

12. Friedrich Hayek, *The Road to Serfdom* (Chicago: University of Chicago Press, 1944; reprint, with an introduction by Milton Friedman and prefaces by the author from the 1956 and 1976 editions, Chicago: University of Chicago Press, 1994), 3 (page citations are to the reprint edition).

13. John Maynard Keynes, *The General Theory of Employment, Interest, and Money* (London: Macmillan, 1936; reprint, San Diego: Harvest, 1964), 383–384 (page citations are to the reprint edition). Hayek's citation of this passage included minor differences in punctuation and wording.

14. Hayek, "The Prospects of Freedom," 2–3, box 5, folder 12, Mont Pèlerin Society Records, Hoover Institution Archives, Stanford, Calif.

15. "The New Attack on Keynesian Economics," *Time,* 10 January 1969, 65.

16. "The Intellectual Provocateur," *Time,* 19 December 1969, 71.

17. Milton Friedman to Ronald Coase, 7 January 1982, box 7, George J. Stigler Papers, Regenstein Library, University of Chicago.

18. Milton Friedman and Rose D. Friedman, "The Tide in the Affairs of Men," in *Thinking about America: The United States in the 1990s,* ed. Annelise Anderson and Dennis L. Bark (Stanford, Calif.: Hoover Institution Press, 1988), 455–468.

19. Friedman referenced the book as early as 1951 in "Neoliberalism and Its Prospects," box 42, folder 8, Milton Friedman Papers, Hoover Institution Archives, Stanford, Calif. (hereafter Friedman Papers). He recommended it as a seminal text for those seeking to understand his ideas in a letter to Troy Allen, 16 November 1976, box 18, folder 25, Friedman Papers. It is also referenced in Friedman and Friedman, "Tide in the Affairs of Men," 456.

20. Dicey's approach to historical analysis and his construction of the Harvard lectures are discussed in Richard A. Cosgrove, "The Lawyer as Historian: *Law and Opinion,*" chap. 8 in *The Rule of Law: Albert Venn Dicey, Victorian Jurist* (Chapel Hill: University of North Carolina Press, 1980).

21. A. V. Dicey, *Lectures on the Relation between Law and Public Opinion in England during the Nineteenth Century* (London: Macmillan, 1905), vii.

22. Milton Friedman, Hoover Foundation Inaugural Lecture, Strathclyde Business School, Glasgow, Scotland, recorded 21 April 1978 for "The Money Programme: Has the Tide Turned?" (BBC), box 56, folder 20, Friedman Papers; Milton Friedman to William Breit, 22 June 1967, box 26, folder 1, Friedman Papers. The other authors Friedman cited in the field of "economic social policy" were Mill, Hayek, and Knight.

23. Dicey, *Lectures on the Relation between Law and Public Opinion,* 21–23.

24. Ibid., 27.

25. Ibid., 34.

26. Milton Friedman, "The Freedom to Listen," Rockford College commencement, 18 May 1969, in *Rockford College: Widening Horizons* 5, no. 2 (1969), box 2, folder 1, Friedman Papers.

27. Milton Friedman, "The Source of Strength," speech delivered to the President's Club of Michigan General Corporation, 2 April 1977, 15, box 56, folder 1, Friedman Papers.

28. Dicey, *Lectures on the Relation between Law and Public Opinion,* 23.

29. Milton Friedman, *Capitalism and Freedom* (Chicago: University of Chicago Press, 1962; reprint, with a preface by the author, Chicago: University of Chicago Press, 1982), viii–ix (page citations are to the reprint edition).

30. Milton Friedman, in Milton Friedman and Rose D. Friedman, *Two Lucky People: Memoirs* (Chicago: University of Chicago Press, 1998), 220.

31. Dicey, *Lectures on the Relation between Law and Public Opinion*, 445.

32. Milton Friedman, *There's No Such Thing as a Free Lunch* (La Salle, Ill.: Open Court, 1975), x.

33. Milton Friedman, "The Battle's Half Won," *Wall Street Journal*, 9 December 2004, A16.

34. See Friedman and Friedman, *Two Lucky People*, 588; Milton Friedman, "Mr. Market: A Nobelist Views Today's Fed, Currencies, Social Security, Regulation," interview by Gene Epstein, *Barron's*, 24 August 1998, 30.

ACKNOWLEDGMENTS

I am grateful for the institutional support that made the research for this book possible, including fellowships from the Mellon Foundation, the Center for American Political Studies, the Edmond J. Safra Center for Ethics, the Charlotte W. Newcombe Foundation, and the American Academy of Arts and Sciences, and grants from the Center for History and Economics, the Project on Justice, Welfare, and Economics, and the Charles Warren Center. I have also benefited from the feedback of scholars at events hosted by the Ecole Normale Supérieure de Cachan, the Radcliffe Institute for Advanced Study, the Center for the History of Political Economy at Duke University, the University of Notre Dame, and the Institute for Applied Economics, Global Health, and the Study of Business Enterprise at Johns Hopkins University, as well as the Smithsonian Contemporary History Colloquium, the Berle Center Symposium, the United States Intellectual History Conference, and the Policy History Conference.

The research for this book was enabled by the prodigious efforts of archivists at the Hoover Institution, the University of Chicago, the London School of Economics and Political Science, the Mudd Library of Princeton University, the Bundesarchiv in Bern, Switzerland, and the Christian Theological Seminary in Indianapolis. Hans Willgerodt at the Institut für Wirtschaftspolitik in Cologne, the staff of the Château de Lourmarin in Lourmarin, France, and Gloria Valentine at the Hoover Institution generously made the materials in their possession available for research. Ellen Viner Seiler and Ken Templeton also shared materials from their paper collections and, along with Kenneth Arrow, Richard Cornuelle, Dorothy Hahn, James Redfield, and Donald Winch, contributed valuable recollections. Barbara Burg and Chella Valdyanathan offered guidance with aspects of the research, Kelly Kelleher Richter provided research assistance in the final stages of the project, Kristin Alise Jones and Susan Husserl-Kapit proofread my translations from German- and French-language sources, and Charles Eberline copyedited the full manuscript with exceptional judgment and care. I would also like to thank J. Daniel Hammond for sharing and granting permission to quote from his unpublished interview with Milton Friedman, Stephen Stigler for granting permission to access and quote from the papers of his father, George J. Stigler, and the Estate of F. A. Hayek for granting permission to quote from his papers.

A number of colleagues provided illuminating comments on sections of the manuscript, including Ben Alpers, Dan Amsterdam, Arthur Applbaum, Roger Backhouse, Bruce Caldwell, Charles Capper, Mary Furner, David Mitch, Jerry Muller, Pat Spacks, and Steven Teles. I am grateful for the insights gleaned from my ongoing conversations with Eduardo Canedo, Ross Emmett, Philip Mirowski, and Thomas Stapleford. The suggestions provided by two anonymous readers for Harvard University Press helped me frame my final revisions to the manuscript, and Brian Distelberg provided vital support in the project's final stages. I am especially grateful for the guidance of my editor, Joyce Seltzer, who shared my vision for the project and worked hard to help me achieve it.

I could not have completed the book without the many kindnesses of family and friends, including Nick Burgin, Robert Collier, Charlotte Douglas, Michael Gitter, Jeff Grappone, Katie Holt, Alex Kauffmann, Hud Morgan, and Hillary Murnighan. Its themes emerged out of my conversations with an extraordinary group of colleagues at Harvard, including Edward Baring, George Blaustein, Daniela Cammack, Tarun Chhabra, Carolyn Dong, Sam Goldman, David Grewal, Katja Guenther, Jo Guldi, Chris Jones, Noam Maggor, Elizabeth More, Yascha Mounk, Ward Penfold, Daniel Shore, Ganesh Sitaraman, Nico Slate, Trygve Throntveit, Ben Waterhouse, Aliza Watters, and Ann Wilson. More recently I have benefited from the insights of the remarkable group of American historians at Johns Hopkins, including Nathan Connolly, Toby Ditz, Louis Galambos, Michael Johnson, Philip Morgan, Dorothy Ross, Mary Ryan, and Ronald Walters. I owe a particular debt to Thomas Meaney, who read the manuscript in its entirety and offered crucial advice as it approached completion.

The book took shape through an extended dialogue with an extraordinarily dedicated committee of advisers. James Kloppenberg inspired me to enter the vocation, guided me through the early years of graduate school with exceptional wisdom and care, and labored to help my writing achieve the high standards he set. Emma Rothschild's advice and judgment informed my research from its earliest stages and, over time, transformed my understanding of the practice of the discipline. Daniel Rodgers responded to each chapter from afar with remarkable perceptiveness, and Peter Gordon's incisive readings remain an example to which I aspire. The book's strengths are due largely to their efforts; its failings are my own.

The love and guidance of my parents made this project possible, and the arrival of Alex Burgin made its final months a joy. It is dedicated to my closest friend and most careful reader, although her gifts to me are not of the kind that words can be expected to repay.

INDEX